The Beginner's Cookbook

The Beginner's Cookbook

Rosemary Wadey

BLACK CAT

To my mother Joan, a splendid cook herself,
who stimulated my interest in cooking, taught me much
and has encouraged me all the way

First published in 1985 in Great Britain by Macdonald & Co
(Publishers) Ltd.

This edition reprinted 1994 by Little, Brown and Co (UK)
under the Black Cat imprint

Little, Brown and Co (UK)
Brettenham House
Lancaster Place
London WC2E 7EN

British Library Cataloguing in Publication Data

Wadey, Rosemary
   The beginner's cookbook.
   1. Cookery
   I. Title
   641.5 TX717

ISBN 0-7481-0091-1

Filmset by Flair plan Photo-typesetting Limited

Printed in Slovakia by Slovart Print, s. r. o.

Editor: Julie Dufour
Designer: Sarah Jackson
Photographers: Paul Webster and Rex Bamber (step-by-step photographs)
Stylist: Dawn Lane
Home Economics: Rosemary Wadey and Heather McCombe
Indexer: Dorothy Frame
Illustrator: Lorna Turpin

Acknowledgements
The publishers would like to thank
the following for the loan of props:
HEFF (UK) Limited
Way In Living, London
David Mellor, Sloane Square, London
Fortnum & Mason, London

OPPOSITE TITLE PAGE: *Carrot and Coriander Soup*
(see page 45), *Brisket Pot Roast* (see page 52) *and*
Charlotte Russe (see page 197)

— Contents —

Introduction

It doesn't matter whether you are a young newly-wed facing the daunting task of cooking everyday meals for the first time, a girl (or boy) learning to cook at school, people suddenly landed with all the cooking for a family when all they had done before was cope with the odd meal for themselves, a man in the kitchen or perhaps a widower who due to circumstances has to begin to cook for himself; this book sets out to help and encourage each and everyone who wants to begin to cook and shows that cooking can be fun and not such a dreary chore as some people think. It won't take long before you will want to begin to experiment with and change the simple everyday recipes and you will soon find you are becoming a competent and adventurous cook.

If you have to start by equipping your kitchen, it can be rather worrying and it is easy to buy all the wrong things – although at the time they probably seem to be just what you will need! It is not easy to select the really basic necessities, so I have given you a list to help sort out this problem and, as you progress, the extra items and equipment can gradually be obtained. Another problem is what do you buy to start a store of food in the larder so there will be items for everyday cooking; again I have given suggestions to get you underway, and as you begin to cook you will gradually be able to add the extras as necessary for the recipes you want to cook that week.

The recipes in this book have been tested in three different weights and measures: these are Metric, Imperial and American cups. It is extremely important to select one of these sets of measurements and then to follow this one only throughout the book. A list of the approximate conversions are given on page 15 which will help if you have any problems, and it should also make it clear why it is necessary not to mix the weights.

Each chapter deals with a particular type of food, e.g. Eggs, Meat, Vegetables, Soups, Baking, etc. In some cases, such as fruit and vegetables, when you might not be familiar with all the different types, information is given on how to store, prepare, cook, etc., and with meats and poultry all the different methods of preparing are provided as well as the basic roasting methods (including carving) and many other ways of cooking and serving. Some recipes are cross-referenced throughout the book so that you have a wider selection of recipes and can follow in detail the instructions for certain processes.

All the recipes have been set out in easy-to-follow steps, which not only makes it simple to find your place, but also to see how you are getting on with the preparation, etc. A note here to remind every cook, whether a beginner or more advanced cook: it is extremely important to read right through the whole recipe before you begin. This not only ensures you have all the ingredients, but tells you what temperature to set the oven at and reminds you to do so in good time so the oven is waiting for the food and not the other way round. It also ensures you know what you are going to have to do and gives you an idea of the time it will take for the preparation and, of course, tells you the actual cooking time so you can plan everything to be ready at the same time.

Don't try to be too ambitious at first; do begin with simple recipes and easy processes – there is plenty of time to move on to all the complicated cooking as you gain experience. It is also a good idea to plan well in advance what you want to cook – this gives plenty of time for shopping and should not put you into a fluster by trying to do something at the last minute. When entertaining, don't try out three new recipes you have never attempted before. It is wise to cook at least two that you have already tried with success, and maybe just experiment with a recipe for one of the courses. Entertaining is meant to be fun, not something that puts the cook into a state of terror as to whether the meal will be perfection or not. Don't panic – if you do make a mistake, you certainly won't be the first cook who has had a disaster at a vital time. Everyone understands and there is usually something that can be done to resurrect a problem. After all, even the greatest of cooks can make mistakes and we all learn from our mistakes.

As a child I was extremely fortunate to have a mother who, quite apart from being an excellent cook herself, loved cooking as well and was keen to pass on her knowledge to me at an early age. I spent hours watching and learning and soon became determined to be able to cook as well as she did. My brother also became interested and watched and learnt as I did and he too has become a very good and exciting cook. But not everyone is as lucky as we were to have someone with the patience and inclination to teach us the basics and then more advanced cooking. I went on to train for several years to learn as much as I could about cooking and now I am trying to pass on some of this knowledge to my two daughters. I hope this book will help them both now as they are beginning to learn and in later years when they need a reference book, and that it will help and encourage an enormous number of other people of whatever age and experience to gain enjoyment and some of the enormous pleasure I have had from simply learning to cook.

Rhubarb Snow (see page 160 *and Lamb and Orange Risotto* (see page 60)

1 General Information

This chapter sets out to help beginners and anybody about to begin cooking in earnest decide on what they will find in a kitchen or will need to buy to equip a kitchen so it will be an easily workable place for them to produce wonderful food in the easiest and most convenient way.

For the beginner it is a daunting thought to try and decide what will be required in the kitchen even for simple cooking. Of course the list of equipment is never ending but the essentials are not so endless and lists are given with these suggestions. Knives are most important when it comes to cooking and can be expensive, so it pays to know a little about what you are buying and equally what each type should be used for.

Main items such as cookers, refrigerators and freezers are very expensive items and need careful thought before buying. Make sure the type and size you select is what you want and fits all your requirements. A freezer is probably not the most important item for many a new cook, but a slow cooker might be just the answer for the young person out at work all day needing to come home to an almost ready-cooked meal. I have described other electrical gadgets to try to help the cook decide if that is what he or she really needs or not.

Next comes the task of filling up the larder or store cupboard with basic ingredients. The choice of goods is huge but, once you have made a selection of the most important items, the extras can be added gradually as they are required for certain recipes.

Finally, a word on the Metric, Imperial and American measurements that are used throughout this book. Here and in other places in the book, I will stress the importance of using and following only one set of measurements. It doesn't matter if it is Metric, Imperial or American but, whichever you choose, do follow that one only and do not jump around using some grammes and some ounces. The recipes have been carefully tested for each type of measurement and, as they all vary slightly when it comes to converting, the correct results will not be achieved if they are mixed. After that warning, don't worry, cooking is fun and whether you are a complete beginner or an experienced cook there is always something new to learn – which is why it is such a rewarding task. So enjoy your cooking – and Good Luck!

KITCHEN EQUIPMENT

Of course you must have the basic essentials of a cooker and refrigerator, sink, etc., in your kitchen but, apart from these large items, there are many other 'musts' to make cooking relatively easy and a pleasure. It is easy to name a long list of items of kitchen equipment but more difficult to name the real basics. Extras can be obtained as and when required.

Saucepans and knives are probably the most difficult to select because of the great variety available, so advice is given below for these items.

POTS AND PANS
3–4 saucepans of assorted sizes
Milk saucepan (preferably non-stick)
Frying pan
Kettle, or electric kettle or electric jug type of kettle
Colander
Large and small roasting tins or pans
1–3 baking or cookie sheets
2 sandwich tins or layer pans (18–20 cm/7–8 inch)
Cake tin or pan (20 cm/8 inch round or square)
Patty tins or muffin pans
Cooling rack
Large mixing bowl
2 basins or bowls (or more as required)
568 ml/1 pint measuring jug, or 8 oz dry measuring cup
300 ml/½ pint measuring jug, or 8 oz liquid measuring cup
Pie dish or plate
2 casseroles (or more as required)
Storage jars and airtight containers

TOOLS AND UTENSILS
Hand-held electric mixer
Set of kitchen knives (see below)
2 kitchen forks
2 kitchen tablespoons
2 kitchen teaspoons
Set of measuring spoons
2 wooden spoons
Slotted spoon
Fish slice or slotted spatula
Potato masher
Skewers
Kitchen scales
Rolling pin
Kitchen scissors or shears
Can opener
Bottle opener/corkscrew
Rotary egg whisk
Flat whisk or balloon whisk
Grater
Lemon squeezer

Mincer or meat grinder
Potato peeler
Apple corer
Chopping board (2 are even better)
2–3 sieves (wire and/or nylon in varying sizes)
Pastry cutters
Pastry brush
Spatula

USEFUL ADDITIONS
Omelette pan
Deep-fat fryer (can be electric)
Large electric mixer, blender or food processor
Electric coffee percolator
Swiss roll tin or shallow rectangular pan
Flan tin or pan
Extra cake and sandwich tins or layer pans (in varying sizes)
Soufflé dish
Ring mould
Spring release cake tin or pan with different bases
Loaf tins or pans
Dariole moulds
Jelly mould
Raised pie tin or mould
Cream horn tins or pans
Double saucepan or boiler
Pressure cooker
Electric frying pan
Electric toaster
Microwave oven
Oven thermometer
Freezer
Grapefruit knife
Ladle
Pie funnel
Flour dredger
Pestle and mortar
Salad shaker
Knife sharpener
Small pastry/petit four cutters
Slow cooker
Kebab skewers

SPECIAL COOKERY EQUIPMENT
Icing bags and assorted icing nozzles
Large vegetable nozzles
Large piping bags
Icing turntable
Icing ruler and scraper
Preserving pan
Jelly bag
Sugar or candy thermometer

SAUCEPANS
The ideal is a set consisting of a 1.2 litre/2 pint, 1.75 litre/3 pint, and 2.75–3.5 litre/5–6 pint saucepans plus a larger one too. These can then be increased as and when required. Always buy a good-quality heavy pan suitable for both gas and electricity (you never know what you may have to cook on if you move flat or house). The base must be flat to ensure even heating and the interior should be slightly rounded where it reaches the base of the pan to make cleaning easier. The lids must be well fitting with non-heating knobs and a comfortable, firmly-fixed handle. Large saucepans containing 4.5 litres/8 pints or more should have a second handle for easy lifting. Don't be tempted to buy cheap lightweight pans – they do not last but become easily distorted with uneven bases, the handles loosen quickly and they can be knocked over much more easily.

Frying pans must also be bought with care. The choice here is between aluminium, stainless steel, cast iron, various non-stick types and others and it really depends on your preference, but remember it should be a fairly solid object and feel firm and heavy. To double up for making omelettes and pancakes, a 20 cm/8 inch pan is best, but it is a bit small for a fry-up so it may be better to buy a larger pan if you are only to have one frying pan.

TYPES OF PANS
Aluminium – cast aluminium with a ground base provides a good solid pan suitable for use on all types of cookers including gas. Medium weight aluminium pans are suitable for modern gas and electric cookers, but be wary of the lightweight cheap pans. These pans tend to discolour during use but this is not harmful and can be removed by boiling up a weak acid solution (e.g. apple peelings or lemon peel in water). Soda will discolour the pan and pit the surface thus encouraging sticking and burning, so a soapy scouring pad is best to use for cleaning.
Copper – these pans are splendid but very expensive. The interior is usually lined with tin to prevent any chemical reactions occurring between the food and copper. Copper is a very good conductor of heat so the contents cook evenly. They do require more care with cleaning than some types of pan, as copper will discolour easily, and therefore a special copper cleaner is recommended.
Stainless steel – good hard-wearing pans, expensive but worthwhile. Steel is not such a good conductor of heat so the base is often covered with aluminium or copper to help even cooking. Easy to clean.
Enamel – pans are made of heavy cast iron, light steel or aluminium to which enamel has been fused. Buy only good quality, heavy pans, as enamel tends to stick and the lightweight ones can be really quite bad.
Non-stick coatings – there are now quite a variety of different non-stick coatings. Some are better than others so again it is best to buy a reputable make and take care with the type of implement you use – avoid anything with sharp edges. Some surfaces recommend using metal implements, but others suggest wood or plastic and these recommendations should be followed. Do not clean with abrasives, as these will rapidly ruin the non-stick surface.
Glass – these are becoming more and more popular and look good, although the foods do tend to stick easily and cook rather unevenly. Follow the manufacturer's instructions carefully and use a heat diffuser mat to lessen the sticking problem. Wash carefully avoiding abrasives, which will scratch and spoil the appearance.
Pyroceram – a special ceramic material that can be taken from the freezer to the oven with no problems. Detachable handles make the pans dual purpose for use on the hob and in the oven.

KNIVES

It is important to buy and use well-made, sharp-edged knives to speed up food preparation. Blades are basically made of steel or stainless steel. Non-stainless steel will take and keep a better edge and it is good to have one of these knives to use for chopping or slicing. Steel does discolour easily but can be cleaned with scouring powder. The handles must be firmly attached to the blade and feel comfortable when held ready for use. Shapes of handles do differ and some 'feel' much better than others.

Knives should ideally be stored separately in a case or rack, or in a special baize-lined drawer for safety and to retain the cutting edge – and to prevent cut fingers, which can happen if they are mixed with all the other kitchen implements in a drawer. A good steel or carborundum is needed for sharpening knives.

The following knives are necessary in a well-equipped kitchen and others can be added in varying sizes as they become necessary.

Vegetable knife – a small knife with a pointed blade about 7.5–10 cm/3–4 inches long, ideal for peeling and dealing with vegetables, boning meat, etc. A similar-sized knife with a serrated or scalloped edge is very good for slicing fruit and tomatoes, which otherwise tend to slip.
Cook's or French knife – this type of knife always has a pointed end and is made in a range of sizes – select one or two to suit yourself. One should be quite large, e.g. a 15–20 cm/6–8 inch blade to use for chopping, slicing etc.
Bread knife – this is a long-bladed knife with a serrated, scalloped or saw edge to make slicing bread and other foods easy.
Palette knife or spatula – this is a flat round-bladed knife, very flexible, which is used for lifting and turning food, spreading and other jobs but not for cutting. They come in varying sizes and the ideal is a small 'spreader' with a blade of about 10 cm/4 inches and a larger palette knife with a blade of 20–25 cm/8–10 inches.
Carving knife – this again is pointed but usually has a narrower blade than the cook's knife. It often comes in a set comprising knife, fork and steel.

HOW TO USE A KNIFE CORRECTLY

1   Always hold the knife blade downwards.
2   Always cut away from you, never towards yourself.
3   Use a proper cutting board or work surface – not formica tops.
4   Always wipe a knife from the back of the blade.
5   Never leave a knife soaking in a bowl of water, it may easily cut the fingers that try to fish it out.

To slice meat, fruit or vegetables, hold the food firmly on a board or the table and with a long-bladed cook's knife, cut in long strokes, keeping the other hand well away from the blade.
To chop vegetables, nuts, dried fruits, parsley, etc, hold a broad-bladed cook's knife firmly at the tip of the blade and cut by moving the knife up and down from the handle end. Work on a special chopping board.
To cut fruit or vegetables into thin slices, hold the item firmly on the board and cut downwards with a sharp cook's knife of the appropriate size. Hold the food well behind the blade to keep fingers out of the way and make

sure your hands are dry, as wet hands can sometimes slip.
To cut bread into neat slices, use a sharp bread knife or bread saw with a serrated edge. Hold the loaf firmly on a board and cut downwards with a sawing movement.
To scrape vegetables, such as carrots, use a small vegetable knife and scrape downwards and away from yourself, holding the vegetable firmly in one hand and turning it as required. You should work on a board. New potatoes are held in one hand and scraped towards you with a small but not too sharp vegetable knife held in the other hand.
Use a palette knife or spatula to turn a pancake or omelette in a pan. The blade is rounded with no sharp edges and its flexibility makes it easy to slip under foods and then lift them up. Use also for spreading and other jobs.

CAKE MAKING EQUIPMENT

A few basic cake tins or pans are essential for every cook but, if you are going to branch out and make a number of everyday and special cakes, then your collection of baking cookware will have to increase.

Cake tins are quite an expensive item and it is wise to buy a good quality make rather than a cheap one which will probably rust and bend out of shape; if good quality and well cared for, they will last for your lifetime and can then be passed on to someone else.

Sandwich tins or layer pans and other small tins can be bought with a variety of 'finishes', some of which are non-stick. These are fine for sandwich or layer cakes and other simple cakes and, in particular, for small individual cakes, but larger cakes and all rich cakes require the tin to be lined with greased wax or greaseproof paper or non-stick baking paper whether the tin is non-stick or not for protection to the actual cake while it is cooking. So a non-stick coating is not necessary for large cake tins.

Always wash cake tins thoroughly in warm soapy water and dry very thoroughly before putting away after use; it is a good idea to stand tins on top of the cooker for an hour or so to make sure they are really dry – they will then keep in good order.

BASIC BAKING EQUIPMENT

2 round sandwich tins or layer pans (about 20 cm/8 inch)
1 deep round cake tin or pan (18–20 cm/7–8 inch)
1 deep square cake tin or pan (18–20 cm/7–8 inch)
1 shallow rectangular tin or pan (about 28 × 18 × 4 cm/11 × 7 × 1½ inch)
1 Swiss roll tin or shallow rectangular pan (about 33 × 23 cm/13 × 9 inch)
1 tray of patty tins or muffin pans
2 baking or cookie sheets
1 loaf tin or pan (23 × 12.5 × 7.5 cm/9 × 5 × 3 inch)
Flan ring or flan tin or pan with loose base, fluted or plain, (about 20 cm/8 inch)
2–3 wire cooling racks

EXTRA BAKING EQUIPMENT

Deep cake tins or pans, round and square, in varying sizes
Extra sandwich tins or layer pans in varying sizes
1 square sandwich tin or layer pan (about 20 cm/8 inch)
1 ring mould (about 1.5 litres/2½ pints)
Extra flan rings, plain and fluted, in varying sizes
Loaf tins or pans in other sizes

1 sponge flan tin or pan
Individual flan tins or pans, or tray of extra deep patty tins or muffin pans
Spring release cake tin or pan, with loose base and extra tubular base

When it comes to making cakes in shapes, it is a good idea to bake the cake in a roasting tin, then whatever shape you require can be cut from this basic shape. There are specialist cake decorating shops that sell numeral cake tins and a variety of other shapes and they will often hire the tins for a couple of days for a nominal sum.

ELECTRICAL EQUIPMENT

A kitchen can be equipped with numerous types of electrical equipment, which is all meant to be labour saving, cut down on time involved and an asset to the cook. However, what equipment you personally will find the most useful does depend a little on the type of household you run, how many you feed and the size of your kitchen, as it is no good cluttering up the place with every conceivable gadget if you are then left with no work surface or space to work in! So do take care when selecting.

The most useful gadget must be an electric mixer or food processor, followed by an electric kettle and toaster and then all the other items, which can be gradually added to your collection if you feel they will be an asset.

ELECTRIC MIXERS AND BLENDERS

These may be one piece of equipment, with mixing and other attachments, or a separate mixer and blender.

The large table-top mixers, which are heavy and not very easy to move around, are frequently very powerful machines and, apart from mixing (usually with a beater, whisk and dough hook), can have many extra attachments, such as a slicer and shredder, mincer, juice extractor, bean slicer, pasta maker, can opener, etc. They are most efficient machines, ideal for a larger family or people who cook in bulk for the freezer, etc. They do require a lot of storage space, so for a kitchen with smaller requirements it may be better to have one of the hand-held electric mixers – some of which also have a small stand, but are dual purpose with the free movement of the mixer. The other type of mixer is simply a hand-held electric mixer which can be used for a great variety of mixing, creaming and whisking jobs.

When buying a blender, it is wise to select the size you will find most convenient to you. However, the bigger ones have larger and stronger motors and thus do the job in the best way. The smallest of the blenders, although efficient, will have limitations, obviously holding small quantities and probably not tackling some of the tasks so efficiently – they will, however, still do the job if allowed to work with small quantities at a time.

FOOD PROCESSORS

These have sprung onto the market in recent years and there are now a wide variety of makes available. They make a very good alternative to a food mixer for some but not all of the processes associated with mixers. They are fairly heavy and again take up quite a bit of space and are not something you can move continually around the kitchen. Most makes cope very efficiently with chopping, slicing, grinding, etc., and the machine comes complete with several of the blades; others can be purchased as required. A food processor does have limitations though: one being the capacity of the bowl, making it possible to purée only small quantities of soup at a time, make smallish quantities of pastry and biscuit dough, etc. It is not so good as a mixer for making creamed cakes and only a few makes can cope with whisking egg whites (using a special blade) and can't whisk anything else. However, apart from this, they are a most useful piece of equipment and the price range makes it possible for many people to own one of them.

DEEP-FAT FRYERS

With the introduction of the electric deep-fat frying machine, this makes the job of deep-frying so much safer, easier and cleaner than by the old method. It also keeps the smell contained for it is used with the lid in position. Simply plug in, select the temperature you require for your cooking and turn on. A light will either come on or go off when it is ready and the food is then put into the fat, the lid replaced and cooking commences. Some machines have a dial on to tell you how long to cook certain types of food. When ready, lift the basket so the fat drains back into the pan and remove the food. The fat will reheat to the same temperature very quickly ready for the next batch. The oil keeps cleaner than with the old method, provided you strain the fat each time after use, once it is cold. If you are a family that does a lot of deep-frying, then an electric deep-fryer will be an absolute boon, but again it is a large item and will take up a lot of valuable storage space in a small kitchen.

ELECTRIC TOASTED SANDWICH MAKER

This is a wonderful invention for preparing toasted sandwiches in a matter of minutes. The machine is not very large and easy to store and, for a family that requires snacks and quick meals, it is ideal. It is a very inexpensive item and the booklets that come with the appliance will show the great versatility of the toasted sandwich!

ELECTRIC FRYING PAN

These are also sometimes called auto-cookers. They consist of a pan with a fairly deep lid and work off an ordinary socket. Although called a frying pan, they can carry out many of the functions of a normal cooker, particularly when cooking for smaller numbers. You cannot grill or broil in an electric frying pan, but you can roast, bake, steam, make stews and casseroles as well as soup – quite apart from using it as a frying pan. The temperature is thermostatically controlled which makes it possible to regulate the heat and prevent overheating and smoking. Some models are made with a non-stick coating, which does make the cleaning process easier. Once the electric connection has been removed from the socket of the pan, the whole pan can be immersed in warm soapy water for cleaning. Take care to dry completely before putting away.

ELECTRIC CARVING KNIFE

This is a rather gimmicky item, but for many a great asset, making the chore of carving much easier. It is marvellous for straightforward carving and slicing, but needs a little practice when it comes to manoeuvring around the bones in a joint. It is not essential to a kitchen, but makes a good present and you will soon find plenty of tasks for it around the kitchen.

ELECTRIC CAN OPENER
Again this is a non-essential piece of equipment to start with, but one which soon makes itself useful if given as a present.

SLOW COOKER
This is really an electric casserole designed for long slow cooking. Slow cookers are usually made of earthenware with an outer case of aluminium and have a low wattage element. They are excellent and economical for stews and casserole dishes, both savoury and sweet, and can be left on safely for 6–10 hours without fear of the food becoming overcooked or the liquid evaporating. It must be pointed out that the manufacturer's instructions must be followed carefully, as each make varies a little. These are ideal for the working wife or single person who wants to prepare a meal in the morning and come home to find it ready cooked.

COOKERS OR STOVES
The cooker is the most important piece of equipment in any kitchen. If you are buying a new cooker, you can probably choose whether you have an electric or gas cooker or buy one powered by oil or solid fuel. However, some kitchens do not have a gas supply so, unless you use calor gas (which means installing a large gas cylinder near the cooker, which in turn needs to be refilled periodically), you may only be able to have an electric cooker, or you may opt for an oil or solid fuel cooker.

Both electric and gas cookers consist of a hob and oven which may be combined in one unit or built into split level ones. The split-level cookers can be combined with rotisseries, etc., and can also be built into the wall along with the refrigerator.

ELECTRIC COOKERS
These have become very much more sophisticated in recent years and practically all models will incorporate an automatic timer for advance cooking while you are out, as well as usually an easy-to-clean surface on the inside of the oven. At least one of the rings on the hob is made so you can use just the inner part, thus saving fuel when you only require to heat a small pan. All models have thermostatic controls for precise cooking results (except sometimes in second ovens when the temperature may not be absolutely accurate). There are also fan-assisted ovens, which give the same temperature throughout the oven, but take care when opening the oven door, as the fan shuts off and allows the oven to cool, so always shut the door quickly.

Watch out with some foreign electric cookers, as they are made with the elements in the top and bottom of the oven instead of at the sides and it may be necessary to adjust your cooking times and temperature to get your usual results.

GAS COOKERS
The main advantage is the instant flame control and when you turn them off they go off instantly instead of taking quite a time to cool down. Gas cookers also often have an automatic cooking switch and there is now an electronic spark ignition, which means the food left in the oven waiting for the automatic cooking to start is not partly warmed by the heat from the pilot light which can start the development of harmful micro-organisms. Again you can find easy-to-clean oven linings and on most models there are large and small hob rings to suit different-sized saucepans and prevent wasted fuel.

SOLID FUEL AND OIL COOKERS
There is a much more limited choice in these types of cookers and they are larger, so are only really suited to a kitchen with plenty of room. They resemble an old-fashioned range and provide constant heat both on top and in the oven. They usually have two large plates on top with plenty of room for several pans on each: one being hot and the other cool. There are two oven and four oven makes, but the two oven is more usual, one oven being hot and the other cool. The main difference with these types of cookers is that you cannot regulate the temperature in the way you can with gas and electric cookers, so you need to follow the manufacturer's handbook carefully until you can adapt your old recipes and cooking times to this new type of heat. Once used to this method of cooking, most people become firm addicts and are loath to change back.

MICROWAVE COOKERS
This is the new revolution in cooking and the sales of microwaves are soaring all over the world. Again, it is a very different method of cooking, one which takes some people a little time to accept. The food is cooked in a fraction of the normal time with microwaves passing through the food. Some cookers have a browning element which makes the food look 'cooked'; others do not and this results in a rather anaemic finished dish which can worry the cook. It is essential to follow the manufacturer's instructions explicitly and to buy yourself a special microwave cookery book that sets out all the do's and don'ts as well as answering numerous other questions. This is obviously the cooking machine of the future and, as sales increase, so the price will drop; although even now there are a wide variety of microwaves at a variety of prices. However, there will still be a place for the controversial cooker – to my mind the microwave will always be an extra, but quite shortly an invaluable extra.

OVEN TEMPERATURE GUIDE

| | Electricity | | Gas Mark |
	°C	°F	
Very cool	110	225	¼
	120	250	½
Cool	140	275	1
	150	300	2
Moderate	160	325	3
	180	350	4
Moderately hot	190	375	5
Fairly hot	200	400	6
Hot	220	425	7
	230	450	8
Very hot	240	475	9

REFRIGERATORS AND FREEZERS

However small your kitchen may be, a refrigerator is a very necessary piece of equipment. In old houses there was always an adequately-sized larder built on a north facing wall, so there was always somewhere cool to store food. Today very few of the modern houses are built with a larder and in flats there simply isn't room for one, so this makes it even more important to have a refrigerator, which in fact doubles up as a storage place along with several other cupboards.

An average domestic refrigerator should be kept at a temperature of 3–7°C/35–45°F, which is sufficiently low to stop micro-organisms developing. It will not destroy any micro-organisms already present in the food so always take care to buy perishable foods when they are as fresh as possible and get them into cool storage as quickly as possible.

REFRIGERATOR TIPS

1 Only open the door when absolutely essential and don't bang the door violently to upset everything in there – most doors have magnetic seals which make them easy to open and close.

2 Don't put hot or warm food into the refrigerator, it will simply raise the temperature and cause condensation which in turn forms frost and makes an insulating layer which stops the refrigerator from working efficiently.

3 Always cover food before you put it in the refrigerator.

4 Store foods correctly in the refrigerator:
(a) Raw foods, such as meat, bacon, poultry, fish, etc., should go in the coldest part, directly under the frozen food compartment.
b) Cooked meats and made-up dishes on the middle shelves.
c) Vegetables and salad ingredients in the special crisper or salad drawer, usually right at the bottom.
d) Butter and fats are usually stored in a special compartment in the door where the temperature is higher, so it doesn't become too hard, otherwise store lower down in the cabinet.

5 Wipe up all spills immediately to cut down on the necessity of cleaning out the cabinet and prevent nasty smells. Also check for small quantities of foods that get hidden behind something larger.

6 Remove cooked foods and cheese about 30 minutes before required to allow them to return to room temperature before serving – this will ensure the maximum flavour.

7 Defrost the refrigerator frequently – do not leave it until it is completely frosted up or it will be working twice as hard as it should but with less results than usual. Don't wipe out with soap or detergent, as they leave an unpleasant smell in the cabinet which the food will pick up. Use a weak solution of bicarbonate of soda in warm water.

THE FROZEN FOOD COMPARTMENT

In Britain there is a star rating given by refrigerator and frozen food manufacturers which is a useful guide as to how long you can keep frozen foods in the frozen food compartment of a domestic refrigerator or in the freezer section of a fridge/freezer.

* *** This is the symbol used to denote the storage temperature of a 3-star compartment plus the ability to freeze a specified weight of fresh food within a 24 hour period at a temperature of −24°C/−12°F. Always check the star markings on commercially frozen food packets.

Maximum temperature of frozen food compartment	Maximum storage time Frozen Foods	Ice Cream
* −6°C/21°F	up to 1 wk	1 day
** −12°C/10°F	up to 1 mth	up to 2 wks
*** −18°C/0°F	up to 3 mths	up to 3 mths

FREEZERS

A deep-freeze has become almost a necessity in many households over the last few years. Freezers are bought for a variety of reasons: usually to make use of abundant supplies of fresh fruit and vegetables and other foods when they are cheap and plentiful; to cut down on frequent shopping, particularly if you live a distance from the shops; and, of course, to enjoy out-of-season delicacies at any time of year. Bulk buying saves on the cost and a freezer is a boon for cooking in advance for everyday and parties.

To freeze fresh food regularly it is essential to use a freezer or frozen food compartment with a 4-star marking. This ensures that the temperature is capable of reaching low enough (e.g. −24°C/12°F) to actually freeze the food and this temperature is lower than the freezer compartment of a 3-star or less refrigerator will reach. Storage in the freezer is quite safe at 18°C/0°F (which is the same as a 3-star refrigerator freezer compartment).

Choose either an upright freezer, which has a front opening door and usually takes up the space of a refrigerator but can also be a small enough cabinet to stand on top of the refrigerator. The larger models often have two doors and usually have at least one shelf with evaporator coils underneath and this is the coldest part, where the food packages to be frozen should be put. If no coils are visible, they will be concealed in the sides of the cabinet, so place packages against the sides. Pull-out baskets are often provided for storing foods and some models have shelves in the doors, but these will not be so cold because of the door being opened, so use for short storage foods.

Chest freezers vary in size from about 100 litres/3.5 cu ft right up to about 450 litres/16 cu ft and larger. They obviously take up much more space than an upright model and are often placed in a garage because of the space required. Some models have baskets, but extra baskets can easily be purchased to fit your particular freezer. The evaporator coils are round the sides of the freezer, so put food to be frozen around the sides or in a special 'fast freeze' compartment in the cabinet. Lids are hinged and open upwards so you cannot store anything on top.

Most modern freezers have a special 'fast freeze' compartment and a special switch which should be turned on several hours before you intend to add a quantity of food to freeze. This lowers the temperature and thus freezes the food as fast as possible to give the best results. Remember to always turn the switch back to normal after 12–24 hours. It is advised to only freeze 10 per cent of the capacity of the freezer in any 24 hours. This means freezing fresh foods, not adding ready-frozen foods.

BASIC RULES OF FREEZING

1 Do not open the freezer door more than necessary and never leave it open. If you have a power cut, do not open it at all.

2 Only freeze really fresh and perfect quality fresh foods, as the quality of the food will not improve in the freezer and poor quality foods are a waste of time and freezer space.

3 Home-frozen foods such as vegetables and many fruits need to be blanched before freezing, they cannot be put into the freezer raw if to be stored for more than 3–4 weeks. It is necessary to buy a specialized freezer book if you are going to do a lot of freezing to find out blanching times, etc. Blanching is in fact putting pre-pared foods into a pan of fast boiling water for a specified time, then draining thoroughly and plunging into iced or very cold water and draining until almost dry.

4 Always cook anything completely and, if possible, chill and then freeze, properly wrapped in an airtight container or polythene bag or foil.

5 Freeze as quickly as possible and in small quantities.

6 Pay special attention to packaging. All air should be expelled and everything must be completely airtight with no tears in the packaging. If using a thin polythene or foil, it is wise to overwrap with a second layer to give proper protection.

7 When freezing liquids, always leave a head space of about 2.5 cm/1 inch as liquids expand when frozen.

8 Label everything clearly with type of food, amount, and date frozen. Also make a list of items in the freezer and when they should be used by.

9 Follow manufacturer's cooking instructions and thaw-ing instructions on packets of bought foods. Vegetables should be cooked from frozen, but all meat and poultry should be properly and completely thawed before cooking and this means until there are no ice crystals left anywhere.

Freezing is a large subject to deal with and I do advise buying a specialized freezing book before you embark on a lot of home-freezing. When freezing ready-frozen foods, always take them home as soon as possible and put them into the coldest part of the cabinet as soon as you can.

BASIC STORE CUPBOARD

When you decide to cook or have to begin to cook, you must start by reading through the recipe carefully. A quick look will tell you which of the ingredients mentioned you have already and those you will need to buy. Shopping lists are essential to make sure you do begin your cooking with all the necessary ingredients – there will be plenty of time for experimenting and adapting recipes to use what is already available when you have mastered the basic arts. There is no need to make problems for yourself too soon.

Your store cupboard should be filled with the basic items that are needed everyday or at least in many recipes. It would be impossible and most time-consuming if everything had to be bought in for each cooking session. A well-stocked store cupboard will mean there is always something to fall back on in an emergency and also to use as the base of a quick meal or snack.

Most dry foods and canned goods will keep well for 6–12 months in suitable storage conditions. This means a cool, dry well-ventilated cupboard or larder that is of suitable size to accommodate your particular needs. If there is a window, it should open easily but must be covered with a fine perforated zinc sheet or gauze to keep out all the insects.

All foods have a definite shelf life, so care must be taken to use items in rotation. If dry ingredients are left uncovered, they will quickly loose their aroma and flavour and spoil your cooking. Items such as dried fruits need cool, dry storage to prevent fermentation, which will happen in damp conditions, and too much warmth will cause shrinkage. Nuts do not store for very long as their high fat content makes them turn rancid. Jams and preserves may grow mould, but this can be carefully removed and the remaining contents used up quickly. When storing canned fruits and other canned goods, keep a regular check for 'blown' cans (bulging ends and leaking seams) and discard these at once.

Remember too to keep the shelves clean, neat and tidy. Always wipe up spillages of any type. Sticky bottles and jars make handling a very messy job and, of course, make everything else that comes in contact with them sticky too.

Always store dry ingredients in airtight containers. Keep in unopened packets on the shelves but, once opened, transfer to an airtight container or put into a polythene bag and secure with a plastic twist tie. All dry ingredients and indeed most other foods should be kept out of direct sunlight.

DRY INGREDIENTS

Plain (all-purpose) flour	Stock cubes
Self-raising flour	Meat and/or vegetable
Cornflour (cornstarch)	extracts
Baking powder	Tea
Bicarbonate of soda	Coffee
Custard powder	Cocoa
Granulated sugar	Currants
Caster (superfine) sugar	Raisins
Brown sugars	Sultanas (golden raisins)
Icing (confectioners') sugar	Cut mixed peel
Salt	Glacé cherries
Peppers	Golden syrup or maple syrup
Spices	Honey
Herbs	Jams
Curry powder	Pickles and chutneys
Mustards	Mayonnaise/salad cream
Tomato purée or paste	or dressing
Tomato ketchup	Rice – patna and pudding
Worcestershire sauce	Macaroni
Oils	Other pasta
Vinegars	Haricot (navy) beans,
Evaporated milk	lentils and other beans
Dried milk	Nuts – walnuts, blanched
Longlife milk	almonds, etc.
Canned fruit juices	Canned vegetables, e.g.
Essences or extracts, e.g.	tomatoes, sweetcorn
vanilla, almond, coffee	Canned fruits, e.g. peaches,
Block chocolate or cooking	mandarins
chocolate	Canned soups
Food colourings and	Canned fish, e.g. tuna,
decorations	sardines
Gelatine	Canned meat, e.g. corned
Jellies	beef, ham

METRIC EQUIVALENTS

It used to be very simple when all British measurements were in Imperial measures and other countries had their own measurements which were either Metric or some type of cup measurement.

In this book the measurements are given first in Metric measures, which are supposed to be simple to follow and easy to use. After the Metric comes the Imperial measure, which many people still prefer to use and many of the older generation will not venture away from for anything, and then, where applicable, a third measurement is given in American measures. Where the measurement is in pounds or a can size or spoon measure, this is the same as the Imperial so the amount has not been repeated.

A chart follows to show the equivalents first in Metric and Imperial for weights, liquids, measurements, etc., and then a list of ingredients showing how they compare with American measures.

SOLID MEASURES

Metric	Imperial	Metric	Imperial
10 g	¼ oz	400 g	14 oz
15 g	½ oz	425 g	15 oz
20 g	¾ oz	450 g	1 lb (16 oz)
25 g	1 oz	550 g	1¼ lb
40 g	1½ oz	675 g	1½ lb
50 g	2 oz	900 g	2 lb
65 g	2½ oz	1.25 kg	2½–2¾ lb
75 g	3 oz	1.5 kg	3–3½ lb
90 g	3½ oz	1.75 kg	4–4½ lb
100 g	4 oz	2 kg	4½–4¾ lb
120 g	4½ oz	2.25 kg	5–5¼ lb
150 g	5 oz	2.5 kg	5½–5¾ lb
165 g	5½ oz	2.75 kg	6 lb
175 g	6 oz	3 kg	7 lb
185 g	6½ oz	3.5 kg	8 lb
200 g	7 oz	4 kg	9 lb
225 g	8 oz	4.5 kg	10 lb
250 g	9 oz	5 kg	11 lb
300 g	10 oz	5.5 kg	12 lb
325 g	11 oz	6 kg	13 lb
350 g	12 oz	6.5 kg	14 lb
375 g	13 oz	6.75 kg	15 lb

MEASUREMENTS

Metric	Imperial	Metric	Imperial
3 mm	⅛ inch	12.5 cm	5 inch
5 mm	¼ inch	15 cm	6 inch
1 cm	½ inch	18 cm	7 inch
2 cm	¾ inch	20 cm	8 inch
2.5 cm	1 inch	23 cm	9 inch
4 cm	1½ inch	25 cm	10 inch
5 cm	2 inch	28 cm	11 inch
6 cm	2½ inch	30 cm	12 inch
7.5 cm	3 inch	33 cm	13 inch
9 cm	3½ inch	35 cm	14 inch
10 cm	4 inch		

LIQUID MEASURES

Metric	Imperial	Metric	Imperial
1.25 ml spoon	¼ teaspoon	400 ml	14 fl oz
2.5 ml spoon	½ teaspoon	450 ml	¾ pint (15 fl oz)
5 ml spoon	1 teaspoon	475 ml	16 fl oz
15 ml spoon	1 tablespoon		(2 US cups)
25 ml	1 fl oz	500 ml	18 fl oz
50 ml	2 fl oz	600 ml	1 pint (20 fl oz)
65 ml	2½ fl oz		(2½ US cups)
85 ml	3 fl oz	750 ml	1¼ pints
100 ml	3½ fl oz	900 ml	1½ pints
120 ml	4 fl oz	1 litre	1¾ pints
135 ml	4½ fl oz	1.2 litres	2 pints
150 ml	¼ pint (5 fl oz)	1.25 litres	2¼ pints
	8 tablespoons	1.5 litres	2½ pints
175 ml	6 fl oz	1.6 litres	2¾ pints
200 ml	7 fl oz (⅓ pint)	1.7 litres	3 pints
250 ml	8 fl oz (1 US cup)	2 litres	3½ pints
275 ml	9 fl oz	2.25 litres	4 pints
300 ml	½ pint (10 fl oz)	2.5 litres	4½ pints
350 ml	12 fl oz	2.75 litres	5 pints

AMERICAN MEASURES

An American cup holds 250 ml or 8 fl oz.
An English cup holds 300 ml or 10 fl oz (½ pint).
1 American tablespoon = 3 teaspoons = ½ fl oz
16 American tablespoons = 1 American cup

All the following measurements are the same as 1 American cup.

225 g/8 oz butter, margarine and lard
110 g/4½ oz shredded suet
225 g/8 oz oil
100 g/4 oz grated Cheddar cheese
100 g/4 oz dry breadcrumbs
50 g/2 oz fresh breadcrumbs
120 g/4½ oz cornflour (cornstarch)
185 g/6½ oz long grain rice
200 g/7 oz pudding rice
100 g/4 oz flour
150 g/5 oz currants
175 g/6 oz raisins and sultanas (golden raisins)
200 g/7 oz glacé cherries
185 g/6½ oz cut mixed peel
165 g/5½ oz whole blanched almonds
110 g/4½ oz chopped walnuts
225 g/8 oz peanut butter
160 g/5⅓ oz powdered gelatine
200 g/7 oz soft brown, caster (superfine) and granulated sugar
110 g/4½ oz icing (confectioners') sugar
325 g/11½ oz golden syrup and treacle
350 g/12 oz honey

In a number of the recipes, particularly the cake recipes, some of the American measurements have been rounded up slightly to make it easier to measure out the ingredients. The results will still be the same.

Where measurements are given in teaspoons and tablespoons they are always level unless otherwise stated.

2 Cooking Terms

It is very important when following a recipe to understand all the special terms given to various processes and – when you know what they are – how to carry them out!

This chapter describes a number of 'processes' and how to do them in detail so that you will know how to proceed when you do meet the term in a recipe, either in this book or some other cookery book. It is a guide which you can refer to when you are in doubt.

To baste – this means to pour or spoon hot melted fat or dripping (or other liquid) from a spoon or with a special meat basting bulb over meat and poultry in a baking tin to keep it moist during roasting. Meat needs to be basted several times during cooking.

To beat – to make a sharp stroking movement with a wooden spoon to remove lumps and turn ingredient(s) into a froth, a paste or a batter – depending on what they are. A spatula or other type of spoon can also be used to beat. Similar to creaming.

To bind – this is to press moistened flour or other ingredients into a sticky ball, using a palette knife and sometimes your fingers, e.g. stuffing, pastry, etc.

To blanch – to put prepared vegetables (usually) or fruit into a pan of boiling water, allow to come back to the boil and then boil for a very short time, such as ½–2 minutes. Drain and plunge immediately into cold water and, when cold, drain again. This process is necessary when preparing vegetables for freezing and can also be used to take the 'edge' off raw vegetables or to tone down an extra strong flavour, such as peppers or leeks.

To blend – this is to mix dry and wet ingredients together smoothly using a wooden spoon or spatula.

To boil – this is to cook ingredients in liquid with the liquid kept at boiling point 100°C/212°F, so that the surface of the water bubbles and turns over continually. There are different degrees of boiling from gently boiling to fast boiling with the surface changing from just gentle bubbling to fairly violent turbulation.

To chop – this is to cut ingredients, such as vegetables, nuts, dried fruits, parsley and other herbs, etc., into very small pieces. Hold a broad-bladed knife firmly at the tip of the blade and cut by moving the knife up and down from the handle end. Work on a special chopping board or wood or other special surface and continue to 'chop' until the ingredient is small enough for the purpose it is required.

To coat – this means to completely cover some ingredient or item with something else. For instance, to coat fish in batter or coat in breadcrumbs after dipping in beaten egg, or to spoon a sauce or mayonnaise over a piece of chicken or vegetable so it is covered.

To combine – to mix together dry ingredients for a cake or the ingredients for a crumble, etc. This refers to anything dry being mixed together using a palette knife, fork or spoon.

To cream – this is a process where you mix a fat, such as butter or margarine, with another ingredient, such as sugar, until it becomes soft, light and very creamy.

To dice – to cut any type of ingredient into small even-sized cubes. The size does vary according to what you want, but is smaller than anything where you would state the size of the cubes.

To dissolve – some ingredients need to be dissolved before they can be added to the other ingredients and this often means dissolving in something else first. For example, powdered gelatine is dissolved in water and is put into a small bowl or basin and placed in a saucepan of very gently boiling water until it becomes transparent. Jelly is also dissolved in water but this can be done in a saucepan because the amount of water used is greater. A microwave oven can also be used for dissolving ingredients.

To dredge with flour (or other ingredients) – this means to shake a small amount of flour over the surface of something; in the case of a greased baking tin it is shaken all over the surface and then the excess is tipped out. Other things are dredged lightly, such as the top of a cake with caster (superfine) or sifted icing (confectioners') sugar, the rolling-out surface for pastry with flour, etc.

To emulsify – when making mayonnaise and other egg-based sauces the process of mixing the egg with the oil by beating hard and adding the oil only drop by drop is called emulsifying.

To fold in – to mix things like dried fruit into a cake mixture or caster (superfine) sugar into stiffly-beaten egg whites. Use a metal spoon or spatula and cut through the mixture turning it over as you cut so the ingredients are gradually and evenly – and most of all lightly – folded in.

To glaze – to brush pastry or other items with beaten egg, milk, or egg white, etc., before baking to give a golden and shiny surface to the cooked item.

To grate – to remove the peel of a lemon or orange in fine little flakes using the finest grating blade on a metal grater. The sizes of blade vary on different sides of the grater: use the medium or coarse blade for cheese and the coarsest blade of all for carrots, vegetables and salad ingredients. Breadcrumbs can also be made by rubbing a piece of bread (not slices) over one of the coarse blades.

To grease a baking tin or pan – rub the surface all over with a piece of butter or margarine paper with a little of the fat still left on it. Or melt a little lard or white fat (or use oil), dip in a pastry brush and spread the fat all over the surface using the pastry brush.

To grease patty tins or muffin pans – brush inside each tin or pan with oil or melted fat using a pastry brush, paying particular attention to the corners where the cake is likely to stick. If you use paper cake cases, no greasing is necessary, simply put the cases into the tins and half to two-thirds fill with the mixture before baking.

To knead – this is to push and mould sticky lumps of dough between your fingers to get them smooth before rolling out, or to punch and fold a yeasted dough to develop the gluten before shaping.

To mash – this is used for potatoes and other vegetables, eggs, fish, etc. The easiest way, if there is sufficient of the ingredients, is to use a special potato masher which presses down onto the food and breaks it up continually until it is smooth. Mashing can also be done with a fork, or with an electric hand mixer, food processor or, for really large amounts, in a large mixer on a stand. Once smooth, butter and/or milk or cream plus seasonings are usually beaten into the mashed mixture to make it creamier.

To melt – this is similar to dissolving but usually nothing else is added to help it. For instance, jam is melted over a low heat; sugar will melt gently before turning to caramel. Fat, sugar and syrup are often melted together when making a gingerbread.

To mince or grind – a special machine called a mincer or meat grinder is fitted onto a table top or is an extra attachment to a large food mixer. Food, especially meat, is put through a coarse or fine blade and comes out as mince. A food processor also chops meat finely so it is similar to mince.

To pare – this means to cut something off very thinly, e.g. the yellow rind from a lemon (free of the white pith), the green skin off a cucumber, etc. A potato peeler is good for this task, although a small vegetable knife can also be used – but mind your fingers.

To peel – this is similar to paring, but to take off all the skin or peel and pith in the case of citrus fruits. Use a vegetable knife for most vegetables, but a potato peeler can obviously be used for potatoes and carrots and also for Jerusalem artichokes, turnips, etc.

To pipe – use a piping bag, either a bought nylon one fitted with a large vegetable nozzle – plain or fluted – suitable for the task to be done, or a small nylon or wax or greaseproof paper piping bag fitted with a small nozzle if it is for cake icing or delicate piping. Half fill with the cream, potato, icing, etc., and fold over the end to enclose the icing or whatever. Hold the bag with one hand to apply pressure on the mixture in the bag as it is piped and use the other hand to guide and steady it so you pipe evenly and where you intend to and pipe out the mixture through the nozzle to give a variety of shapes, including stars, whirls, shells, etc., for decoration.

To purée – this is to make something that has been cooked and is either full of lumpy ingredients or is just lumpy completely smooth! Either put a sieve over a bowl, add some of the mixture and press it through the sieve with the help of a wooden spoon, or put into a food processor or blender and switch on until smooth and puréed.

To rub in – in pastry making and with some cakes and buns, the dry ingredients are put into a bowl and the fat is added in small pieces. These pieces are literally rubbed into the flour by rubbing them with the fingertips. The finished mixture looks like breadcrumbs.

To shred – this means to slice cabbage and other vegetables into very thin slices or strands. Shredding can also be done on a large electric mixer or in a food processor using one of the shredding blades.

To skim – a casserole may sometimes have a layer of fat appear on the surface when it is cooked; bone stock gets a scum on the surface when it first comes to the boil. Use a spoon to carefully take off the layer of fat or a slotted spoon to remove the scum from the stock. If the fat persists, skim it by laying sheets of absorbent kitchen paper towel on the top, which will soak up excess fat.

To skin a tomato – bring a saucepan of water to the boil. Put the tomato into the water for about 30 seconds. Remove it immediately to a bowl of cold water. Using a sharp knife make a tiny nick in the skin and the skin should split and peel off easily. Alternatively, if you have a gas hob, impale the tomato on a fork and hold carefully over the naked flame, turning it until it is evenly browned and the skin splits, again it should peel off easily.

To slake – this is a term given to mixing arrowroot or cornflour (cornstarch) with the minimum of cold water before it is added to the rest of the sauce. Both arrowroot and cornflour (cornstarch) have a rather strange texture and the mixing with water is a sort of dissolving process. Once mixed, a little of the hot sauce should then be added to the slaked mixture before it is all stirred back into the sauce and brought to the boil until thickened.

To slice – use a sharp knife and put the item to be sliced onto a chopping board and cut downwards in neat even strokes to give the thickness of slice you require. Some items such as bread are better sliced using a serrated-edged knife; others are fine with an ordinary knife, but it must be sharp.

To sieve – to pour something through a wire mesh or nylon mesh strainer of suitable size, or to put something thicker into the strainer (or sieve) and push it through with a wooden spoon.

To sift – similar to sieve but only used for dry ingredients such as flour, icing (confectioners') sugar, etc. Simply tip into the sieve and shake it through to remove any lumps and incorporate air as it is shaken.

To simmer – this is again to cook in a liquid in a saucepan on a hob, but is a very, very slow boil, so the liquid is only barely shimmering, not bubbling.

To strain – to pour something in a liquid through a sieve, or strainer or colander to drain off all the liquid. It can be used for vegetables when the vegetable itself is the important part, although some or all of the liquid can be saved to use for sauces, soups, etc., or for a stock or something when the liquid is the important part and the bones, etc., are to be discarded.

To turn a cake out of a tin or pan – usually leave for a few seconds in the tin to allow it to shrink from the sides of the tin a little, or in some cases for up to 10 minutes for the cake to settle, or with very rich fruit cakes until cold, before attempting to turn out. First tip the tin from side to side to check it is loosened and, if visibly stuck in certain places, loosen with the help of a small round-bladed palette knife or spatula. Invert the cake onto a wire cooling rack, peel off the paper and then turn back using another cooling rack so the cake is the right way up. Leave until cold.

To test if a cake is cooked – warm a straight-sided skewer, as fine as possible, and insert straight down into the centre of the cake. If it comes out completely clean, the cake is ready; if it is at all sticky, it is not, so leave the cake in the oven for 5 minutes or so before testing again. Remember to keep the door closed while the cake is out of the oven being tested or the temperature of the oven will drop rapidly.

To whip – to beat eggs or cream with a hand whisk or fork using a light circular stroke. This is the way you make egg yolks and their whites blend evenly together among other things.

To whisk – a faster way of beating a batter or whipping cream or egg whites until just frothy or until really stiff. Use a rotary whisk or hand-held electric mixer for preference, but a balloon or flat whisk can also be used – provided you have plenty of strength in your arm.

To weigh – to measure dry ingredients, meat, vegetables, etc., in fact anything that is not liquid. Most sets of scales have both Metric weights and Imperial weights marked on the dial of the scales. Proper sets of scales using metal weights are more accurate and the weights come in Metric and Imperial sizes and either can be used on the same machine. American cup measures are also available – remember an American cup is 8 fl oz/250 ml while a British cup is 10 fl oz or ½ pint/300 ml.

To measure liquid – use a jug with the measurements on the side. Metric measurements are in mililitres and litres; Imperial measures are in pints and fluid ounces; American measures are in cups and, if you can't find an American cup, use the 8 fl oz/250 ml mark on the side of the jug.

To measure a level spoonful – use a set of measuring spoons for ease; they come in sets of 1 tablespoon, 1 teaspoon, ½ teaspoon and ¼ teaspoon and make measuring so much easier. Fill the spoon with the dry ingredient and use a knife or palette knife or spatula to level off the surface to be really accurate. Liquid measures will level themselves.

To measure syrup or honey – warm the spoon or jug, then brush lightly all over with oil. The measured syrup will then slowly slide off the spoon or pour out of the jug without sticking and altering the measurement. For larger weights, particularly if the syrup is to be warmed, put the saucepan on the scales, note the weight and then add sufficient syrup to give the required amount.

3 Eggs

Eggs are a most versatile and nutritious food, invaluable for numerous quick snacks as well as for inclusion in a multitude of other meals and are indeed an essential ingredient in a great many recipes, especially cakes, puddings and desserts. They are available all the year round and always remain cheap in comparison to meat and fish, although the prices do fluctuate. Eggs are high in protein and fat and contain good amounts of Vitamin A, several of the B group Vitamins and useful amounts of calcium and iron.

Eggs are best stored in a cool larder and not in the refrigerator, unless really essential, as their porous shells can absorb other strong flavours if placed too close. If it is necessary to keep them chilled, they should be stored in the rack provided in the refrigerator and kept well away from the ice box. It is recommended that they are allowed to return to room temperature before use otherwise, when used in cake making and mayonnaise, etc., they are liable to curdle, the shells will definitely crack when boiled and the whites are difficult to whisk. Fresh eggs will keep in a cool place for 2–3 weeks and a little longer in the refrigerator. They are still often usuable after this time in cooking but will not be so good for boiling as they become stale.

HOW TO TEST FOR FRESHNESS
There is always a small air space inside an egg and this increases as the egg ages. Therefore, the fresher the egg, the heavier it should be. To test this, fill a bowl or tumbler with water and put in the egg. If it sinks to the bottom and stays there, it is fresh; if it tilts slightly, it is beginning to stale, and should it rise to the surface, then it is more than likely to be bad!

Egg shells vary in colour according to the breed of chicken and the colour makes no difference to the flavour or food value of the egg. Sometimes the yolks are extra rich in colour and this is usually due to the type of feed given to the birds.

EGG SIZES
Eggs are graded in sizes which range from 1–7 or extra large to very small.

Size 1 – extra large	Size 5 – small
Size 2 – large	Size 6 – small
Size 3 – medium	Size 7 – very small
Size 4 – medium	

Size 1 or extra large eggs are obviously the most expensive and are good to serve as boiled eggs, etc. Sizes 2, 3 and 4 or large to medium eggs are most popular and many cookery books base their recipes using large or medium eggs.

Recipes will usually state the grade or possibly large, medium or small and the appropriate size should be used. If the size is not indicated, it is safer to use size 2 or 3 or large or medium eggs to ensure satisfactory results.

OTHER TYPES OF EGGS
Most of the time eggs refer to hen's eggs but there are other eggs that can be used for boiling and in cooking.

Duck's eggs – these are larger and richer than hen's eggs and have a stronger flavour. They must be thoroughly cooked for safety, e.g. at least 10 minutes boiling, and are good used in most cakes (simply weigh against hen's eggs and use accordingly). However, do not use in whisked sponges or meringues or dishes that require little or low temperature cooking. Do not preserve, store or freeze them.

Goose eggs – the flavour is similar to hen's eggs but the size of course is considerably larger. Use exactly as you would hen's eggs – all you need to do is work out how much you need by weighing against hen's eggs. One good egg should make sufficient scrambled egg for 3–4 people!

Turkey eggs – smaller than goose eggs but can be used in the same way. Allow about 6–7 minutes for soft-boiled or 15 minutes plus for hard-boiled. These are readily available at farm shops that sell fresh turkeys, or turkey farms.

Quail's, gull's, plover's eggs – these are usually served hard-boiled as an hors d'oeuvre. They are a delicacy, but are becoming more popular and easier to obtain. Boil for 10–15 minutes.

FREEZING EGGS
Whole eggs do not freeze either in the shell or out of it as they are. However they can be separated and frozen.

Egg whites can be frozen as they are in small containers or ice cube trays. Clearly label with quantities. Thaw out completely and use as if fresh egg whites within 2 days of thawing.

Egg yolks will coagulate during freezing but can be frozen if salt or sugar is added as a stabilizer. Add ½ teaspoon salt or caster (superfine) sugar to each 6 egg yolks, beating well. Label clearly whether for sweet or savoury use. Thaw completely and use immediately they are thawed for such dishes as soufflés, omelettes, cakes, etc.

Eggs will keep in the freezer for up to 6 months.

MAIN USES OF EGGS

Apart from cooking eggs for main dishes, they are used for three main reasons in cooking and these are raising, thickening and binding, and emulsifying.

Raising – eggs form the raising agent to a great extent in cake and batter mixes. The egg whites are often whisked and folded into mixtures such as soufflés and other extra light cakes as well as airy mixtures and desserts, and also form the basis of meringues, icings and frostings.

Thickening and binding – beaten eggs or egg yolks are used for thickening sauces and custards either to make in a saucepan or bake in the oven and for binding all types of ingredients together for stuffings and croquettes, burgers, etc., and also for coating foods that are to be covered in breadcrumbs and fried or whatever, to prevent the food from falling apart.

Emulsifying – the yolk of the egg only is used to emulsify the other ingredients in such sauces as mayonnaise and hollandaise.

HOW TO CRACK AND SEPARATE EGGS

To crack an egg, take the egg in one hand and give it a sharp tap on something firm, such as the side of a basin, the edge of the working surface, etc., and then break the shell in half using two hands. This should be done so the egg is held over a basin and the contents will drop into it. Prolonged gentle tapping of the shell will only cause the shell to crush and probably break the yolk.

To separate eggs, having broken the shell evenly and, holding the egg over a basin, pass the yolk back and forth from one half of the shell to the other, allowing the white to fall into the basin. Put the yolk in another basin. It is advisable to have a third basin if you are separating more than one egg to allow for the possibility of a bad or stale egg or if the yolk should break and mix with the white. Each egg is broken into one bowl and the yolks and whites then added to those already cracked. This will avoid any disaster or wastage.

BASIC COOKING METHODS

BOILED EGGS

1 Bring a saucepan of water to boiling point. A little salt or vinegar added to the water helps prevent the shells from cracking.
2 Put the eggs slowly into the water using a tablespoon or slotted kitchen spoon and bring back to the boil. Boil for 3–5 minutes depending on size of egg and how you like to eat your egg. The average is 4 minutes for a medium size egg. The shorter cooking time gives a lightly set egg and the longer a firm but not hard egg. Fresh eggs take a little longer for the whites to set.
3 Using a draining spoon, put into egg cups with the pointed end upwards and crack the tops gently to prevent overcooking. Serve with bread and butter.
4 For hard-boiled eggs, put into cold water, bring to the boil and boil for 10–12 minutes. Run immediately under cold water and leave in the cold water until cool. Crack shells and peel. Hard-boiled eggs will keep in the refrigerator in their shells for 4–5 days before use.

Eggs Mornay
Serves 2

4 eggs
300 ml/½ pint/1¼ cups cheese sauce (see page 31)
½ teaspoon French or Dijon mustard
25 g/1 oz/¼ cup grated Cheddar cheese
1 tablespoon grated Parmesan cheese
1 tablespoon breadcrumbs
To garnish
1 tomato, sliced
a few sprigs of parsley (optional)

1 Hard-boil the eggs, do not run under cold water but shell and cut in half. Lay in a shallow ovenproof dish and keep warm.
2 While the eggs are boiling, make the cheese sauce. When ready, stir in the French mustard and pour over the eggs.
3 Combine the grated cheeses and breadcrumbs and sprinkle over the eggs. Place under a moderate grill or broiler and cook until golden brown.
4 Garnish with slices of tomato and sprigs of parsley. Serve hot.

Note: If liked, a 225 g/8 oz packet of frozen spinach (leaf or chopped) can be cooked, following the instructions on the packet, drained well and placed in the dish with the eggs and the sauce poured over the top.

Curried Eggs
Serves 2

4 eggs
50 g/2 oz/¼ cup butter or margarine
1 onion, peeled and thinly sliced
1 clove garlic, crushed (optional)
½–1 small dessert apple, peeled, cored and chopped
2 teaspoons curry powder
3 tablespoons flour
300 ml/½ pint/1¼ cups beef or chicken stock (made using ¾–1 stock cube)
salt and pepper
2 tablespoons tomato ketchup
100 g/4 oz/¾ cup long grain rice

1 Melt the fat in a pan and fry the onion and garlic (if used) gently until soft. Add the apple and continue cooking for a minute or so longer, stirring from time to time.
2 Stir in the curry powder and flour and cook for about a minute, stirring continuously – take care it does not overbrown or burn.
3 Gradually add the stock and bring to the boil, stirring frequently. Season lightly, add the ketchup, cover and simmer for about 20 minutes giving the pan an occasional stir.
4 Put a pan on to boil with salted water – add a good pinch of salt. When boiling, add the rice, stir until the water returns to the boil, lower the heat and simmer, uncovered, for 12–14 minutes or until the rice is just tender. It should be tender but still feel firm when pinched between the fingers and still have a bit of a 'bite' to it. Do not overcook, as soggy rice is awful. Give the rice a stir two or three times during cooking.
5 When ready, strain through a sieve and hold under a hot

running tap to rinse out the excess starch and drain.

6 The eggs should be put on to boil for 10–12 minutes when the rice has just been added to the water.

7 Place the rice around the edge of two plates. Peel and halve the eggs and stand in the centre of the rice. Spoon the sauce over the eggs and serve. Either mango chutney or lime pickle makes a good accompaniment.

Stuffed Eggs Serves 2

4 eggs, hard-boiled
25 g/1 oz/2 tablespoons softened butter
1 tablespoon mayonnaise
95 g/3 1/2 oz can tuna fish, salmon, or prawns or shrimp, drained
salt and pepper
To garnish
sprigs of parsley or slices of stuffed olives

1 Halve the cold eggs and carefully remove the yolks. Stand the whites on a plate, cut side upwards. Mash the yolks finely in a basin with a fork and beat in the butter and mayonnaise.

2 Mash the tuna or salmon or finely chop the prawns or shrimp, add to the yolks and beat well, then season to taste.

3 Either spoon the filling back into the whites using a teaspoon or put into a piping bag fitted with a large plain vegetable nozzle and pipe back into the whites.

4 Garnish each stuffed egg with a sprig of parsley or a slice of stuffed olive and serve with salads.

Note: There are a great variety of other fillings you will be able to think of yourself to make very interesting stuffed eggs. Try mashed avocado with lemon juice; finely chopped watercress, freshly chopped herbs and minced or ground chicken; minced or finely chopped smoked salmon, etc.

POACHED EGGS

There are two ways of poaching eggs, either with a special egg poacher or in a frying pan.

1 Put water in the base of a poaching pan and bring to the boil. Put a knob of butter into each cup required and, if not non-stick, brush around the cup until coated.

2 Crack eggs and add one to each poacher pan. Cover the pan and simmer gently for 3–4 minutes or until the yolks and whites are sufficiently set – a knife inserted into the egg white will tell how set the egg is.

3 Serve the eggs turned out, with the help of a palette knife or spatula, onto buttered toast, toasted cheese, or creamed spinach, etc., and serve at once.

4 If you don't have an egg poacher, fill a frying pan to about half full with water and bring to the boil. Turn down so the water just shimmers. Either put greased pastry cutters into the water and break an egg into each and cook as above, or using a spoon swirl the water in the pan fairly vigorously and drop the egg carefully into the centre of the 'swirl'. Cook gently for 3–4 minutes until set. Lift out carefully, drain well on a slotted spoon and repeat with further eggs.

Florentine Eggs Serves 4

4–8 eggs
450 g/1 lb frozen spinach (leaf or chopped), or 900 g/2 lb fresh spinach
salt and pepper
ground or freshly grated nutmeg
40 g/1 1/2 oz/3 tablespoons butter or margarine
25 g/1 oz/1/4 cup flour
300 ml/1/2 pint/1 1/4 cups milk
75 g/3 oz mature Cheddar cheese, grated

1 Either cook the spinach following the directions on the packet if using frozen, or strip off tough stalks from fresh spinach and wash thoroughly in several changes of water to remove mud and grit. Place in a saucepan with a good pinch of salt and 3–4 tablespoons water. Cover the pan and cook gently for 12–15 minutes or until the spinach is tender.

2 Drain the spinach very thoroughly and chop roughly. Heat 15 g/1/2 oz/1 tablespoon butter in a pan, toss in the chopped spinach, a little salt and pepper and a good pinch of nutmeg and heat through thoroughly, stirring frequently. Keep warm.

3 Meanwhile, melt the remaining fat in a pan and make a white sauce as usual (see page 29). Add 50 g/2 oz/1/2 cup of the grated cheese, stir until melted and then season to taste.

4 Poach the eggs. Arrange the spinach in an ovenproof dish, or four large individual dishes, put the eggs on top and coat with the sauce. Sprinkle with remaining cheese and brown quickly under the grill or broiler.

Egg Piperade Serves 2–4

2–4 eggs
1 large onion, peeled and thinly sliced
1 clove garlic, crushed
2 tablespoons oil
1 red pepper, deseeded and sliced
1 green pepper, deseeded and sliced
225 g/8 oz can peeled tomatoes
salt and pepper
1 teaspoon tomato purée
1 teaspoon Worcestershire sauce

1 Fry the onion and garlic gently in the heated oil in a saucepan until soft but only lightly coloured, stirring from time to time.

2 Add the peppers and continue to cook for 3–4 minutes, stirring occasionally.

3 Add the tomatoes and their juice, seasonings, tomato purée and Worcestershire sauce, bring to the boil, cover the pan and simmer very gently for about 15 minutes or until thick and tender, stirring occasionally.

4 When the tomato mixture is almost ready, poach the eggs.

5 Serve the piperade in two soup plates or shell dishes and top each portion with 1–2 eggs. Serve with hot fingers of toast.

Omelette (see page 25)

1   *Pull the sides of the omelette to the centre of the pan, allowing the liquid egg to run out to the sides.*

2   *Tilt the pan away from you and fold about one-third of the omelette to the centre.*

3   *Having folded over the other third, slip the folded omelette onto a warm plate, turning it so the folds are underneath.*

SCRAMBLED EGGS

Allow 2 eggs and 1–2 tablespoons milk per person.

1   Gently melt a knob of butter (about 1–1½ teaspoons) in a saucepan and add the milk and salt and pepper.
2   Beat the eggs with a fork until evenly mixed, then pour into the saucepan. Cook gently over a low heat, stirring continuously with a spatula or wooden spoon as the egg begins to thicken.
3   Continue to cook and stir until just thickened and creamy. Do not overcook or the egg will become dry and hard and sometimes begin to separate. Do not be tempted to cook quickly over a fierce heat.
4   Serve immediately on hot buttered toast.

Note: For quantities using more than 8 eggs, it is better to cook in two separate amounts.

VARIATIONS

Add any of the following ingredients to a 4-egg mixture just before turning onto the plates.
Mushroom – 50 g/2 oz/1 cup fried chopped mushrooms.
Ham – 50 g/2 oz/½ cup chopped ham or fried chopped bacon rashers.
Cheese – 50–75 g/2–3 oz/½–¾ cup grated cheese.
Prawn or Shrimp – 50 g/2 oz peeled prawns or shrimp or melted potted shrimp.
Smoked Fish – 50 g/2 oz/½ cup flaked smoked cod, haddock or mackerel.
Tomato – 2 tomatoes, peeled and chopped.
Asparagus – 4–8 cooked asparagus spears, chopped.
Herb – ½ teaspoon dried mixed herbs or 1 tablespoon freshly chopped mixed herbs.

Stuffed Rolls   Serves 4

6 eggs
4 crisp round rolls
8 rashers streaky bacon, derinded
6 tablespoons milk
salt and pepper
25 g/1 oz/2 tablespoons butter
2 tablespoons snipped chives or chopped spring onion
   (scallion) tops
4 sprigs parsley

1   Heat the rolls gently in a warm oven, then cut off the tops and scoop out the crumb; save this for breadcrumbs. Keep the rolls warm.
2   Roll up the rashers of bacon, spear on wooden cocktail sticks or skewers and cook under the grill or broiler until browned and cooked through.
3   Use the eggs, milk and seasonings to make into scrambled egg in a saucepan with the melted butter. Stir in the chives or spring onions and spoon into the rolls.
4   Top each roll with 2 bacon rolls, the lid of the roll and a sprig of parsley. Serve hot.

OPPOSITE: *Stuffed Eggs* (see page 21) *and Florentine Eggs* (see page 21)

Egg Sandwich and Roll Fillings

Scramble 2, 3 or 4 eggs as usual, turn into a basin and leave to get cold. When cold, mash thoroughly, season well and beat in 1 tablespoon thick mayonnaise. Use to fill rolls or sandwiches together with cress or lettuce, or chopped peeled tomatoes, or chopped smoked salmon or ham.

For cocktail snacks, simply spread the mixture onto buttered biscuits, pieces of toast or pumpernickel bread and garnish with a slice of stuffed olive, sprig of parsley, slice of cucumber, whole prawn or large shrimp, etc.

BAKED EGGS

These are baked in ovenproof cocotte or other small dishes in a moderate oven (180°C/350°F/Gas Mark 4).

1   Stand the required number of dishes on a baking sheet and brush the insides liberally with melted butter. Break an egg into each dish and season lightly.
2   Cook in the centre of the oven until just set – about 6–8 minutes. Serve at once with fingers of hot toast.

Note: Recipes for more sophisticated baked eggs that include other ingredients and cream, etc., appear below. They are sometimes cooked in a hotter oven.

Mushroom Baked Eggs

Serves 4 as a starter

4 eggs
175 g/6 oz button mushrooms, chopped
25 g/1 oz/2 tablespoons butter or margarine
1/4 teaspoon ground coriander
salt and pepper
4 tablespoons double (heavy) cream
50 g/2 oz Cheddar cheese, grated

1   Fry the mushrooms gently in the melted fat, stirring frequently, until tender – about 2 minutes. Season with coriander, salt and pepper.
2   Lightly grease four ovenproof ramekin or cocotte dishes and divide the mushroom mixture between them. Stand on a baking sheet.
3   Carefully break an egg into each dish and pour 1 tablespoon cream over each one. Sprinkle with cheese.
4   Cook in a moderate oven (180°C/350°/Gas Mark 4) for about 12–15 minutes or until the eggs are just set. Serve hot with brown toast and butter or granary rolls.

VARIATIONS

Ham and Tomato – 2 slices cooked ham, finely chopped, and 2–3 peeled tomatoes, chopped.
Tomato and Herb – 4–6 peeled and sliced tomatoes and 1 teaspoon dried basil or oregano.
Potted Shrimp – divide 2 individual portions of potted shrimp between the four dishes.
Curried – fry 1 small chopped onion in 1 tablespoon oil until lightly browned. Add 25 g/1 oz/1/4 cup raisins, 1 teaspoon curry powder and 40 g/1 1/2 oz/1/4 cup rice, boiled, and mix well together.

Potato Eggs

Serves 4

4 eggs
450 g/1 lb creamed potatoes (or use instant potato)
1 onion, peeled and thinly sliced
25 g/1 oz/2 tablespoons butter or margarine
1 tablespoon oil
100 g/4 oz mushrooms, sliced
salt and pepper
1/2 teaspoon dried mixed herbs (optional)
50 g/2 oz Cheddar cheese, grated

1   Either spread or pipe the potato (using a piping bag and large star vegetable nozzle) around the edge of four greased scallop shells or individual ovenproof dishes.
2   Fry the onion in the melted fat and oil in a small pan until soft. Add the mushrooms and continue for a minute or so. Season well and add the herbs (if used).
3   Divide between the dishes, placing in the centre of the potato. Break an egg into each and sprinkle with the cheese.
4   Cook in a moderate oven (180°C/350°F/Gas Mark 4) for 10–15 minutes until the eggs are set. Serve at once.

Note: 4 rashers bacon, chopped, may be fried with the onion, or add 50 g/2 oz cooked ham, chopped, at the end.

FRIED EGGS

Use about 3 tablespoons oil, dripping or bacon fat, or 40–50 g/1 1/2–2 oz/3–4 tablespoons lard for frying eggs.

1   Melt your chosen fat in a frying pan but don't let it get too hot. Break eggs, one at a time, into a cup and pour into the pan leaving a space between each one.
2   Cook gently, tilting the pan from time to time so the fat can be spooned over the eggs to baste them.
3   When the eggs are set, remove from the pan carefully using a fish slice or spatula and place on toast, fried bread or a warmed plate.

Framed Eggs

Serves 4

4 eggs
8 rashers bacon, derinded
dripping, lard or oil
4 slices bread (brown or white), about 2 cm/3/4 inch thick
watercress to garnish

1   Fry the bacon in dripping, lard or oil until well browned and crispy. Drain and keep warm.
2   Using a glass or pastry cutter, cut out a circle from the centre of each slice of bread leaving a rim of at least 1 cm/1/2 inch.
3   Fry the bread in the fat in the pan until browned on one side and then turn over. Break an egg into each piece of bread and cook until the egg is set and the bread browned on the underside.
4   Serve the eggs, well drained, on warmed plates with a slice of bacon on each side of the egg and garnished with watercress.

Meringue Eggs on Haddock Serves 4

4 eggs, separated
4 fillets smoked haddock or golden cutlets
150 ml/¼ pint/⅔ cup milk
dripping, lard or oil for frying

1 Place the fish in a saucepan with the milk and sufficient water to barely cover it. Bring to the boil, cover the pan and simmer gently for 5–8 minutes until tender. Drain the fish, using a fish slice or slotted spatula, put onto four plates and keep warm. Discard the cooking liquid.
2 Whisk the egg whites until very stiff. Heat a little fat in a frying pan and when hot place four even piles of whisked egg white in it. Make a hollow in each pile of meringue and drop an egg yolk into each one. Cook gently until set.
3 Drain well and serve 1 egg on each portion of fish. Serve at once.

OMELETTES

Your first omelette may not be as perfect as you had hoped, but take heart, they do need a little practice to make perfect. Omelettes make an ideal snack or supper dish, are extremely quick to make and can have fillings of almost anything you like to add. Always serve an omelette straight from the pan to the table; they do not like to be kept waiting and will only become tough and rubbery if kept.

Ideally, use a special omelette pan, which is like a small frying pan, about 20 cm/8 inches in diameter, but an ordinary frying pan can be used so long as it has a heavy base. The thick base is necessary so it will hold the heat and cook the omelette evenly, without burning, as soon as the mixture is poured into the pan.

It is necessary to 'season' a new omelette pan, provided it does not have a non-stick surface. This is done by adding a knob of butter to the pan and heating it very slowly until hot but not browned, then rubbing vigorously with kitchen paper towel so the butter is well 'in' to the surface of the pan. If the pan is to be kept for omelettes alone, it should never be washed. Simply rub over with kitchen paper towel and then with a clean cloth. If it doesn't seem clean enough, heat the pan gently with a good sprinkling of salt in it and rub thoroughly with a pad of kitchen paper towel until clean; the grittiness will clean the surface and leave it smooth and ready for use.

Before use, heat the pan over a gentle heat until really evenly hot – if it is heated too quickly or over a fierce heat the pan will be unevenly hot.

Plain Omelette Serves 1

Use butter, unsalted margarine or bacon fat for the best omelettes. (See step-by-step illustrations, page 22.)

2 eggs
salt and pepper
1–2 tablespoons water
about 15 g/½ oz/1 tablespoon butter

1 Whisk the eggs lightly with a fork with salt and pepper to taste and the water. Do not overwhisk, they should not be frothy or completely beaten.
2 Heat the pan and, when ready, add a knob of butter, twisting the pan until it has melted and the surface of the pan is evenly coated.
3 Pour in the egg mixture, leave for a few seconds until it begins to set in places then, using a small knife or fork, gently pull the sides of the omelette to the centre of the pan, allowing the liquid egg to run out to the sides. Continue until all the egg has just set then cook for a few seconds longer, undisturbed, until the underside is golden brown.
4 Using a palette knife or spatula loosen the omelette, tilt the pan away from you and fold about one-third of the omelette to the centre. Next fold over the other third and slip the folded omelette out of the pan onto a warm plate, turning it so the folds are underneath. Serve at once.

VARIATIONS AND FILLINGS

There are many fillings that can be added to omelettes; these are just a few:

Ham – chop 50 g/2 oz ham, cooked bacon or tongue and either add to the beaten egg before cooking or sprinkle over the egg when it is about half set.

Bacon – fry 2 derinded and chopped bacon rashers in a small pan in their own fat until crisp. Drain and spoon over the omelette before folding.

Cheese – grate 40–50 g/1½–2 oz mature Cheddar cheese, mix half of it with the beaten eggs and sprinkle the remainder over the omelette just before it is folded. Other types of cheese may be used, or a combination of two varieties. For a strong flavour, add grated Parmesan cheese.

Tomato – peel and chop 2 tomatoes and heat in 15 g/½ oz/1 tablespoon butter in a small pan. Add to the omelette just before folding.

Herb – add 1 teaspoon dried mixed herbs or 1 tablespoon freshly chopped mixed herbs (or any one preferred herb) to the beaten eggs.

Prawn or Shrimp – use 40–50 g/1½–2 oz peeled prawns or shrimp (thawed out if frozen) and tossed in 15 g/½ oz/1 tablespoon melted butter. Add to the omelette just before folding.

Basic Soufflé (see page 28)

1   *Separate the eggs, putting the whites into a large bowl.*

3   *Whisk the egg whites until very stiff and standing in peaks.*

2   *Stir the flour into the melted butter and cook for a minute or two, stirring constantly, then gradually add the milk, stirring continuously, and bring to the boil.*

4   *Fold the egg whites into the sauce.*

Spanish Style Omelette
Serves 2

4 eggs
1 small onion, peeled and chopped
1–2 tablespoons oil
1 tomato, peeled and chopped
1 small red pepper, deseeded and chopped, or 1–2 canned pimientos, chopped
2 cooked potatoes, roughly chopped
2–3 tablespoons cooked peas
salt and pepper

1   Fry the onion gently in the heated oil in a frying pan (not a small omelette pan) until soft. Add the pepper and continue for a few minutes.

2   Add the rest of the vegetables and cook for a minute or so, stirring frequently.

3   Beat the eggs with a little salt and pepper and pour over the vegetables. Cook slowly, shaking the pan occasionally, until set. This omelette is left to cook undisturbed.

4   Put the omelette still in the pan under a moderate grill or broiler until lightly browned to finish off the cooking. Alternatively, the omelette can be carefully turned over to brown the second side, but this can be a little difficult as the omelette is rather thick and unwieldy.

5   Cut the omelette in half and slide onto two warmed plates. Serve hot.

Note: Crisply-fried chopped bacon or ham may also be added to the omelette if liked.

OPPOSITE: *Tomato and Sweetcorn Soufflé* (see page 28) *and Spanish Style Omelette*

Soufflé Omelette
Serves 1

2 eggs, separated
2 tablespoons water
1 teaspoon caster (superfine) sugar for sweet, or salt and
*   pepper to taste for savoury*
15 g/½ oz/1 tablespoon butter

1   Put the egg yolks in one bowl and the whites in another. Add the water and sugar or seasonings to the yolks and beat until smooth.
2   Whisk the egg whites until very stiff so that they stand in peaks and will stay in position when the bowl is turned upside down.
3   Heat the butter in an omelette or small frying pan.
4   Add the egg whites to the yolks and fold in gently using a metal spoon, but take care not to overmix.
5   Brush the fat round the sides of the heated pan and pour in the egg mixture. Cook over a gentle heat, undisturbed, until the underside is golden brown.
6   Immediately place under a moderate grill or broiler and cook until browned on top.
7   Move immediately from under the grill, run a spatula around the sides of the pan and under the omelette and spread or spoon any filling onto it. Double over carefully and slide onto a warmed plate. Serve at once.

FILLINGS
Use any of the savoury fillings suggested for plain omelettes, simply spooning onto it before folding in half.
Jam – spread the cooked omelette with warmed jam, jelly, marmalade, honey, lemon cheese or curd, etc., fold over and sprinkle with sugar.
Liqueur – add 1 tablespoon rum, brandy or any liqueur to the egg yolks before cooking. When on the serving plate, pour over 2–4 tablespoons warmed rum and ignite.
Fruit – add the finely grated rind of 1 orange or lemon to the egg yolks before cooking and spread some warmed fruit purée, e.g. apricot, raspberry, strawberry, blackberry and apple, etc., over the omelette before folding up. Sprinkle with sugar and serve.
Nut – fry 25 g/1 oz/¼ cup chopped nuts in 15 g/½ oz/ 1 tablespoon butter until golden brown, stirring frequently. Stir in 1 tablespoon demerara sugar and a little spice and spoon over the omelette before folding up.

SOUFFLÉS
Hot soufflés are quite delicious to eat and are really simple to make; the most important point to remember is that a hot soufflé must be taken straight from the oven to the table to eat immediately. If left to stand at all, it will simply sink and look sad and most unappetizing.

The base of a hot soufflé is a thick sauce – a panada (see sauces chapter) – egg yolks are beaten into this sauce and, finally, the stiffly-beaten whites are folded in. Flavourings are added to the sauce or laid under the soufflé mixture. Do not be tempted to add too much filling to the actual sauce or a tough and heavy soufflé will result.

Soufflés are usually baked in a special soufflé dish. It has a fluted exterior but smooth inside and usually stands 7.5–10 cm/3–4 inches high and in sizes ranging from very small up to a diameter of 23–25 cm/9–10 inches.

Basic Cheese Soufflé
Serves 3–4

(See step-by-step illustrations, page 26.)

3 eggs, separated
25 g/1 oz/2 tablespoons butter or margarine
25 g/1 oz/¼ cup flour
150 ml/¼ pint/⅔ cup milk
salt and pepper
good pinch of dry mustard
75 g/3 oz mature Cheddar cheese, grated, or 50 g/2 oz
*   Cheddar, grated, and 2 tablespoons grated Parmesan*

1   Grease an 18 cm/7 inch soufflé dish. Separate the eggs, putting the whites into a large bowl.
2   Melt the fat in a saucepan (not too small or there will not be room to fold in the egg whites), stir in the flour and cook for a minute or two, stirring continuously.
3   Gradually add the milk, stirring continuously, and bring to the boil. Remove from the heat and beat in seasonings, the mustard and cheese followed by the egg yolks, one at a time.
4   Whisk the egg whites until very stiff and standing in peaks. Beat 2 tablespoons of the egg whites into the sauce and then fold in the remainder quickly and evenly using a metal spoon or plastic spatula.
5   Pour into the soufflé dish and cook at once in a fairly hot oven (200°C/400°F/Gas Mark 6) for about 35 minutes or until well risen and browned. Do not be tempted to look in the oven for the first 30 minutes or the soufflé will surely sink and, when you do look, close the door very carefully. A blast of cool air or sudden jolt will also cause it to sink. Serve immediately.

VARIATIONS
Ham – finely chop or mince 75 g/3 oz ham and beat into the sauce in place of the cheese and add 1 teaspoon creamed horseradish, if liked.
Salmon or Smoked Fish – finely flake 75 g/3 oz cooked or canned fish, or salmon or mackerel and add to the sauce in place of the cheese. Omit the mustard and add 1 tablespoon chopped parsley, if liked.
Cauliflower, Cheese and Mushroom – cook a small cauliflower cut into florets in boiling salted water until barely tender, about 8–10 minutes, then drain. Fry 100 g/4 oz/2 cups sliced mushrooms in 40 g/1½ oz/3 tablespoons butter or margarine for 1–2 minutes. Mix the cauliflower with the mushrooms and put in the base of 20–23 cm/8–9 inch soufflé dish. Make up the basic cheese soufflé mixture, pour into the dish over the vegetables and cook as above but for about 5 minutes longer.
Tomato and Sweetcorn – fry 1 large sliced onion in 25 g/ 1 oz/2 tablespoons butter until soft. Add 3–4 peeled and sliced tomatoes, a 200 g/7 oz can drained sweetcorn kernels, salt and pepper and ½ teaspoon dried thyme or mixed herbs. Cook gently for 2–3 minutes, then pour into a 20 cm/8 inch soufflé dish. Make up the basic cheese soufflé mixture and pour into the dish. Cook as above.

4 Sauces

The saying that the sauce makes the dish is often quite true for, if well made, the flavour and consistency should enhance the food it is served with. Sauces vary from being very simple to wildly exotic, but basically they are grouped into white, brown, egg-based and miscellaneous.

For white sauces, the liquid used is either milk, white stock or a mixture of the two, plus additions such as white wine or cider which can be added to vary the flavours when you have mastered the art of making a simple sauce. Brown sauces require a brown stock made from meat or poultry bones or good vegetable stocks and additions of wine, cider or sherry. Fish sauces are enhanced by using a fish stock made from simmering the bones and skin from the fish for a short while. Recipes for making stock are given in the soups chapter, however there are excellent stock cubes available in a wide variety of flavours and these make very good substitutes for the real thing, still providing a well-flavoured sauce.

ROUX-BASED AND BLENDED SAUCES

Basic sauces are made in one or two ways. (Egg sauces and miscellaneous ones are dealt with separately further on in the chapter). Either use the roux method, which is the most usual, or the blended method.

For a roux sauce, the fat is melted in a saucepan, the flour stirred in and then this is cooked and thoroughly combined without colouring for a white sauce or, for a brown sauce, cooked until browned (but not burnt!), stirring constantly. The liquid is gradually added, stirring continuously – for the beginner, this is best done off the heat, as cooking is stopped while the liquid is added. It is then brought slowly to the boil, stirring frequently until thickened. Once boiling, it should simmer for a minute or so to ensure the flour is cooked properly, otherwise the flavour will be impaired and taste 'raw'.

A blended sauce is made by blending the flour or cornflour (cornstarch) with a little of the measured liquid until quite smooth while the remainder of the liquid is brought to the boil. The hot liquid is stirred into the blended flour, the whole thing returned to the saucepan and brought to the boil for a few minutes, stirring continuously, until thickened and the flour is cooked.

The main problem with making sauces is that, if less than constant care is given to it, the sauce will become lumpy and unpalatable. There are various methods to try and correct this – firstly, if there are only a few lumps, strain through a sieve into a clean pan and continue. If this fails, whisk very hard with a small hand flat or balloon whisk, which may remove the lumps, or, finally, turn the sauce into a blender or food processor and switch on until smooth. Return to a clean pan and continue to cook, but stir constantly! Most sauces may be made in advance and either left in the saucepan or turned into a bowl, provided a disc of wet wax or greaseproof paper is pressed onto the surface of the sauce to prevent a skin from forming. Reheat gently when required.

For preference, use a roux-based sauce, the flavour is always much better; blended sauces tend to be more glutinous and are more often used for sweet sauces. Butter will also give a better flavour than margarine but is more likely to 'catch' on the bottom or burn. A non-stick saucepan is excellent for most sauces apart from those that need a double saucepan or basin standing over a pan of very gently simmering water. Use an appropriately-sized pan; a huge pan for a small amount of sauce is not a good idea. The type of flour, whether plain (all-purpose) or self-raising, does not matter with these types of sauces.

SIMPLE WHITE SAUCES
There are three basic thickness of sauce – pouring, coating, and binding (also known as a panada).

Pouring Sauce

20 g/¾ oz/1½ tablespoons butter or margarine
20 g/¾ oz/3 tablespoons flour
300 ml/½ pint/1¼ cups milk or milk and white stock
salt and pepper

1   Melt the fat in a small saucepan. Add the flour and stir until completely blended using a wooden spoon or small spatula.
2   Cook over a gentle heat for 2–3 minutes, stirring continuously, until the mixture (roux) begins to bubble – this cooks the flour.
3   Remove the pan from the heat and gradually add the liquid, stirring continuously to prevent lumps forming.
4   Return the pan to a gentle heat and bring to the boil, stirring continuously until thickened. Allow to simmer gently for 1–2 minutes.
5   Season to taste with salt and pepper and your sauce is ready for use or to add one of the flavourings given below.

Velouté Sauce (see page 33)

1   *Melt the fat in a pan and stir in the flour.*

3   *Gradually add the stock and bring to the boil, stirring continuously until thickened.*

2   *Cook for a few minutes, stirring continuously, until golden brown and bubbling.*

4   *Strain the finished sauce into a sauce boat.*

Coating Sauce

25 g/1 oz/2 tablespoons butter or margarine
25 g/1 oz/¼ cup flour
300 ml/½ pint/1¼ cups milk or milk and white stock
salt and pepper

Make in exactly the same way as for the pouring sauce. For an even thicker sauce, increase the proportions of fat and flour to 40 g/1½ oz/3 tablespoons butter and 40 g/1½ oz/⅓ cup flour but keep the amount of liquid the same.

Binding Sauce (Panada)

50 g/2 oz/¼ cup butter or margarine
50 g/2 oz/½ cup flour
300 ml/½ pint/1¼ cups milk or milk and white stock
salt and pepper

Make the sauce in the same way but the sauce will be really thick and must be stirred all the time it is on the heat or it will definitely stick and burn. Use for binding ingredients together for use in fish cakes, croquettes, etc.

Blended White Sauce

Suitable for savoury and sweet sauces.

1½ tablespoons cornflour (cornstarch)
300 ml/½ pint/1¼ cups milk
salt and pepper or caster (superfine) sugar to taste
15 g/½ oz/1 tablespoon butter or margarine

1   Put the cornflour in a small bowl with 2–3 tablespoons of the milk and blend together until quite smooth.
2   Heat the remainder of the milk in a small saucepan to just below boiling point.

Hollandaise Sauce (see page 36)

1   *Put the egg yolks into a bowl or top of a double saucepan and strain in the reduced vinegar mixture, beating well.*

3   *Heat gently, stirring continuously, until the sauce thickens.*

2   *Put the bowl over a saucepan part-filled with hot water.*

4   *Cut the butter into knobs and beat into the sauce, one at a time, until well incorporated and smooth.*

3   Pour onto the blended cornflour, stirring continuously, then return the whole of it to the saucepan. Put on a gentle heat and bring to the boil, stirring continuously.
4   Allow to simmer for 1–2 minutes, add salt and pepper or sugar, depending on whether it is to be a savoury or sweet sauce, and stir in the butter until melted.

Note: For a coating consistency, increase the amount of cornflour (cornstarch) to 2 tablespoons.

VARIATIONS

Parsley – use all milk and add 3 tablespoons freshly chopped or 1½ tablespoons dried parsley to the sauce when it has come to the boil. Simmer a minute or so longer.
   Serve with fish, chicken, eggs, ham, etc.
Anchovy – use all milk or, if to serve with fish, half milk and half fish stock. When ready, remove from the heat and stir in 2–3 teaspoons anchovy essence (or to taste) and a good squeeze of lemon juice.
   Serve with fish or eggs.

Egg – use all milk or, if to serve with fish, half milk and half fish stock, if possible. When ready, stir in 1–2 finely chopped hard-boiled eggs and, if liked, 1 tablespoon freshly chopped parsley or 2 teaspoons dried parsley and/or 2 teaspoons freshly chopped or 1 teaspoon dried chives.
   Serve with fish, kedgeree, etc.
Cheese – make the sauce using all milk and add 50–100 g/ 2–4 oz/½–1 cup grated mature Cheddar cheese and ½ teaspoon made English mustard to the sauce, stirring until the cheese has melted. A touch of cayenne pepper or Tabasco sauce may be added to give a 'bite'. Combinations of cheeses may also be used for flavouring, and for a really strong flavour add 1–2 tablespoons grated Parmesan cheese.
   Serve with fish, pasta, vegetables, eggs, etc.
Mustard – use all milk or half milk and half stock and, when ready, stir in 1 tablespoon dry mustard blended with 2 teaspoons sugar and 1–2 tablespoons wine vinegar. For a stronger flavour, increase the mustard or add 2–3

teaspoons Dijon or French mustard as well. For a mild-flavoured sauce, use German mustard. Also try one of the blended or mixed mustards that are widely available for varying the flavours and vary textures by using the whole grain varieties.

Serve with fish, ham, vegetables, poultry, eggs, etc.

Mushroom – use all milk or half milk and half white stock. Lightly fry 50–100 g/2–4 oz/1–2 cups sliced or chopped mushrooms in 25 g/1 oz/2 tablespoons butter or margarine and add to the sauce just before serving. Herbs may also be added for variety.

Serve with meat, poultry, fish, eggs, pasta, vegetables, etc.

Onion – peel and finely chop 2 onions and cook in boiling water until tender – about 15 minutes. Drain, reserving the liquid, and use 150 ml/¼ pint/⅔ cup of it together with milk to make the sauce as usual. When thickened, add the drained onions and a squeeze of lemon juice and simmer for 2 minutes before serving.

Serve with lamb, vegetables, eggs, or add 2 teaspoons dried sage and use to serve with boiled ham or chicken.

Shrimp or Prawn – use milk or half milk and half white or fish stock to make the sauce and when ready stir in a squeeze of lemon juice, 1 teaspoon tomato purée or 1 tablespoon tomato ketchup (if liked) and 50 g/2 oz peeled shrimp, prawns or potted shrimp. Heat through thoroughly before serving.

Serve with fish, eggs and pasta.

SWEET WHITE SAUCES

These are more often made using a blended sauce but the roux method may be used, provided you remember to omit the salt and pepper and add sugar to taste!

Add one of the following to the basic sweetened blended white sauce:

Fruit – add the finely grated rind of an orange or lemon and a little juice, if liked, just before serving.

Rum or Brandy – add 2–4 tablespoons rum or brandy (or other liqueur) to the made sauce.

Spiced – add 1 teaspoon mixed spice, ground cinnamon, ground ginger or apple pie spice to the made sauce.

Cream – add 2–4 tablespoons double (heavy) cream, soured cream or natural yogurt to the made sauce and reheat gently.

Chocolate Sauce

1 tablespoon cornflour (cornstarch)
1 tablespoon cocoa powder
300 ml/½ pint/1¼ cups milk
2 tablespoons caster (superfine) sugar
15 g/½ oz/1 tablespoon butter or margarine
a few drops of vanilla essence (optional)

Make as the basic blended white sauce by blending the cornflour and cocoa together with a little of the milk. Add the sugar, butter and vanilla essence (if used) at the end.

Custard Sauce

1½ tablespoons custard powder
300 ml/½ pint/1¼ cups milk
2 tablespoons caster (superfine) sugar

Make in the same way as for a blended white sauce to give a pouring custard. For a thick coating custard, increase the custard powder to 2–2½ tablespoons.

BROWN SAUCES

The main brown sauces are gravy and espagnole sauce (a slightly tomato-flavoured sauce) and most of the other sauces are based on these.

Gravy is made according to personal taste and should vary from very thin to quite thick depending on what it is to be served with. But as some people hate thin gravy and others detest thick gravy, I leave the choice to you. To be correct, roast beef and roast game should have clear or very thin gravy and everything else should be served with a thickened gravy of some sort. Gravy is best made using the pan juices left after removing the roasted meat: simply pour off the excess fat leaving about 1–2 tablespoon fat in the pan plus all the juices.

Clear Gravy

For a clear gravy, no flour is used but, for a thin gravy, a small amount of flour is used.

1   Pour all the fat from the pan juices in the roasting tin, then add 300 ml/½ pint/1¼ cups meat or vegetable stock and seasonings and bring to the boil.
2   Scrape all the sediment from the tin and boil for 2–3 minutes.
3   Strain into a sauce boat and serve very hot.

Thin or Thick Gravy

(See step-by-step illustrations, page 34.)

1   Pour off all but 1–2 tablespoons fat from the tin, leaving the sediment and juices still in the tin.
2   Add 1 tablespoon flour (for a thin gravy) or 2 tablespoons flour (for a thicker gravy) and cook for about 2 minutes, stirring continuously, until beginning to brown.
3   Gradually add 300 ml/½ pint/1¼ cups meat or vegetable stock and bring to the boil.
4   Add a dash of Worcestershire sauce and ½ teaspoon tomato purée and season with salt and pepper. Simmer for 2–3 minutes, stirring to make sure all the sediment has been loosened.
5   Strain into a sauce boat.

Espagnole Sauce

This is the classic brown sauce to which many variations can be made.

1 rasher bacon, chopped
½ onion, peeled and chopped
1 clove garlic, crushed (optional)
25 g/1 oz/2 tablespoons butter or margarine
25–50 g/1–2 oz mushrooms, chopped (stalks alone give the best flavour)
1 carrot, peeled and chopped
2–3 tablespoons flour
300 ml/½ pint/1¼ cups beef stock
1 bay leaf or a bouquet garni (see page 37)
2 tablespoons tomato purée
salt and pepper

1 Fry the bacon, onion and garlic (if used) in the melted fat in a saucepan until soft, stirring occasionally – about 5 minutes. Add the mushrooms and carrot and continue cooking for about 5 minutes or until lightly browned, stirring occasionally.
2 Add the flour (depending upon thickness required) and mix well. Continue cooking until it begins to brown, stirring continuously.
3 Gradually add the stock, preferably off the heat, and bring to the boil, stirring. Add the bay leaf or bouquet garni, tomato purée and seasonings. Cover the pan and simmer very gently for about 45 minutes, giving an occasional stir.
4 Strain the sauce into a clean pan through a sieve, taking care to push through all the liquid. Skim off any fat from the surface and adjust the seasonings. If to be served as it is, add a little extra stock if the sauce appears rather thick. Reheat and serve.

VARIATIONS
Bigarade (orange) – put the prepared espagnole sauce into a saucepan and add the grated rind of 1 orange, the juice of 1 orange and 1 lemon, 3–4 tablespoons port, and 1–2 tablespoons redcurrant or cranberry jelly. Bring to the boil and simmer for 2–3 minutes, stirring frequently.
   Serve with roast duck, lamb or venison.
Reforme – boil 3–4 tablespoons vinegar with 6–8 whole black peppercorns until reduced by half. Discard the peppercorns, and add the basic espagnole sauce, 2–3 tablespoons port or red wine and 1 tablespoon redcurrant jelly or orange-shred marmalade. Bring slowly back to the boil and simmer gently for 5–10 minutes, then strain.
   Serve with lamb, steaks, beef, etc.
Madeira or Marsala – add 6–8 tablespoons Madeira or Marsala to the prepared espagnole sauce and simmer very gently for about 5 minutes. Sharpen the sauce to taste with a little lemon juice, if necessary, and adjust the seasonings.
   Serve with veal, any roast meats or game.

RICH WHITE SAUCES
These are roux-based sauces but are made with flavoured stock or milk or have extra ingredients added for flavour and richness.

Béchamel Sauce

This is a classic white sauce on which many sauces are based.

300 ml/½ pint/1¼ cups milk
½ small onion, peeled and roughly chopped
½ stick celery, sliced
1 small carrot, peeled and sliced
½–1 bay leaf
3–6 whole black peppercorns
25 g/1 oz/2 tablespoons butter or margarine
25 g/1 oz/¼ cup flour
salt and pepper

1 Put the milk into a saucepan with the onion, celery, carrot, bay leaf and peppercorns and bring slowly to the boil. Remove the pan from the heat, cover and leave to cool for about 15 minutes to allow the ingredients to infuse with the milk.
2 Strain the liquid and use with the other ingredients to make a roux-based sauce as for basic white sauce (see page 29). Season to taste before serving.

VARIATIONS
Mornay – to 300 ml/½ pint/1¼ cups béchamel sauce, add 50–100 g/2–4 oz/½–1 cup grated Cheddar, Parmesan, Gruyère or other cheese, ½ teaspoon made English mustard and seasoning to taste.
   Serve with fish, chicken, veal, eggs, vegetables, etc.
Aurore – to 300 ml/½ pint/1¼ cups béchamel sauce, add 2 tablespoons tomato purée, a few drops of Tabasco or Worcestershire sauce and a knob of butter.
   Serve with fish, chicken, veal, etc.

Velouté Sauce

This is a rich pouring white sauce made with white stock and cream. (See step-by-step illustrations, page 30.)

25 g/1 oz/2 tablespoons butter or margarine
2 tablespoons flour
300–450 ml/½–¾ pint/1¼–2 cups white stock
3–4 tablespoons cream, single (light) or double (heavy)
½–1 teaspoon lemon juice
salt and pepper

1 Melt the fat in a pan, stir in the flour and cook for a few minutes, stirring continuously until golden brown and bubbling.
2 Gradually add the stock and bring to the boil, stirring continuously until thickened. Simmer for 2 minutes.
3 Stir in the cream followed by lemon juice and seasonings to taste and reheat without boiling. Strain into a sauce boat.
   Serve with fish, poultry, veal, etc.

Thin or Thick Gravy (see page 32)

1   *Having drained off most of the fat, stir in the flour.*

2   *Add the stock gradually and bring to the boil.*

3   *Strain the gravy into a sauce boat.*

VARIATION

Supreme –this is an even richer version of velouté sauce – excellent served with veal, poultry, fish, etc.

Beat in to the prepared velouté sauce 1–2 egg yolks, 3–4 tablespoons cream, single (light) or double (heavy), and 15–25 g/½–1 oz/1–2 tablespoons butter. Heat gently without boiling, adjust seasoning and serve.

EGG-BASED SAUCES

These are made in a completely different way from the other sauces already mentioned and do need extra care taken when making them. They must in no way be hurried or curdling is likely.

Mayonnaise

The oil used for mayonnaise is a matter of choice. Olive oil used on its own makes a rather heavy mayonnaise with a strong flavour, so is probably best used in conjunction with a lighter one such as sunflower or vegetable. You will soon get to know which oil gives the mayonnaise you prefer. Other dressings and variations to mayonnaise are given in the chapter on salads (see page 141).

2 egg yolks
1 teaspoon dry mustard
300 ml/½ pint/1¼ cups salad oil
1 tablespoon lemon juice
1–2 tablespoons wine vinegar
salt and pepper (use white pepper for preference)
½–1 teaspoon caster (superfine) sugar

1   Put the egg yolks into a slightly warmed but thoroughly dry basin with the mustard and mix thoroughly.
2   Add the oil drop by drop while whisking continuously until about half of the oil is incorporated and the sauce is very thick. A hand-held electric mixer makes the job of whisking easier but a balloon whisk or even a wooden spoon can be used, provided you whisk hard enough.
3   Whisk in the lemon juice and then continue adding the rest of the oil in the same way as before, although towards the end the oil may be poured in a little faster.
4   Add vinegar to taste and the seasonings and sugar. Add these gradually, tasting as you go to prevent over-seasoning or oversweetening the mayonnaise.
5   Mayonnaise will store in an airtight jar or plastic container in the refrigerator for 2–3 weeks. Do not freeze mayonnaise.

Note: Do not use eggs straight from the refrigerator, they will cause the mayonnaise to curdle. If the mayonnaise should curdle during making, it is probably due to adding the oil too quickly. Simply put a fresh egg yolk into a clean bowl and gradually add the curdled mixture, whisking it in the same way as the oil, drop by drop.

OPPOSITE: *Prawn Sauce on fish rolls* (see page 32) *and Apple Sauce with pork* (see page 36)

Hollandaise Sauce

This is served with salmon and other fish, asparagus, broccoli, etc. (See step-by-step illustrations, page 31.)

2 tablespoons wine vinegar or tarragon vinegar
1 tablespoon water
3–4 whole black peppercorns
2 egg yolks
75–100 g/3–4 oz/⅓–½ cup butter, softened
salt and pepper

1   Put the vinegar, water and peppercorns into a small pan, bring to the boil and boil until reduced by half.
2   Put the egg yolks into a bowl or the top of a double saucepan or boiler – if you have one – and strain the vinegar mixture onto the egg yolks beating hard.
3   Stand the bowl over a saucepan of very gently simmering water and heat gently. Stir continuously until the sauce thickens. Too much heat will cause curdling.
4   Cut the butter into knobs about the size of a fingernail and beat into the sauce, one at a time, until well incorporated and smooth.
5   Season to taste and, if too sharp, add a little more butter, or add a touch of lemon juice if extra piquancy is required. The sauce should be thick enough to hold its shape and is usually served warm.

Béarnaise Sauce

4 tablespoons wine vinegar or tarragon vinegar
¼ onion or 1 shallot, peeled and very finely chopped
a few sprigs of fresh tarragon, chopped, or ½ teaspoon dried tarragon
2 egg yolks
75 g/3 oz/⅓ cup butter, softened
salt and pepper

1   Put the vinegar, onion and tarragon into a small saucepan, bring to the boil and boil until reduced to about 1 tablespoon.
2   Continue from step 2 of Hollandaise sauce. This sauce should be a little thicker than Hollandaise.
     Serve with steaks, chops, grills, etc.

OTHER SAUCES
Cranberry Sauce

175 g/6 oz/¾ cup sugar
200 ml/7 fl oz/⅞ cup water
225 g/8 oz/2 cups cranberries, fresh or frozen

1   Dissolve the sugar in the water in a saucepan over a low heat, stirring occasionally, then bring to the boil and boil for about 5 minutes.
2   Add the cranberries, cover the pan and simmer for about 10 minutes or until all the berries have 'popped' and are tender.

3   Add 1–2 tablespoons port, if liked, and leave to cool.
     Serve with roast turkey, lamb, game, etc.

Note: Once made, this sauce will store in the refrigerator in an airtight container for about 10 days.

Bread Sauce

1 medium onion, peeled
5 whole cloves
450 ml/¾ pint/scant 2 cups milk
1 bay leaf (optional)
6 black peppercorns
15 g/½ oz/1 tablespoon butter or margarine
75 g/3 oz/1½ cups fresh white breadcrumbs
salt and pepper

1   Stud the onion with the cloves. Put into a saucepan with the milk, bay leaf (if used) and peppercorns. Bring to the boil, remove from the heat and leave in a cool place to infuse for about 20 minutes.
2   Remove the peppercorns and bay leaf and add the butter and breadcrumbs. Bring slowly to the boil, stirring continuously, and cook very gently for about 10 minutes until creamy, stirring from time to time.
3   Discard the onion and season to taste.
     Serve hot with poultry and game.

Mint Sauce

3 tablespoons finely chopped fresh mint
1 tablespoon caster (superfine) sugar
2 tablespoons boiling water
1–2 tablespoons malt vinegar

1   Put the mint into a small bowl and add the sugar.
2   Pour on the boiling water and stir until the sugar has dissolved.
3   Add vinegar to taste, stirring well.
     Serve with lamb.

Note: Mint sauce will store in a small screw-top jar in the refrigerator for 2–3 weeks.

Apple Sauce

450 g/1 lb cooking apples
2–3 tablespoons water
25 g/1 oz/2 tablespoons butter
a little sugar (optional)

1   Peel, core and slice the apples into a pan. Add the water, cover the pan and cook gently until very soft and pulpy – about 10 minutes – stirring occasionally.
2   Beat the apple until quite smooth with a wooden spoon, or rub through a sieve or purée in a blender.
3   Return to a clean pan and beat in the butter and a little sugar to taste if too tart.
     Serve with pork, duck, etc.

5 Soups

It is very simple, quick and convenient to open a can or reconstitute a packet of soup, but good though they are, the home-made element is missing. This is easily corrected by making your own wide variety of soups. Soup making is a satisfying occupation and, although to achieve the very best results it is necessary to start from the beginning and make your own stock, a very adequate stock can be made by using bought stock cubes. A word of warning though: watch the salt content when using stock cubes for they tend to be already seasoned and slightly on the salty side. So taste before you add too much extra salt to the completed soup. Should you find the soup is very salty, add something like raw potato, which will help to absorb the excess.

Stock is made from bones and vegetables. A white stock requires veal bones or chicken bones, which are put straight into a saucepan with the water and other ingredients. Poultry or game stocks can use the carcass and odd bones plus any skin and trimmings, either raw or cooked, from any type of poultry or game; brown stock requires good beef marrow bones, which should be browned in the oven before adding to the stock pan for extra flavour and colour (although a touch of gravy browning will add the extra colour if it is missing). Vegetable stocks can be made from the trimmings of one or more varieties of vegetables (but not potato) cooked to give a well-flavoured concentrated vegetable water.

Extra ingredients are required for making the stock in the form of root vegetables: e.g. onions, carrots, turnips, leeks, etc., but not potato, and often a bay leaf (fresh or dried) is added or, in some cases, a bouquet garni (see below), which is a collection of herbs, is used to give flavour. Do not season the ingredients for stock.

Stock cubes are available in beef, chicken, lamb and vegetable flavours. Follow the directions on the packet for reconstituting but with most brands 1 cube makes 450 ml/ ¾ pint/scant 2 cups stock when dissolved in boiling water. Powdered stock is also available in jars; again, follow the instructions.

Soups vary tremendously in texture; they may be clear, thin or from thick up by stages to very chunky and full of bits and pieces, making them almost a knife and fork affair. Some soups are smooth, others are really creamy; some may be purely puréed vegetables, others may include chopped meat; and types vary from vegetable and meat-based to fish, seafood and even fruit soups.

Almost all soups can be frozen either in the completed stage or somewhere along the way. Stocks also freeze well. So it is a good idea to cook larger quantities at a time, as the cooking time will only be minimally longer yet the time saved is exceptional.

It is important to serve soup in an attractive manner, whether as a quick hot snack or for an elegant dinner party, or chilled for a warm summer evening. Garnishes are simple to make, can be prepared in advance and are simply sprinkled over the surface of each bowl of soup before it is taken to the table, but what a difference they make to the presentation. Ideas for garnishes are given at the end of this chapter.

Remember too that it is important to serve a hot soup really piping hot and a chilled soup really cold; lukewarm soups or room-temperature soups do not do justice to the time and effort spent in preparing them.

Bouquet Garni

These are used widely in many other dishes, not only stocks and soups..

1 bay leaf (fresh or dried)
1 sprig parsley
1 sprig thyme
6 black peppercorns
1 clove
small piece of blade of mace (optional)

Tie all these ingredients together in a small piece of muslin, leaving a short length of string so it can be easily removed from the pan when required.

Dried Bouquet Garni

1 bay leaf
good pinch of dried mixed herbs
1 whole clove
6 black peppercorns
pinch of dried parsley

Tie these together in a small piece of muslin as above.

Basic White Stock

1   *Prepare all the ingredients.*

2   *Skim off any scum from the surface that forms.*

3   *Remove any excess fat from the surface by blotting with kitchen paper towel.*

SOUPS BASED ON WHITE STOCK
Basic White Stock

900 g/2 lb veal bones, chopped into 5–10 cm/2–4 inch
   pieces
2.25 litres/4 pints/10 cups cold water
1 onion, peeled and sliced
2 carrots, peeled and sliced
1 bay leaf or bouquet garni
1 teaspoon lemon juice

1   Put the bones and water into a saucepan and bring to
    the boil. Skim off any scum from the surface that forms
    and add the remainder of the ingredients.
2   Return to the boil, cover the pan and simmer gently for
    3–4 hours.
3   Strain into a bowl and either remove any excess fat
    from the surface by blotting with kitchen paper towel
    or leave until cold and lift off the set layer of fat.
4   The stock is now ready for use.
Makes about 1.7 litres/3 pints/7½ cups

Note: Stock can be made in a pressure cooker too. You
must follow the method and instructions with your particular make of pressure cooker. Use ingredients as above
but only 1.7 litres/3 pints/7½ cups water. Bring to high
pressure and cook for 1–1¼ hours. Release pressure
slowly before removing the lid.

Cream of Celery Soup   Serves 6

1 head celery
50 g/2 oz/¼ cup butter or margarine
1 onion, peeled and sliced
1 tablespoon flour
900 ml/1½ pints/3¾ cups white stock
salt and pepper
1 bouquet garni
good pinch of ground mace or nutmeg
300 ml/½ pint/1¼ cups milk
4 tablespoons cream, single (light) or double (heavy)
paprika to garnish

1   Trim the celery, wash and remove about 6 small leaves
    for garnish. Chop the remainder of the celery including
    any outer leaves.
2   Melt the fat in a large saucepan, add the celery and
    onion and cook gently for about 5 minutes, stirring
    occasionally. Do not allow the vegetables to brown.
3   Sprinkle the flour over the vegetables and stir in
    gradually, add the stock and bring to the boil.
4   Add seasonings, bouquet garni and mace or nutmeg,
    cover the pan and simmer gently for about 45 minutes
    or until everything is very tender.
5   Discard the bouquet garni and either rub the soup
    through a sieve or purée in a blender or food processor.
6   Return to a clean saucepan, add the milk and bring
    back to the boil. Season to taste and simmer for 2
    minutes, then stir in the cream and heat without boiling.

7   Turn into warm soup bowls, sprinkle each portion lightly with paprika and float a celery leaf on each. Serve piping hot.

To freeze: Work to the end of step 5. Cool, then pour into a rigid container and freeze. Add milk and cream when reheating ready to serve. Store for up to 3 months.

Cream of Cucumber Soup   Serves 6

This is another way to make a creamed soup. It is a matter of preference whether you peel the cucumber or not. I prefer to leave the skin on as it gives an attractive, slightly mottled appearance to the finished soup and a slightly stronger flavour.

1 ½ cucumbers
1 medium onion, peeled and chopped
900 ml/1½ pints/3¾ cups white stock
40 g/1½ oz/3 tablespoons butter
40 g/1½ oz/6 tablespoons flour
salt and pepper
2 teaspoons lemon juice
1–2 egg yolks
150 ml/¼ pint/⅔ cup single (light) cream or natural yogurt
To garnish
a few cucumber slices
sprigs of fresh mint or parsley.

1   Peel the cucumber, if liked, or wipe over and chop into roughly-diced pieces. Place in a saucepan with the onion and stock.
2   Bring to the boil, cover the pan and simmer gently for about 20 minutes or until tender. Cool the soup a little, then rub through a sieve or purée in a blender or food processor.
3   Melt the fat in a clean saucepan and stir in the flour. Cook for a minute or two to form a roux and then gradually beat in the cucumber purée. Bring to the boil and simmer for 2–3 minutes, stirring occasionally, until thickened and smooth.
4   Add seasonings to taste. Blend the egg yolks into the cream or yogurt, then whisk in a little of the soup.
5   Return to the rest of the soup and reheat gently to just below boiling point. If allowed to boil, the eggs and cream will cause the soup to curdle.
6   Pour into warmed soup bowls and serve garnished with 1–2 thin slices of cucumber and a small sprig of mint or parsley.

Note: This soup is also excellent served chilled. After adding the eggs and cream reheat gently, then cool quickly, cover and chill.
To freeze: Make the soup as far as the end of step 3. Season lightly, allow to cool, then pour into a rigid container and freeze. Store for up to 3 months. Add egg yolks and cream when reheating ready to serve.

Cream of Celery Soup

1   *Gradually add the stock to the sautéed vegetables.*

2   *Discard the bouquet garni and rub the soup through a sieve.*

3   *Sprinkle each bowl of soup with paprika and float a celery leaf on top.*

Vichyssoise
Serves 6

3 leeks
40 g/1½ oz/3 tablespoons butter or margarine
1 onion, peeled and thinly sliced
450 g/1 lb potatoes, peeled and chopped
900 ml/1½ pints/3¾ cups white stock
salt and pepper
½ teaspoon ground coriander
1 egg yolk
150 ml/¼ pint/⅔ cup single (light) cream
snipped chives or chopped parsley to garnish

1 Trim the leeks, removing most of the green part (see note below), and slice the remainder thinly.
2 Melt the fat in a saucepan, add the leeks and onion and fry gently for about 5 minutes, stirring frequently, without allowing to brown.
3 Add potatoes, stock, salt and pepper and coriander, bring to the boil, cover and simmer gently for about 30 minutes or until all the vegetables are very tender.
4 Rub the soup through a sieve, or purée in a blender or food processor, and return to a clean saucepan.
5 Blend the egg yolk with the cream, add a little of the soup and whisk back into the residue in the saucepan. Reheat gently without boiling and adjust the seasonings.
6 Cool and chill the soup thoroughly. Serve in bowls sprinkled with snipped chives or chopped parsley.

Note: Most of the green part can be left on the leeks and used in this soup to serve hot, when it is called leek and potato soup.

SOUPS BASED ON BROWN STOCK
Brown Stock

900 g/2 lb marrow bones, chopped up
1.7 litres/3 pints/7½ cups water
1 bouquet garni
1 large onion, peeled and chopped
1–2 tablespoons oil or dripping
1 carrot, peeled and sliced
1–2 sticks celery, sliced

1 Put the bones into a roasting tin and place in a fairly hot oven (200–225°C/400–424°F/Gas Mark 6–7) for about an hour or until well browned. Transfer the bones to a large saucepan.
2 Fry the onion in the oil or dripping until well browned. Drain off all the fat and add the onion to the saucepan.
3 Add all the other ingredients, bring to the boil and skim off any scum that appears.
4 Continue as for the white stock (see page 38).
Makes about 1.5 litres/2½ pints/6¼ cups

Note: To make in a pressure cooker see note under white stock using 1.5 litres/2½ pints/6¼ cups.

Rich Brown Stock

For a really rich brown stock to use for making consommé, replace 450 g/1 lb bones with finely chopped shin (shank) of beef and brown this all in the oven.

Consommé
Serves 4–6

This is an absolutely clear soup, free of flour. To clear it properly, the crushed egg shells and whisked whites should form a filter to catch all the bits and pieces in the soup.

1.2 litres/2 pints/5 cups rich brown stock
175 g/6 oz/¾ cup lean minced or ground beef
2 tomatoes, peeled, deseeded and chopped
1 carrot, peeled and chopped
1 onion, peeled and chopped
1 bouquet garni
2 egg whites
shells of 2 eggs
salt and pepper
1 tablespoon sherry (optional)
To garnish
1 cooked carrot, cut into very narrow strips

1 Place the stock in a saucepan with the minced or ground beef, tomatoes, carrot, onion and bouquet garni and well-beaten egg whites.
2 Crush the egg shells and add to the pan with plenty of salt and pepper.
3 Bring the mixture almost to the boil, whisking the mixture all the time. Allow to boil without further whisking and then simmer very gently, uncovered, taking care not to break the frothy layer on top.
4 Pour through a scalded jelly bag or piece of double muslin or a scalded tea or dish towel keeping the froth back until last. Taste and adjust the seasonings and add the sherry (if used).
5 Pour the liquid through the filter of egg shells left in the muslin into a clean saucepan. If still cloudy, pour it through the filter again.
6 Reheat the soup carefully, add the cooked carrot sticks and serve very hot.

Thick Vegetable Soup
Serves 6

50 g/2 oz/¼ cup butter or margarine
225 g/8 oz carrots, peeled and chopped
2 onions, peeled and chopped
1 leek, washed, trimmed and sliced
2 sticks celery, chopped
1 parsnip, peeled and chopped
25 g/1 oz/¼ cup flour
2 large tomatoes, peeled and sliced
1–2 teaspoons tomato purée
1.3 litres/2¼ pints/5⅔ cups brown stock
2 bay leaves
good pinch of ground nutmeg
salt and pepper
freshly chopped parsley to garnish

1 Melt the fat in a saucepan. Add the carrots, onions, leek, celery and parsnip and cook gently for about 10 minutes, stirring occasionally, without browning.
2 Stir in the flour until evenly blended, then stir in the tomatoes and tomato purée followed by the stock. Bring to the boil, add the bay leaves, nutmeg and seasonings, cover and simmer for about 30 minutes or until very tender.
3 Discard the bay leaves and put the soup through a sieve or purée in a food processor. Return to a clean pan.
4 Bring back to the boil and adjust seasonings. If too thick, add a little extra stock or water. Serve in warmed bowls sprinkled with chopped parsley.

Note: For a vegetarian soup use a vegetable stock made with about 900 g/2 lb mixed vegetables and vegetable trimmings, chopped, a bouquet garni, and 1.5 litres/2½ pints/6¼ cups water, simmered gently for 45–60 minutes. Strain and use.

Mulligatawny Soup   Serves 6

The curry flavour can be adapted to your individual taste.

50 g/2 oz/¼ cup dripping or margarine
1 large onion, peeled and chopped
2 carrots, peeled and chopped
3 sticks celery, chopped
1 apple, peeled and chopped
2 tablespoons flour
2–4 teaspoons curry powder
1.2 litres/2 pints/5 cups brown stock
225 g/8 oz can peeled tomatoes
salt and pepper
100 g/4 oz lean leftover cooked beef, lamb or poultry, minced or very finely chopped
50 g/2 oz/1 cup cooked rice (about 20 g/¾ oz/¼ cup raw rice)
2–3 teaspoons lemon juice
freshly chopped parsley to garnish

1 Melt the fat in a saucepan and add the onion, carrots, celery and apple. Fry gently until soft and just beginning to turn a pale brown, stirring from time to time.
2 Stir in the flour and curry powder and cook for a few minutes, stirring continuously.
3 Add the stock, tomatoes and their liquid and seasonings and bring up the boil. Cover the pan and simmer gently for about 45 minutes, stirring occasionally.
4 Cool the soup, then rub through a sieve or purée in a blender or food processor.
5 Return to a clean saucepan with the meat and rice and bring to the boil. Adjust seasoning and stir in the lemon juice.
6 Serve in warmed bowls sprinkled with chopped parsley. Poppadums or chapatis or naan bread make a good accompaniment.

Note: This soup can be left without sieving or puréeing provided the vegetables are chopped very finely before frying. It is best not to freeze this, or for only up to 1 month, as strong curry flavours tend to turn musty.

Oxtail Soup   Serves 6–8

1 oxtail, jointed
25 g/1 oz/2 tablespoons butter or margarine
2 onions, peeled and very finely chopped
½–1 leek, washed, trimmed and finely sliced
1 carrot, peeled and very finely chopped
2 sticks celery, finely chopped
25 g/1 oz/¼ cup flour
2 litres/3½ pints/8¾ cups brown stock
1 bouquet garni
salt and pepper
1 tablespoon lemon juice
sherry (optional)

1 Wash and dry the oxtail and cut off any excess fat. Melt the fat in a saucepan and fry the pieces of oxtail until browned, stirring from time to time.
2 Add the onions, leeks, carrot and celery and continue to fry for a few minutes, stirring frequently.
3 Sprinkle the flour over the meat and vegetables, mix well and gradually add the stock and bring to the boil.
4 Skim off any scum from the surface and add the bouquet garni, seasonings and lemon juice. Cover the pan and simmer gently for about 3 hours or until the oxtail is very tender and simply falls off the bones. Skim any fat from the surface of the soup as it appears during cooking.
5 Remove the oxtail from the pan and discard the bouquet garni. Either leave the soup as it is or rub through a sieve or purée in a blender of food processor. Return to a clean pan.
6 Chop the meat from the bones and return to the soup. Add sherry to taste (1–2 tablespoons), if liked, and adjust the seasonings. Bring back to the boil, skim off any fat that remains and serve piping hot.

SOUPS BASED ON POULTRY AND GAME STOCK
Basic Poultry or Game Stock

The flavour of the finished stock will vary depending on the type of poultry or game used. Venison and hare stock should be made as for a white stock.

carcass, bones, skin and trimmings of 1 chicken or turkey or 1–2 pheasant, partridge, grouse, etc
1 large onion, peeled and chopped
2 carrots, peeled and sliced
2 sticks celery, sliced
1–2 bay leaves
1–2 slices lemon
1.5–1.7 litres/2½–3 pints/6¼–7½ cups water

Make in the same way as for a white stock (see page 38) but boil for only 2–2½ hours. To make in a pressure cooker, use only about 1.2 litres/2 pints/5 cups water and cook at high pressure for about 45–60 minutes.
Makes about 1.2 litres/2 pints/5 cups

Cock-a-leekie Soup

Serves 6–8

2 chicken portions
1.5 litres/2½ pints/6¼ cups chicken stock
4 leeks, trimmed, washed and finely sliced
salt and pepper
1 teaspoon ground coriander
1 bouquet garni
12 'no need to soak' prunes (optional)

1 Put the chicken portions into a saucepan with the stock, leeks, seasonings, coriander and bouquet garni. Bring to the boil and skim off any scum.
2 Cover the pan and simmer gently for about 1½ hours or until the chicken is so tender it is falling off the bones.
3 Remove the chicken portions, strip off the flesh, discarding the skin and bones, and chop the flesh. Return the chopped meat to the pan with the prunes.
4 Bring back to the boil, adjust seasonings and simmer for 10 minutes.
5 Serve very hot in warmed bowls with crusty bread.

Note: 150 ml/¼ pint/⅔ cup single (light) cream may be stirred into the soup just before serving to give a creamy taste.

Cream of Pheasant Soup

Serves 6

This recipe can be used for any of the game birds.

1.2 litres/2 pints/5 cups pheasant stock made as for poultry stock using 1 pheasant carcass, raw or cooked (see page 41)
50 g/2 oz/¼ cup butter or margarine
1 onion, peeled and very finely chopped
40 g/1½ oz/⅓ cup flour
salt and pepper
½ teaspoon ground coriander
good pinch of ground nutmeg
1 bay leaf
150 ml/¼ pint/⅔ cup single (light) cream
2 tablespoons freshly chopped parsley
fried croûtons to garnish

1 Make the pheasant stock and strain. Remove any pieces of meat from the carcass and chop finely.
2 Melt the fat in a pan and fry the onion gently until soft but not coloured. Stir in the flour and cook for a minute or so. Gradually add the stock and bring to the boil.
3 Season well, add coriander, nutmeg and bay leaf. Cover the pan and simmer gently for about 20 minutes.
4 Discard the bay leaf, stir in the pheasant meat and adjust the seasonings. Simmer for a further 3–4 minutes.
5 Stir in the cream and parsley and bring back to just boiling.
6 Serve very hot sprinkled with fried croûtons.

Note: This recipe can be used for many other types of game. If using wild duck carcass, it is a good idea to add about ½ teaspoon finely grated orange rind.

Potato and Bacon Soup

Serves 6

175 g/6 oz streaky bacon rashers, derinded and thickly chopped
1 large onion, peeled and finely chopped
350 g/12 oz peeled potatoes, diced
1.2 litres/2 pints/5 cups poultry or game stock
2 bay leaves
salt and pepper
pinch of ground nutmeg
¼ teaspoon celery salt
200 g/7 oz can sweetcorn kernels, drained
1 tablespoon freshly chopped parsley

1 Fry the bacon gently in a saucepan with no added fat. As it heats, the fat will run out allowing it to fry.
2 Add the onion and continue to cook for 3–4 minutes, stirring occasionally, until beginning to lightly colour.
3 Add potatoes, stock, bay leaves, a little salt and pepper, nutmeg and celery salt and bring to the boil. Cover the pan and simmer gently for about 30 minutes or until very tender, but the potato should still be visible.
4 Discard the bay leaves. Add the sweetcorn and simmer for 5 minutes. Adjust the seasonings, watching the salt content because of the bacon. Stir in the parsley and serve very hot.

SOUPS BASED ON FISH STOCK

It is not always possible to make a fish stock for soups and some do not need it as the fish cooking in water with the rest of the soup ingredients provides a strong enough flavour. However, using a fish stock when cooking fish recipes will make the finished dish far better.

Fish Stock

1 cod's head or fish bones and trimmings
salt
1 bouquet garni
1 onion, peeled and sliced
water

1 Wash the fish head and/or trimmings. Place in a saucepan with a little salt, bouquet garni and onion and add about 1.2 litres/2 pints/5 cups cold water, or to cover.
2 Bring to the boil, remove any scum from the surface, cover the pan and simmer for 20 minutes. Longer cooking will tend to make the stock bitter.
3 Strain and use at once, or within 2 days if kept in the refrigerator.
Makes about 900 ml/1½ pints/3¾ cups

Herb Bread (see page 47), *Potato and Bacon Soup* (see page 42), *Crab Bisque* (see page 44) *and French Onion Soup* (see page 46)

Smoky Haddock Soup   Serves 6

225 g/8 oz smoked haddock fillet
1 onion, peeled and finely chopped
600 ml/1 pint/2½ cups fish stock or water
600 ml/1 pint/2½ cups milk
salt and pepper
225 g/8 oz hot mashed potato
25 g/1 oz/2 tablespoons butter or margarine
1 tablespoon lemon juice
freshly chopped parsley

1 Put the fish into a saucepan with the onion and stock or water. Bring to the boil, cover the pan and simmer very gently for about 15 minutes or until the fish is tender.
2 Using a fish slice or slotted spoon, remove the fish from the cooking pan. Cool the fish a little, remove the skin and any bones and flake the fish finely.
3 Return the skin and bones to the cooking liquor and simmer gently for 10 minutes.
4 Strain the fish liquor and put 450 ml/¾ pint/scant 2 cups into a clean pan with the milk and flaked fish and season to taste. Take care when adding salt as smoked fish tends to be salty.
5 Bring back slowly to the boil and then gradually whisk in the mashed potato to give the required consistency.
6 Return to the boil, add the lemon juice and adjust the seasonings. Either stir in about 2 tablespoons freshly chopped parsley or serve the soup in warmed bowls thickly sprinkled with parsley.

Prawn or Shrimp Chowder Serves 5–6

Chowders are thick hearty soups suitable to be served as a snack meal or light lunch, perhaps followed by cheese and fruit. They are really too heavy to serve as a starter for a dinner party.

2 tablespoons oil
1 large onion, peeled and finely chopped
2 rashers lean bacon, derinded and finely chopped
1 clove garlic, crushed
1 large red pepper, deseeded and finely chopped
225 g/8 oz can peeled tomatoes
900 ml/1½ pints/3¾ cups fish stock
1 tablespoon tomato purée
1 bay leaf
good pinch of ground mace or nutmeg
40 g/1½ oz/¼ cup long grain rice
1 tablespoon wine vinegar
salt and pepper
75–100 g/3–4 oz/¾–1 cup peeled prawns or large shrimp, roughly chopped
1–2 tablespoons freshly chopped parsley

1 Heat the oil in a pan and fry the onion, bacon and garlic gently for about 3 minutes until soft, without allowing to brown.
2 Add almost all the pepper and continue to fry gently for 2–3 minutes.
3 Chop the tomatoes and add to the pan with their juice,

together with the stock, tomato purée, bay leaf, mace or nutmeg, rice, vinegar and seasonings.
4 Bring to the boil, cover and simmer gently, stirring occasionally, for 25–30 minutes or until all the ingredients are very tender.
5 Discard the bay leaf. Add the prawns or shrimp and parsley, adjust the seasonings and simmer for a further 2–3 minutes.
6 Serve very hot sprinkled with the remaining pepper and with anchovy or garlic bread (see page 47).

Crab Bisque   Serves 6

25 g/1 oz/2 tablespoons butter or margarine
1 onion, peeled and finely chopped
2 sticks celery, finely chopped
25 g/1 oz/scant ¼ cup long grain rice
600 ml/1 pint/2½ cups fish stock
3 tomatoes, peeled and finely chopped
900 ml/1½ pints/3¾ cups milk
salt and pepper
1 teaspoon anchovy essence
2 teaspoons tomato purée
225 g/8 oz crab meat (fresh, frozen or canned), flaked
150 ml/¼ pint/⅔ cup single (light) cream or natural yogurt, or soured cream
4–6 tablespoons brandy (optional)
fried croûtons to garnish

1 Melt the fat in a pan and fry the onion and celery gently until soft, about 3–4 minutes, stirring occasionally. Do not allow to brown.
2 Add the rice, stock and tomatoes. Bring to the boil, cover the pan and simmer gently for about 20 minutes or until tender, stirring occasionally.
3 Cool the soup a little, then rub through a sieve or purée in a blender or food processor. Return to a clean saucepan.
4 Add the milk, seasonings, anchovy essence, tomato purée and crab meat, bring back to the boil and simmer gently for 5 minutes.
5 Add the cream and reheat. Adjust seasonings and serve very hot in warmed bowls. A tablespoon of brandy may be stirred into each portion, if liked. Sprinkle with croûtons and serve.

OTHER VEGETABLE SOUPS

These soups are all based on vegetables and, although one type of stock is specified for each type, it does not really matter which you use (except fish!), but, of course, the flavour will obviously vary with each one.

Carrot and Coriander Soup   Serves 6

450 g/1 lb carrots, peeled and chopped
1 onion, peeled and chopped
100 g/4 oz peeled potatoes, chopped
225 g/8 oz can peeled tomatoes
900 ml/1 ½ pints/3 ¾ cups stock (chicken, white or brown)
1 ½ teaspoons ground coriander
salt and pepper
300 ml/ ½ pint/1 ¼ cups milk
1–2 teaspoons lemon juice
To garnish
6 tablespoons natural yogurt or soured cream

1 Put the carrots, onion, potatoes, tomatoes and their juice, stock, coriander and seasonings into a saucepan. Bring to the boil, cover the pan and simmer gently for about 30 minutes or until everything is very tender.
2 Cool a little, then rub through a sieve or purée in a blender or food processor.
3 Return to a clean saucepan with the milk and bring back to the boil. Adjust the seasonings and add lemon juice to taste. Carrots tend to be rather sweet and need something sharp to counteract this.
4 Serve very hot in warmed bowls and, just before taking to the table, put a tablespoon of natural yogurt or soured cream into each one and swirl with a spoon to give a marbled effect.

Note: Suitable to freeze as for Cream of Celery Soup (see page 38).

Vegetable Soup with Oatmeal

Serves 6

50 g/2 oz/ ¼ cup butter or margarine
1 large onion, peeled and very finely chopped
1 turnip, peeled and very finely chopped
3 large carrots, peeled and finely chopped
2 sticks celery, chopped
1 leek, washed, trimmed and thinly sliced
25 g/1 oz/ ¼ cup medium oatmeal
900 ml/1 ½ pints/3 ¾ cups white or poultry stock
salt and pepper
1 bouquet garni
450 ml/ ¾ pint/scant 2 cups milk or milk and single (light) cream mixed
To garnish
3–4 tablespoons toasted oatmeal, medium or coarse (see below)

1 Melt the fat in a saucepan and add all the vegetables. Fry very gently for about 5 minutes, stirring frequently, without allowing them to colour.
2 Stir in the oatmeal and continue to cook for a few minutes longer, stirring frequently.
3 Gradually add the stock, seasonings and bouquet garni and bring to the boil. Cover the pan and simmer gently for about 45 minutes or until all the vegetables are very tender. Stir occasionally.
4 Discard the bouquet garni, add the milk and bring back to the boil. Adjust the seasonings, adding plenty of freshly ground black pepper. Serve piping hot sprinkled with toasted oatmeal.

Note: Oatmeal is available fine, medium and coarse and each is best for specific dishes. To toast the oatmeal, spread it on a piece of foil and put under a medium grill or broiler for a few minutes, turning as necessary so it is evenly browned. Watch out, as it will suddenly catch and burn black! Cool and store in an airtight container.

Minestrone   Serves 6

50 g/2 oz/ ½ cup haricot (navy) beans
1.7 litres/3 pints/7 ½ cups any stock (except fish)
2 tablespoons oil
25 g/1 oz/2 tablespoons butter or margarine
2 carrots, peeled and finely chopped
1 large onion, peeled and finely chopped
1 clove garlic, crushed
2 leeks, washed, trimmed and sliced or finely chopped
425 g/15 oz can peeled tomatoes
1 tablespoon tomato purée
1 bouquet garni
salt and pepper
50 g/2 oz spaghetti, broken up
freshly grated Parmesan cheese to garnish

1 Soak the beans in 600 ml/1 pint/2 ½ cups of the stock in a cool place overnight.
2 Next day put the beans and their soaking stock and a further 600 ml/1 pint/2 ½ cups of the stock into a saucepan and bring to the boil. Cover and simmer for about an hour.
3 Heat the oil and butter in a saucepan and add the carrots, onion, garlic and leeks. Fry gently for about 5 minutes, stirring frequently, until they are just beginning to colour.
4 Chop up the tomatoes and add to the pan with their juice, tomato purée, bouquet garni and seasonings. Pour in the beans in their liquid and the remaining stock. Bring back to the boil and simmer for an hour.
5 Add the spaghetti, adjust the seasonings and simmer for a further 5–10 minutes.
6 Discard the bouquet garni and serve very hot, sprinkling each portion liberally with Parmesan cheese.

Note: For an untraditional but even chunkier soup, add 75–100 g/3–4 oz finely chopped or coarsely minced or ground cooked meat, poultry or game.

Cream of Mushroom Soup   Serves 6

75 g/3 oz/⅓ cup butter or margarine
1 large onion, peeled and chopped
1 clove garlic, crushed
350 g/12 oz open or cup mushrooms
50 g/2 oz/½ cup flour
900 ml/1½ pints/3¾ cups vegetable stock
salt and pepper
good pinch of ground mace or nutmeg
300 ml/½ pint/1¼ cups milk
2–3 teaspoons lemon juice
150 ml/¼ pint/⅔ cup single (light) or soured cream
freshly snipped chives or spring onion (scallion) tops

1 Melt the fat in a saucepan, add the onion and garlic and fry very gently for about 5 minutes or until soft.
2 Roughly chop about 225 g/8 oz of the mushrooms, add to the pan and continue to cook for a few minutes until quite soft.
3 Stir in the flour and cook for a minute or two, stirring continuously, then gradually add the stock and bring to the boil. Season with salt and pepper and add the mace or nutmeg. Cover the pan and simmer gently for 15–20 minutes or until tender.
4 Cool a little, then rub the soup through a sieve or purée in a blender or food processor. Return to a clean pan.
5 Finely chop the remaining mushrooms and add to the soup with the milk and lemon juice. Bring back to the boil and simmer gently for 5–10 minutes.
6 Stir in the cream or soured cream, adjust seasonings and serve very hot sprinkled with chives or spring onion tops.

Note: Freeze without adding the milk or cream as for Cream of Celery Soup (see page 38).

SPECIAL SOUPS

There are quite a number of soups that should be classed as miscellaneous or, as I prefer, 'special'. They don't seem to fall into any particular category but are excellent and that little bit different to use as a starter for a dinner party as well as at other times.

French Onion Soup   Serves 6

65 g/2½ oz/⅓ cup butter or margarine
450 g/1 lb onions, peeled and very thinly sliced
1 tablespoon flour
1.5 litres/2½ pints/6¼ cups brown stock
salt and pepper
2 bay leaves
6 slices French or Vienna bread
75 g/3 oz Gruyère or Emmenthal cheese, grated

1 Melt the fat in a heavy-based saucepan, add the onions and fry gently until browned all over. This may take up to 20 minutes. Stir from time to time.

2 Stir in the flour until evenly blended and gradually add the stock and bring to the boil, stirring frequently.
3 Add seasonings and bay leaves, cover the pan and simmer gently for about 30 minutes or until tender.
4 Discard the bay leaves and adjust the seasonings.
5 Lay the pieces of bread on a foil-lined grill rack and cover with the cheese. Place under a moderate grill or broiler until melted.
6 Ladle the soup into warmed bowls and place a piece of bread on each one. Serve immediately.

Cream of Mussel Soup   Serves 6

2.25 litres/4 pints/10 cups mussels (see below)
½ bottle dry white wine
2 large onions, peeled and finely chopped
50 g/2 oz/¼ cup butter or margarine
50 g/2 oz/½ cup flour
600 ml/1 pint/2½ cups fish stock
450 ml/¾ pint/scant 2 cups milk
salt and pepper
1 tablespoon lemon juice
2 tablespoons freshly chopped parsley
150 ml/¼ pint/⅔ cup single (light) cream

1 Wash and scrub the mussels thoroughly, using several bowls of cold water to remove all traces of grit and sand. Discard any mussels that do not close when given a sharp tap with the back of a knife (these are dead and will make you ill). Also pull off any pieces of 'beard' or weed that protrude from the shells.
2 Put the mussels into a saucepan and add the wine and onions. Bring to the boil, cover the pan and simmer gently for about 10 minutes or until all the mussels have opened. Discard any that don't open.
3 Remove the mussels and take most of them out of their shells. Leave about 6 mussels on their half shells for garnish. Make sure you catch all the juices from them as they are removed.
4 Melt the butter in a pan and stir in the flour. Cook for 1–2 minutes, stirring frequently to form a roux.
5 Gradually add the mussel liquor followed by the stock and milk and bring to the boil. Season to taste and simmer for 5 minutes.
6 Add the mussels and simmer for a further 5 minutes, then stir in the parsley and cream and reheat without boiling. Serve topped with a mussel in its half shell.

Note: Mussels are only available at certain times of the year fresh but can be obtained frozen without their shells all the year round.

Gazpacho

Serves 6

This is a famous chilled summer soup from Spain. It varies widely in ingredients and flavourings but most often has a fairly strong taste of garlic! This recipe has tomato juice as a base.

900 ml/1 1/2 pints/3 3/4 cups tomato juice, well chilled
4 teaspoons wine vinegar
3 tablespoons lemon juice
3/4 teaspoon Worcestershire sauce
3–4 cloves garlic, crushed
salt and pepper
450 g/1 lb tomatoes, peeled and chopped
1/2 small onion, peeled and grated
10 cm/4 inch piece cucumber, grated
1/2 green pepper, deseeded and finely chopped
1/2 small red pepper, deseeded and finely chopped
To garnish
1/2 red pepper, deseeded and finely chopped
1/2 green pepper, deseeded and finely chopped
10 cm/4 inch piece cucumber, thinly diced

1 Put the tomato juice in a bowl and add the vinegar, lemon juice, Worcestershire sauce and garlic and season to taste.
2 Add the tomatoes, onion, cucumber and peppers and mix well. Cover the bowl securely with plastic cling film or foil and chill for several hours or until required.
3 Ladle the soup into bowls and add an ice cube or two to each bowl, if liked. Serve the chopped vegetables separately for the guests to help themselves.

SOUP GARNISHES AND ACCOMPANIMENTS

There are many types of garnish that can be added to soups just before taking to the table. They can usually be prepared in advance and are really only used to add the final touch to the soup so that it looks attractive. The flavour should obviously enhance the type of soup, not clash with it, but there are often several different garnishes that will 'go' with one particular soup.

Croûtons – serve sprinkled over the soup or in a separate bowl for guests to help themselves.

Fried Croûtons: cut slices of bread 5 mm–1 cm/1/4–1/2 inch thick, remove the crusts and then cut into dice of about 5 mm–1 cm/1/4–1/2 inch. Fry quickly in melted lard or heated shallow oil in a frying pan. Stir and turn with a slotted spoon – they brown quickly and need to be turned to prevent burning. Remove quickly onto absorbent kitchen paper towel to drain off the excess fat. Serve warm or cold.

Toasted Croûtons: toast slices of bread evenly, cut off all the crusts and dice or cut into small shapes. Serve cold.

Lemon – cut a lemon into water-thin slices, making sure all the pips are removed. Float on the top of all clear soups, vegetable soups, most chilled soups and fishy soups.

Raw Leek – cut a leek into paper-thin slices and scatter over vegetable soups.

Fried Onion Rings – peel and slice an onion thinly and fry in heated oil or dripping until golden brown. Drain on absorbent kitchen paper towel and float on the surface of most vegetable soups.

Bacon – use streaky or back bacon and either crisply fry or cook under a moderate grill or broiler until crispy but not burnt. Drain on absorbent kitchen paper towel and finely chop or crumble. Bacon rinds only can also be fried, finely chopped or crumbled. Sprinkle over vegetable soups or those containing bacon in the ingredients.

Cucumber – thinly sliced cucumber, either peeled or with the skin left on, can be floated on the surface of many chilled soups and chicken-based soups.

Cream – 1–2 tablespoons double (heavy) or single (light) cream, soured cream or natural yogurt can be swirled into the soup just before serving. Simply pour or spoon into the bowl and swirl around with a fork or knife. This can be used in most soups.

Celery – use the small pale green celery leaves from the centre of the head to garnish soups.

Herbs – any type of freshly chopped herbs can be sprinkled into soups. Obviously some of the herbs blend better with certain types of soups than others: parsley goes with everything; try mint or basil with tomato; and fresh coriander with cucumber or potato.

Almonds – toast a few flaked almonds and sprinkle over soups, particularly poultry-based ones.

Garlic Bread

100–175 g/4–6 oz/1/2–3/4 cup butter
2–4 cloves garlic, crushed
1 Vienna or small French loaf

1 Soften the butter and beat in the garlic to taste.
2 Using a sharp bread knife or any saw-edged knife, cut the loaf into slanting slices almost through but leaving a 'hinge' on the bottom crust.
3 Spread each slice with the garlic butter and reassemble the loaf. Wrap in foil.
4 Put into a moderate to hot oven (180–220°C/350–425°F/Gas Mark 4–7) for 10–20 minutes.
5 Serve with the foil folded back so each person can pull off one or more slices as he or she wants.

VARIATIONS

Herb Bread – use 1 tablespoon dried mixed herbs or 2 tablespoons freshly chopped mixed herbs in place of some or all of the garlic.

Anchovy Bread – finely chop or pound a drained can of anchovies and beat into the butter in place of the garlic.

Curry Bread – beat 2–3 teaspoons curry powder into the butter in place of the garlic.

6 Meats

For many of us meat is the most important, satisfying and versatile of all foods. There are, of course, those who disagree and to my mind everyone is entitled to their own favourites or horrors when it comes to eating meat – it is far too expensive an item to be wasted. However, for the large proportion of the people who do like and enjoy eating meat it is a tremendous supply of protein and also a good source of iron and some of the B vitamin group. The fat provides energy and also helps to bring out much of the flavour of the meat and keeps the leaner parts of it succulent during cooking.

The variety and quality of meat available is better now than it ever has been, but then it has never been so expensive before, which is why it is so important to take a little time and trouble when selecting a roast or any cut of meat to ensure you get the very best value for your money, and to know what you are looking for and why.

As a general guide to buying, meat should not have an undue amount of fat on it – but must have some. The fat should be firm and free from discolouration with a fine grain and have no visible bruising.

Never store meat tightly wrapped in anything after purchase (unless to be put straight into the freezer). It must be kept in the cold and have a good air circulation. It is often best to put the meat on a plate, cover lightly but keep the ends open, and store in the refrigerator or a cold larder until required. Fresh meat should not be kept for more than 3–4 days even in the refrigerator and minced (ground) meat and offal should be cooked within 24 hours because they are extremely perishable. Cooked meats should be wrapped in plastic cling film or foil to prevent drying out and leftover casseroles and pies, etc., must be cooled quickly before covering and then stored in the refrigerator until the next day. Remember that reheated meat dishes must be completely reheated through to boiling point before serving again – not just warmed up, as that is where the trouble of food poisoning can start.

The carcasses of all types of animal have prime cuts and lesser cuts too. It is probably easiest to roast the best pieces and grill or broil or fry steaks and chops, but these are the most expensive parts of the carcass. The cheaper cuts are very important too and often by pot roasting, stewing or long casseroling the finished dish will be far more flavoursome and is sure to be tender for much less than half the cost of the other more expensive cuts. Often the meat on the cheaper cuts is sweeter and has much more flavour, so don't disregard it but take a little extra time and trouble to produce a really good dish.

ROASTING

There are basically two methods of roasting meat. One is to use a hot oven (220°C/425°F/Gas Mark 7), which quickly seals the outside of the joint and keeps the juices in. This gives a good meaty flavour and a well-browned outside. The other is to use a moderate to moderately hot oven (180–190°C/350–375°F/Gas Mark 4–5), which gives a moister joint with less shrinkage, but in my opinion not such a good flavour. The joint should be put into a roasting tin with the thickest layer of fat upwards so that it will automatically baste itself. Often dripping is spread over the meat before putting in the oven but oil or lard can also be used. Take care not to prick the meat while cooking or you will lose many of the valuable juices. Basting (or spooning the fat over the meat) will help keep the meat moist during cooking and this should be done several times during the cooking time.

Roasting meat using roaster bags or plastic film or foil is preferred by some people, but the meat remains pale in colour and doesn't develop such a good flavour as with open roasting. However, you will get good results so long as you follow the instructions on the packs.

A meat thermometer can also be used and this is inserted into the deepest part of the meat, not anywhere near a bone, and the meat is cooked as recommended until the thermometer reaches the specified temperature.

Whatever method of roasting you choose, the meat should be put into the centre of the oven for cooking. Vegetables such as potatoes, parsnips, sweet potatoes, etc. can be put around the joint to roast alongside it. They are often put into a saucepan and brought to the boil and drained before adding to the pan. They need about an hour to cook, so may have to be added some time after the meat has been put in the oven; remember to baste them at the same time as the meat.

When the meat is cooked, transfer it to a warmed serving dish and leave to 'set' for at least 5 minutes. It must not be allowed to get too cold during this time, so a cool oven or warming drawer is the best place but it does help to make carving easier. Spoon or pour away all the fat from the roasting tin, but reserve the juices from the meat and use as a base for the gravy.

POT ROASTING

This is a method of cooking joints of meat in a covered pan in the oven and is particularly suitable for small compact pieces of meat and for any cuts that are likely to be tough when roasted. Breast of lamb, which is boned, stuffed and rolled up, brisket of beef, etc., are greatly improved by this method of cooking – a little liquid is put in with the meat plus flavourings such as vegetables and herbs.

BRAISING

This is a combination of stewing, steaming and roasting. The meat is cooked in a saucepan or casserole over a bed of vegetables, with sufficient liquid to just keep it moist. Boned and stuffed joints of meat are particularly good cooked by this method, as are large pieces of stewing or braising meat which are cut to individual portion size. The lid can be removed from the pan for the last 30 minutes or so to brown the surface.

STEWING

This is a long slow method of cooking in a liquid which is kept at simmering point throughout the cooking time. The meat is cooked in a saucepan or heavy heatproof casserole and the liquid in which it is cooked is served with the meat, so none of the flavours are lost. Many extras can be added for flavour and the meat is usually one of the cheaper or cheapest cuts of meat. The lid must fit tightly to prevent evaporation, which would allow the pot to 'boil dry' and spoil it. The temperature must be only simmering – that is below boiling point – as boiling can cause the meat to toughen and become coarse and stringy. All the ingredients can be put straight into the saucepan and cooked, but for a better colour and texture it is better to fry the meat in hot fat to seal it before adding to the pan.

CASSEROLING

This is very similar to stewing but the ingredients are put into an ovenproof casserole and cooked in a slow to moderate oven until tender. Again it is best to seal the meat before putting into the casserole. Add all types of flavourings, but not quite so much liquid as for stewing, as the evaporation is not so great.

GRILLING OR BROILING

A quick method of cooking meats is under a grill or broiler or over a hot fire. This is only suitable for best quality prime cuts of meat – steaks, chops, cutlets, liver, kidneys, gammon or ham, bacon and sausages. The meat should be seasoned before putting under the grill and brushed with melted fat or oil before cooking, unless it is a particularly fatty meat, such as pork, when little or no extra fat is required. Always preheat the grill before you put the meat under it so the meat will begin to cook immediately and seal in the juices as soon as possible. It is not worth trying to grill cheap cuts of meat, as they will only become tougher – they need liquid and long slow cooking for tenderizing.

Many foods that are to be grilled can be soaked in a mixture of oil, wine or vinegar, seasonings, herbs and perhaps a touch of chopped onion to add flavour and juiciness to the meat – this is called marinating. Various types of marinade can be made and it is usual to put the meat into it for not less than an hour and up to 24 hours, turning it over several times while soaking. Drain off the excess liquid and put the meat under the grill – the marinade can be brushed over the meat during cooking and added to a sauce. A marinade is nearly always used when barbecuing meat, either to soak the meat in prior to cooking or for brushing over the meat while cooking.

FRYING

This is another quick method of cooking, but this time in hot fat or oil instead of by radiant heat. Only the better quality cuts of meat should be fried, as for grilling. Use either butter and/or oil for quick frying, and oil or lard or fat for shallow or deep-frying. This method of cooking is not, of course, good for anyone trying to lose weight.

FREEZING MEAT

Most meats can be frozen, but do check whether you are buying fresh meat or something that has been bought in ready frozen by the butcher and then thawed out before cutting up to sell. Joints and cuts can also be bought ready frozen from the butcher or supermarket to simply transfer to your own freezer. However, if you do freeze your own, it is important to wrap it very securely with polythene or foil, making sure there are no tears in the wrapping – if there are sharp bones, pad these first with a piece of foil before wrapping – and that all the air has been excluded from the pack. Label clearly with the meat, amount and date of freezing. Meat keeps well but the fat on the joint will turn rancid after a time so it is wise to remove any excess fat or lumps of fat that are attached to the meat. Joints of beef, lamb and veal will freeze well for up to 1 year; steaks and chops are best used within 6–8 months. Pork does keep well but the flavour can begin to deteriorate quicker than the other meats so is best to keep joints for only up to 6–8 months and chops, etc., for 4–6 months. Bacon and cured meats are best used within 2 months and the same time is recommended for all offal and minced or ground meats.

Thaw meat out slowly and completely before cooking, so the meat to be served is at its best. Hasty thawing will not improve the flavour, so it pays to remember to take it out of the freezer in good time. Joints can be roasted from frozen but this can be a tricky process which takes a long time and the use of a meat thermometer is essential.

Once cooked, meat and meat dishes can be frozen for up to 2 months. It doesn't matter if the meat was originally frozen; once it has been cooked it is then treated as fresh meat. Thaw out completely and recook the meat before serving – do *not* simply warm it through.

BEEF

When you buy beef, the lean should be a bright red to dark red with the fat a creamy yellow. Small flecks of fat should be visible throughout the lean. Flesh that has a dark red colour indicates that the carcass has been well hung and is more likely to have a good flavour and be very tender.

CUTS OF BEEF

Sirloin – boned and rolled into a joint, or left on the bone. Joints can be cut to the size required. Roast.

Ribs – wing, corner and top. These cuts can be on the bone or boned and rolled. They have an excellent flavour, especially when on the bone. Roast, for preference, but they can also be pot roasted or braised.

Topside or top round – usually boned and rolled, this is a very lean joint often with a strip of extra fat tied on to it by the butcher to prevent it being overdry. Can be roasted, but pot roasting gives a better result.

Silverside or round – a boneless joint which may be salted.

It needs long, slow cooking, such as boiling or braising.

Aitchbone or rump – boned and rolled, although it can be left on the bone. It is a little fatty on the top but has a good flavour, and can be salted. Roast, pot roast, braise or boil.

Brisket – this has an excellent flavour but may be fatty so look for a lean piece. Best boned and rolled but can also be on the bone. It needs long slow cooking, such as braising, pot roasting or slow roasting.

Stewing meats – leg and shin need very long, slow cooking; chuck and blade are better quality and cook more quickly. Stew, casserole or braise.

Minced or ground beef – can be cooked in many ways but is best if started in a heavy-based pan, without any extra oil, over a low heat until the fat runs. Any excess fat can then be drained off instead of left for the meat to cook in.

Steaks – rump, fillet, entrecôte, sirloin and other cuts may be grilled or broiled or fried as you prefer. The steaks with a strip of fat around them need less fat added for cooking but fillet steak, which is completely fatless, must be cooked with butter or some other fat to keep it moist.

Roast Beef

prime joint of beef on the bone, e.g. sirloin, ribs, aitchbone or rump (about 1.25–2.75 kg/2½–6 lb), or a prime joint of beef, boned and rolled, e.g. sirloin, ribs, topside or top round (about 1.25–2.25 kg/2½–5 lb)
50 g/2 oz/¼ cup dripping
salt and pepper (optional)

1 Wipe the meat and trim if necessary. Weigh and calculate the cooking time from the chart below.
2 Place the joint in a roasting tin with the thickest layer of fat upwards. Spread all over with the dripping and season lightly with salt and pepper, if liked.
3 Cook in a hot oven or moderately hot oven (see chart below) for the recommended time, basting the joint with the fat in the tin several times during cooking. Potatoes may be placed around the joint for the last hour of cooking time, turn over once and baste at the same time as the meat.
4 When ready, remove the meat to a serving dish and keep warm. Allow to stand and 'set' for at least 5 minutes before carving.
5 Serve with horseradish sauce, gravy (see page 32) and Yorkshire puddings (see page 52).

CARVING BEEF

Carving is an art and one which can be easily mastered, provided you have a suitable sharp knife and some practice. The butcher will prepare the joint in the easiest way for it to be carved and will often give hints on how and where to begin carving. The blade of the carving knife should be slightly flexible and made of best stainless or carbon steel. It should be well balanced and feel 'comfortable' in the hand. It is equally important to have a good carving fork with a guard – in case the knife slips – and a steel for sharpening the knife. It should be sharpened each time it is to be used for carving so it will cut straight through the meat instead of sawing and tearing at the fibres. Where possible cut across the grain of the meat to shorten the fibres and make the meat seem more tender. Boned and rolled joints are obviously easier to carve than those on the bone, but do try to carve even-sized slices of medium thickness so it looks attractive as well as tasting good.

1 Always stand up to carve a joint – it is so much easier than sitting down.
2 Let the joint 'set' for 5–10 minutes before carving.
3 Make sure your knife is well sharpened.
4 Remove any string and/or skewers which will be in the way as you start to carve.
5 Stand the joint on a flat slip-proof surface, such as a wooden board, or on a plate with spikes to hold it in position.
6 Remove any outer bones, which will be in the way of carving – not the main bone which the flesh is attached to.

Beef on the bone – remove the string, run the knife down either side of the bone to loosen the meat and carve in slices. Alternatively, run the knife down either side of the bone, lift off the meat onto a board and then carve in slices.

Rib roasts – remove the chined bone, run the knife between the meat and ribs to loosen the meat, but only as far as you think you will need to carve, then carve straight down in slices.

ROASTING TIMES FOR BEEF

Meat on the Bone	Moderately hot 190°C/375°F/ Gas Mark 5	Hot 220°C/425°F/ Gas Mark 7
Rare	20 mins per 450g/1 lb plus 20 mins	15 mins per 450 g/1 lb plus 15 mins
Medium	25 mins per 450 g/1 lb	20 mins per 450 g/1 lb plus 20 mins
Well done	30–35 mins per 450 g/ 1 lb plus 30 mins	25–30 mins per 450 g/ 1 lb plus 25 mins

Meat Boned and Rolled		
Rare	25 mins per 450 g/1 lb plus 25 mins	20 mins per 450 g/1 lb plus 20 mins
Medium	30 mins per 450 g/1 lb plus 30 mins	25 mins per 450 g/1 lb plus 25 mins
Well done	35–40 mins per 450 g/ 1 lb plus 35 mins	30–35 mins per 450 g/ 1 lb plus 30 mins

HOW MUCH TO ALLOW

For beef on the bone, allow 225–350 g/8–12 oz raw per person, plus a little extra for some to serve cold.

For boned and rolled beef, allow about 175 g/6 oz raw per person, plus a little extra for some to serve cold.

For steaks, allow 150–175 g/5–6 oz per portion for those with fat attached, or 100–175 g/4–6 oz per portion for fillet steak.

For braising beef on the bone, allow 175–225 g/6–8 oz raw per portion.

For braising beef without bone, allow 100–175 g/4–6 oz raw per portion.

Sweet and Sour Pork Balls (see page 64), Beef Olives with Pecan Stuffing (see page 54) and Bean Sprouts with Peppers and Mushrooms (see page 120)

Yorkshire Puddings

50 g/2 oz/¹/₂ cup plain (all-purpose) flour
pinch of salt
1 egg
150 ml/¹/₄ pint/²/₃ cup milk
a little dripping

1 Sift the flour and salt into a bowl and make a well in the middle.
2 Add the egg and a little of the milk and gradually work in the flour to give a smooth batter. Add the rest of the milk and continue to beat until smooth.
3 Add a little dripping or oil to 4 Yorkshire pudding tins or 8–10 patty tins or muffin pans and put in to a hot oven (220°C/425°F/Gas Mark 7) until the fat is really hot.
4 Pour the batter into the tins so they are not more than two-thirds full and bake in the oven (above the joint) for 20–25 minutes (or a little less for the smaller ones) until well puffed up and golden brown.
5 Put onto a plate and keep warm to serve with the roast.

COOKING STEAKS

Very little needs to be done when cooking steaks as far as preparation is concerned because they are bought 'ready to cook'. If there is excess fat, this may be trimmed off, but do not cut it all off, as it is essential to help with the cooking and for the flavour. Salt and pepper and/or crushed garlic may be rubbed over the steaks before cooking, but this is basically all that is required.

To grill or broil steaks, brush with melted butter or a good oil and put under a preheated medium grill. Either stand on the grill rack or in the pan. Cook following the chart below, turning once or twice. If possible, serve at once.

To fry steaks, cook in melted butter with a touch of oil added to prevent burning and, if the steak is large, brown it quickly on both sides and then lower the heat and cook gently until the required 'doneness' is achieved. With small steaks, fry on one side and then the other until done and serve as soon as possible. .

Thickness	Rare	Medium	Well done
2 cm/³/₄ inch	5 mins	9–10 mins	12–15 mins
2.5 cm/1 inch	6–7 mins	10 mins	15 mins
4 cm/1¹/₂ inches	10 mins	12–14 mins	18–20 mins

TYPES OF STEAK

Rump – this is the joint next to the sirloin and one of the commonest cuts used for grilling or broiling or frying. The 'point' is considered the best part for flavour and tenderness. There is a layer of fat all along the top edge of this steak. It is usually cut from 2–3 cm/³/₄–1¹/₄ inches thick.
Fillet – this is the undercut of the sirloin; probably one of the best-known and most expensive of the cuts used for grilling or broiling or frying. It is very tender, although probably has not such a good flavour as rump steak. The centre or 'eye' of the fillet is the prime part, but none of it has any fat. It is cut into slices of 2.5–5 cm/1–2 inches thick and these can be formed into rounds known as tournedos,

weighing from 150–175 g/5–6 oz each.
Sirloin – this is cut into two parts to give the porterhouse steak which is cut from the thick end of the sirloin. If it is cooked on the bone this is called a T-bone steak. The upper part of the sirloin is cut into very thin steaks called 'minute' steaks – these are very good and need only a short cooking time.
Chateaubriand – this is a thick slice taken from the middle of the fillet, weighing about 350 g/12 oz which can be grilled or broiled or roasted – a marvellous cut.
Entrecôte – this is really the part of the meat between the ribs of beef, but a slice cut from the sirloin or rump which is thin rather than thick can also be termed as an entrecôte steak.

Brisket Pot Roast

Serves 4–6

1.5 kg/3 lb lean piece of brisket, boned and rolled
150 ml/¹/₄ pint/²/₃ cup red wine
2 tablespoons oil or dripping
8 small onions, peeled
4 carrots, peeled and thickly sliced
4 sticks celery, cut into thick slices
10 whole cloves
2 bay leaves
salt and pepper
150 ml/¹/₄ pint/²/₃ cup beef stock
1 tablespoon cornflour (cornstarch)

1 Put the joint in a deep dish. Pour the wine over it and leave to marinate for at least 4 hours and preferably overnight, turning the meat several times. Keep in a cool place.
2 Remove the meat from the marinade and dry off. Heat the oil in a pan and fry the joint all over until it is well sealed and a good brown colour.
3 Put the joint into a deep casserole and arrange the onions, carrots and celery around it. Add the cloves and bay leaves, season well and then pour over the marinade and stock.
4 Cover the casserole tightly and cook in a moderate oven (160°C/325°F/Gas Mark 3) for 3–3¹/₂ hours or until very tender.
5 Remove the meat to a serving plate and the vegetables to a serving dish and keep warm. Strain the cooking juices into a saucepan, skim off any fat and bring back to the boil. Blend the cornflour with a little cold water, add to the sauce and bring back to the boil until thickened and clear. If it is too thick, add a little more beef stock. Adjust the seasonings, pour into a gravy boat and serve with the joint.
6 Boiled or mashed potatoes and a green vegetable should be served with this.

Boiled Beef and Carrots

Serves 6–8

1.75 kg/4 lb joint of silverside or round, salted
4–6 small onions, peeled
6–8 medium carrots, peeled
1 leek, trimmed and cut into 5 cm/2 inch lengths, or 3
* sticks celery, thickly sliced*
1–2 turnips, peeled and quartered (optional)
Herb Dumplings
100 g/4 oz/1 cup self-raising flour
good pinch of salt
1/2–1 teaspoon dried mixed herbs
50 g/2 oz/1/4 cup shredded suet

1 Wash the beef and place in a saucepan leaving a little room around the meat. Bring to the boil, remove any scum from the surface, cover the pan and simmer, allowing 45 minutes per 450 g/1 lb.
2 An hour before the end of the cooking time, prepare the vegetables and add to the saucepan placing them evenly round the joint.
3 For the dumplings, sift the flour and salt into a bowl and mix in the herbs and suet. Add sufficient cold water (about 4 tablespoons) to mix to an elastic dough. Divide into 10–12 small pieces and roll into balls.
4 About 15 minutes before the meat is ready add the dumplings to the pan, arranging them around the top. If the pan is too full, boil some water in another pan and cook the dumplings separately in that. Cover the pan and simmer for 15–20 minutes or until they swell and rise to the top of the pan.
5 Remove the dumplings and the meat and place on a serving dish. Strain the vegetables and either arrange around the joint or put into a separate serving dish. Serve the cooking juices as they are as a thin sauce or use to make a mustard or parsley sauce (see page 31) but use half cooking liquor and half milk.

Spaghetti Bolognese

Serves 4

450 g/1 lb lean raw minced or ground beef
1 large onion, peeled and finely chopped
1–2 carrots, peeled and finely chopped
1–2 cloves garlic, crushed
2 tablespoons tomato purée
1 tablespoon flour (optional)
425 g/15 oz can peeled tomatoes
1 teaspoon Worcestershire sauce
salt and pepper
4 tablespoons red wine or beef stock (optional)
100 g/4 oz mushrooms, sliced or chopped
1 tablespoon oil
225 g/8 oz spaghetti
grated Parmesan cheese, fresh or dried

1 Put the minced beef into a heavy-based saucepan with no added fat. Heat gently until the fat begins to run and the mince begins to cook. Stir frequently to prevent sticking.
2 Add the onion, carrots and garlic and continue to cook gently for about 5 minutes, stirring occasionally.
3 Stir in the tomato purée and flour (if used) and cook for

about a minute stirring all the time. Add the tomatoes, Worcestershire sauce, seasonings and wine and bring to the boil. Cover the pan and simmer gently for about 20 minutes, giving an occasional stir. Add the mushrooms and a little more stock, if getting too dry, and cook for a further 10 minutes.
4 Put a saucepan of water on to boil and add a good pinch of salt and 1 tablespoon oil (to help keep the pasta from sticking together). Add the spaghetti a little at a time, allowing it to be gently pushed into the pan so it curls around. Boil gently for about 12–14 minutes or until almost tender – *al dente* – do not overcook it. Drain thoroughly and, if liked, run under a hot tap to remove any excess starch and drain again.
5 Serve the spaghetti on four hot plates, leaving a dip in the middle and then spoon the meat sauce into the dip and over most of the spaghetti. Serve the grated cheese separately for each person to help himself.

Steak and Kidney Pie

Serves 4–5

675 g/1 1/2 lb stewing steak or braising steak, cut into
* 2 cm/3/4 inch cubes*
100 g/4 oz ox kidney, chopped
2 tablespoons oil or dripping
1 large onion, peeled and thinly sliced
1 tablespoon flour
1 meat extract cube or stock cube
1 tablespoon tomato purée
600 ml/1 pint/2 1/2 cups water
1 teaspoon Worcestershire sauce
salt and pepper
1/2 recipe quantity puff or flaky pastry (see pages 173–4),
* or 1 recipe quantity shortcrust pastry (see page 165)*
beaten egg to glaze

1 Heat the oil or dripping in a pan and fry the onion until soft. Add the steak and kidney and continue to cook until the meat is well sealed, stirring occasionally.
2 Stir in the flour and cook for 1 minute, then add the crumbled stock cube, tomato purée and water and bring to the boil. Add the Worcestershire sauce, and plenty of seasonings and cover the pan and simmer gently for about 1 1/2 hours or until tender. Extra stock may be needed, but it must only simmer and not boil, and should be stirred occasionally.
3 Put a pie funnel into the centre of a pie dish and pour or spoon the meat and juices around it so it is full. If there is too much liquid, save this to serve separately. Leave to cool. At this stage the pie may be chilled in the refrigerator until the next day.
4 Roll out the pastry and use to cover the pie (see page 164). Decorate with pastry trimmings and glaze with beaten egg.
5 Bake in a hot oven (220°C/425°F/Gas Mark 7) for 25 minutes or until beginning to brown. Reduce the temperature to moderately hot (190°C/375°F/Gas Mark 5) and continue cooking for about 30 minutes or until the filling is piping hot and the crust well risen and browned. If the filling was taken straight from the refrigerator, increase the cooking time by about 10 minutes.

VARIATIONS

Mushroom – add 100 g/4 oz/2 cups halved or sliced mushrooms to the meat just before turning into the pie dish.

Steak and Herb – replace the kidney with the equivalent in stewing or braising steak and add 1 teaspoon dried mixed herbs. 150 ml/¼ pint/⅔ cup of the water may be replaced with red or white wine or cider.

Tomato and Caper – add 4 peeled and chopped tomatoes and 2 tablespoons drained capers to the meat just before turning the meat into the pie dish.

Chestnut – omit the kidney and add 175 g/6 oz/1 cup lightly roasted or canned whole chestnuts to the meat halfway through the initial cooking process. Replace up to half the water with red or white wine.

Carbonnade of Beef   Serves 4–6

675 g/1½ lb braising beef
3 tablespoons flour
salt and pepper
2 tablespoons oil or dripping
2 large onions, peeled and thinly sliced
1 clove garlic, crushed
300 ml/½ pint/1¼ cups brown ale
300 ml/½ pint/1¼ cups beef stock
2 large carrots, peeled and sliced
¼ teaspoon ground nutmeg or mace
1 teaspoon sugar
1 tablespoon tomato purée
1 teaspoon vinegar
1 bay leaf
100 g/4 oz button mushrooms, trimmed

1   Trim the meat free of any excess fat or gristle and cut either into eight even-sized pieces or into 2.5 cm/1 inch cubes.
2   Combine the flour with plenty of seasonings and use to coat the meat, reserving the surplus.
3   Heat the oil in a pan and fry the pieces of meat until well sealed and browned all over, then transfer to a casserole.
4   Fry the onions and garlic in the same fat until golden brown, stirring occasionally, then stir in the rest of the seasoned flour and cook for a minute or so.
5   Gradually stir in the ale and stock and bring to the boil, stirring frequently. Add the carrots, nutmeg, sugar, tomato purée, vinegar and bay leaf and pour into the casserole.
6   Cover the casserole and cook in a moderate oven (160°C/325°F/Gas Mark 3) for 1½ hours.
7   Add the mushrooms (cutting into halves or quarters if very large), mix well and adjust the seasonings. Re-cover the casserole and return to the oven for a further 30–60 minutes or until very tender. Discard the bay leaf and serve with boiled rice or noodles and a green vegetable or a salad.

Beef Olives with Pecan Stuffing

Serves 4

4 thin slices of topside or top round of beef
1 tablespoon oil
25 g/1 oz/2 tablespoons butter or margarine
2 tablespoons flour
300 ml/½ pint/1¼ cups beef stock
4 tablespoons medium dry sherry, Marsala or white wine
Stuffing
40 g/1½ oz/¼ cup long grain rice
salt and pepper
25 g/1 oz/2 tablespoons butter or margarine
1 onion, peeled and finely chopped
1 tablespoon freshly chopped parsley
½ teaspoon dried thyme
40 g/1½ oz/¼ cup pecan nuts, chopped
¼ teaspoon ground coriander
1 egg, beaten
To garnish
a little soured cream or natural yogurt
sprigs of parsley

1   Beef olives are made from slices of beef taken off a topside joint. They need to be beaten between two sheets of plastic cling film or damp wax or greaseproof paper to give them their characteristic thinness. The butcher will usually beat them for you.
2   For the stuffing, cook the rice in boiling salted water for 12–14 minutes until tender. Drain well and put into a bowl.
3   Melt the fat in a pan and fry the onion gently until soft but only lightly coloured. Add the parsley, thyme, nuts, seasonings, coriander and cooked rice and mix well. Add the egg and bind to a fairly slack consistency.
4   Divide the stuffing between the slices of meat spreading it evenly over them, then roll up carefully to enclose the filling and secure with wooden cocktail sticks or by tying with thin string.
5   Heat the oil and fat in a frying pan and fry the olives until browned all over. Transfer to a shallow casserole.
6   Stir the flour into the pan juices and cook for a minute or so. Gradually add the stock and sherry and bring to the boil. Season well and strain the sauce over the olives.
7   Cover tightly with a lid or foil and bake in a moderate oven (180°C/350°F/Gas Mark 4) for about 1½ hours or until tender.
8   Remove the cocktail sticks or string and serve each olive topped with a spoonful of soured cream or yogurt and garnished with parsley.

Crown of Lamb (see page 59) and Almond Croquettes (see page 119)

Beefy Burgers

Serves 4

450 g/1 lb hamburger mince (fine lean mince)
1 small onion, peeled and very finely chopped or minced
1 clove garlic, crushed (optional)
salt and pepper
1 egg or egg yolk (optional)
a little fat or oil for frying
watercress or salad to garnish

1 Put the mince into a bowl with the onion, garlic (if used) and salt and pepper. Mix thoroughly and then, if liked, add the egg or egg yolk. Divide into four equal portions and press out to make flatish round cakes about 1.5 cm/½ inch thick. Burgers may be chilled in the refrigerator with plastic cling film between each one at this stage until ready to cook later in the day. They may also be frozen – in foil – for up to 3 months.
2 Heat a little fat or oil in a frying pan and add the burgers. Fry slowly for 5–8 minutes, then turn over carefully using a fish slice and/or palette knife or spatula and cook the second side for about 5 minutes. Alternatively, the burgers may be placed on a grill rack and cooked under a moderate grill or broiler for 5–7 minutes each side.
3 Drain the burgers on absorbent kitchen paper towel and serve in a split bap or hamburger bun with slices of raw or fried onion, tomato slices and, if liked, a spoonful of chutney. Serve garnished with watercress or salad.

VARIATIONS

Herby – add 1–2 teaspoons dried mixed herbs or any individual herb to the raw mince mixture before shaping.
Peanut – add 50 g/2 oz/⅓ cup finely chopped salted peanuts to the raw mince and bind with the egg.
Curry – add 2–3 teaspoons curry powder to the raw mince.
Chilli – add 2–3 teaspoons chilli seasoning or ½–1 teaspoon chilli powder to the raw mince.

Steak Diane

Serves 4

8 slices fillet steak (5 mm/¼ inch thick), or 4 thin sirloin or entrecôte steaks
25 g/1 oz/2 tablespoons butter
2 tablespoons oil
1 clove garlic, crushed
2 tablespoons very finely chopped onion
2 tablespoons Worcestershire sauce
1 tablespoon lemon juice
salt and freshly ground black pepper
2 tablespoons freshly chopped parsley

1 Melt the butter and oil in a large frying pan. When hot, add the steaks and fry for 1–2 minutes on each side. Remove from the pan.
2 Add the garlic and onion, and fry for about a minute, then add the Worcestershire sauce, lemon juice, seasonings and parsley and bring to the boil. Replace the steaks and cook for about 2 minutes, spooning the sauce over the steaks. Serve immediately with fried potatoes and a salad.

Beef Strogonoff

Serves 4

450 g/1 lb rump steak or end of the fillet
3 tablespoons seasoned flour
50 g/2 oz/¼ cup butter
1 tablespoon oil
1 onion, peeled and very thinly sliced
225 g/8 oz button mushrooms, thinly sliced
salt and pepper
good pinch of ground coriander
150–300 ml/¼–½ pint/⅔–1¼ cups soured cream
freshly chopped parsley to garnish

1 Slice the steak thinly, then beat it with a rolling pin or the blade of a meat chopper. Cut into strips about 5 mm × 5 cm/¼ × 2 inches and coat in the seasoned flour.
2 Heat half the butter and the oil in a frying pan and fry the pieces of steak until golden brown, about 5–7 minutes, stirring frequently.
3 Heat the remaining butter in another pan and fry the onion gently until soft but not coloured. Add the mushrooms and continue cooking for 2–3 minutes.
4 Add the onion mixture to the beef and season well with salt, pepper and coriander. Cook for about a minute, stirring frequently.
5 Stir in soured cream to taste, reheat gently and serve at once with plain boiled rice and a green salad or vegetable.

Hungarian Goulash

Serves 4–6

675 g/1½ lb stewing steak, cut into 1 cm/½ inch cubes
3 tablespoons seasoned flour
2 tablespoons oil or dripping
2 onions, peeled and chopped
1 large green pepper, deseeded and sliced
2–3 teaspoons paprika
3 tablespoons tomato purée
a little grated nutmeg or ground coriander
salt and pepper
50 g/2 oz/½ cup flour
300 ml/½ pint/1¼ cups beef stock
225 g/8 oz can tomatoes
1 bay leaf
150 ml/¼ pint/⅔ cup beer, cider or wine

1 Coat the pieces of meat evenly with the seasoned flour.
2 Heat the oil in a frying pan and fry the onions and pepper for about 3 minutes, without colouring. Add the meat and continue until it is well sealed all over, stirring frequently.
3 Add the paprika, tomato purée, nutmeg or coriander, seasonings and flour and mix well. Gradually add the stock, tomatoes, bay leaf and beer and bring to the boil.
4 Transfer to a casserole, cover tightly and cook in a moderate oven (180°C/350°F/Gas Mark 4) for 1½–2 hours until very tender. Discard the bay leaf.
5 Serve with boiled noodles, which can be tossed in melted butter with ½–1 teaspoon caraway seeds added, if liked, and a green salad.

LAMB

The age of the animal is indicated by the colour of the lean meat. Pale pink denotes young lamb and this turns to light red as the age increases. Mutton, which used to be so popular in Britain and is one of its traditional dishes, is now hard to obtain because the demand for it is so low but, if you can find it, the flavour is distinctive and extremely good. Legs and shoulders of lamb should be plump with a layer of fat covering the flesh. If you buy New Zealand lamb that is still frozen, do take time to thaw it out slowly – the butcher always does – so the meat is in prime condition when you cook it. Fast thawing will not help the flavour and tenderness. Some people prefer to serve roast lamb very slightly underdone so it is just pink – this is in the French style and is very good, but it is a matter of taste. The cooking times do allow for a completely cooked roast joint.

CUTS OF LAMB

Leg – often sold cut in half as it is a large and expensive joint. It is suitable for roasting and can have leg steaks cut off the top of it. The fillet (or top) half of the leg is good for making kebabs. Can also be pot roasted.

Shoulder – this joint can also be cut in half to give the blade and knuckle ends. It is a good-flavoured joint, very succulent and sweet with more flavour than the leg but also more fat. Usually roasted on the bone, but can be boned and rolled with stuffing added if liked. Shoulder meat can also be cut off for casseroling, etc.

Loin – a prime cut which is usually roasted (or served as chops) either cooked on the bone or boned and rolled with or without a stuffing. Also can be pot roasted. Loin chops and butterfly (or double loin) chops are cut from this joint and sometimes noisettes are cut from loin.

Best end of neck – can be roasted or pot roasted as a joint, or cut into cutlets to grill or broil or fry. This cut is also made into a crown roast, guard of honour, etc.

Breast of Lamb – this is a versatile, cheap and tasty cut, scorned by many but thoroughly enjoyed by those prepared to buy and cook it properly. It is fatty, but much of the fat can be removed either before cooking or when cooked by allowing to cool so the solid layer of fat is easy to remove. It can be boned, stuffed and rolled and then roasted or pot roasted, or cut into pieces to roast, casserole or fry.

Middle and scrag end of neck – these are cheap cuts with rather a high percentage of bone and some fat, but well flavoured. Excellent for casseroles and stews.

Chops – loin chops are cut from the loin as single or double chops; chump chops are cut from nearest the leg and are the largest and leanest. All chops are suitable for grilling or broiling or frying as well as braising or in casseroles.

Cutlets – these are taken from the best end of neck; they have a small eye of meat and a long bone which can be left with meat on it or scraped clean before cooking. Grill or broil or fry, or use in a casserole. Noisettes can be made from best end of neck, which is boned, rolled up and secured with cocktail sticks and then cut into slices the thickness required. Again, fry or grill or broil.

Roast Lamb

prime joint of lamb, e.g. leg, shoulder, loin or best end of neck
25 g/1 oz/2 tablespoons dripping or lard
salt and pepper (optional)
Optional flavourings
garlic
fresh or dried rosemary

1 Trim the meat, if necessary, and weigh. Lamb can either be cooked on the bone or boned and rolled with or without stuffing. If the joint is to be stuffed, this should be added before the joint is weighed.
2 Calculate the cooking time from the chart below. Stand the joint in a roasting tin with the thickest layer of fat upwards and season with salt and pepper (if used), or rub all over with a cut clove of garlic and then spread all over with the dripping.
3 If liked, small slits can be cut in the fat and small sprigs of rosemary inserted to give extra flavour during roasting. Alternatively, simply sprinkle the joint with dried rosemary.
4 Roast the lamb in a hot oven (220°C/425°F/Gas Mark 7) or in a moderate oven (180°C/350°F/Gas Mark 4) for the time recommended in the chart below. Baste the joint several times during cooking. Potatoes may be roasted around the joint for the last hour of cooking; turn them over once and baste when you baste the meat.
5 When cooked, remove the meat to a serving dish, keep warm and allow to set for at least 5 minutes before carving.
6 Serve with mint sauce or jelly, or redcurrant jelly. Onion sauce can also be served as an accompaniment. Use the pan juices to make a slightly thickened gravy.

ROASTING TIMES FOR LAMB

	Moderate oven 180°C/350°F/ Gas Mark 4	Hot Oven 220°C/425°F/ Gas Mark 7
Meat on the bone	30–35 mins per 450g/ 1 lb depending on the thickness of the joint	20 mins per 450 g/ 1 lb plus 20 mins
Meat boned and rolled	40–45 mins per 450 g/ 1 lb depending on the thickness of the joint	25 mins per 450 g/ 1 lb plus 25 mins

CARVING LAMB

Follow the basic rules for carving beef and note these hints too. Lamb should not be carved too thinly; try to aim for about 5 mm/¼ inch. With loin or best end of neck, ask the butcher to chine the joint first. This means to partly chop through the backbone lengthwise so the bone can easily be removed before carving to make it easier to carve between the rib bones. If removed before cooking, the meat would simply shrink from the bones, making it a very unattractive joint.

Loin or best end of neck – stand the joint squarely on a plate and remove the backbone and then carve between the ribs to

Roast Pork (see page 61)

1   Make sure the rind is well scored.

3   Baste the meat and potatoes several times during cooking.

2   Rub the rind well with oil and then with a good layer of salt.

4   Serve the pork with balls of stuffing and apple sauce and with roast potatoes and freshly cooked vegetables.

divide the joint into cutlets. Either cut between each bone or every other one for a 'mini' joint for each serving.

Shoulder – before cooking you can loosen around the blade bone with a small sharp knife, but do not remove it. When cooked, this bone can then be twisted and pulled out to make the carving easier. The shoulder is probably the most difficult joint to carve and you have to get used to carving it both ways for there is a left and right shoulder! Turn the joint so the skin side is uppermost and firmly hold the shank end with a carving fork. Carve a wedge-shaped slice about 5 mm/¼ inch thick from the centre, then continue carving slices from either side of this cut. Carve horizontal slices from the shank end, then small vertical slices from beside the bone. Turn the joint over, remove any fat, then carve in horizontal slices.

Leg – hold the knuckle end firmly with a carving fork and carve a wedge-shaped slice from the centre of the meatiest side. Carve slices from each side of the cut, gradually turning the knife to get larger slices and ending parallel to the bone. Turn the joint over and carve in long horizontal slices.

HOW MUCH TO ALLOW
For leg, loin, shoulder and best end of neck on the bone, allow 350 g/12 oz raw per portion; when boned and rolled, allow about 175 g/6 oz raw per portion.
For chops and cutlets, allow 1–2 of each per portion, but with double loin and chump chops, one is sufficient.
For noisettes, allow 1–2 depending on size.
For stewing lamb or breast of lamb, allow 225–350 g/8–12 oz raw per portion.

Minted Lamb Chops   Serves 4

4 large loin, butterfly or chump chops, or 8 small loin
  chops or cutlets
about 2–3 tablespoons mint jelly
4 tomatoes, halved
watercress to garnish

1   Trim the chops and place in the grill pan. They may be

lightly seasoned with salt and pepper, if liked.

2 Add 1 heaped teaspoon mint jelly to each chop or cutlet and spread out a little.

3 Cook under a moderate grill or broiler for about 8–10 minutes, depending on the size of the chops, and then turn over. Add another teaspoon of mint jelly to each one and add the halved tomatoes to the pan.

4 Cook for a further 8–10 minutes or until cooked through and the chops have a lovely glaze, but take care they do not overbrown or burn.

5 Remove to a serving dish and, after spooning off any excess fat, spoon some of the pan juices over the chops and garnish with the tomatoes and watercress.

VARIATIONS

Ginger – use ginger preserve in place of the mint jelly
Orange – use a fairly smooth orange marmalade in place of the mint jelly.

Crown of Lamb
Serves 6–7

1 crown of lamb
a little oil
vegetables to garnish (e.g. peas, carrots, courgettes (zucchini) celery, etc.)
Stuffing
25 g/1 oz/2 tablespoons butter
1 large onion, peeled and finely chopped
2 sticks celery, finely chopped
100 g/4 oz/2 cups fresh brown breadcrumbs
salt and pepper
50 g/2 oz/1/2 cup walnut halves, chopped
75 g/3 oz/3/4 cup cooked rice (see page 134)
1 teaspoon curry powder
1 egg, beaten

1 A crown can be ordered in advance from the butcher or can often be found in larger supermarkets. It is in fact two best ends of neck of lamb that are turned inside out, scored and sewn together so the boney structure is on the outside and the meaty part inside. Brush lightly all over with oil.

2 For the stuffing, melt the butter in a pan and fry the onion and celery until soft, then stir in all the other ingredients, binding together with the egg. Use to fill the centre of the crown giving it a domed top.

3 Weigh the stuffed joint and stand in a roasting tin. Wrap foil around the bone tips to prevent burning and cover the stuffing with a small piece of foil.

4 Cook in a moderate oven (180°C/350°F/Gas Mark 4) allowing 30 minutes per 450 g/1 lb plus 30 minutes over. Baste the outside of the joint once or twice during cooking and remove the foil from the stuffing for the last 30 minutes of cooking.

5 To serve, place the crown on a serving dish and remove the foil from the bone tips. Put a cutlet frill on top of each one for decoration. Arrange cooked vegetables around the base of the crown and serve with a gravy made using the pan juices. Serve with redcurrant jelly.

Noisettes of Lamb with Tomato Sauce
Serves 4

4 large noisettes of lamb or kidney cutlets (or 8 small ones)
salt and pepper
50 g/2 oz/1/4 cup butter or margarine
Tomato Sauce
1–2 cloves garlic, crushed
100 g/4 oz mushrooms, finely chopped
150 ml/1/4 pint/2/3 cup red wine
150 ml/1/4 pint/2/3 cup tomato ketchup
To garnish
fried bread triangles
watercress

1 Season the noisettes with salt and pepper. (Noisettes are boned cutlets rolled into a round.) Heat almost all the butter in a frying pan and fry the noisettes gently for 8–10 minutes. Turn over and cook for a further 10 minutes or until cooked through.

2 Meanwhile, to make the sauce, heat the remaining fat in a pan and fry the garlic until soft. Add the mushrooms followed by the wine and tomato ketchup. Bring to the boil and simmer, uncovered, for 10–15 minutes until thickened and much darker in colour. Stir occasionally. Adjust the seasonings.

3 Serve the noisettes with the tomato sauce spooned over them and garnish with fried bread and watercress.

Moussaka
Serves 4

450 g/1 lb lean lamb, minced or ground (use leg, shoulder or fillet)
2 aubergines (eggplant)
salt and pepper
2 large onions, peeled and thinly sliced
225 g/8 oz can tomatoes
2 tablespoons tomato purée
Topping
2 eggs
150 ml/1/4 pint/2/3 cup single (light) cream

1 Wipe the aubergines and cut into slices about 2 cm/3/4 inch thick. Place on a board or tray, sprinkle lightly with salt and leave to stand for about 30 minutes. Rinse off the salt under cold water and dry on a cloth or kitchen paper towel.

2 Arrange the slices of aubergine over the base and up the sides of a casserole.

3 Put the minced or ground lamb into a heavy-based saucepan and heat gently until the fat begins to run, stirring frequently. Add the onions and cook gently for about 5 minutes.

4 Add the tomatoes and tomato purée and season well. Mix well, bring to the boil and pour into the casserole.

5 Cook in a moderate oven (180°C/350°F/Gas Mark 4) for about 45 minutes.

6 Beat together the eggs and cream and season, then pour over the meat and aubergines. Return to the oven, still uncovered, for about 15–20 minutes or until the custard has set and is lightly browned.

Stuffed Breast of Lamb
Serves 4

2 large breasts of lamb, boned
salt and pepper
25 g/1 oz/2 tablespoons butter or margarine
2 sticks celery, finely chopped
1 small onion, peeled and finely chopped
1 small dessert apple, peeled, cored and coarsely grated
50 g/2 oz/1 cup fresh white breadcrumbs
1 tablespoon freshly chopped parsley
$1/2$ teaspoon dried thyme
grated rind of 1 lemon
1 egg yolk
Sauce
40 g/1$1/2$ oz/$1/3$ cup flour
300 ml/$1/2$ pint/1$1/4$ cups beef stock
150 ml/$1/4$ pint/$2/3$ cup dry cider

1 Trim off the excess fat from the pieces of lamb and cut out any gristle or membrane. Cut each one in half and season lightly.
2 For the stuffing, melt the fat in a pan and fry the celery and onion gently until soft but not coloured. Turn into a bowl and mix in the apple, breadcrumbs, parsley, thyme, lemon rind and egg yolk. Mix to bind together.
3 Divide the stuffing between the four pieces of lamb spreading it out evenly over the inside, then roll up each piece carefully and secure with wooden cocktail sticks.
4 Place in a greased roasting tin and roast (without adding further fat) in a hot oven (220°C/425°F/Gas Mark 7) for 45–60 minutes or until well browned and cooked through. Baste several times during cooking with the fat which will emerge from the lamb.
5 Remove the rolls to a serving dish and keep warm. Spoon off all but 2 tablespoons fat from the pan, stir in the flour and cook for a minute or so, stirring frequently. Gradually add the stock and cider and bring to the boil, still stirring. Simmer for 2 minutes, adjust the seasonings and strain into a sauce boat. Serve with the lamb.

Lamb and Orange Risotto
Serves 4

675 g/1$1/2$ lb lean boneless lamb (top of leg, leg or shoulder), cut into 2.5 cm/1 inch cubes
2 oranges
salt and pepper
1 tablespoon oil
1 large onion, peeled and sliced
450 ml/$3/4$ pint/scant 2 cups beef stock
50 g/2 oz/$1/3$ cup raisins
$1/4$ teaspoon ground coriander
175 g/6 oz/1 cup long grain rice
100 g/4 oz/1 cup frozen peas, cooked
To garnish
25 g/1 oz/2 tablespoons toasted almond slivers
watercress and slices of orange

1 Pare the rind thinly from 1 orange and free of white pith, using a potato peeler. Cut the rind into very thin strips (called julienne strips). Cut away the white pith

from the orange and ease out the segments. Squeeze the juice from the second orange.
2 Season the lamb lightly with salt and pepper. Heat the oil in a frying pan and fry the lamb until it is well browned all over. Remove from the pan.
3 Fry the onion in the same pan until golden brown, then add the strips of orange rind, segments and juice and the stock and raisins and bring to the boil. Season well and add the coriander.
4 Lay the rice in an ovenproof dish or casserole, add the onion mixture and lamb and mix well. Cover with foil or a lid and cook in a moderate oven (180°C/350°F/Gas Mark 4) for an hour.
5 Remove the lid and stir in the cooked peas. Serve sprinkled with the toasted almonds and garnished with watercress and twisted slices of orange.

Lancashire Hotpot
Serves 4–6

8–12 middle neck of lamb chops or best end chops
225 g/8 oz onions, peeled and finely chopped
2–3 carrots, peeled and sliced
2 lambs' kidneys, skinned, cored and diced (optional)
salt and pepper
$1/2$ teaspoon dried mixed herbs (optional)
450–675 g/1–1$1/2$ lb potatoes, peeled and thinly sliced
300 ml/$1/2$ pint/1$1/4$ cups stock
25 g/1 oz/2 tablespoons butter or margarine
chopped parsley to garnish

1 Remove any excess fat from the chops and layer them in a casserole with the onions, carrots, kidneys (if used), seasonings and herbs (if used).
2 Cover the ingredients with an even layer of sliced potato, overlapping to give an attractive finish.
3 Pour the stock over the potatoes, then brush the potatoes with melted fat.
4 Cover the casserole with a lid or foil and cook in a moderate oven (160°C/325°F/Gas Mark 3) for 2 hours. Remove the lid, increase the oven temperature to hot (220°C/425°F/Gas Mark 7) and return to the oven for about 20 minutes to give a brown top to the potatoes.

Lamb Kebabs
Serves 4

1.25 kg/2$1/2$ lb piece top of leg of lamb, or 2 lamb fillets
8 bay leaves
8 thick slices raw onion
8 slices pepper (optional)
Marinade
4 tablespoons oil
2 tablespoons wine vinegar
2 tablespoons lemon juice
1 clove garlic, crushed
salt and pepper
1 small onion, peeled and very finely chopped
To garnish
lemon wedges
sprigs of parsley

1 Trim the lamb and cut into 2.5 cm/1 inch cubes keeping them as neat as possible as you cut around the bone.

2 Put the oil into a bowl with the vinegar, lemon juice, garlic, seasonings and chopped onion and mix well. Add the cubes of meat, cover and leave to marinate in a cool place for at least 2 hours. Give the meat a stir once or twice, if possible.

3 Drain the cubes of meat and thread onto four long skewers, alternating with the bay leaves, slices of onion and pepper (if used).

4 Cook under a moderate grill or broiler for about 10 minutes each side until well browned and cooked through. Brush with the marinade when you turn them over. Alternately, cook on a barbecue over charcoal.

5 Serve the kebabs on a bed of freshly boiled rice, garnished with lemon wedges and parsley.

PORK

Pork should have a good layer of firm white fat with thinnish elastic skin around the pale pink and moist lean, which may be slightly marbled with fat. The skin for any joint that is to be roasted should be scored to give a good crackling. At one time pork was considered to be seasonal and only available at its best when there was an 'R' in the month, this myth has now been dispelled and excellent pork is available all the year. However, although a roast of pork may not be very acceptable on a boiling hot summer's day, grilled or broiled chops or a delicate dish using pork fillet will be instantly acceptable. Pork is cheaper than some of the other meats, but the prices do fluctuate rather widely.

CUTS OF PORK

Leg – a large lean joint often boned and rolled and cut into smaller joints but it is very good on the bone when it can be halved as for lamb. Roast.

Loin – a prime roasting joint either on or off the bone. Can include the kidney and may be stuffed if boned and rolled. Also cut into chops to grill or broil, fry or casserole.

Spare rib – a fairly lean joint moderately priced, sometimes with more fat than the other roasting joints and a good flavour. Roast, or cut up and casserole, braise or stew.

Fillet or tenderloin – a prime piece of meat with no fat. Very versatile and excellent for kebabs, strogonoff-type dishes and for grilling or broiling and frying.

Hand and spring – this is the foreleg of the pig and is suitable for roasting, boiling and stewing and is good to mince or grind.

Belly – cheap and fatty, but full of flavour. Can be used on or off the bone, either rolled and stuffed or cut into slices. Roast, pot roast, casserole, grill or broil, or fry.

Spare ribs – taken from the belly, they are removed in one piece and then cut up into ribs with meat left all around the bones. Usually barbecued, grilled or broiled, or casseroled.

CARVING PORK

Follow the basic rules for carving as for beef, including leaving the meat to stand for 5–10 minutes to set.

Boned and rolled pork – remove the string from each part of the joint as it is carved. Cut through the crackling where it was scored halfway along the joint, lift off and cut into portions, then carve downwards into fairly thin slices.

Loin – sever the chined bone from the chop bones and put aside. Divide into chops cutting between the rib bones and the scored crackling and serve as chops. Alternatively, loosen the meat from the bones (after cutting off the chined backbone) and then cut off in slices without dividing into chops. It is probably easier to cut off the crackling in portions before slicing the meat if you use this method.

Leg – use the knife to cut through the crackling and remove it before actually carving the meat; this makes it much easier. Do not take off more crackling than meat to be carved. Carve in a similar way as for leg of lamb keeping the slices fairly thin. For half legs, it is probably easier to start at one end of the joint and work to the other end, then turn over and carve the under side.

Spare rib – cut between the score marks into fairly thick slices.

Roast Pork

Make sure the butcher scores the rind of the pork joint well. (See step-by-step illustrations, page 58.).

prime joint of pork, e.g. leg, loin or spare rib, on the bone
*   *or boned and rolled*
oil
salt

1 Trim the pork then weigh and calculate the cooking time from the chart below.

2 Rub the well-scored rind of the pork with oil and then rub in a good layer of salt to give a good crackling.

3 Stand the joint in a roasting tin and cook for the time suggested below either in a hot oven (220°C/425°F/Gas Mark 7) for a joint on the bone or a fairly slim boned and rolled joint, or in a moderately hot oven (190°C/375°F/Gas Mark 5) for a boned and rolled joint, particularly if it is stuffed.

4 Baste several times during cooking and roast potatoes alongside the joint for the last hour of cooking if liked.

5 When ready, transfer to a serving dish and keep warm. Leave to stand for at least 5 minutes for the meat to 'set' before carving. Serve with apple sauce or a gooseberry sauce and sage and onion stuffing (see below), if the joint is not already stuffed. Make a fairly thick gravy from the pan juices after spooning off the excess fat.

ROASTING TIMES FOR PORK

	Moderately hot 190°C/375°F/ Gas Mark 5	Hot 220°C/425°F/ Gas Mark 7
Pork on the bone		25–30 mins per 450 g/1 lb plus 25 mins
Pork boned and rolled	30–35 mins per 450 g/1 lb plus 30 mins	

HOW MUCH TO ALLOW

For joints on the bone, allow 225–350 g/8–12 oz raw pork per portion.

For joints that are boned and rolled, allow about 175 g/ 6 oz raw pork per portion.

For chops, allow 1 per portion; for cutlets or boneless pork slices, allow 1–2 or about 100–175 g/4–6 oz per portion.

For hand and spring, allow 350 g/12 oz raw per portion.

For pork tenderloin, allow 100–175 g/4–6 oz raw per portion.

For belly, allow 100–225 g/4–8 oz raw per portion.

Sage and Onion Stuffing

2 large onions, peeled and chopped
25 g/1 oz/2 tablespoons butter
100 g/4 oz/2 cups fresh breadcrumbs
2 teaspoons dried sage
salt and pepper

1 Put the onions into a pan of cold water and bring to the boil. Simmer for about 5 minutes, then drain well.
2 Melt the fat in a pan, stir in the onions and fry for a minute or so.
3 Put the breadcrumbs, sage and seasonings into a bowl. Add the onions and the fat and mix well together.
4 Press lightly into a greased ovenproof dish and cook in the oven below the joint of pork for 35–45 minutes or until lightly browned on top and crisp. Cut into wedges to serve.

Corsican Pork Chops   Serves 4

4 lean pork chops
salt and pepper
25 g/1 oz/2 tablespoons butter or margarine
1 green pepper, deseeded and thinly sliced
1 teaspoon dried rosemary
4 tomatoes, peeled and sliced
50 g/2 oz/½ cup grated Cheddar cheese

1 Trim the chops and season lightly with salt and pepper. Put into the grill pan or on the grill rack.
2 Cook under a moderate heat for about 10 minutes.
3 Meanwhile, melt the fat in a small saucepan and fry the pepper gently for a few minutes.
4 Turn the chops over, sprinkle with rosemary and cook for a further 8–10 minutes or until cooked through.
5 Spoon the peppers on top of the chops, then cover with sliced tomatoes and put under the grill or broiler for a minute or so. Sprinkle with the cheese and continue to cook until the cheese melts and is bubbling.

Pork Fillet in a Crust   Serves 4–5

450 g/1 lb pork fillet or tenderloin
2–3 tablespoons oil
15 g/½ oz/1 tablespoon butter or margarine
1 small onion, peeled and finely chopped
4 lean bacon rashers, rinds removed and chopped
75 g/3 oz mushrooms, chopped
1 medium cooking apple, peeled, cored and chopped
¼ teaspoon dried mixed herbs
salt and pepper
about ½ recipe quantity puff or flaky pastry (see pages 173–4)
beaten egg to glaze
watercress to garnish
Sauce
1 tablespoon plain (all-purpose) flour
300 ml/½ pint/1¼ cups stock
2–3 tablespoons wine or cider
1 tablespoon tomato purée

1 Cut the pork fillets to about 23 cm/9 inches long to make an even-sized joint, then tie together with fine string in a neat shape. Heat the oil in a pan and fry the pork very gently for about 20 minutes, turning it regularly, until evenly browned. Remove from the pan and allow to cool. Reserve the pan and its drippings for the gravy.
2 For the stuffing, melt the butter in a pan and fry the onion and bacon gently until soft. Add the mushrooms and continue for a minute or so. Stir in the apple, herbs and plenty of seasonings. Leave to cool.
3 Roll out the pastry on a floured surface large enough to enclose the pork fillet. Spread the mushroom mixture down the centre of the pastry, remove the string from the pork and place this on the stuffing.
4 Wrap the pastry around the pork, dampen the edges with water and seal together, folding the ends neatly under the joint. Place in a lightly greased roasting tin with seams and joins underneath and decorate the top with pastry leaves cut from the pastry trimmings. Glaze all over with beaten egg and make a hole in the centre for the steam to escape.
5 Bake in a hot oven (220°C/425°F/Gas Mark 7) for 30 minutes. Reduce the temperature to moderate (180°C/ 350°F/Gas Mark 4) and cook for a further 15–20 minutes until well puffed up and golden brown. If getting overbrown, lay a sheet of wax or greaseproof paper over the pastry.
6 Meanwhile, make the sauce. Stir the flour into the reserved pan juices and cook for a minute. Gradually add the stock, wine or cider and tomato purée and bring to the boil. Simmer for 2 minutes, adjust the seasonings and strain into a sauce boat. Garnish the pork with watercress and serve.

Fried Veal Escalopes Viennoise (see page 68) and Crispy-topped Pork Casserole (see page 65)

Somerset Pork

Serves 4

4 large boneless pork slices
2 tablespoons seasoned flour
40 g/1½ oz/3 tablespoons butter or margarine
175 g/6 oz tiny button mushrooms, trimmed
300 ml/½ pint/1¼ cups dry cider
good dash of Worcestershire sauce
salt and pepper
150 ml/¼ pint/⅔ cup single (light) or double (heavy)
  cream
To garnish
1 dessert apple
a little lemon juice
chopped parsley

1   Trim the pork and coat in seasoned flour, reserving the excess. Melt the butter in a frying pan and add the slices of pork. Cook gently until browned on both sides and almost cooked through – about 10–15 minutes. Remove from the pan and keep warm.
2   Add the mushrooms to the pan and cook gently for a minute or so. Stir in the remaining seasoned flour and cook for another minute. Gradually add the cider and bring to the boil.
3   Add the Worcestershire sauce and seasonings and replace the pork. Simmer gently in a covered pan for about 10 minutes.
4   Stir in the cream and reheat without boiling. Adjust the seasonings and serve garnished with slices of unpeeled apple, which have been dipped in lemon juice to prevent them turning brown, and chopped parsley.

Sweet and Sour Pork Balls

Serves 4

450 g/1 lb lean pork, minced or ground
1 clove garlic, crushed
50 g/2 oz/1 cup fresh white breadcrumbs
salt and pepper
1 egg, beaten
flour for coating
2 tablespoons oil
Sauce
1 green pepper, deseeded and thinly sliced
1 red pepper, deseeded and thinly sliced
225 g/8 oz can pineapple rings
75 g/3 oz/scant ½ cup brown sugar
4 tablespoons cider or wine vinegar
3 tablespoons soy sauce
300 ml/½ pint/1¼ cups chicken stock
4 teaspoons cornflour (cornstarch)

1   Combine the pork with the garlic, breadcrumbs and plenty of seasonings in a bowl. Add the egg and bind together. Divide into 16–20 pieces and roll each piece into a ball.
2   Heat the oil in a frying pan and fry the pork balls gently until they are evenly browned and cooked through – this will take from 15–20 minutes. Remove the cooked balls from the pan and keep warm.
3   Meanwhile, put the peppers into a pan of cold water

and bring to the boil for 1 minute. Drain. Drain the pineapple rings and chop and mix with the peppers.
4   Put the sugar into a saucepan with the vinegar, soy sauce and stock and bring to the boil. Add the peppers and pineapple and simmer for 5 minutes.
5   Blend the cornflour with a little cold water and add the sauce. Bring back to the boil for a minute or so and adjust the seasonings.
6   Serve the pork balls on plain boiled rice with the sauce spooned over them.

Indonesian Pork

Serves 4

550 g/1¼ lb pork fillet or tenderloin
65 g/2½ oz/good ¼ cup butter or margarine
1 large onion, peeled and finely chopped
2 carrots, peeled and diced
1 clove garlic, crushed
1½ teaspoon curry powder
1 tablespoon soy sauce
½ teaspoon ground coriander
salt and pepper
225 g/8 oz/1⅓ cups long grain rice, boiled (see page 134)
225 g/8 oz/2 cups frozen peas, freshly cooked
1 large egg

1   Cut the pork into narrow strips about 4 cm/1½ inches long. Melt 50 g/2 oz/¼ cup of the fat in a pan and add the pork. Fry gently for about 10 minutes, stirring frequently.
2   Add the onion, carrots and garlic and continue to cook for 5–8 minutes until tender and the pork is cooked.
3   Stir in the curry powder, soy sauce, coriander and seasonings and mix thoroughly, then add the rice and heat through completely.
4   Stir in the peas, mix well and arrange in a warmed shallow serving dish. Keep warm.
5   Whisk the egg with 1 tablespoon water and seasonings. Melt the remaining fat in a frying pan, pour in the egg mixture and cook, without stirring, until set. Turn out of the pan onto a plate and cut into narrow strips. Either arrange in a lattice over the pork dish, or just scatter over the top. Serve at once.

Barbecued Pork

Serves 4–5

900 g/2 lb pork spare ribs, or 675 g/1½ lb lean belly of
  pork cut into thin slices
25 g/1 oz/2 tablespoons butter or margarine
2 teaspoons oil
2 large onions, peeled and sliced
4 tablespoons demerara sugar
1½ teaspoons salt
1 teaspoon paprika
1 tablespoon tomato purée
1 tablespoon Worcestershire sauce
2 tablespoons vinegar
4 tablespoons lemon juice
425 g/15 oz can apricot halves
2–3 teaspoons cornflour (cornstarch)
black olives to garnish

1 Melt the fat and oil in a pan and quickly fry the pork ribs or slices until browned. Transfer to a casserole.
2 Fry the onions in the same fat until lightly browned, then drain off any excess fat from the pan.
3 Add the sugar, salt, paprika, tomato purée, Worcestershire sauce, vinegar, lemon juice and about 200 ml/7 fl oz/scant cup of water to the pan and bring to the boil.
4 Pour over the pork, cover the casserole and cook in a fairly hot oven (200°C/400°F/Gas Mark 6) for about 45 minutes.
5 Drain the apricots over a bowl and add to the casserole. Blend the cornflour with 2 tablespoons of the apricot juice and stir into the casserole. Re-cover and cook for a further 15–20 minutes.
6 Skim off any excess fat from the surface of the casserole and serve garnished with black olives.

Crispy-topped Pork Casserole

Serves 5–6

675 g/1½ lb lean pork, cut into 2.5 cm/1 inch cubes
50 g/2 oz/¼ cup butter or margarine
1 onion, peeled and finely chopped
4 sticks celery, thinly sliced
1 large red pepper, deseeded and thinly sliced
1–2 cloves garlic, crushed
4 tablespoons medium sherry
2 tablespoons soy sauce
1 tablespoon lemon juice
about 175 ml/6 fl oz/¾ cup beef stock
salt and pepper
325 g/11 oz can sweetcorn kernels, drained
Topping
50 g/1½ oz/3 tablespoons butter
40 g/1½ oz/¾ cup fresh breadcrumbs
40 g/1½ oz/⅓ cup blanched almonds, chopped
freshly chopped parsley to garnish

1 Melt half the butter in a pan and fry the pork cubes until browned all over. Drain well and transfer to a casserole.
2 Add the rest of the fat to the pan and add the onion, celery, red pepper and garlic. Fry for 2–3 minutes, then add to the casserole.
3 Combine the sherry, soy sauce and lemon juice and make up to 300 ml/½ pint/1¼ cups with the stock. Bring to the boil, season well and add the sweetcorn. Pour over the pork, mix well and cover tightly.
4 Cook in a moderate oven (180°C/350°F/Gas Mark 4) for 50–60 minutes or until the meat is tender.
5 Meanwhile, melt the butter for the topping in a frying pan and fry the breadcrumbs until beginning to brown. Add the nuts and continue frying until they are golden brown.
6 To serve, remove the lid from the casserole, give the contents a good stir then spoon the nut mixture over the top and sprinkle with parsley.

Sage and Bacon Stuffed Pork

Serves 5–6

1.5 kg/3 lb loin of pork, boned and rolled
salt and pepper
6–8 rashers lean bacon, derinded
2 teaspoons freshly chopped sage, or 1 teaspoon dried sage
40 g/1½ oz/¾ cup fresh white breadcrumbs
1 egg yolk
fresh sage leaves or parsley sprigs to garnish

1 Unroll the pork and cut the flesh a little to open it out. Season the inside of the meat lightly and lay the bacon evenly over the surface.
2 Mix the sage, breadcrumbs and a little seasoning together and bind with the egg yolk. Spread over the bacon.
3 Reroll the pork to enclose the filling. Secure with string and skewers (if necessary) and weigh the joint. Place in a roasting tin, rub the rind with oil and then liberally with salt.
4 Cook as for roast pork (see page 61), roasting potatoes alongside the joint.
5 Serve the joint surrounded with potatoes and sprigs of sage and parsley and with a gravy made from the pan juices (see page 32). Apple sauce can be served as an accompaniment.

VEAL

As veal should come from a very young calf the flesh should be comparatively light in colour – a pale pink meat that is soft and moist with a very little firm pinkish or white fat. Avoid veal that is overflabby and really wet. As the animal ages, the flesh tends to take on a bluish tinge and become mottled. Veal has a lot of bone in proportion to the meat and this makes excellent jellied stock or gravy when it is boiled, so do not discard veal bones if they come with your joint. They may be used raw or cooked for stock.

As veal has very little fat, it is important that it is not allowed to dry out during cooking. If roasting, extra fat or liquid must be added to counteract this and, when casseroling or cooking by any method, make sure there is plenty of liquid and that the meat is not cooked too fast or overcooked, as it is very easy to make it dry and tasteless and therefore a waste of money – for it is an expensive meat.

CUTS OF VEAL
Leg – a prime joint, boned and often stuffed before rolling, although it can be cooked on the bone. Suitable for roasting and pot roasting.
Loin – a prime cut for roasting, usually boned and rolled but again it can be cooked on the bone. Also cut into cutlets from the neck end and chops as you get further down – these can be fried, grilled or broiled, braised, etc.
Fillet – can be sold as a very expensive joint for roasting but is more usually cut into escalopes to fry, grill or broil.
Shoulder – often boned, rolled and roasted. It is also cut into pieces to use for pies, fricassées, casseroles, etc. It is a more economical joint as it is a rather awkward shape.

Knuckle or hind – a cheaper cut from the foreleg. Good for stewing veal for pies, etc., or to casserole, or can be boned, rolled and stuffed to pot roast or braise.

Breast – another fairly cheap cut that is usually boned, stuffed and rolled and then roasted or pot roasted.

Chops – the loin can be divided into chops – those from the bottom end with just a small round bone in are known as chump chops. Chops are suitable for grilling or broiling and frying with plenty of fat or marinade.

Cutlets – these are prime cuts from the top or neck end of the loin to use for grilling or broiling, or frying.

Shin – this is often cut into slices about 2.5 cm/1 inch thick by sawing through the bone to provide the meat for Osso Bucco; otherwise the meat is used as pie veal and the bone for stock.

Roast Veal

Remember that veal is a very dry meat with little fat of its own to help keep the flesh moist. It is one of the joints that takes well to being roasted in foil or pot roasted or, if to be roasted in the normal way, it is best to wrap streaky or fat bacon rashers around it to help counteract the lack of fat. It may also be partly cooked in an open tin and then covered with foil to complete the cooking.

prime roasting joint of veal (about 1.25–2.25 kg/2½–5 lb), on the bone or boned and rolled
8–10 rashers streaky or fat bacon
about 50 g/2 oz/¼ cup dripping or other fat
salt and pepper

1 Trim the joint and weigh, then stand in a roasting tin.
2 Lay the rashers of bacon over the joint, tying loosely with string if necessary. Season lightly with salt and pepper and spread the fat liberally over the whole joint.
3 Roast in a hot oven (220°C/425°F/Gas Mark 7), allowing 30 minutes per 450 g/1 lb, and baste every 15 minutes for the first 1½ **hours**. For a larger joint which takes more than 1½ hours, it is wise to cover the whole joint with foil for the rest of the cooking time.
4 Remove the joint to a serving dish – the bacon can be taken off, if liked, or left in position – and allow 5–10 minutes for it to 'set'. Use the pan juices to make a fairly thin gravy and serve with grilled or broiled bacon rolls, and a veal forcemeat.

Veal Forcemeat

100 g/4 oz lean veal or pork
75 g/3 oz lean bacon, derinded and finely chopped
1 small onion, peeled
25 g/1 oz/2 tablespoons butter
75 g/3 oz/1½ cups fresh breadcrumbs
25 g/1 oz mushrooms, finely chopped
1 tablespoon finely chopped fresh parsley
salt and pepper
pinch of ground nutmeg, mace or coriander
1 egg, beaten

1 Finely mince or grind the veal or pork, bacon and onion and put into a bowl.
2 Add the melted butter, breadcrumbs, mushrooms, parsley and seasonings and mix well. Add a touch of lemon juice, if too dry.
3 Add the egg and bind together. Either press lightly into a greased ovenproof dish or form into balls about the size of a large walnut and stand in a greased ovenproof dish.
4 Cook in the oven below the roasting joint for about 40 minutes or until lightly browned.

CARVING VEAL

Veal is similar in shape to beef or lamb when it comes to carving. It is also a lot more tender than some meats so it should cut much more easily. Follow the directions for the other meats.

HOW MUCH TO ALLOW

For roasting joints on the bone, allow 225–350 g/8–12 oz raw per portion.
For fillet or escalopes (boneless), allow 100–150 g/4–5 oz raw per portion.
Allow 1 veal chop taken from the loin or 1–2 cutlets from neck end or top of the loin, depending on size.
For breast of veal on the bone, knuckle on the bone and best end of neck on the bone, allow about 450 g/1 lb raw, or when boned, allow 100–175 g/4–6 oz.

Pot Roast Veal Provençal   Serves 4–6

1.25 kg/2½ lb shoulder of veal, boned and rolled
1 tablespoon dripping or margarine
salt and pepper
1 large onion, peeled and sliced
1 tablespoon tomato purée
425 g/15 oz can peeled tomatoes
150 ml/¼ pint/⅔ cup dry white wine
good pinch of sugar
about 16 black olives
a little garlic powder
sprigs of parsley to garnish

1 Fry the joint in the melted dripping or margarine until well browned all over. Remove from the pan, season well and place in a casserole.
2 Fry the onion in the same fat until soft, add the tomato purée, tomatoes and their juice, wine and sugar and bring to the boil. Season well and pour around the veal. Add the olives to the casserole and sprinkle the garlic powder over the joint.
3 Cover the casserole tightly and cook in a moderately hot oven (190°C/375°F/Gas Mark 5) for an hour. Baste the joint thoroughly, replace the lid and return to the oven for a further hour or until tender. Taste and adjust the seasonings.
4 To serve, place the joint on a serving plate and put the vegetables and juices into a serving dish or large sauce boat with a ladle for serving. Garnish the joint with parsley and serve it cut into fairly thin slices.

Saltimbocca

Serves 4

*8 small thin veal escalopes, or 4 large escalopes, halved and
    beaten*
1 tablespoon lemon juice
salt and pepper
8 fresh sage leaves, or a little dried sage
8 small, thin slices prosciutto or ham
40 g/1½ oz/3 tablespoons butter
3–4 tablespoons Marsala or dry sherry
3 tablespoons light stock
To garnish
fried croûtons (see page 47)
freshly chopped parsley

1   Ask the butcher to flatten the veal, or place the pieces
    between two sheets of plastic cling film and beat flat
    with a mallet or the side of a chopper. Rub each piece
    with lemon juice and season lightly.
2   Lay a sage leaf on each piece of veal or sprinkle with a
    little dried sage. Cover with the prosciutto or ham and
    roll up neatly. Secure with wooden cocktail sticks or tie
    with fine string.
3   Melt the butter in a frying pan and fry the rolls gently
    until golden brown all over. Add the Marsala or sherry
    and stock and bring to the boil. Cover the pan and
    simmer very gently for about 20 minutes, or until
    tender.
4   Adjust the seasonings and serve with the juices poured
    over the rolls and garnished with fried bread croûtons
    and chopped parsley.

Raised Veal and Ham Pie

Serves 6

450 g/1 lb pie veal or other lean veal
350 g/12 oz cooked ham
1 small onion, peeled
salt and pepper
¼ teaspoon ground coriander
2 teaspoons powdered gelatine
300 ml/½ pint/1¼ cups chicken stock
Hot water pastry
100 g/4 oz/½ cup lard or white fat
150 ml/¼ pint/⅔ cup water
350 g/12 oz/3 cups plain (all-purpose) flour
salt
1 egg, beaten

1   Finely mince or grind the veal with 100 g/4 oz of the
    ham and the onion. Season well with salt, pepper and
    the coriander. Cut the remaining ham into small cubes
    or strips.
2   For the pastry, put the fat and the water into a
    saucepan and heat gently until the fat melts. Bring to
    the boil. Sift the flour and a good pinch of salt into a
    bowl.
3   Pour the boiling liquid over the flour and mix to form
    a softish dough. Knead lightly, using clean rubber
    gloves if the mixture is too hot to handle.
4   Roll out almost three-quarters of the dough on a
    lightly floured surface and use to line a lightly greased

18–20 cm/7–8 inch round cake tin, preferably with a
loose bottom. Keep the rest of the pastry covered with
a cloth.
5   Put half the minced meat mixture in the pastry case,
    cover with the chopped ham and then with the rest of
    the mince. Press down only lightly until even.
6   Roll out the remaining pastry for a lid. Damp the
    edges, position on the pie and press the edges firmly
    together. Trim off the excess pastry and crimp the
    edges. Roll out the trimmings and cut into leaves.
7   Brush the top of the pie with beaten egg, arrange the
    leaves and glaze again. Make a hole in the centre of
    the pie for the steam to escape and stand on a baking
    sheet.
8   Cook in a fairly hot oven (200°C/400°F/Gas Mark 6)
    for 30 minutes. Glaze the top of the pie again and
    reduce the oven temperature to moderate (160°C/
    325°F/Gas Mark 3). Continue to cook for 1¼ hours,
    laying a sheet of wax or greaseproof paper over the
    pie when it is sufficiently browned.
9   Leave the pie in the tin to cool for about 20 minutes.
    Dissolve the gelatine in the stock in a small saucepan
    and season well. Insert a small funnel into the hole
    made in the centre of the pie and fill up the pie
    gradually with the stock. You may need to leave the
    pie for 10 minutes and repeat filling it several times.
    Leave until cold and then refrigerate for at least 12
    hours.
10 Carefully remove the pie from the tin and serve in
    slices with a selection of salads.

Osso Bucco

Serves 4–6

1–1.25 kg/2–2½ lb shin of veal, sawn into 4–5 pieces
salt and pepper
2 tablespoons oil
1 large onion, peeled and chopped
4 sticks celery, sliced
4 carrots, peeled and sliced
150 ml/¼ pint/⅔ cup dry white wine
1 tablespoon lemon juice
300 ml/½ pint/1¼ cups chicken stock
½ teaspoon dried rosemary
425 g/15 oz can tomatoes
2 teaspoons cornflour (cornstarch) (optional)

1   Trim the pieces of veal and season lightly. Heat the oil
    in a saucepan and fry the pieces of meat until well
    browned all over. Remove from the pan.
2   Add the onion, celery and carrots to the pan and fry
    gently until they are just beginning to colour, stirring
    occasionally. Pour off any excess fat from the pan.
3   Add the wine and lemon juice and replace the veal.
    Bring the pan to the boil, cover and simmer very gently
    for about 40 minutes.
4   Add the stock, rosemary, tomatoes and seasonings,
    bring back to the boil and simmer for a further hour, or
    until the meat is tender.
5   The juices may be thickened by blending the cornflour
    with a little water, add to the pan and bring back to the
    boil for a few minutes. Adjust the seasonings and serve.

Fried Veal Escalopes

Serves 4

4 veal escalopes, beaten
2 eggs, beaten
about 100 g/4 oz/2 cups fresh white breadcrumbs
100 g/4 oz/½ cup butter
4–6 tablespoons oil
Wiener Schnitzel
lemon wedges
watercress
Viennoise
1 hard-boiled egg
1 tablespoon capers
a few anchovy fillets

1 The escalopes should be beaten really thin either by the butcher or by yourself by putting them between two sheets of plastic cling film and beating with a mallet or the flat side of a chopper.
2 Season the beaten egg, if liked, and dip each escalope into it. Immediately coat each one in fresh breadcrumbs, pressing in where necessary. Once coated, the escalopes may be chilled until ready to cook.
3 Melt the butter and about half the oil in a frying pan and fry the veal gently (with only 2 escalopes in the pan at a time) for about 5 minutes on each side. Turn over carefully so the coating does not pull off. When ready, the coating should be a good golden brown, but not too dark! Drain on absorbent kitchen paper towel and keep warm while frying the others.
4 For Wiener Schnitzel, serve the fried escalopes garnished with wedges of lemon and watercress.
5 For Veal Viennoise, serve the fried escalopes garnished with a small pile of sieved egg yolk in the centre of the meat with finely chopped egg white and capers each side and 2 or 3 fillets of anchovy laid over the garnish.

Veal and Lemon Cobbler

Serves 4–6

675 g/1½ lb pie veal
1 large onion, peeled and sliced
25 g/1 oz/2 tablespoons butter
1 tablespoon oil
25 g/1 oz/¼ cup flour
450 ml/¾ pint/scant 2 cups chicken stock
salt and pepper
finely grated rind of 1 lemon
½ teaspoon dried mixed herbs
1 tablespoon lemon juice
100 g/4 oz button mushrooms, trimmed and quartered
Scone topping
200 g/8 oz/2 cups self raising flour
50 g/2 oz/¼ cup butter or margarine
finely grated rind of ½ lemon
1 egg, beaten
3–4 tablespoons milk
milk or beaten egg to glaze

1 Fry the onion in a mixture of the melted butter and oil in a deep frying pan or heatproof casserole until soft.
2 Trim the veal, and cut into 2 cm/¾ inch cubes. Add to the pan and fry for about 5 minutes or until well sealed.

3 Stir in the flour and cook for about a minute, then gradually add the stock and bring to the boil. Season well, add the lemon rind, herbs and lemon juice and cover the casserole. If necessary, transfer to a casserole.
4 Cook in a moderate oven (180°C/350°F/Gas Mark 4) for 1¼ hours or until tender. Stir in the mushrooms.
5 For the scone topping, sift the flour into a bowl, add a little salt and pepper and rub in the fat until the mixture resembles fine breadcrumbs. Stir in the lemon rind, then bind to a soft dough with the beaten egg and sufficient of the milk.
6 Pat out the dough on a floured surface to about 1 cm/½ inch thick and cut into 4 cm/1½ inch rounds. Arrange these scones in an overlapping circle round the edge of the casserole over the meat to form a border. The scones should just overlap. Brush the scones with milk or beaten egg.
7 Increase the oven temperature to hot (220°C/425°F/Gas Mark 7) and replace the casserole for about 15 minutes or until the scones are well risen, firm to the touch and golden brown. Serve at once.

Veal Fricassée

Serves 6

675 g/1½ lb pie or stewing veal, cut into 2.5 cm/1 inch cubes
225 g/8 oz back bacon, cut into 2 slices
50 g/2 oz/¼ cup butter or margarine
1 tablespoon oil
1 onion, peeled and finely chopped
300 ml/½ pint/1¼ cups chicken stock
salt and pepper
2 tablespoons flour
2 tablespoons lemon juice
about 4 tablespoons cream, double (heavy) or single (light)
To garnish
fried mushrooms
watercress

1 Cut the rind off the bacon and cut into small cubes. Melt half the butter and the oil in a pan and fry the bacon and veal until well sealed. Do not allow them to brown at all. Transfer to a casserole.
2 Add the onion to the fat in the pan and fry very gently, again without browning. Add to the casserole.
3 Bring the stock to the boil, season well and pour over the veal. Cover the casserole and cook in a moderate oven (180°C/350°F/Gas Mark 4) for 1½ hours.
4 Strain off the liquor and keep the rest of the casserole ingredients warm.
5 Melt the remaining butter in a pan, stir in the flour and cook for a minute or so. Gradually add the strained cooking liquor and bring to the boil. Add the lemon juice and simmer for about 2 minutes. Stir in the cream and adjust the seasonings and reheat without boiling.
6 Pour the sauce over the veal and serve garnished with fried mushrooms and watercress.

BACON AND HAM

Bacon is the flesh of the pig which has been salted or cured in brine and then smoked. Green or unsmoked bacon is cured but not smoked and is consequently less strong in flavour, and will not keep for as long as its smoked counterpart. Gammon is the hind leg of the pig which is cured on the side of bacon, then cut off and cooked and served cold as ham. There are several special cures given to hams such as York, Bradenham, etc., and for these the legs are cut off and then cured in special ways, which are usually manufacturers' secret recipes. Shoulder and collar joints are far less expensive than gammon and they can be served in a similar way and are again called ham.

Bacon pigs are specially bred to have small bones, a long back, small shoulders and large plump gammons or hams. Good fresh bacon should have a pleasant aroma with firm, white fat, and pink-coloured lean, that is firm with a good bloom. The rind should be a good pale cream colour if unsmoked, or light to dark golden brown for smoked bacon, depending on the type of smoking process used.

CUTS OF BACON

The cuts and joints do vary from region to region with bacon more than any other type of meat and in one place the cut or rasher will be called one thing and somewhere else it will have a different name.

Back bacon – this is obviously taken from the back and is boned out. When cut into rashers, the prime back should have a good eye of meat and a distinct layer of fat. Back can be used rolled in a joint for boiling or baking. Use the rashers for frying and grilling or broiling.

Middle or through cut – these are long rashers that combine back and streaky rashers to give reasonably-priced rashers. They are in fact 'cut through' the whole or in fact half side of the pig. This also makes a good joint with or without stuffing.

Streaky bacon – these are narrow rashers which are lean and fat combined in one long rasher. The amount of fat to lean does differ and the length of the rashers varies from very short to long. Good for frying and grilling or broiling and for adding in strips or cubes to casseroles for flavouring. Can also be used for laying over joints or poultry that are short of fat to prevent drying out during cooking. Joints can be made from streaky bacon but they tend to be rather on the fatty side.

Collar – prime collar when boned and rolled makes one of the best boiling joints with plenty of flavour and just the right amount of fat around it. Collar rashers are fairly substantial and basically lean with fat around the outside and can be grilled or fried. Collar joints vary in size from about 450 g/1 lb upwards to a whole joint which weighs about 3.5 kg/8 lb and can be boiled, baked and braised.

Gammon or ham – the most prized part of the bacon side for leanness and fine texture with little fat. It is often sold ready cooked, but can be bought raw as a whole or half gammon, or as small cuts which are known as slipper, middle, corner and gammon knuckle – most are boned.

Gammon or ham steaks and rashers – steaks being cut from the prime of the meat are very lean, about 1 cm/ ½ inch thick (or thicker), good to grill or broil or fry but are expensive. Gammon rashers are the same but cut very much thinner.

Bacon chops – these are boneless slices taken from the back and cut from 5 mm–2.5 cm/¼–1 inch thick depending on taste. Grill or broil or fry.

Forehock – whole hocks can be bought very inexpensively with the bone still in ready to cook and, including the knuckle, weigh about 3–3.5 kg/7–8 lb. However, they are often sold boned and rolled so the joints can be cut to size as required. Both whole or boned joints can be boiled, braised, baked or cut into pieces to use in other ways.

Vacuum-packed bacon – both joints and more usually rashers are sold in vacuum packets, which are hygienic and convenient both for the customer and the shopkeeper. This method of packing extends the keeping qualities of the bacon and the pack will have a 'sell by' and 'use by' date stamped on it. Once opened, use as loose cut bacon.

Store bacon in the refrigerator or at a very cool temperature. Wrap it in plastic cling film or foil or put into an airtight plastic container. If vacuum-packed, leave in the packet until opened, then treat as above. Wax or grease-proof paper should not be used as it is porous and allows dehydration of the bacon and drying, resulting in surface saltiness. Store bacon for 7–10 days. Smoked bacon will probably store for longer if treated correctly.

BOILING BACON

When dealing with large smoked joints it is advisable to soak them in cold water for 8–12 hours. Small joints may be cooked unsoaked unless you are susceptible to saltiness. With the milder cures and green or unsmoked joints, there should be no need to soak – or for a maximum of 4 hours. After soaking, remove from the soaking water, rinse under fresh cold water and always cook in fresh cold water.

Instead of soaking, the joint may be placed in a pan of cold water and brought to the boil. Throw away the water (including the excess salt) and start again with fresh water.

The joint should always be weighed, for the length of cooking time depends on the weight. For joints up to 4.5 kg/10 lb, allow 20–25 minutes per 450 g/1 lb plus 20 minutes over – giving the longer time for really thick joints. For larger joints, allow 15–20 minutes per 450 g/1 lb plus 15 minutes over.

Place the bacon in a large saucepan, skin side down, cover with cold water and bring to the boil. Remove any scum that appears on the surface. For flavour, you can add 1–2 onions, peeled and roughly chopped, 2 carrots, peeled and sliced, 1 bay leaf and 4–6 peppercorns. Start timing the cooking from when the water reaches the boil. Cover and simmer gently – do not fast boil – and add extra boiling water, if necessary. When cooked, if to serve cold, leave in the water – off the heat – for an hour, then remove and leave until cold. Remove the skin when cold. For a hot joint, drain well and carefully ease away the rind. Serve as it is with a parsley or mustard sauce (see page 31) or, if to serve cold, the fat may be sprinkled with brown breadcrumbs (or the bought variety) and served with salads.

BAKING AND GLAZING BACON

Weigh the joint and calculate the cooking time as for boiling. Boil for half the cooking time, then drain the joint and wrap loosely in foil and stand in a roasting tin. Bake in a moderate oven (180°C/350°F/Gas Mark 4) until 30 minutes before the end of cooking. Increase the oven to hot

(220°C/425°F/Gas Mark 7), unwrap the joint and strip off the skin. Cut (or score) the fat into diamonds, stick a clove into each diamond if liked, and sprinkle the surface liberally with demerara sugar. Pat the sugar in and return to the oven to complete the cooking and give a crisp and golden brown coating to the joint.

COOKING RASHERS OF BACON

Bacon has plenty of fat so needs very little added fat to cook it, unless you want to pile on the calories. For grilling or broiling, or frying, the rind may be cut off or left on as preferred. Lay the rashers on a grill rack or in a grill pan and cook under a preheated moderate grill or broiler, with no added fat or oil, until the fat is beginning to colour. Turn over and continue cooking the other side. Some people prefer their bacon almost raw; others almost a crispy cinder, so the time really depends on taste.

For frying the lean rashers, a smidgeon of fat heated in the pan will prevent them from sticking, but the fat will soon run from the fat actually on the rasher; with streaky or fat bacon rashers, no fat at all is needed – simply put into a cold pan and as it heats up so the fat will start to run and the rashers begin to cook. Again fry on both sides to the degree of 'doneness' required. Drain on absorbent kitchen paper towel before serving.

For bacon rolls, the rind must be cut off and the bacon rolled up neatly but not too tightly. They are best cooked under the grill or broiler or in a moderate to hot oven until just browned all over. For frying, they should be impaled on skewers or wooden cocktail sticks so they don't unroll when they are turned over.

CARVING HAM

All cooked ham and bacon should be carved thinly; thick slices and chunks do not do justice to the flavour and texture of the meat. Use a special ham carving knife or a fairly large cook's knife, which must be very sharp. Boned and rolled joints are easy to carve but those with bones can be a little more tricky.

Prime forehock – this is best carved keeping the fat side underneath. Hold the protruding bone firmly with the fork or a cloth and carve in vertical slices up to the bone, then repeat from the other end. When the bone is reached, carve long, downward-slanting slices at an angle to the bone. Turn over and carve the remaining slices down to the bone.

Gammon hock – firmly hold the shank end (or bone) with a fork or a cloth and carve in wedge-shaped slices from one side of the bone. turn the joint over and repeat.

Corner gammon – begin at the thicker end and carve in wedge-shaped slices which are thicker on the wider curve and thinner on the side from which the bone has been removed.

Whole gammon or ham – there are several methods of carving a gammon or ham, this is probably the simplest. Remove a small slice from the knuckle end of the bone. Carve in long oblique slices to the bone on either side.

HOW MUCH TO ALLOW

With rashers, allow 2–4 depending on size and what else is to be served. Allow 1–2 bacon chops depending on size; 1 gammon steak depending on size; 1 gammon rasher.

For meat on the bone, allow 225–350 g/8–12 oz raw per portion; for boned meat, allow 175–225 g/6–8 oz.

Bacon and Onion Pudding   Serves 4–5

550 g/1¼ lb piece lean bacon, derinded and diced
225 g/8 oz/2 cups self-raising flour
½ teaspoon salt
100 g/4 oz/1 cup shredded suet
about 150 ml/¼ pint/⅔ cup cold water to mix
black pepper
1 teaspoon dried mixed herbs
2 onions, peeled and sliced
4 tablespoons stock or water

1   Put a large saucepan of water to boil with sufficient water to come halfway up the side of a basin. Thoroughly grease a 1 litre/2 pint/5 cup basin.
2   Sift the flour and salt into a bowl. Mix in the suet and mix to a soft dough with the water. Cut off a quarter of the dough and keep for the lid. Roll out the remainder on a floured surface to a circle about twice the diameter of the top of the basin.
3   Carefully lower the pastry into the basin, pressing into the sides but without tearing or creasing.
4   Season the bacon with pepper only, then mix with the herbs and onions. Spoon into the pastry-lined basin, pressing it down evenly but not too hard or it will tear the pastry. Add the stock or water.
5   Roll out the reserved pastry for a lid to fit the top of the basin. Damp the edges with water and put into position. Trim and then press the edges well together.
6   Thoroughly grease a sheet of wax or greaseproof paper and lay over the basin. Fold round the basin tucking it under the rim, then cover with a sheet of foil and tie this in position with string. Add a piece of string over the top to make it easier to remove from the saucepan.
7   Lower the basin gently into the pan of boiling water, cover and allow to simmer gently for about 3 hours. Check the water level occasionally and refill to halfway up the basin with boiling water when necessary.
8   To serve, remove the coverings of foil and paper and serve straight from the basin. Creamed potatoes and a green vegetable make good accompaniments.

Ham and Leeks au Gratin   Serves 4

4 slices cooked ham
4 leeks, trimmed and well washed
salt and pepper
450 ml/¾ pint/scant 2 cups cheese sauce (see page 31)
50 g/2 oz/½ cup grated mature Cheddar cheese
1 tablespoon grated Parmesan cheese
2 tablespoons fresh white breadcrumbs

1   Cook the leeks in boiling salted water for 5 minutes, then drain very thoroughly.
2   Wrap a slice of ham around each leek and place in a shallow, lightly greased ovenproof dish.
3   Make up the cheese sauce and pour over the leeks. Combine the cheese and breadcrumbs and sprinkle over the top.
4   Cook in a hot oven (220°C/425°F/Gas Mark 7) for about 30 minutes or until the top is crispy and well browned.

Kidneys with Orange (see page 75) and Ham and Leeks au Gratin

Pot Roast Collar Bacon   **Serves 6**

1.5 kg/3 lb prime collar joint of bacon
16–20 cloves
350 g/12 oz button onions, peeled
15 g/¹/₂ oz/1 tablespoon butter
450 g/1 lb tomatoes, peeled and quartered
1 teaspoon dried basil
150 ml/¹/₄ pint/²/₃ cup dry white wine
2 tablespoons dried breadcrumbs
salt and pepper

1 If the bacon is smoked and you do not like a strong flavour, soak the joint in cold water for 6–8 hours. Put the bacon into a saucepan and cover with cold water. Bring to the boil and simmer for an hour.

2 Drain the bacon and carefully strip off the skin. Stud the fat with the cloves and stand the joint in a casserole.

3 Fry the onions in the melted butter until they are lightly browned and then arrange around the joint. Add the tomatoes, sprinkle with basil and pour on the wine.

4 Cover and cook in a moderately hot oven (190°C/ 375°F/Gas Mark 5) for 40 minutes, or until tender.

5 Remove the lid and sprinkle the breadcrumbs over the clove-studded fat. Return to the oven for 10 minutes.

6 Remove the joint to a serving dish and the vegetables to another serving dish. Adjust the seasonings, then strain the juices into a sauce boat.

OFFAL

The word offal to most people means liver and kidney and this is right, but it also covers a wide selection of other parts of the animal that do not fit into any other category. These include hearts, heads, tails, brains, tongues, etc., which may not sound very exciting, but are in fact quite delicious and very rich in nutrients that are essential to the body – not least of all iron. Offal is relatively inexpensive, but it is essential to eat it very fresh, that is on the day bought or, at the latest, on the next day, provided it has been kept in the refrigerator. There is very little waste on offal and most of it is quick to cook and easy to prepare. Offal, if bought fresh, can be frozen to use when required but it must only be stored in the freezer for up to 2 months, and thawed out thoroughly before cooking. Cooked offal dishes can on the whole be frozen, but should be stored for only up to 1 month.

LIVER

There are several types of liver available; all are excellent value but vary in flavour and texture. Whatever type it is, it should be smooth and glossy. Wash it and remove any loose pieces of skin and veins. Take care not to overcook liver as it can become hard and uninteresting.

Ox liver – this is fairly cheap but has a strong flavour and can be tough. The texture is quite coarse so it is best to use it in a casserole rather than for grilling or broiling or frying.

Calves' liver – this is the best and most expensive liver but is not always readily available. It is very tender and delicately flavoured and is best lightly fried or grilled or broiled with extra butter to prevent it drying. If over-cooked, it will become tough and hard.

Pigs' liver – cheaper than lambs' liver, it has a very pronounced flavour and rather soft texture which many people dislike. It can be fried or grilled or broiled and is very good used in casseroles. It is the best liver (along with chicken livers) to use for making pâtés and terrines. Some of the strong flavour can be removed by soaking the liver in milk for an hour before cooking.

Lambs' liver – cheaper than calves' liver and with a stronger flavour but not nearly so strong as pigs' liver. Probably the most popular and most versatile type of liver. Fry or grill or broil, or add to casseroles and stews.

KIDNEYS

With any type of kidney, remove the skin and core before cooking – a pair of scissors is best to use for this task. Kidneys can be grilled or broiled or fried, as well as using for casseroles and pan fries. They can be blended with beef and other meats for casseroles, puddings and pies.

Ox kidney – the cheapest and obviously largest of the kidneys. It has a fairly strong flavour and needs slow gentle cooking to make it tender. The kidney is made up of many joined lobes and a whole one weighs about 675 g/1½ lb.

Calves' kidneys – much the same as ox kidney but of course smaller and more tender, but used in the same way.

Lambs' kidneys – these are usually the best and most popular of all the kidneys. They are small and well flavoured without being strong or overbearing and are tender enough to grill or broil or fry whole, halved, or cut into pieces. Do remove the thin outer skin and the core before cooking and take care not to overcook or they will become very hard.

Pig's kidneys – these are a little larger than lambs' and rather more elongated. They are also stronger in flavour and can be cooked as for lambs', but are usually halved or cut into smaller pieces. Also good to add to casseroles.

SWEETBREADS

These must be bought when they are really fresh and should be used at once. Calves' sweetbreads are the best apart from lambs', which are the most expensive and usually even better. Allow one pair per portion and keep them as white as possible by soaking them for at least 4 hours in cold water, which should be changed several times, then put into cold salted water and bring to the boil. Remove the veins and skin, place the blanched sweetbreads between two plates to flatten them and allow to cool. To cook, either coat in egg and breadcrumbs and shallow-fry in butter or cook in a sauce.

TRIPE

This comes from the stomach lining of an ox. It is a light easily-digested meat but it must be prepared carefully. There are two types – ordinary or blanket and 'Honey-comb' – and they come from the first and second stomach respectively. Tripe is usually sold 'dressed' or cleaned and parboiled, but it requires further cooking. Tripe is often served in a white onion sauce but can also be dipped in egg and breadcrumbs and deep or shallow-fried or be simmered in a spicy tomato and garlic sauce. It is not the flavour of which people are wary, but more the texture, which almost melts in the mouth.

HEARTS

Hearts used to be very popular as a tasty stew or casserole, but their popularity has dwindled somewhat. However, it is an economical meat with no fat, although being a strong muscle itself, it does require long slow cooking to tenderize it. The gravy it makes has a marvellous flavour and is full of nutrients. Wash thoroughly and remove all the tubes and arteries.

Ox heart – is the largest and toughest so should be cut into strips or cubes and casseroled slowly. It can also be parboiled and then stuffed and pot roasted with plenty of good flavouring vegetables and stock. A whole heart will weigh from 1.5–2 kg/3–4½ lb.

Calves' hearts – smaller and therefore more tender than the ox heart, but they still need slow cooking for preference, such as pot roasting or braising, although they can also be stuffed and roasted, preferably under a lid of foil.

Lambs' hearts – these are the smallest and most tender of all the hearts with a very pleasant flavour. They are usually stuffed and roasted, pot roasted or braised.

BRAINS

These must be bought when really fresh and used as soon as possible after purchase. Often a butcher will ask a customer to order brains when they are required for they will not keep and it is up to him to make sure he only sells them when they are very fresh. Calves' are the best and are usually poached and served with a delicately-flavoured sauce. Lambs' can be cooked as calves' but are more often casseroled. Calves' brains should be soaked in cold water for 15 minutes before being put into a pan of cold water and brought to the boil. Remove and take off the membrane before continuing. Allow 1–1½ sets of brains per portion.

TONGUE

When buying a tongue make sure that the skin is smooth, for the tongue becomes rough as it ages. Salted and smoked tongues are available as well as fresh (although they may need to be ordered 7–10 days in advance) and they are best soaked in cold water overnight before cooking. Salted and smoked tongues require only about half the cooking time of fresh ones.

Ox tongue has the best flavour and texture and can be boiled or braised to serve hot or cold. Calves' and lambs' tongues are much smaller and are usually sold fresh. They are usually poached or braised and more often served hot. The small tongues, once cooked, can be skinned, if preferred, and then returned to the casserole before serving.

OXTAIL

This has a high proportion of bone and is usually rather fatty but it is an inexpensive meat with an excellent flavour and with slow cooking becomes very tender and ideal for rich hearty stews and soup. It should look fresh when bought with good red flesh and creamy white fat and the butcher will cut it (if it isn't already cut) into thick slices ready for use. It is a good idea to make an oxtail dish the day before required and allow it to chill, so the layer of fat can be easily removed before it is served.

HOW MUCH TO ALLOW

Liver – allow 100 g/4 oz raw per portion.
Kidneys – Ox: allow 100 g/4 oz raw per portion; Calves': 1 kidney will serve 1–2 portions; Lambs': allow 2 kidneys per portion; Pigs': allow 1–2 depending on size.
Hearts – Ox: a whole one will serve 4–6 portions; Calves': one will serve 2 portions; Lambs': allow one per portion.
Sweetbreads – allow about 100 g/4 oz or one pair per portion.
Tripe – allow 100–175 g/4–6 oz raw per portion.
Brains – allow 1–2 sets per portion.
Tongue – Ox tongue weighs about 1.8 kg/4 lb so will serve about 8 hot, or more if served cold; Calves' tongues weigh 450–900 g/1–2 lb each so will serve 3–4 portions; with Lambs' tongues, allow one per portion.
Oxtail – 1 oxtail will serve 4–5 portions.

Oxtail Casserole　　　Serves 4

1 oxtail, cut up
40 g/1½ oz/3 tablespoons dripping
25 g/1 oz/¼ cup flour
600 ml/1 pint/2½ cups water or stock
2 large onions, peeled and chopped
4 carrots, peeled and sliced
3–4 sticks celery, sliced
1 leek, trimmed and sliced (optional)
salt and pepper
1 teaspoon paprika
1 teaspoon Worcestershire sauce
2 bay leaves
freshly chopped parsley to garnish

1　Trim any excess fat from the pieces of oxtail. Heat the dripping in a large heavy-based saucepan and fry the pieces of oxtail until browned all over. Remove from the pan. Pour off all but 2 tablespoons of fat from the pan.
2　Stir the flour into the fat in the pan and cook for 1 minute. Gradually add the water or stock and bring to the boil.
3　Replace the oxtail in the pan and add all the other ingredients except the parsley. Cover the pan tightly and simmer very gently for about 3 hours or until tender. Alternatively, the contents of the saucepan can be transferred to a large casserole and cooked in a moderate oven (160°C/325°F/Gas Mark 3) for about 4 hours. The oxtail must be very tender before serving.
4　If possible, cool the casserole and chill overnight so the layer of fat that forms on the surface can be easily removed. Discard the bay leaves.
5　If reheating, this must be done thoroughly either in a saucepan by bringing to the boil and simmering gently for about 20 minutes, or in the same temperature oven for about an hour. Sprinkle with parsley and serve.

Note: 150 ml/¼ pint/⅔ cup of the water or stock may be replaced with red or white wine, if preferred.

Creamy Sweetbreads

Serves 6

675 g/1½ lb calves' sweetbreads, prepared and blanched
pinch of dried thyme
2 slices lemon
300 ml/½ pint/1¼ cups stock
150 ml/¼ pint/⅔ cup dry white wine
salt and pepper
100 g/4 oz button mushrooms, sliced
65 g/2½ oz/good ¼ cup butter
50 g/2 oz/½ cup flour
150 ml/¼ pint/⅔ cup single (light) cream
chopped parsley to garnish
fried circles of bread

1   Put the blanched and prepared sweetbreads into a saucepan with the thyme, lemon, stock, wine and seasonings and bring to the boil. Cover the pan and simmer very gently for about 15 minutes. Add the mushrooms and simmer for a minute or so longer.
2   Strain off the cooking liquor and keep the sweetbreads and mushrooms warm.
3   Melt the butter in another saucepan, stir in the flour and cook for a minute or so. Gradually add the cooking liquor and bring to the boil, stirring continuously. Return the sweetbreads and mushrooms to the sauce, adjust the seasonings and simmer for 2 minutes. Stir in the cream and heat to just below boiling point.
4   Serve sprinkled liberally with chopped parsley and with fried circles of bread.

Tripe and Onions

Serves 5–6

675 g/1½ lb tripe
568 ml/1 pint/2½ cups milk
salt and pepper
1 bay leaf
450 g/1 lb onions, quartered or roughly chopped
25 g/1 oz/2 tablespoons butter
25 g/1 oz/¼ cup flour
1 tablespoon freshly chopped parsley
1 teaspoon freshly chopped or a good pinch of dried thyme

1   Cut the tripe (which has been prepared and blanched by the butcher) into 4 cm/1½ inch cubes. Put into a saucepan, cover with cold water and bring to the boil for 5 minutes. Drain well.
2   Put the tripe back into the saucepan with the milk, seasonings and bay leaf. Bring to the boil, cover and simmer very gently for an hour.
3   Add the onions and continue to simmer gently for about 45 minutes.
4   Strain off the cooking liquor and make it up to just under 600 ml/1 pint/2½ cups with milk, if necessary.
5   Melt the butter in a pan, stir in the flour and cook for a minute or so. Gradually stir in the cooking liquor and bring to the boil, stirring frequently. Return the tripe and onions to the sauce (discarding the bay leaf), and reheat until piping hot.
6   Adjust the seasonings, stir in the parsley and thyme and serve at once with mashed potatoes and carrots.

Pressed Tongue

Serves about 10

1 salted or pickled ox tongue (about 1.5 kg/3–3½ lb)
1–2 onions, peeled and studded with 3–4 cloves
2 bay leaves
2 carrots, peeled and sliced
salads to garnish (e.g. lettuce, cucumber, tomatoes or radishes, spring onions (scallions), etc.)

1   Soak the tongue in cold water for 12–24 hours if you do not want it to be very salty. Drain the tongue and place in a saucepan of clean cold water. Add the onions, bay leaves and carrots and bring to the boil.
2   Cover the pan and simmer very gently for about 3½ hours, adding more boiling water if necessary, until very tender. Test to check it is tender with a fine skewer.
3   Drain the tongue and immediately plunge into a bowl of cold water. Remove the skin, and any bones and gristle from the thick end of the tongue.
4   Put the tongue onto a board and cut in half lengthwise. Place one half, cut side downwards, in a round 15 cm/6 inch cake tin, curling it round to fit it.
5   Arrange the second half of the tongue with the cut side upwards on top of the first piece. Cover with a saucer and put a heavy weight on the saucer. Leave until quite cold and chill overnight at least.
6   Turn the tongue out carefully onto a serving dish and garnish with salads. Slice thinly to serve.

Crispy Fried Brains

Serves 4

450 g/1 lb calves' or lambs' brains
1 small onion, peeled and chopped
salt and pepper
3 tablespoons vinegar
a little seasoned flour
1–2 eggs, beaten
50 g/2 oz/1 cup fresh white breadcrumbs
oil or fat for shallow-frying
lemon wedges
watercress

1   Soak the brains in cold water for 30 minutes, then rinse under cold running water and drain well. Remove any arteries and membranes with a sharp knife, and make sure all traces of blood have been removed.
2   Put the brains in a saucepan and add the onion, plenty of seasonings, the vinegar and cold water to cover. Bring to the boil very slowly and then cover the pan and simmer very gently for 5 minutes.
3   Drain the brains and plunge into a bowl of cold water. Drain well.
4   Cut the brains into smaller pieces, if preferred, and roll in seasoned flour. Dip in beaten egg and then roll in breadcrumbs.
5   Fry in shallow fat, turning once, until a pale golden brown all over and crispy. Drain on absorbent kitchen paper towel and keep warm while frying the remainder.
6   Serve hot garnished with lemon wedges and watercress and with tartare sauce.

Liver and Bacon Pâté
Serves 6–8

450 g/1 lb pigs' liver
300 g/10 oz streaky bacon rashers, derinded
1 onion, peeled
2 cloves garlic, crushed
salt and pepper
1 egg, beaten
2 tablespoons red wine or brandy
stuffed olives to garnish

1 Put the liver, half the bacon, the onion and garlic through the fine blade of a mincer or meat grinder twice or process in a food processor until very finely chopped.
2 Season very well and mix in the beaten egg and the wine or brandy.
3 Stretch the remaining bacon rashers with the back of a knife and use to line a greased 450 g/1 lb loaf tin.
4 Spoon in the liver mixture, pressing down well and fold the ends of the bacon over the filling.
5 Stand the tin in a roasting pan containing 4 cm/1½ inches water and cook in a moderate oven (180°C/350°F/Gas Mark 4) for about 1¼ hours. Cool in the tin then stand a weight on the tin and chill thoroughly.
6 Turn the pâté out carefully. Garnish the top with slices of stuffed olives and serve in slices with hot toast and butter.

Liver Marsala
Serves 4

450 g/1 lb lambs' liver
a little seasoned flour
40 g/1½ oz/3 tablespoons butter
8 rashers streaky bacon, derinded
4–6 tablespoons Marsala
150 ml/¼ pint/⅔ cup beef stock
1 tablespoon lemon juice
salt and pepper
freshly chopped parsley or mixed herbs to garnish

1 Trim the liver and coat in seasoned flour.
2 Melt the butter in a pan and fry the bacon until lightly coloured. Remove from the pan.
3 Fry the liver in the same pan until browned on both sides. Add the Marsala, stock and lemon juice and bring to the boil. Season well and replace the bacon.
4 Cover the pan and simmer gently for about 15 minutes or until tender. Adjust the seasonings and serve sprinkled with parsley or herbs.

Stuffed Lambs' Hearts
Serves 4

4 lambs' hearts
1 small onion, peeled and finely chopped
2 rashers bacon, derinded and finely chopped
2 small sticks celery, finely chopped
25 g/1 oz/2 tablespoons butter
50 g/2 oz/1 cup fresh breadcrumbs
salt and pepper
½ teaspoon ground coriander
40 g/1½ oz/⅓ cup raisins or sultanas (golden raisins)
300 ml/½ pint/1¼ cups stock
1 tablespoon vinegar
1 tablespoon cornflour (cornstarch)

1 Wash the hearts very thoroughly, slit open a little and remove any tubes and gristle. Wash again and dry.
2 Fry the onion, bacon and celery in the melted butter until soft, but only lightly coloured. Add the breadcrumbs, seasonings, coriander and raisins and mix well.
3 Use the mixture to stuff the cavities of the hearts, tying into shape with fine string. Place the hearts in an ovenproof casserole just large enough to hold them.
4 Bring the stock to the boil, season well and add the vinegar. Pour over the hearts, cover tightly and cook in a moderate oven (160°C/325°F/Gas Mark 3) for 2–2½ hours or until tender.
5 Strain off the liquor and thicken with half or all of the cornflour blended with a little cold water. Bring back to the boil, season to taste and pour back over the hearts. Serve with creamy potatoes, peas and carrots.

Kidneys With Orange
Serves 4

8–10 lambs' kidneys, skinned, halved and cored
4 rashers streaky bacon, derinded and chopped
2 onions, peeled and thinly sliced
40 g/1½ oz/3 tablespoons butter
2 tablespoons seasoned flour
½ teaspoon paprika
300 ml/½ pint/1¼ cups beef stock
finely grated rind and juice of 1 large orange
salt and pepper
2 teaspoons tomato purée
chopped parsley and orange slices to garnish

1 Fry the bacon and onions in the melted butter in a frying pan until soft.
2 Coat the kidneys in the seasoned flour, reserving the excess. Add to the pan and cook gently for 5 minutes, turning frequently, until well sealed.
3 Stir in the remaining flour and paprika and cook for about a minute. Gradually add the stock, orange rind and juice and bring slowly to the boil. Season well and add the tomato purée.
4 Cover the pan and simmer gently for 15–20 minutes, stirring occasionally and adding a little more stock, if necessary. Adjust the seasonings.
5 Serve sprinkled with parsley and with orange slices. Boiled rice or noodles and salad are good with this.

7 Poultry and Game

Poultry includes quite a large variety of birds apart from the different types of chicken, such as ducks, geese, guinea fowl and, of course, turkeys. Game covers an even larger selection of birds, water fowl and furred animals that, unlike poultry, can only be shot and sold during certain times of the year or 'seasons'.

Most poultry is sold ready for cooking, that is cleaned, plucked and trussed. It may be fresh or frozen and in some cases both these methods of preparation can be broken down even further with different types of chilling, additions to freezing, etc. Chickens, ducks and turkeys are also sold in portions and pieces as well as, in the case of turkeys particularly, a number of boneless pieces and joints. Again, these portions can be fresh or frozen.

Ideally, poultry should be hung for 2–3 days after killing before it is drawn and cooked. In cold weather this time can be increased by several days, while in warm conditions the length of time has to be watched. Game is very different as it is necessary to hang it to achieve the gamey flavour and tenderize the flesh. Poultry is usually hung ready plucked, whereas game is hung in the feather. Hang in a cool airy larder and protect it from flies by using something like muslin.

As most poultry is bought oven ready, the worry of plucking and drawing the bird is removed and, if bought from a butcher, he will do it for you when you buy or order the bird. Always ask for the giblets, because they can be used to make an excellent stock for the gravy or to add to the carcass for making soup. The giblets include the heart, liver, neck and gizzard, all of which need to be thoroughly washed in cold water before cooking. It is also essential to cut off any yellow portions of the liver or gizzard for they contain bile which is very bitter and will spoil the flavour of the stock. The crop should be removed intact from the gizzard and any fat should be removed from any of the giblets.

When using frozen poultry and game birds, it is essential to thaw properly and completely before cooking. Problems can occur when frozen birds are only partly thawed because some of the ice crystals remain in the bird and slow down the normal cooking time quite dramatically.

REHEATING POULTRY

All cooked poultry can be served hot a second time, but it is essential to recook it and not just gently warm it through. Whatever the dish, make sure the meat is properly recooked in a hot oven or boiled in a sauce, then there will be no danger of food poisoning. It is also extremely important to cool the cooked bird as rapidly as possible and then to refrigerate it immediately.

Cooked poultry meat can be refrozen, even if it was a frozen bird to start with, but again do thaw properly and recook it. Made-up dishes can also be frozen, but it is better to thaw and recook rather than try to recook from frozen.

CHICKEN

If you are buying a fresh chicken (one that has not been frozen in any way), feel the tip of the breastbone with the thumb and finger – it should be soft and flexible to indicate it is young. The feet should also be small with smooth small scales, not rough scaly legs and feet. There are several categories of chickens mainly used to describe the size and age of the bird.

Poussins – these are very small chickens, weighing from 450–900 g/1–2 lb each and usually 6–8 weeks old. The smaller ones are served one per portion but the larger ones will sometimes serve two. Roast, pot roast or casserole, but remember they are tender and have a very delicate flavour. Also good to grill or broil.

Broilers – these are small birds that are usually sold as frozen chickens. They tend to be about 12 weeks old and weigh from 1.2–1.6 kg/2½–3½ lb. They are very versatile and can be cooked by almost any method. One bird should serve 3–4 portions.

Large Roasters – these are usually young cockerels or hens that have been specially fed so they grow larger. Good flavoured and tender, they vary in size from 1.8–2.3 kg/4–5 lb and will serve from 5–6 portions.

Boiling fowl – these are older tougher birds, often over 18 months or even older, and can be former egg-laying birds. They are best boiled or stewed as they will be tough if just roasted. The flavour, however, is excellent. They usually weigh from 1.8–3.2 kg/4–7 lb.

Capons – these birds, which used to be specially injected after castrating and then fattened, are not supposed to be available now, but large specially-fattened birds are available called 'capon-style' chickens. They usually weigh from 3.5–4.5 kg/8–10 lb and make a good family meal to serve up to 10 portions.

Fresh chickens are more expensive than frozen ones and are thought to have a better flavour, but, if thawed carefully and then cooked properly, the frozen birds are excellent value. A fresh chicken will keep for up to 2 days in the refrigerator before cooking, but do remember to thaw a frozen one completely. Leave in the wrappings at room temperature or a cool place for about 10–12 hours for a 900 g/2 lb bird. If you want to thaw in the refrigerator, the time allowed must be at least doubled – i.e. 24–30 hours. Chicken joints take about 4–9 hours to thaw.

PREPARING AND COOKING CHICKENS
Chickens can be cooked by most of the methods used for meat (see pages 48–50) including roasting, pot roasting, casseroling, stewing, boiling, grilling or broiling, barbecuing, etc. Of these methods, roasting is probably the most popular.

With roasting and pot roasting, it is often usual to add a stuffing to the neck end of the bird. The stuffing should be added before weighing the bird and calculating the cooking time necessary. A chicken also needs trussing before cooking or the wings and legs will stick out at strange angles giving an untidy finished dish.

TO TRUSS A CHICKEN
There are several ways of trussing a bird but this is one of the simplest.
1 Insert a skewer right through the body of the bird just below the thigh bone and turn the bird over on its breast.
2 First, catching in the wing tips, pass the string under the ends of the skewer and cross it over the back.
3 Turn the bird over and tie the ends of the string together round the tail, at the same time securing the drumsticks.

TO TEST IF THE BIRD IS COOKED
1 Take a fine skewer and pierce the thickest part of the thigh. If the juices run clear, all is well; if they are tinged pink, return to the oven for a further 10 minutes and test again.
2 Always allow at least 15 minutes for possible 'extra cooking' time when roasting a chicken, as some birds are much thicker and will take longer than other 'slimline' birds.
3 If taking the bird straight from the refrigerator to the oven, increase the cooking time by about 10–15 minutes to ensure it is cooked properly.
4 As with meat, all poultry should be allowed to stand and 'set' for about 10 minutes to make carving easier.

ROASTING TIMES
For both chicken and guinea fowl, allow 20 minutes per 450 g/1 lb plus 20 minutes over in a fairly hot oven (200°C/400°F/Gas Mark 6). When over 2.7 kg/6 lb the extra 20 minutes is not necessary and the cooking temperature may be lowered to moderately hot (190°C/375°F/Gas Mark 5).

ROASTING CHICKEN
1 If frozen, make sure the chicken is completely thawed – the legs are flexible and there are no ice crystals left in the body cavity. Remove the giblets.
2 Stuff the neck end of the bird only (make the remainder of stuffing into balls to roast around the joint). Fold the neck skin over the stuffing to enclose it, then truss as

above. A quartered onion or lemon may be put into the cavity for extra flavour.
3 Weigh the bird and calculate the cooking time from the above guide allowing time to 'set', etc. Stand the bird in a roasting tin and brush all over with melted butter or oil. Season lightly with salt and pepper, if liked. A few streaky rashers of bacon may be laid over the breast to help keep it moist during cooking. Add a little oil to the roasting pan.
4 Roast in a preheated fairly hot oven (200°C/400°F/Gas Mark 6) until cooked through, basting occasionally. Potatoes may be roasted around the bird for about an hour.
5 Remove the bird to a serving plate and the potatoes to a dish. If extra stuffing balls are to be cooked, they should be added to the roast about 20 minutes before it is ready. Spoon off the fat from the pan juices and use to make a thin gravy (see page 32).

Note: To roast a chicken in foil, wrap the bird loosely in foil, weigh and cook as above but increase the cooking time by about 5 minutes per 450 g/1 lb and fold back the foil for the last 15 minutes of cooking to brown the bird.

TRADITIONAL ACCOMPANIMENTS
Bacon rolls
Stuffing balls (if there is not sufficient in the neck of the bird)
Bread sauce
Thin gravy

CARVING CHICKEN
Special poultry carvers are smaller than ordinary carvers and make it easier to carve all poultry and game.
1 Place the bird so that one wing is towards your left hand, with the breast diagonally towards you. Stand it on a board or firm dish.
2 Steadying the bird with the flat of the knife held against the breast, prise the leg outwards with the fork to expose the thigh joint. Cut through this cleanly to remove the leg. The leg is usually cut in half to give the thigh and drumstick and, if the bird is very large, the thigh can be cut into smaller pieces.
3 Hold the wing with the fork and cut through the outer layer of the breast, trying to judge where the wing joint is so that the wing joint is cut through cleanly in one go.
4 Cut the breast into thin slices parallel with the breast-bone. When stuffing has been cooked in the bird, it should be sliced from the front of the breast and the remainder removed with the help of a spoon.
5 Repeat with the other side, removing first the leg and then the wing, etc.

HOW MUCH TO ALLOW
Allow at least 8 oz/225 g raw oven-ready chicken per portion, therefore a 1.2–1.5 kg/2½–3 lb oven-ready chicken will serve 3–4 portions.
Allow 1 quarter or breast portion of chicken per portion.
Allow 2–3 drumsticks or wings per portion.
Allow 2 thighs per portion.

Pot Roast Peanut Chicken   Serves 4–6

1.5–1.75 kg/3½–4 lb oven-ready chicken
25 g/1 oz/2 tablespoons butter or margarine
1 onion, peeled and finely chopped
75 g/3 oz/1½ cups fresh white breadcrumbs
2 tablespoons freshly chopped parsley
½ teaspoon dried thyme
grated rind of ½ small lemon
50 g/2 oz/½ cup salted peanuts, finely chopped
salt and pepper
1 egg yolk
lemon juice (optional)
300 ml/½ pint/1¼ cups boiling chicken stock or half stock
    and half white wine
sprigs of parsley to garnish
2 tablespoons double (heavy) cream

1   Wipe the chicken inside and out. Melt the fat and fry
    the onion until soft but not coloured. Turn into a bowl.
2   Add the breadcrumbs, parsley, thyme, lemon rind,
    peanuts and seasonings to the onions, mix well and
    bind together with the egg yolk and a little lemon juice.
3   Use some of the stuffing to stuff the neck end only of
    the bird, tuck under the flap of skin and truss the bird
    loosely. Make the rest of the stuffing into balls. Put into
    a lightly greased ovenproof dish.
4   Stand the bird in a deep casserole just large enough to
    hold it. Season the stock or stock and wine and pour
    over the bird. Cover tightly and cook in a moderate
    oven (180°C/350°F/Gas Mark 4) for 1¼ hours.
5   Remove the lid from the casserole and return to the
    oven. Put the stuffing balls into the oven also and cook
    for a further 15–25 minutes or until the chicken is well
    browned and tender and the stuffing balls cooked.
6   Remove the chicken to a serving dish and arrange the
    stuffing balls and parsley around it. Skim off any fat
    from the juices, stir in the cream, adjust the seasonings
    and strain into a sauce boat.

Creamy Chicken   Serves 4

4 large chicken portions, halved, or 8 small boned chicken
    portions
salt and pepper
50 g/2 oz/¼ cup butter
150 ml/¼ pint/⅔ cup milk
¼ teaspoon dried sage
175 g/6 oz button mushrooms, trimmed and halved
150 ml/¼ pint/⅔ cup double (heavy) cream
2 teaspoons cornflour (cornstarch)
¼ teaspoon dried basil
watercress or parsley to garnish

1   Season the chicken pieces well with salt and pepper.
    Melt the butter in a pan and fry the pieces of chicken
    gently all over until golden brown. Transfer to a
    casserole with the butter from the pan.
2   Pour the milk over the chicken and sprinkle with
    seasonings and sage. Cover and cook in a moderate
    oven (180°C/350°F/Gas Mark 4) for 45 minutes.
3   Uncover the casserole, give the contents a stir and add

the mushrooms to the sauce. Blend the cream with the
cornflour and stir into the casserole with the basil.
Cover again and return to the oven for 15–20 minutes
or until tender. Garnish with watercress or parsley.

Pollo Cacciatore   Serves 4

4 large chicken portions, halved
3 tablespoons oil
2 large onions, peeled and sliced
2 cloves garlic, crushed
425 g/15 oz can tomatoes
2 tablespoons freshly chopped parsley
1 teaspoon dried basil
1 tablespoon tomato purée
150 ml/¼ pint/⅔ cup red wine
salt and pepper

1   Wipe the chicken joints and, if liked, remove the skin.
2   Heat the oil in a frying pan and fry the pieces of chicken
    until they are well browned all over. Remove from the
    pan to a casserole.
3   Fry the onions and garlic in the same fat until they are
    golden brown, stirring occasionally. Add the tomatoes,
    with their juice, the parsley, basil, tomato purée and
    wine. Bring to the boil, season well and pour over the
    chicken.
4   Cover and cook in a moderate oven (160°C/325°F/Gas
    Mark 3) for about an hour or until tender.
5   Remove any fat from the surface of the casserole with a
    spoon, taste and adjust the seasonings. Serve the
    chicken with any type of boiled pasta.

Chicken with Coconut   Serves 4

4 part-boned chicken breasts
4 tablespoons desiccated coconut
150 ml/¼ pint/⅔ cup boiling water
salt and pepper
25 g/1 oz/2 tablespoons butter or margarine
1 tablespoon oil
1 onion, peeled and thinly sliced
1 clove garlic, crushed
2 tablespoons flour
300 ml/½ pint/1¼ cups chicken stock
¼ teaspoon turmeric
½ teaspoon ground coriander
4–6 gherkins, sliced
chopped parsley to garnish

1   Put the coconut into a jug and pour on the boiling
    water. Leave to stand for 10 minutes.
2   Trim the chicken and season well. Heat the fat and oil
    in a frying pan and fry the pieces of chicken until
    browned. Transfer the pieces to a casserole.
3   Add the onion and garlic to the pan and fry gently in
    the same fat until soft but only lightly coloured. Stir in
    the flour and cook for 1 minute, stirring continuously.
4   Add the stock followed by the coconut mixture and
    bring to the boil. Stir in the turmeric, coriander and
    plenty of seasonings. Pour over the chicken and cover.

Chicken Kiev

1 Beat the pieces of chicken between two sheets of plastic cling film until a little thinner and of an even thickness all over.

3 Coat the chicken rolls first in seasoned flour, and then dip in beaten egg and finally coat in breadcrumbs.

2 Roll and fold up the pieces of chicken to enclose the flavoured butter completely and secure with wooden cocktail sticks.

4 Remove the cocktail sticks and serve with a salad and savoury rice.

5 Cook in a moderate oven (180°C/350°F/Gas Mark 4) for about 40 minutes. Stir in the gherkins, re-cover the casserole, and return to the oven for about 20 minutes.
6 Spoon off any fat from the surface and serve sprinkled with chopped parsley.

Chicken Kiev

Serves 4

4 large boneless chicken breasts
100 g/4 oz/½ cup butter
grated rind of ½ lemon
salt and pepper
1 tablespoon chopped parsley
1–2 cloves garlic, crushed
a little seasoned flour
1 egg, beaten
100 g/4 oz/2 cups fresh white breadcrumbs
oil or fat for deep-frying

1 Put the pieces of chicken between two sheets of plastic cling film and beat out carefully until a little thinner and of an even thickness all over.
2 Work the butter until slightly softened, then beat in the lemon rind, seasonings, parsley and garlic. Cut into four pieces and place one on each piece of chicken.
3 Roll up the pieces of chicken to enclose the butter completely and secure with wooden cocktail sticks.
4 Coat the chicken rolls first in seasoned flour and then dip in beaten egg and finally coat in breadcrumbs. Pat the crumbs well in and chill thoroughly.
5 For a better coating, dab the coating with beaten egg and coat a second time in the crumbs and chill again.
6 To serve, heat the oil to about 160°C/325°F. Place two chicken portions in a frying basket and gently lower into the hot fat. Fry for about 12–15 minutes until a good golden brown. Do not pierce to see if the chicken is cooked or the butter will spurt out. Drain well and keep warm while frying the remaining pieces.
7 Serve the chicken with a salad and savoury rice.

Chicken Rossini

Serves 4

4 boneless chicken breasts
salt and pepper
100 g/4 oz firm liver pâté
40 g/1½ oz/3 tablespoons butter
175 g/6 oz button mushrooms, sliced
3 tablespoons brandy or port
6 tablespoons chicken stock
3 tablespoons double (heavy) or single (light) cream
To garnish
4 circles of toast
watercress

1   Flatten the chicken breasts a little as for Chicken Kiev and season lightly.
2   Cut the pâté into four even-sized pieces and roll up one piece in each breast of chicken. Secure with wooden cocktail sticks.
3   Melt the butter in a pan and fry the chicken rolls until lightly browned all over and partly cooked. Remove the chicken from the pan and keep warm.
4   Fry the mushrooms in the remaining fat in the pan for a few minutes. Add the brandy or port and stock and bring to the boil. Season well and replace the chicken rolls. Cover the pan and simmer very gently for about 20 minutes, turning once or twice, or until tender.
5   Stir the cream into the pan, adjust the seasonings and reheat gently.
6   Remove the cocktail sticks and serve the chicken rolls on the circles of toast with the sauce spooned over and garnished with watercress.

Chicken Marengo Pot Roast

Serves 4–6

1.75 kg/4 lb oven-ready chicken
salt and pepper
50 g/2 oz/¼ cup butter or margarine
2 tablespoons brandy
1 onion, peeled and sliced
1–2 cloves garlic, crushed
2 tablespoons flour
425 g/15 oz can tomatoes, puréed or very finely chopped
150 ml/¼ pint/⅔ cup dry white wine
1 tablespoon tomato purée
100 g/4 oz button mushrooms, trimmed and halved
To garnish
8 large whole prawns or shrimp
2 hard-boiled eggs, quartered
8 black olives

1   Season the chicken all over. Melt the fat in a frying pan and fry the chicken until browned all over. Transfer the chicken to a casserole.
2   Warm the brandy, pour over the chicken and ignite.
3   Add the onion and garlic to the fat remaining in the pan and fry gently until soft and lightly browned.
4   Stir the flour into the pan and cook for a minute or so. Gradually add the puréed tomatoes, wine and tomato

purée. Bring to the boil and season well. Pour over the chicken and cover the casserole.
5   Cook in a moderate oven (160°C/325°F/Gas Mark 3) for an hour. Stir the mushrooms into the sauce around the chicken, baste it well and return to the oven, uncovered, for about 15 minutes or until the chicken is cooked through and crisp on top.
6   Remove the chicken to a serving dish and arrange the prawns, quarters of hard-boiled egg and olives around the chicken. Adjust the seasonings in the sauce and pour into a sauce boat.

Chicken Goujons with Curry Dip

Serves 4

4 boneless chicken breasts
a little seasoned flour
2 eggs, beaten
golden breadcrumbs
25 g/1 oz/¼ cup shelled walnuts, very finely chopped
oil or fat for deep frying
mustard and cress or watercress to garnish
Curry Dip
4 tablespoons thick mayonnaise
4 tablespoons soured cream
1½–2 teaspoons curry powder
½ teaspoon Worcestershire sauce
good dash of soy sauce
8 stuffed green olives, chopped
3–4 spring onions (scallions), finely chopped
salt and pepper

1   Cut the chicken breasts into narrow strips about 4 cm/ 1½ inches long. Dip in the seasoned flour.
2   Dip the goujons of chicken into the beaten eggs.
3   Combine about 8 tablespoons golden breadcrumbs with the finely chopped walnuts and use to coat the chicken pieces.
4   Heat the fat or oil until a cube of bread will brown in 30 seconds, then deep-fry the chicken strips, a few at a time until golden brown and cooked through – about 5 minutes. Drain on absorbent kitchen paper towel and keep warm while frying the remainder.
5   To make the dip, put all the ingredients into a bowl and mix very well. Season to taste and put into a bowl.
6   Serve the chicken goujons piled up on a plate garnished with the mustard and cress. Hand the dip separately.

Coq au Vin
Serves 4

1.75 kg/4 lb oven-ready chicken
225 g/8 oz piece streaky bacon, derinded
350 g/12 oz button onions, peeled
1–2 cloves garlic, crushed
25 g/1 oz/2 tablespoons butter
2 tablespoons oil
salt and pepper
450 ml/¾ pint/scant 2 cups red wine
150 ml/¼ pint/⅔ cup chicken stock
1 bouquet garni or bay leaf
¼ teaspoon dried oregano
175 g/6 oz button mushrooms, trimmed
2 teaspoons cornflour (cornstarch)

1   Cut the streaky bacon into neat dice about 1 cm/ ½ inch. Fry with the onions and garlic in a frying pan with the butter and oil until lightly browned, stirring frequently. Remove to a casserole.
2   Cut the chicken into eight even pieces and season well with salt and pepper. Fry in the same fat until well browned all over. Transfer to the casserole.
3   Pour off the excess fat from the pan, then add the wine, stock, bouquet garni or bay leaf, oregano and plenty of seasonings and bring to the boil. Pour over the chicken and cover the casserole.
4   Cook in a moderate oven (180°C/350°F/Gas Mark 4) for 45 minutes.
5   Add the mushrooms to the casserole. Blend the cornflour with the minimum of cold water and add to the casserole. Re-cover and return to the oven for 20–25 minutes until quite tender. Discard the bouquet garni or bay leaf and serve.

Chicken à la King
Serves 4–5

350 g/12 oz cooked chicken meat, diced
50 g/2 oz/¼ cup butter or margarine
100 g/4 oz mushrooms, sliced
½ green pepper, deseeded and chopped
40 g/1½ oz/⅓ cup flour
450 ml/¾ pint/scant 2 cups milk or milk and chicken stock mixed
salt and pepper
½ teaspoon ground coriander
2 tablespoons sherry
freshly chopped parsley to garnish

1   Melt the butter in a frying pan and fry the mushrooms and pepper together very gently until soft.
2   Stir in the flour and cook for a minute or so, stirring all the time.
3   Gradually add the milk and bring to the boil, stirring continuously. Add the chicken, seasonings, coriander and sherry and simmer gently for about 10 minutes or until really well heated through. Adjust the seasonings.
4   Serve on a bed of freshly boiled rice, sprinkled with chopped parsley.

DUCK

Duck or duckling is now available all the year both fresh or frozen and whole (oven ready) or in portions. It has an excellent flavour, but is a dark-fleshed bird with plenty of fat on it, quite the opposite of chicken. It also has a boney carcass with much less flesh on it than is apparent. Cooking has to be done carefully so it is not overfatty or, on the other hand, dry.

The name 'duckling' refers to a bird between 6 weeks and 3 months old and the majority of ducks sold are duckling. The duck should be young with soft pliable feet, not tough old ones, and the feet and bill should be yellow. An average duck will weigh about 1.75 kg/4 lb, but anything under 1.5 kg/3 lb is likely to be all bone and no flesh. Larger birds are available and ducks are being bred so they are larger. Allow at least 450 g/1 lb raw dressed weight of duck per person.

Ducks are not usually stuffed, although a sage and onion stuffing can be added if liked. It is more usual to cook the stuffing separately in a dish to serve as an accompaniment. Potatoes may be roasted around the duck in the fat that comes out of the bird as it cooks.

ROASTING DUCK
As with all poultry, if frozen, make sure it is completely thawed before cooking.
1   Truss the duck, if it is not already done, by trussing as for chicken but not pulling the wings across the back, leave at the sides, and tie the legs with fine string. Weigh.
2   Season the skin of the duck with salt (and a little pepper if liked), then prick all over the skin with a fine skewer.
3   Stand a rack (a grill rack will do) in a roasting tin and put the duck on the rack. As the duck is very fatty it is not necessary to add any extra fat or oil to the pan.
4   Roast in a fairly hot oven (190°C/375°F/Gas Mark 5) allowing 30 minutes per 450 g/1 lb. It is not necessary to baste the duck at all, but I prefer to do so once or twice during the cooking time. Add the potatoes an hour before required, when there is some fat in the pan from the duck.
5   Remove the duck to a serving dish with the potatoes and keep warm. It is essential to remove almost all the fat from the pan juices, if there are any, before using to make the gravy or sauce or it will taste very fatty.

Note: The duck should be tested in the same way as a chicken to see if it is ready, that is with a skewer in the deepest part of the thigh to check that the juices run clear.

TRADITIONAL ACCOMPANIMENTS
Sage and onion stuffing
Apple sauce (see page 36) or Bigarade sauce
Thin gravy
Orange salad
Peas

CARVING DUCK

The easiest way is to cut the duck into quarters. Beginning at the neck end, use a sharp knife, kitchen scissors or poultry shears to cut along the length of the breastbone. Split the duck in half by cutting through the backbone. Make a diagonal cut between the wings and legs to give four portions.

A duck can also be carved by removing the legs and wings in more or less the same way as a chicken and then carving the breast meat in long slices the whole length of the body.

Bigarade Sauce

This can be used as an alternative to gravy.

3 oranges
2 lemons
1 tablespoon sugar
1 tablespoon vinegar
2 tablespoons brandy
150 ml/¼ pint/⅔ cup dry white wine
1 tablespoon cornflour (cornstarch)
salt and pepper

1   Finely grate or pare the rind from one of the oranges, free of white pith and cut into thin (julienne strips). Cook the strips in boiling water for 5 minutes and drain.
2   Squeeze the juice from all the oranges and lemons.
3   Put the sugar and vinegar into a small pan and heat gently until melted, then continue to cook until the mixture turns brown.
4   Quickly add the brandy and fruit juices, followed by the wine. Heat gently until the sauce comes to the boil.
5   Spoon off all the fat from the pan juices, add the orange sauce to it and bring to the boil. Blend the cornflour with a little cold water and add to the sauce. Bring back to the boil, adjust the seasonings and strain into a jug. Stir in the orange rind and serve with the duck.

Plum Duck   Serves 4

2.25 kg/5 lb oven-ready duck
salt and pepper
a little garlic powder, or a cut clove of garlic
550 g/1¼ lb can red plums in syrup
2 teaspoons Worcestershire sauce
1 tablespoon wine vinegar
2 teaspoons soy sauce
watercress to garnish

1   Trim the duck and remove any excess fat. Place in a large casserole or roasting tin and prick the skin all over. Season well with salt and pepper and sprinkle with garlic powder or rub with a cut clove of garlic.
2   Cook, uncovered, in a fairly hot oven (200°C/400°F/ Gas Mark 6) for 30 minutes. Spoon off any fat from around the duck, leaving just the pan juices.

3   Drain the juice from the plums, add the Worcestershire sauce, vinegar, soy sauce and seasonings and make up to 300 ml/½ pint/1¼ cups with water. Pour over the duck, cover with a lid or foil and return to the oven for 45 minutes.
4   Baste the duck with the juices and put the plums around the bird. Cover and return to the oven for 15 minutes or until tender. The lid may be removed for the last 10 minutes to crisp up the skin again.
5   Transfer the duck to a serving dish and arrange the plums around it. Spoon off the fat from the cooking juices and serve in a sauce boat. Alternatively, the plums may be stoned and liquidized or puréed with the sauce and served as a thicker sauce. Garnish with watercress.

Duck Montmorency   Serves 4

4 breast portions of duck
salt and pepper
425 g/15 oz can black cherries
grated rind of 1 orange
juice of 2 oranges
1½ teaspoons cornflour (cornstarch)
4 tablespoons stock
To garnish
orange slices or wedges
watercress

1   Trim the duck, removing any excess fat and protruding bones. Season well with salt and pepper and prick the skin all over with a fork. Put into a lightly greased roasting tin.
2   Cook in a fairly hot oven (200°C/400°F/Gas Mark 6) for 10 minutes.
3   Drain the cherries and make the juice up to 200 ml/ 7 fl oz/scant cup with stock or water. Add the orange rind and juice to the cherry juice and pour over the duck. Return to the oven for 20 minutes, basting the duck at least once.
3   Add the cherries to the roasting tin, baste the duck again and continue to cook for 10–20 minutes or until the duck is tender and the skin crisp.
4   Remove the duck to a serving dish and keep warm. Blend the cornflour with a little of the stock and add to the pan juices, after skimming off any fat from the surface. Bring to the boil and simmer for about 2 minutes, adding further stock if necessary.
5   Season to taste and spoon over the duck, or spoon some of the sauce and the cherries over the duck and serve the remainder in a sauce boat. Garnish with the orange and watercress.

Apricot Duck (see page 84) and Chicken Rossini (see page 80)

Apricot Duck
Serves 4

2.25 kg/5 lb oven-ready duck
100 g/4 oz dried apricots
grated rind and juice of 1 orange
150 ml/¼ pint/⅔ cup water
1 onion, peeled and very finely chopped
40 g/1½ oz/⅓ cup flour
450 ml/¾ pint/scant 2 cups chicken stock
2 teaspoons demerara sugar
salt and pepper
425 g/15 oz can apricot halves
4 tablespoons brandy
25 g/1 oz/¼ cup shelled walnuts, chopped

1 Roast the duck by the usual method (see page 81).
2 Meanwhile, gently stew the dried apricots in the orange juice with the orange rind and water for 20 minutes until soft. Purée in a blender or food processor.
3 Remove the duck from the roasting tin, cut into quarters and put into a shallow casserole.
4 Put 2 tablespoons of the fat from the roasting tin into a pan and fry the onion in it until soft and lightly browned. Stir in the flour and cook for a minute or so. Gradually add the stock, apricot purée and sugar and bring to the boil. Season well and pour over the duck.
5 Drain the apricots, put into a frying pan and pour on the brandy. Ignite and heat gently until the apricot halves are quite hot. Spoon over the duck in the casserole and sprinkle with the walnuts.

Duck and Orange Casserole
Serves 4

2.25–2.75 kg/5–6 lb duck, quartered, or 4 duck portions
a little seasoned flour
1 tablespoon oil
2 onions, peeled and chopped
40 g/1½ oz/⅓ cup flour
300 ml/½ pint/1¼ cups chicken stock
300 ml/½ pint/1¼ cups orange juice (not squash)
salt and pepper
100 g/4 oz mushrooms, sliced
grated rind of ½–1 orange

1 Trim the duck and coat in seasoned flour. Heat the oil in a frying pan and fry the duck until browned all over. Transfer to a casserole.
2 Add the onions to the pan and fry gently until golden brown. If there is not enough fat, add another tablespoon of oil.
3 Stir in the flour and cook for a minute or so, stirring continuously. Gradually add the stock and orange juice and bring to the boil. Season well and pour over the duck.
4 Cover the casserole and cook in a moderate oven (180°C/350°F/Gas Mark 4) for an hour.
5 Remove the lid from the casserole and spoon off any fat from the surface. Stir in the mushrooms and orange rind, re-cover and return to the oven for about 15 mintues or until very tender.

Duck with Cumberland Sauce
Serves 4

2.25 kg/5 lb oven-ready duck
salt and pepper
Sauce
grated rind of 1 orange
4 tablespoons redcurrant jelly
250 ml/8 fl oz/1 cup port or red wine
juice of 2 oranges
2 tablespoons lemon juice
1–2 teaspoons cornflour (cornstarch) (optional)

1 Trim the duck, season well, prick the skin and stand on a rack in a roasting tin. Roast following the basic method (see page 81).
2 Mix the orange rind with the redcurrant jelly, port or wine and orange and lemon juices.
3 When the duck is cooked, transfer to a warm serving dish and keep warm. Skim off all the fat from the pan juices.
4 Add the orange mixture to the pan juices. Heat gently until the jelly has completely dissolved, stirring frequently, then bring to the boil and simmer for about 2 minutes. If liked, the sauce may be thickened with a little cornflour blended in the minimum of cold water, added to the sauce and brought back to the boil until thickened and clear.
5 Season to taste and spoon some of the sauce over the duck. Put the rest of the sauce in a sauce boat.

GOOSE

This bird is becoming more popular again and rather easier to find, both fresh and frozen, although the price still remains rather high. This is again a bird with a large bony carcass with little flesh on it for its size, but what flesh there is has a splendid flavour and is usually very tender – although it can be a little greasy if due attention is not paid to the cooking. An oven-ready goose weighing about 4.5 kg/10 lb will feed 7–8 people so it is an extravagant meat. Again, the bird must be young with soft yellow feet, a yellow bill and with yellowish fat and a pinkish-coloured flesh. Truss the bird with skewers and string after cutting off the feet and wings at the first joint. Put a skewer through the wing, then through the body and out again through the outer wing. Put a second skewer through the end of the wing joint on one side, through the thick part of the leg, through the body and out the other side in the same way. Put a third skewer through the loose skin near the end of the leg through the body and out the other side in the same way. Wind string around the skewers to keep the body in shape, but do not take the string over the breast. Tuck the neck skin under the string. A goose can be stuffed with sage and onion stuffing, but the stuffing is more often cooked and served separately.

Serve with a thin gravy made using the giblet stock and with a gooseberry or apple sauce. Fried apple rings also make a good accompaniment.

ROASTING GOOSE

1 Sprinkle the oven-ready bird all over with salt and put into a roasting tin standing on a rack – as for duck, as the flesh tends to be greasy. The skin may be lightly pricked with a pin or fine skewer to help the fat run out. Lay a sheet of greased wax or greaseproof paper over the bird.

2 To cook the bird by the hot method, roast in a fairly hot oven (200°C/400°F/Gas Mark 6) allowing 15 minutes per 450 g/1 lb plus 15 minutes over; or cook in a moderate oven (180°C/350°F/Gas Mark 4) allowing 25–30 minutes per 450 g/1 lb. The goose may be basted once or twice, if liked, and the wax or greaseproof should be removed for the last 30 minutes or so of cooking time to brown the bird.

3 Pour off almost all the fat from the pan and use the juices to make a thin gravy, preferably with the giblet stock.

CARVING GOOSE

Carve with the breast upwards. First remove the legs or at least one leg and then the wings or wing. If the bird is stuffed, cut thick slices across the body from the neck end. Carve thickish slices from either side of the breast bone taking the slices the length of the body. Carve the meat off the legs and wings and serve with the breast meat.

TURKEY

Turkey is one of the most versatile of the poultry meats. Although it is large, it can be cooked whole, in halves and in a variety of 'pieces' in ways to suit all types of everyday and party eating. Although turkey used to be a seasonal bird, it is now very readily available all the year both fresh and frozen. Larger fresh birds are more readily available at Christmas time in Britain, but they can be ordered from butchers and farm fresh shops all the year. Portions of turkey that are available include thighs, drumsticks, wings, breast fillets, escalopes and steaks, and many areas also offer their own turkey speciality cuts. Fresh turkey will keep for up to 3 days in the refrigerator before cooking. Sometimes confusion arises between the fresh and frozen birds along with the chilled and other methods of preparation. Basically a fresh turkey is one that is seen hanging up, ready plucked, but with head still on and has not been drawn. When bought, it is then dressed ready to eat. Fresh turkeys are always hung before preparation. Frozen turkeys are killed, plucked, drawn and prepared all in one continuous process which ends with them being sealed into polythene bags and blast frozen. A chilled turkey goes through the same process but is packed into a different type of bag and is then chilled and despatched immediately to the stores, as its shelf life is very limited. Once bought, it should be treated in the same way as a fresh bird. Frozen turkeys will keep in the frozen state for up to 1 year. When bought, they should be taken home immediately and, if to be stored, put right away into the deep freeze. If to be thawed out, put onto a large plate, still in the wrapping, and leave at room temperature or a cool place (but preferably not the refrigerator, unless the bird is under about 3.5 kg/8 lb) for the time recommended in the chart.

Turkey joints and roasts (boneless) are also widely available, both fresh and frozen. Follow the thawing and cooking instructions on the packets.

Turkeys vary in size tremendously from the mini birds of around 2.25 kg/5 lb right up to the giants of 13.5 kg/30 lb plus. An average domestic cooker can handle a turkey of up to about 10.5 kg/23 lb.

As with all poultry, it is desperately important to make sure the turkey is completely thawed out before cooking. Do check the legs are flexible and that there are no ice crystals left in the body. If you are caught out and the bird is taking longer to thaw than you anticipated, then it can be soaked in a bowl of cold water for a few hours, which will help to hasten the thawing process.

THAWING TIMES AND SERVINGS

Oven-ready weight	Thawing time at room temperature	Approximate number of servings
2.25–3.35 kg/5–8 lb	15–18 hours	6–10
3.5–5 kg/8–11 lb	18–20 hours	10–15
5–6.75 kg/11–15 lb	20–24 hours	15–20
6.75–9 kg/15–20 lb	24–30 hours	20–28
9–11.25 kg/20–25 lb	30–36 hours	28–36

These servings are based on a 75–100 g/3–4 oz portion of white and dark meat, including skin, per person.

TO TRUSS A TURKEY

Put the stuffing in the neck end only and fold the neck flap over to completely enclose it. If necessary, secure with a small skewer or wooden cocktail stick. Truss in a similar way as for a chicken with the wings folded under the bird and the legs tied together. Do not be tempted to truss too tightly or the heat of the oven will find it hard to penetrate the deepest parts of the thighs, thus increasing the cooking time, which can spoil the breast meat. A quartered peeled onion or lemon can be inserted in the body cavity for extra flavour and to keep the bird moist.

PREPARING AND COOKING TURKEY

Once completely thawed, or if a fresh bird, first wipe inside and out with a clean cloth. Remove the giblets including the neck, wash these and use to make a stock for the gravy. Stuff the neck end of the bird only – it is dangerous to stuff the cavity, as when the actual turkey is cooked the stuffing may not be and this can cause food poisoning – and extra stuffing or a second stuffing is best cooked separately in an ovenproof dish below the turkey. Weigh the stuffed bird and put into a greased baking tin. Rub all over with melted or softened butter or margarine and season, if liked. Cook in a moderate oven, following the chart below, either as it is or wrapped in foil. Baste the turkey several times during cooking and, if a large bird, lay a sheet of wax or greaseproof paper or foil over the breast when sufficiently browned; if cooking in foil, fold back the foil for the last 20 minutes of cooking time to allow the bird to brown.

Check the bird is cooked by inserting a skewer into the deepest part of the thigh to check that the juices run clear. If at all pink tinged, return to the oven for 15 minutes and test again. It is advisable to calculate so the cooking time is completed at least 20 minutes before required. This will allow for extra cooking time should it be necessary and allow the bird to stand and set for easier carving. If taking the turkey straight from the refrigerator to the oven, increase the cooking time by about 15 minutes to allow the bird to warm up before starting to cook.

RECOMMENDED COOKING TIMES

Weight	Without Foil	Wrapped in Foil
2.25–3.5 kg/5–8 lb	2–2½ hours	2½–3½ hours
3.5–5 kg/8–11 lb	2½–3¼ hours	3½–4 hours
5–6.75 kg/11–15 lb	3¼–3¾ hours	4–5 hours
6.75–9 kg/15–20 lb	3¾–4¼ hours	5–5½ hours
9–11.25 kg/20–25 lb	4¼–4¾ hours	Not recommended

When the turkey is cooked, stand it on a large serving dish and keep warm. Spoon off the fat from the pan juices and use the juices with giblet stock to make a gravy. Other traditional accompaniments are bacon rolls, chipolata sausages, bread sauce and cranberry sauce or jelly.

CARVING TURKEY

Carve with the breast upwards. Remove a drumstick, leaving the thigh on the bird, and slice the meat from it. Carve slices from the thigh and then remove the wings and strip off the meat from these. Carve thin slices from the breast, taking in slices from the stuffing. Serve a mixture of white and dark meat plus stuffing for each portion. When the first side has been carved, turn the bird around and start on the other side.

Turkey Beanpot
Serves 4–5

675 g/1½ lb raw boneless turkey thigh meat
25 g/1 oz/2 tablespoons butter or margarine
1 tablespoon oil
1 large onion, peeled and chopped
1 clove garlic, crushed
2 carrots, peeled and diced
1 red pepper, deseeded and sliced
1 tablespoon flour
150 ml/¼ pint/⅔ cup red or white wine or cider
425 g/15 oz can tomatoes
150 ml/¼ pint/⅔ cup chicken stock
salt and pepper
½ teaspoon ground coriander
good pinch of ground cinnamon
1 tablespoon Worcestershire sauce
425 g/15 oz can red kidney beans, drained
freshly chopped parsley to garnish

1 Trim the turkey meat, remove the skin and cut into 2 cm/¾ inch cubes.
2 Heat the butter and oil in a pan and fry the turkey until well sealed. Transfer to a casserole. Fry the onion and garlic in the same fat until soft, then add the carrots and pepper and cook for a minute or so longer.
3 Stir in the flour and cook for a minute, then gradually add the wine, tomatoes, stock, seasonings, spices and Worcestershire sauce and bring to the boil. Stir in the beans, pour over the turkey and cover tightly.

4 Cook in a moderate oven (180°C/350°F/Gas Mark 4) for about an hour or until very tender. Adjust the seasonings, sprinkle with parsley and serve with freshly boiled rice, jacket or creamed potatoes and a salad.

Turkey Véronique
Serves 4

4 turkey escalopes
salt and pepper
25 g/1 oz/2 tablespoons butter or margarine
1 tablespoon oil
25 g/1 oz/¼ cup flour
150 ml/¼ pint/⅔ cup medium white wine
150 ml/¼ pint/⅔ cup chicken stock
grated rind of ½ lemon
1 tablespoon lemon juice
1 bay leaf
150 ml/¼ pint/⅔ cup single (light) cream
1 egg yolk
100 g/4 oz green grapes, peeled, halved and deseeded
To garnish
green grapes
watercress

1 Trim the escalopes and season lightly. Heat the butter and oil in a pan and fry the turkey all over until lightly browned and partly cooked. Remove from the pan.
2 Stir the flour into the fat in the pan, cook for 1 minute, then gradually add the wine and stock and bring to the boil, stirring continuously. Add the lemon rind, lemon juice, bay leaf and seasonings to taste.
3 Replace the turkey, cover and simmer gently for about 20 minutes, turning the pieces once or twice.
4 Blend the cream and egg yolk together, stir in a little of the sauce and then return it all to the sauce. Add the grapes and simmer very gently for about 4–5 minutes. Adjust the seasonings.
5 Serve the escalopes with the sauce spooned over and garnished with small bunches of green grapes and watercress.

Turkey Kebabs
Serves 4

450 g/1 lb raw turkey meat, white or dark, cut into
    2.5 cm/1 inch cubes
8 lean rashers bacon, derinded and rolled
8 button onions, peeled and blanched
2 tablespoons apricot jam
4 tablespoons tomato ketchup
1 tablespoon soy sauce
1½ teaspoons Dijon or French mustard
1 clove garlic, crushed
1 tablespoon Worcestershire sauce
grated rind of ½ lemon
1 tablespoon lemon juice
2 tablespoons oil
pinch of cayenne pepper
salt and pepper

1 Thread the cubes of turkey onto four long skewers alternating with the bacon rolls and onions.

2   Put the jam, ketchup, soy sauce, mustard, garlic, Worcestershire sauce, lemon rind and juice, oil and seasonings into a saucepan and bring slowly just to the boil, stirring frequently. Remove from the heat.

3   Stand the kebabs in a foil-lined grill pan and brush liberally with the sauce.

4   Cook under a preheated moderate grill or broiler for 8–10 minutes each side, or until cooked through. Brush the kebabs at least once more with the sauce during cooking. The kebabs may also be cooked on an open barbecue in the same way.

5   Serve with the remaining sauce, reheated gently, with jacket potatoes or savoury rice, or in pitta bread.

Turkey Escalopes with Sweetcorn
Serves 4

4 turkey escalopes
salt and pepper
25 g/1 oz/2 tablespoons butter or margarine
1 onion, peeled and thinly sliced
1 clove garlic, peeled and crushed
about 150 ml/¼ pint/⅔ cup chicken stock
juice of 1 orange
2 teaspoons flour
275 g/10 oz can cream-style sweetcorn
Stuffing
50 g/2 oz/¼ cup butter or margarine
½ onion, peeled and finely chopped
1 stick celery, finely chopped
2 rashers bacon, derinded and finely chopped
50 g/2 oz/1 cup fresh breadcrumbs
grated rind of ½ lemon
To garnish
lemon slices
stuffed green olives or black olives
sprigs of watercress or parsley

1   Beat the turkey escalopes between two sheets of plastic cling film until they are a little thinner and will roll up easily. If they are very thick, cut them in half horizontally and then beat out. Season lightly.

2   For the stuffing, melt the butter in a pan and fry the onion, celery and bacon until soft. Mix with the breadcrumbs, the lemon rind and plenty of seasonings.

3   Divide the stuffing between the turkey pieces and roll up or fold into three to enclose the filling. Secure with wooden cocktail sticks.

4   Melt the butter or margarine in a frying pan and fry the turkey rolls or parcels until golden brown. Transfer to a shallow casserole.

5   Fry the onion and garlic in the pan until golden brown.

6   Combine the stock and orange juice. Stir the flour into the onions, cook for a minute or so and then gradually add the liquid. Bring to the boil, stir in the creamed sweetcorn and season well. Bring back to the boil again and pour over the turkey.

7   Cover and cook in a moderate oven (180°C/350°F/Gas Mark 4) for about 45 minutes or until tender.

8   Turn onto a serving dish, discard the cocktail sticks and garnish with lemon, olives and watercress or parsley.

Cidered Turkey
Serves 4

550 g/1¼ lb raw boneless turkey meat, cubed
25 g/1 oz/2 tablespoons butter or margarine
2 tablespoons oil
1 onion, peeled and sliced
1 green pepper, deseeded and sliced
2 tablespoons flour
300 ml/½ pint/1¼ cups cider
300 ml/½ pint/1¼ cups chicken stock
200 g/7 oz can sweetcorn kernels, drained
100 g/4 oz mushrooms, sliced
salt and pepper
1 large dessert apple, peeled, cored and sliced
freshly chopped parsley to garnish

1   Melt the butter and oil in a frying pan, add the turkey and fry until lightly browned. Put in a casserole.

2   Add the onion and green pepper to the frying pan and fry in the same fat until soft, stirring occasionally. Stir in the flour and cook for 1 minute. Gradually add the cider and stock and bring to the boil, stirring frequently. Add the sweetcorn, mushrooms and seasonings and pour into the casserole.

3   Cover the casserole and cook in a moderate oven (180°C/350°F/Gas Mark 4) for about an hour or until tender. Adjust the seasonings, stir in the apple and return to the oven for about 15 minutes. Serve sprinkled with chopped parsley.

Potted Turkey
Serves 4–6

225 g/8 oz cooked turkey meat
100 g/4 oz/½ cup butter
1 onion, peeled and very finely chopped
1–2 cloves garlic, crushed
2 tablespoons sherry or port
about 3 tablespoons chicken stock
salt and pepper
pinch of ground nutmeg, mace or coriander
good pinch of dried mixed herbs (optional)
To garnish
stuffed olives
sliced tomatoes

1   Mince or grind the turkey meat finely twice, or put into a food processor until almost puréed.

2   Melt half the butter in a frying pan, add the onion and garlic and fry gently until soft and lightly coloured, stirring frequently.

3   Stir in the turkey meat followed by the sherry or port and just sufficient stock to moisten. Season to taste with salt, pepper and spices and add the herbs (if used). Mix very thoroughly.

4   Press the potted turkey into a lightly greased dish or individual ones and level the tops. Chill until firm.

5   Melt the remaining butter and pour a thin layer over the potted turkey. Chill again.

6   Serve garnished with stuffed olives and tomatoes and with fingers of toast or fresh crusty bread. The potted turkey will keep for 2–3 days only in the refrigerator.

GAME

The name 'game' is given to a variety of wild animals and birds that live in the wild and mainly depend on the food available to them in their native environment. They are hunted and killed for food but they are protected by game laws, which allow only certain times when they can be shot. There are quite a wide variety of feathered game, plenty of different water fowl and, of course, the different types of venison and the hare.

The most important thing to know is the game seasons, so that you can plan your game eating around these times. These obviously differ slightly from country to country, so either look in a book specializing on game, or ask a poulterer or a shop selling sporting guns and equipment.

SELECTING AND PREPARING GAME

Try to choose a young bird or animal, as when they begin to age they can be particularly tough and hard, although the flavour will probably be good. All game needs hanging but the length of time can vary greatly depending firstly on the type of game, secondly on the weather conditions – cold frosty weather will slow down the ripening process, while warm and muggy weather will hasten it and can help the game become overripe without due attention – and thirdly on the type of flavour and degree of ripeness you like in your game. Hanging is essential to improve the flavour of the game, to help to tenderize it and to give the characteristic taste associated with game.

Birds are hung still in the feather and undrawn. Hare is hung in the fur unpaunched, but rabbit is paunched first and then hung in the fur. Birds are hung by the neck, rabbits and hares by the feet.

Game will mostly be bought ready prepared, i.e. plucked and drawn and oven-ready as for other poultry, or as joints or cuts of meat for venison. If fresh, game should be kept in a refrigerator for only a short while before cooking, as the hanging has bought the bird to its correct degree of ripeness and it should therefore be cooked without further delay. If it is frozen, allow it to thaw out slowly, again as for poultry or meat, but once thawed completely it should be cooked without undue delay.

Fresh game can be home frozen, but it should be hung and prepared ready for cooking before it is frozen. Most game will freeze satisfactorily for 8–12 months.

COOKING GAME

Each type of game can be roasted and this is the basic method of cooking. There are also many other ways of cooking and serving all types of game, but each type of game has its traditional accompaniments. Remember all game tends to be dry, so, when roasting, it is essential to add plenty of fat for basting and quite often a strip of pork fat or fatty bacon laid over the breast of a bird or tied round a joint of venison will give extra moistness. The different varieties of game are dealt with and described separately with several recipes given for each main type.

PHEASANT

This is probably the best known of British game birds and many people only think of pheasant when referring to game. They should be hung in a cool, dry, well-ventilated place for 1–3 weeks, but the average time is 7–10 days. Young birds are best roasted, but the more mature they get the more important it is to casserole or braise them to ensure they will be tender. They can often be bought cheaper by the brace, that is as a cock and hen. The cock has the brightly-coloured plumage and the hen is muted shades of brown. A pheasant will serve from 2–4 people.

Roast Pheasant   Serves 2–4

1 oven-ready pheasant
a knob of butter or margarine
a quarter of lemon or wedge of onion
salt and pepper
melted dripping, butter or margarine
a few rashers of fat or streaky bacon, or a piece of pork fat,
*   beaten thinly*
watercress to garnish

1   Wipe the pheasant inside and out and place a knob of butter and a piece of lemon or onion in the cavity. Truss lightly (as for a chicken) and stand in a roasting tin.
2   Pour or spoon melted fat over the bird and season lightly. Lay the bacon or piece of pork fat over the breast of the bird.
3   Cook in a hot oven (220°C/425°F/Gas Mark 7) for ¾–1¼ hours depending on the size. Baste the bird regularly every 15 minutes until cooked through and tender. Check the deepest part of the thigh with a skewer as for chicken and turkey to make sure the juices run clear.
4   The bacon or pork fat can be removed 15 minutes before the end of cooking time to brown the skin. Unlike some game, pheasant should be completely cooked, not served slightly underdone.
5   Remove the trussing string and serve the pheasant on a warmed dish with game chips and garnished with watercress. Spoon the fat from the pan juices and use to make a thin gravy. Also serve fried crumbs (see below), and/or bread sauce.

Fried Crumbs

50 g/2 oz/¼ cup butter
2 tablespoons oil
75 g/3 oz/1½ cups fresh white breadcrumbs

1   Melt the butter and oil together in a frying pan and fry the breadcrumbs until golden brown all over, stirring almost continuously.
2   Drain on absorbent kitchen paper towel and serve with roast game.

Pheasant with Walnuts and Cranberries

Serves 4

1 large mature pheasant, oven ready
1 tablespoon oil
25 g/1 oz/2 tablespoons butter
salt and pepper
1 large onion, peeled and thinly sliced
4–5 sticks celery, sliced
1 1/2 tablespoons flour
300 ml/1/2 pint/1 1/4 cups stock
150 ml/1/4 pint/2/3 cup red or white wine
75 g/3 oz whole cranberries, fresh or frozen
2 tablespoons demerara sugar
50 g/2 oz/1/2 cup walnut halves

1 Cut the pheasant into quarters and season lightly. Heat the oil and butter in a frying pan and fry the pheasant pieces until browned all over. Transfer to a casserole.
2 Fry the onion and celery gently in the same fat until soft but not coloured, stirring frequently. Stir in the flour and cook for 1 minute, then gradually add the stock and wine and bring to the boil. Season well and pour over the pheasant. Cover the casserole.
3 Cook in a moderate oven (180°C/350°F/Gas Mark 4) for 45 minutes. Adjust the seasonings, stir in the cranberries, sugar and walnuts and a little more boiling stock, if necessary, and re-cover the casserole. Return to the oven for 20–30 minutes or until very tender.

Pot Roast Pheasant with Chestnuts

Serves 3–4

1 large pheasant, oven ready
salt and pepper
1 tablespoon oil
25 g/1 oz/2 tablespoons butter or margarine
225 g/8 oz button onions, peeled
425 g/15 oz can whole chestnuts, drained
25 g/1 oz/1/4 cup flour
150 ml/1/4 pint/2/3 cup red wine
450 ml/3/4 pint/scant 2 cups stock
grated rind and juice of 1 orange
2–3 tablespoons coarse orange marmalade or cranberry
*   sauce*

1 Wipe the pheasant all over and season with salt and pepper. Heat the oil and butter in a pan and fry the pheasant all over until golden brown. Transfer to a casserole or small roasting tin.
2 Fry the onions in the same fat until golden brown and then lay around the pheasant with the chestnuts.
3 Stir the flour into the fat in the pan and cook for 1 minute. Gradually add the wine, stock, orange rind and juice and the marmalade and bring to the boil. Season well, pour over the pheasant and cover the casserole tightly with a lid or foil.

4 Cook in a moderate oven (160°C/325°F/Gas Mark 3) for 1 1/2 hours or until very tender. Remove the pheasant to a serving dish, ready to carve. Strain the sauce and put the onions and chestnuts into a serving dish and the sauce into a jug.

PARTRIDGE

These are small birds and they normally serve only one portion, although the larger red-legged variety can sometimes be split in half to serve two. Partridges should be hung for 4–8 days depending on the weather conditions and personal taste, but they are not normally served as 'high' as a pheasant. They are not nearly so plentiful as pheasant and consequently more expensive, but the flavour is excellent and well worth the cost.

Casserole of Partridge

Serves 4

4 oven-ready partridges
salt and pepper
25 g/1 oz/2 tablespoons butter or margarine
2 tablespoons oil
1 onion, peeled and chopped
175 g/6 oz cooked ham, chopped
1 cooking apple, peeled, cored and sliced
1 clove garlic, crushed
1 bay leaf
4 tablespoons stock or cider
150 ml/1/4 pint/2/3 cup single (light) cream
2 tablespoons brandy
watercress to garnish

1 Truss the birds and season lightly. Melt the butter and oil in a frying pan and fry the partridges until browned all over. Remove to a plate.
2 Fry the onion in the same fat for a few minutes until soft and lightly browned. Add the ham, apple and garlic and cook for a few minutes longer, stirring.
3 Spoon the ham mixture into a casserole and stand the partridges on top. Add the bay leaf and the stock or cider. Season lightly and cover the casserole.
4 Cook in a moderate oven (160°C/325°F/Gas Mark 3) for an hour. Discard the bay leaf, add the cream to the casserole and pour the brandy over the birds. Cover again and return to the oven for about 30 minutes or until tender.
5 Serve from the casserole, garnished with watercress.

Roast Partridge   Serves 2–4

2–4 oven-ready partridges
salt and pepper
melted butter or dripping
streaky or fat bacon rashers
To garnish
watercress
lemon wedges

1 Wipe the birds inside and out and add a knob of butter to the cavity. Truss the birds lightly or simply tie the legs together and season lightly. Stand in a roasting tin and pour or spoon melted fat over them. Lay 2 rashers bacon over the breast of each bird.
2 Roast in a hot oven (220°C/425°F/Gas Mark 7) for 30–45 minutes depending on the size. Baste several times during cooking. The bacon may be removed for the last 10 minutes of cooking, if liked.
3 Remove the trussing string and serve the birds on a warmed dish garnished with watercress and lemon. Also serve matchstick potatoes or game chips and bread sauce. Make a thin gravy from the pan juices.

GROUSE

There are several species of grouse, but the best known and most popular is the Red Grouse. Shooting of this bird begins in Britain on August 12th – a day known to all shooting people as the 'Glorious Twelfth'. Grouse need to hang for about a week. Again only roast or grill or broil the young birds; keep the mature ones to make a very handsome casserole. Grouse has a very unique gamey flavour which most people crave for, but there are a few people who are not so keen on this bird. Allow ½–1 bird per portion depending on size.

Roast Grouse   Serves 2–3

2–3 young grouse
salt and pepper
a knob of butter for each bird
2–3 slices or rounds of toast
melted dripping or butter
streaky bacon rashers
a little flour (optional)
watercress to garnish

1 Wipe the birds inside and out, truss lightly, season well and put a knob of butter in the cavity of each bird. Stand each on a piece of toast and put into a roasting tin.
2 Pour the melted fat over the breasts of the birds and then lay rashers of bacon over each bird. Cook in a hot oven (220°C/425°F/Gas Mark 7) for 30–45 minutes until tender and cooked through. Baste several times during cooking.
3 If liked, the bacon can be removed from the birds about 10 minutes before ready and the breasts lightly dredged with flour. Grouse should be just cooked but on no account overcooked.

4 Remove the birds to a serving dish, still on the rounds of toast, garnish with watercress and serve with matchstick potatoes. Use the pan juices to make a thin gravy to which a little port or red wine may be added. Also serve with fried crumbs (see page 88) and/or bread sauce. A celery and apple salad is also another good accompaniment.

Spatchcock of Grouse with Almonds   Serves 4

4 plump young grouse, oven ready
1 clove garlic, crushed
1 tablespoon oil
3 tablespoons lemon juice
salt and pepper
75 g/3 oz/⅓ cup butter
50 g/2 oz/½ cup flaked almonds
grated rind of ¼ lemon
1 tablespoon freshly chopped parsley
fried bread triangles to garnish

1 Cut the grouse open along the backbone and press it out so that it lays flat with the flesh upwards. Rub lightly with garlic and then brush with a mixture of 1 tablespoon each of oil and lemon juice. Season with salt and pepper and leave to stand for 30 minutes.
2 Place the grouse in a grill pan lined with foil and cook under a moderate heat until well browned. Turn over and cook the other side, brushing with the marinade from time to time. The grouse should take about 15 minutes to cook through.
3 Meanwhile, melt the butter and fry the almonds until lightly browned. Remove from the heat and stir in the remaining lemon juice followed by the lemon rind, parsley and seasonings.
4 Arrange the grouse on a serving dish and spoon the almond butter sauce over the top. Garnish with triangles of fried bread and serve with a green salad.

WILD DUCK

The title of wild duck covers a wide variety of species of ducks. Of all the ducks that can be shot, the mallard is the largest and best known. The other well-known varieties are the teal and wigeon but these are much smaller and will only serve 2–3 people. Wild ducks should only be hung for 1–3 days and may in fact be eaten unhung. The flesh of all wild ducks is dry and virtually fat free, so great care must be taken when cooking them to see that they do not dry out completely. Roast wild duck should be served only barely cooked. This does not mean so underdone as to be raw, but the flesh should be tinged with pink; once overcooked it becomes so dry that the whole bird is spoilt. Wild ducks freeze well, but take care you don't freeze birds that have been feeding in marshy areas for they can pick up this marshy or fishy flavour which will intensify in the freezer and completely spoil the cooked bird.

Roast Wild Duck

Serves 2–6

2 wild duck (any variety), oven ready
butter
2 orange quarters
salt and pepper
a little port or orange juice (optional)
To garnish
watercress
orange wedges

1 Prepare the ducks and wipe inside and out. Truss lightly in a similar way to a domestic duck and place a knob of butter and piece of orange in the cavity of each bird. Season lightly, rub all over liberally with softened butter and place in a roasting tin.

2 Cook in a hot oven (220°C/425°F/Gas Mark 7) allowing 30–50 minutes for mallard, 30–40 minutes for wigeon and 20–30 minutes for teal or other small birds. Baste regularly and on no account allow them to overcook. Halfway through the cooking time, a little port or orange juice may be poured over the birds.

3 Serve on a warmed dish, garnished with watercress and orange wedges and serve with an orange salad and thin gravy made from the pan juices with the excess fat spooned off, or with a Bigarade sauce (see page 33).

Wild Duck with Ginger

Serves 6

2 wild ducks, oven ready
50–75 g/2–3 oz/¼–⅓ cup butter
salt and pepper
½ teaspoon ground ginger
1 bay leaf
1 clove garlic, crushed
4 dessert apples
4 tablespoons redcurrant jelly
2 tablespoons wine vinegar
2–3 pieces stem ginger, finely chopped
juice of 1 large orange
100 ml/4 fl oz/½ cup port or red wine
watercress to garnish

1 Brown the ducks in the melted butter in a large frying pan. Transfer to a roasting tin. Season the skins well with salt, pepper and ginger and then pour half the fat from the pan over the ducks.

2 Add the bay leaf and garlic and cover with foil. Cook in a fairly hot oven (200°F/400°F/Gas Mark 6) for about 40 minutes.

3 Peel the apples, remove the cores with an apple corer and cut in half. Fry the apples in the remaining fat in the pan until lightly browned and then place around the ducks. Return to the oven, uncovered, for 10–20 minutes or until the birds are tender and browned.

4 Melt the redcurrant jelly in the vinegar and keep warm. Remove the ducks to a serving dish and surround with the apples. Glaze both the ducks and apples with the redcurrant glaze and keep warm.

5 Skim the fat from the pan juices and add the chopped ginger, orange juice, port and any remaining redcurrant glaze. Bring to the boil and simmer for a minute or so, then adjust the seasonings.

6 Garnish the ducks with watercress and serve the sauce separately in a sauce boat.

VENISON

There are several species of deer, but really only three that are regularly eaten as venison. These are the red deer, fallow deer and roe deer. The red deer is the largest and said by some to be the only deer meat that should rightly be called venison. However, venison is the name given to all deer meat, and very good it is too. In recent years, deer farms have been springing up all over the country and this has helped to increase the supply of this popular meat.

Very young animals may be roasted and eaten almost unhung but, as with all meat, both the flavour and tenderness are vastly improved by them being well hung, and they should be hung for up to 2 weeks. Venison is a very dry meat and therefore needs all the help it can have, so lay extra fat over the joint and baste regularly.

Venison freezes extremely well because of its lack of fat and, in fact, I feel it is often improved by storage in the freezer. It is recommended to freeze it for only up to a year, but I have successfully kept venison in my freezer for over 2 years with excellent results.

ROASTING VENISON

The best joints to roast are the saddle, haunch or loin of venison. The haunch may be roasted on the bone or boned and rolled with stuffing added if liked. Remember all venison is virtually fat free so it needs plenty of dripping or oil to cook it in and rashers of fatty bacon or slices of pork fat tied over the joint. Venison joints may be marinated for 24–48 hours, if liked and indeed this is necessary if the venison is known to be over 18 months old. Young venison can be roasted quite satisfactorily without a marinade. Either roast in foil as it is, or pot roast adding wine, cider or stock to the roasting pan and covering with foil which is removed for the last 30 minutes of cooking.

To Roast a Venison Joint in Foil
Prepare the joint, add the stuffing, if to be used, and secure with string and/or skewers. Wrap rashers of streaky bacon around the joint and weigh. Place on a sheet of well-greased foil, spread some dripping or butter over the joint, season and close the foil. Stand in a roasting tin and cook in a hot oven (220°C/425°F/Gas Mark 7) allowing 30–35 minutes per 450 g/1 lb (depending on the depth of the joint). Fold back the foil for the last 30 minutes of cooking and baste the joint a couple of times.

To Roast Venison without Foil
Prepare the joint as above and stand in a roasting tin with plenty of dripping or oil over and around the joint. Cook in a fairly hot oven (200°C/400°F/Gas Mark 6) allowing about 30 minutes per 450 g/1 lb and basting very regularly.

Serve roast venison with a thickish brown gravy made from the pan juices, after the fat has been spooned off the surface, and flavoured with some of the marinade and/or red wine or port and redcurrant jelly. Also serve with redcurrant, cranberry or gooseberry jelly, and possibly braised chestnuts, and with a green vegetable and potatoes.

Marinade for Venison

1 carrot, peeled and sliced
1 onion, peeled and chopped
1 stick celery, sliced
6 black peppercorns
1 bouquet garni
450 ml/¾ pint/scant 2 cups red wine
3–4 tablespoons oil

1   Mix all the ingredients together. Place the venison in a large dish or bowl and pour the marinade over.
2   Cover with plastic cling film or a clean cloth and leave to marinate in the refrigerator or a cold place for at least 8 hours and up to 48 hours. Turn the joint several times while in the marinade.
3   Remove the venison and dry well before beginning to cook.

Venison Steaks with Curry Butter

Serves 4

4 venison steaks
salt and pepper
4 tablespoons oil
½ teaspoon ground coriander
2 tablespoons white wine vinegar
Curry Butter
100 g/4 oz/½ cup butter, softened
1 teaspoon coarse-grain mustard
1–2 teaspoons curry powder
good pinch of turmeric
1–2 tablespoons freshly chopped parsley

1   Put the venison steaks in a shallow dish and season well. Combine the oil, coriander and vinegar and pour over the steaks. Cover and leave to marinate for 2–3 hours.
2   For the savoury butter, put the butter into a bowl and gradually work in all the other ingredients. Shape into a roll, wrap in plastic cling film and chill until firm.
3   When ready to cook, stand the steaks on a foil-lined grill rack and cook under a preheated moderate grill or broiler for about 10 minutes each side, brushing the venison frequently with the marinade during cooking.
4   Serve immediately, topping each steak with two slices of curry butter. Boiled potatoes and a salad make good accompaniments.

Note: Venison steaks should be eaten immediately they are cooked for they tend to become hard and rather tough if made to wait for any length of time after cooking.

Pot Roast Venison

Serves 6

1.5 kg/3 lb venison, cut from the thick end of the haunch
300 ml/½ pint/1¼ cups oil
600 ml/1 pint/2½ cups white wine or white wine vinegar or cider
1 large onion, peeled and chopped
2 sticks celery, chopped
salt and pepper
1 teaspoon paprika
3 dried bay leaves, crumbled
a little flour
25 g/1 oz/2 tablespoons butter or margarine
To garnish
freshly cooked cauliflower florets and courgettes (zucchini)
watercress

1   Put the venison into a bowl. Put the oil, wine, onion, celery, seasonings, paprika and bay leaves into a saucepan and bring to the boil. Pour the hot marinade over the venison. Cover and leave to stand overnight in a cold place.
2   Drain the meat, dry off and then coat with flour. Heat the fat in a frying pan and fry the meat until well sealed and browned all over. Transfer to a casserole or roasting tin.
3   Add half the marinade plus the chopped vegetables to the venison and cover tightly. Cook in a moderate oven (180°C/350°F/Gas Mark 4) for 1½–2 hours or until tender.
4   Blend 1–2 tablespoons flour with a little water and use to thicken the rest of the marinade. Bring to the boil, add the juices from the pot roast and adjust the seasonings. Spoon off any excess fat from the surface of the sauce and strain into a sauce boat.
5   Place the venison on a warmed serving dish and arrange the cauliflower florets and courgettes around it. Garnish with watercress and serve.

WOODPIGEON

It is the woodpigeon, of the several varieties of pigeon that can be eaten, that tastes rather like game, but is not strictly classed as game – and there are no close seasons. Try always to find young pigeons to cook and, when they are plentiful, do not bother to pluck them, simply cut along the breastbone with a sharp knife and peel off the skin and feathers together so that the bird can be lifted out. The breasts alone may be removed in this way too, as there is really only flesh on the breast of the birds. Pigeons freeze well and are available widely both fresh and frozen. Allow a whole bird per portion, but if using only the breasts, then allow 1½–2 per person. Only roast very young birds, so if in doubt use for a casserole or delicious pie.

Pigeons Louisette   Serves 4

4 plump pigeons, oven ready
1 small orange, quartered
salt and pepper
8 rashers streaky or fat bacon, derinded
1 tablespoon oil
25 g/1 oz/2 tablespoons butter or margarine
1 large onion, peeled and chopped
1 tablespoon flour
6–8 tablespoons Marsala or red wine
300 ml/½ pint/1¼ cups stock
100 g/4 oz mushrooms, thickly sliced
6 juniper berries, crushed
3–4 tablespoons cream (optional)

1   Insert a piece of orange inside the cavity of each pigeon and season lightly all over. Lay 2 rashers of bacon over each bird and secure with cotton or fine string.
2   Heat the oil and butter in a frying pan and fry the pigeons until well browned all over. Transfer to a casserole.
3   Fry the onion in the same fat until beginning to brown, then stir in the flour and cook for 1 minute. Gradually add the Marsala or wine and stock and bring to the boil, stirring frequently.
4   Add the mushrooms and juniper berries to the sauce and season well. Pour over the pigeons, cover tightly and cook in a moderate oven (180°C/350°F/Gas Mark 4) for 1–1½ hours or until very tender.
5   Adjust the seasonings, stir in the cream (if used) and remove the birds to a serving dish. Take off the string or cotton. Put the sauce into a jug and serve with creamed potatoes and green vegetables.

HARE

Try to find a young hare if you want to roast it, otherwise it is better to 'jug' or casserole it to ensure it will be tender. Hare is cut into portions to casserole, but can be roasted or baked whole. The blood from the hare is caught in a container while the hare is hanging and this is used to thicken the sauce and add flavour, but it must not be allowed to boil once it has been added to the sauce or it will curdle. The hare should be hung for about a week before being skinned and paunched. More blood will be found between the membrane and the ribs. Hare can be bought frozen but will not then have the blood for thickening.

Jugged Hare   Serves 6

1 hare, skinned and jointed
300 ml/½ pint/1¼ cups red wine
4 tablespoons oil
½ teaspoon dried marjoram or oregano
1 onion, peeled and sliced
2 bay leaves
4 whole cloves
salt and pepper
3 carrots, peeled and sliced
3 sticks celery, sliced
1 bouquet garni
grated rind and juice of 1 orange
600 ml/1 pint/2½ cups good beef stock
15–25 g/½–1 oz/1–2 tablespoons cornflour (cornstarch)
2 tablespoons redcurrant jelly
4 tablespoons port or red wine
hare's blood (if available)
sprigs of parsley to garnish
Forcemeat balls
75 g/3 oz/1½ cups fresh breadcrumbs
1 onion, peeled and finely chopped
1 apple, peeled, cored and grated
2 sticks celery, finely chopped
grated rind of 1 lemon or orange
1 teaspoon lemon juice
1 egg beaten

1   Put the wine, 2 tablespoons oil, marjoram or oregano, onion, bay leaves, cloves and seasonings in a bowl. Add the pieces of hare, cover and leave to marinate for at least 12 hours, turning several times.
2   Remove the hare from the marinade and dry. Fry the pieces of hare in the remaining oil until browned all over. Transfer to a casserole.
3   Wipe out the pan, add the marinade, carrots, celery, bouquet garni, orange rind and juice, stock and seasonings to the pan and bring to the boil. Pour over the hare and cover the casserole tightly.
4   Cook in a moderate oven (160°C/325°F/Gas Mark 3) for 3–3½ hours until very tender.
5   For the forcemeat balls, combine all the ingredients and form into small balls about the size of a walnut. Place on a greased baking sheet and cook alongside the hare for the last 30 minutes of cooking time.
6   Discard the bay leaves, strain off the cooking juices and put into a saucepan. Thicken the juices with the cornflour blended in a little cold water. Add the redcurrant jelly and port and adjust the seasonings. Bring back to the boil, then blend a little of the sauce with the hare's blood (if available) and stir it back into the sauce. Do not allow to boil after adding the blood or it will curdle.
7   Pour the sauce back over the hare and serve garnished with the forcemeat balls and parsley.

RABBIT

This should not really appear at all in the game section, but there is no other place for it in this book, and in many game books it does appear because it can be cooked in many of the 'gamey' ways. Make sure you buy fresh young rabbit, otherwise buy frozen which should be good quality. Thaw it out slowly before cooking. Although rabbit is a cheap meat, it is extremely tasty and is increasing in popularity. Young rabbit can be roasted, but it is more usual to stew or casserole rabbit or make it into the famous Rabbit Pie.

Rabbit Pie
Serves 4–6

1 young rabbit (about 900 g/2 lb), jointed
225 g/8 oz collar bacon, derinded and chopped
450 ml/³⁄₄ pint/scant 2 cups stock or water
1 large onion, peeled and chopped
2 carrots, peeled and chopped
1 bay leaf
juice of ¹⁄₂ lemon
salt and pepper
25 g/1 oz/¹⁄₄ cup flour
1 tablespoon freshly chopped parsley
12 no-need-to-soak prunes
1 recipe quantity shortcrust pastry (see page 165)
beaten egg to glaze

1. Soak the rabbit in cold salted water for 2 hours, then drain and dry. Put into a saucepan with the bacon, stock, onion, carrots, bay leaf, lemon juice and seasonings. Bring to the boil, cover and simmer for ³⁄₄–1 hour until tender.
2. Remove the rabbit from the pan, strip off the meat from the bones.
3. Blend the flour with a little cold water, whisk into the cooking liquor and bring to the boil, stirring all the time. Adjust the seasonings and stir in the parsley, cooked rabbit and prunes. Pour into a pie dish and leave to cool.
4. Roll out the pastry and use to cover the pie dish (see page 164). Glaze with beaten egg, make a hole in the centre for the steam to escape and cook in a fairly hot oven (200°C/400°F/Gas Mark 6) for 20 minutes.
5. Reduce the temperature to moderate (180°C/350°F/Gas Mark 4) and continue for a further 20–25 minutes. Serve hot.

Rabbit with Mustard
Serves 4–5

1 rabbit, jointed
1 tablespoon flour
1 tablespoon dry mustard
2 tablespoons oil
25 g/1 oz/2 tablespoons butter or margarine
1 onion, peeled and sliced
150 ml/¹⁄₄ pint/²⁄₃ cup light ale or cider
300 ml/¹⁄₂ pint/1¹⁄₄ cups chicken stock
salt and pepper
1 tablespoon vinegar
1 tablespoon demerara sugar
1 tablespoon Dijon mustard
Topping
50 g/2 oz/1 cup fresh breadcrumbs
2 tablespoons oil
50 g/2 oz/¹⁄₄ cup butter
1 teaspoon snipped chives
1 tablespoon freshly chopped parsley

1. Wipe the rabbit over and then toss in a mixture of the flour and dry mustard. Heat the oil in a pan and fry the pieces of rabbit until well browned all over. Transfer to a casserole.
2. Add the butter to the pan and fry the onion until soft. Stir in the remaining flour and mustard mixture and cook for a minute or so. Gradually add the ale or cider and stock and bring to the boil, season well and add the vinegar, sugar and Dijon mustard and pour over the rabbit.
3. Cover the casserole and cook in a moderate oven (180°C/350°F/Gas Mark 4) for about an hour or until tender.
4. Meanwhile, fry the crumbs in a mixture of oil and butter until golden brown, stirring frequently, and mix, with the chives and parsley.
5. Remove the lid from the rabbit, adjust the seasonings and sprinkle with the crumb mixture. Serve at once.

Rabbit Pie and Pigeons Louisette (see page 93)

8 Fish and Shellfish

There are numerous types of fish available today, both fresh and frozen, from fishmongers, supermarkets and frozen food shops. And if you live near the coast there are usually opportunities to buy off the beach, which means the fish is straight from the sea!

Fish can be grouped in various ways and probably a simple method is into freshwater and sea fish and, of course, shellfish. These, apart from shellfish, can be broken down further into white fish and oily fish, flat fish and round fish. It may sound complicated but it really is not so.

White fish have a characteristic white flesh and low fat content with a high protein content. Obviously this makes it an ideal food for slimmers and those who need to be on a light or low fat diet, but white fish should not be disregarded in any way because of this – indeed some of the finest dishes are prepared from one or other of the better white fishes.

Oily fish as it suggests is much higher in fat and has a darker or coloured flesh. It is also a good source of vitamins A and D as well as being high in protein. Because it is called oily fish it does not mean it is unsuitable for those watching their diet; it is still a lot lower in calories and fat than many types of meat. It simply needs to be watched a little more carefully when used in diets.

Shellfish is a different category altogether, for most of the varieties are encased in some sort of horny shell or body. They are again low in calories, although rather more expensive to buy than white fish.

FRESHWATER FISH

SALMON (OILY)

Imported frozen salmon, especially from Canada, Norway and Alaska, are available all year but they are not so well flavoured or good textured as freshly caught fish. They can be bought as whole fish, pieces, steaks and cutlets. A whole fish should have a small head and broad shoulders with bright silvery scales and deep pink flesh when raw and on cooking this turns to a delicate pale pink. The size of the fish is no indication of its age, only that it has spent a longer time at sea feeding well. Salmon is best served simply cooked; its unique and delicate flavour should not be overpowered with other flavours.

TROUT (OILY)

There are several types of trout, the best known being rainbow and brown or river trout. The largest is the sea trout which is dealt with in the sea fish section. In all trout the flesh is delicate and, apart from sea trout which has a creamy-pink cooked flesh, the others are normally a pale cream. Individual trout are usually served with head and tail still intact but the eyes (which turn white when cooked) can be removed if preferred and filled in with a sprig of parsley.

Rainbow trout – these are available all year round fresh and frozen. Trout farms mainly stock this variety of trout and feed them on a diet containing shrimps which gives the flesh a pink tinge. The average length is 25–45 cm/10–18 inches but they more usually serve just one portion. Cook by grilling or broiling, frying, poaching or baking.

Brown or River trout – these live in rivers and mountain streams and are often thought to have a superior flavour to the rainbow trout. Sizes vary from 20–50 cm/8–20 inches in length and they may serve one or more portions depending on size, although in large lakes they can grow really big to about 7 kg/15 lb.

CARP (OILY)

This is a round fish which tends to have a slightly muddy flavour acquired from feeding off the muddy floors of streams. It is wise to soak it in salted water for 3–4 hours before cooking to help counteract any muddiness. Grill or broil or fry small fish, but bake larger ones, preferably stuffed.

PIKE (WHITE)

This fish has a fine flavour but it is best to use fish of around 900 g/2 lb – larger fish tend to be dry and rather tough. Cook carefully as the flesh breaks up easily and take care not to swallow any bones which are rather dangerous and do not dissolve in the stomach as many others do.

Other freshwater fish include perch, graying, char and freshwater eel.

SEA FISH

There are a great many of these, some of which are much more common than others. Fishmongers usually stock a fairly wide selection but will, of course, concentrate on the types that sell most easily. Sea fish fall into categories of flat or round fish. If you come across a fish you don't know, ask your fishmonger who will always be willing to tell you more about the fish he has for sale.

Flat Fish

These can again be categorized as small and very large fish. The small, such as sole, plaice, flounder, dabs, etc., are cooked whole or filleted while the very large fish (halibut and turbot) are cut into steaks or cutlets to cook.

SOLE (WHITE AND SMALL)

The best of the variety of sole is the Dover; other varieties include lemon, witch and Torbay. The flavour of the Dover sole is delicate and delicious and quite firm textured. The others are slightly inferior in flavour, but are still an excellent buy and much cheaper than the Dover sole. Sole can be obtained fresh or frozen all year round. They are good to grill or broil, fry, bake and steam and the fillets are often poached in flavoured stocks. Sole forms the base of many well-known fish dishes. Serve whole fish on the bone or remove the fillets after cooking. A sole is sufficient to feed 1–2 people – sizes do vary, so some of the larger lemon soles may feed more.

PLAICE (WHITE AND SMALL)

This fish is a favourite with many people. It has soft white flesh with a delicate flavour and is available all the year either fresh or frozen. Cook it whole or filleted by grilling or broiling, frying, baking, poaching, etc. Sizes vary from small to sufficient to feed 2–3 people.

DAB (WHITE AND SMALL)

This is a small member of the plaice family, only sufficient for one portion. Usually cooked on the bone, it can be cooked as for plaice.

FLOUNDER (WHITE AND SMALL)

This is similar to plaice but with not such a good texture; it can be substituted for plaice in any recipe.

TURBOT (WHITE AND LARGE)

This is described as the finest of the flat fish on the same level as salmon. It is usually cut into steaks and grilled or broiled, baked, poached or fried in many ways. The flesh is creamy white, firm and quite delicious, but it is rather expensive.

HALIBUT (WHITE AND LARGE)

Almost on a par with turbot, this fish also has a splendid flavour and texture. Sold cut into steaks, it is most often grilled or broiled, or baked, but can be cooked as for turbot and cod.

BRILL (WHITE AND LARGE)

Good-flavoured with a good texture resembling turbot but not such a high class fish and therefore cheaper. The flesh should be slightly yellowish – avoid anything that has a blue tinge, which means it is stale. Cook like turbot. Good served cold with mayonnaise.

Round Fish

BREAM (WHITE)

A good-flavoured fish with lean firm flesh and a delicate flavour, but very coarse skin. It can be poached, baked, grilled or broiled, fried, etc., and is also good boned, stuffed and baked.

BASS (WHITE)

Similar in shape to a salmon but with very white flesh. Can be small to cook whole and serve as one portion or large, when it is usually poached or baked. It has a good flavour, particularly the larger fish, and is very versatile in the ways it can be cooked.

HADDOCK (WHITE)

This has firm, white flesh and good flavour. Sizes vary from small to very large. Sold filleted, in cutlets, steaks and pieces. Cook as for any white fish.

COD (WHITE)

This is a large fish with good close-textured white flesh but with less flavour than some other white fish. Best cooked with flavouring ingredients. Sold filleted, in pieces, cutlets and steaks. Can be poached, grilled or broiled, fried, baked and is excellent for use in made-up dishes.

COLEY (WHITE)

A fish of the cod family with greyish flesh which turns white during cooking. It is good to cook with strong-flavoured ingredients. Best poached or baked with liquids, as the flesh tends to dry out if dry-cooked.

HERRING (OILY)

Fairly small with creamy-coloured flesh and a fairly strong distinctive flavour. Usually sold whole, but can be bought filleted. Normally grilled or broiled, fried or baked.

Herrings are also sold prepared in many other guises (see cured fish below).

HUSS (WHITE)

Also known as 'rock' or rock salmon. The flesh is firm with a slight pinkish tinge. Popular for deep-frying in batter and also good to cook with stronger-flavoured ingredients and vegetables. Always sold skinned.

MACKEREL (OILY)

This is rather larger than herring with creamy flesh and a strong individual flavour. It must be eaten very fresh. Cook either whole or filleted, in similar ways to herrings. Good filleted, stuffed and baked. Can also be smoked.

SEA TROUT (OILY)

Also known as Sewin and, rather incorrectly, as Salmon Trout. Similar to salmon but a less solid-looking fish in shape. When cooked it has a creamy pink flesh and thought by many to have a flavour equal to, if not finer than, salmon. Usually cooked whole, but can be cooked in pieces or steaks if a large fish. Sizes range from about 900 g/2 lb upwards. Poach or bake whole fish; small pieces may be grilled or broiled.

HAKE (WHITE)

Similar in shape and size to cod – the cooked flesh is closer-textured and better-flavoured than cod. Cook as for cod.

JOHN DORY (WHITE)

This has an excellent flavour and firm white flesh. It can be cooked whole, once the head and fins have been removed, by baking or poaching, but it is more often filleted and can then be cooked as for sole.

Filleting Fish (see page 100)

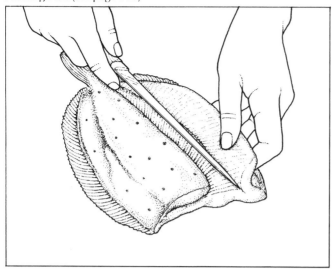

1   *To fillet a flat fish, cut off the head and make a cut down the back of the fish. Insert a knife at the tail end and using long smooth strokes cut the fillets from the bone.*

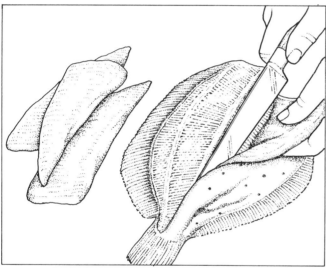

2   *Turn the fish round and take the fillet from the right side in the same way.*

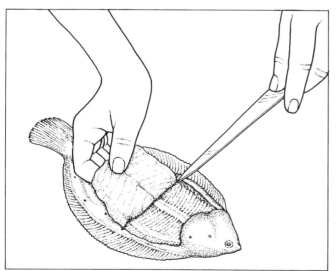

3   *For smaller fish, starting at the head end, ease the fillet away from the bone on either side of the fish to give two fillets only.*

MULLET (WHITE)

The red mullet is easily recognized by its red skin; the grey mullet is larger with coarser-textured flesh than the red variety, but has a good flavour. Bake, poach or grill or broil.

SARDINE (OILY)

These are really the young of pilchard or herrings and when available are excellent grilled or broiled or fried. In summer, fry them on the barbecue as they do in Portugal.

SKATE (WHITE)

A strange shaped fish with 'wings'. It is only the wings that are edible. Cook by poaching, frying or baking in a sauce.

WHITING (WHITE)

A fish of delicate flavour but rather a lot of small bones. Cook whole or filleted by any of the methods used for white fish.

WHITEBAIT (OILY)

These are the 'fry' or young of several types of fish, particularly herrings and sprats. They are very small and silvery and are served whole deep-fried; the whole fish, head and all, is consumed.

SPRATS (OILY)

A fairly small fish of the herring family. They are eaten whole after removing the entrails by making a cut with scissors just below the gills and pressing them out. Fry or grill or broil.

SMOKED FISH

Haddock, cod, herrings, mackerel and salmon are also sold in several ways after curing or smoking; some processes give their name to the fish.

HADDOCK AND COD

Finnan haddock – named after the Scottish village of Findon the fish are split open, lightly brined and then smoked. The fish tend to be straw coloured after smoking and turn a darker colour when cooked.

Smokies – Arbroath in Scotland used to provide 'THE' smokies but they are now widely produced. They are small haddock or whiting with heads removed and hot smoked, keeping the fish round and not split open. They are really ready cooked and just need careful reheating to serve.

Smoked cod or haddock fillets – these are often taken from large fish with large coarse flakes; the smaller fillets are best. They are brined and dyed a bright yellow before smoking.Cod has the skin removed, but haddock has it left on – as does whiting, which can also be found smoked.

Golden fillets or cutlets – these are small haddock with their heads removed, and are split and boned before brining, dying and smoking.

HERRINGS

Kippers – the best known of the smoked or cured herrings, these fish are split, brined and smoke-cured over wood chips. They vary tremendously depending on the area from where they come and the type of smoke-cure used. Available with the bones in, boned, or in fillets in boil-in-the-bags, fresh or frozen.

Bloaters – these are lightly smoked, dry salted herrings, which are left whole. As they are only lightly smoked they do not keep like most of the other smoked fish and should be used within 24 hours of purchase.

Buckling – this is a whole herring smoked for longer and at a higher temperature than kippers; the flesh thus becoming lightly cooked.

MACKEREL

These are smoked whole, split open and in fillets. They are ready to eat and do not need further cooking, although they can be added to other fish dishes for flavour.

SALMON

Scotch salmon is the supreme smoked salmon. It should be moist and of a good deep pink colour and is available in slices, trimmings, etc. Canadian and Pacific salmon tend to be much drier, are much cheaper and not of such good quality. Many fishermen have their own smoking equipment and some of the freshly caught home-smoked salmon are absolutely delicious. Available fresh and frozen.

PREPARING YOUR FISH

Before cooking any fish a certain amount of preparation is necessary – even if it is only washing and drying it after the fishmonger has done the main preparation for you. Sometimes fish are given as presents and need gutting and cleaning – it is not as difficult as you may think. And, depending on the type of fish, it may need filleting or boning or cutting up to freeze if it is too large to eat all at once.

TO CLEAN FISH

Remove any scales by using a knife and scraping the skin from tail to head, rinsing it under cold water frequently.

To gut a round fish, such as herring, trout, salmon, etc., either cut the head off first and make a slit along the abdomen to about halfway to the tail, then draw out the entrails scraping away any clotted blood with a knife. If there is dark skin inside, rub with a little salt to loosen, and then rinse under cold running water and dry. Or for fish such as trout that are more often served with the head still on, make a slit along the abdomen from the gills as before and slide out the entrails, etc. Rinse thoroughly, particularly the head. The eyes are usually removed but again for trout you leave them in place. They can always be removed after cooking if you wish.

Flat fish, such as plaice, sole, flounder, etc., usually have the heads cut off and then a small cut is made into the cavity under the gills and the entrails are scraped out. Wash thoroughly and dry. The fins and gills should be cut off if the fish is to be served whole and the tail may be trimmed or cut off.

Fillets and cutlets or steaks of fish should be rinsed in cold water and dried with an absorbent kitchen paper towel.

Cleaning and Skinning Fish (see page 100)

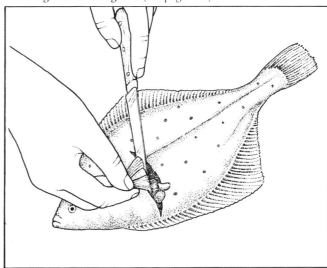

1   To *clean a flat fish, make a small cut into the cavity under the gills and scrape out the entrails.*

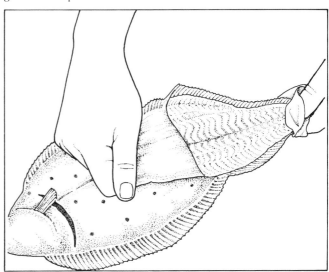

2   *Loosen the skin around the sides of the fish, then, holding the fish firmly, strip off the skin towards the head fairly sharply.*

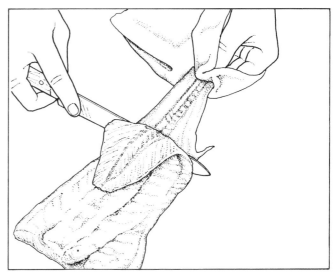

3   *To skin a fillet, hold the tail end of the skin very firmly, press a sharp knife firmly and flatly against the skin and gradually work it towards the head with a sawing action.*

TO FILLET FISH

Flat fish – four fillets are taken from these fish, two from each side. (See step-by-step illustrations, page 98).

1   Using a small, sharp-pointed knife (a filleting knife) cut off the head and then make a cut straight down the back of the fish to the bone.
2   Insert a knife under the flesh at the tail end of the fish and, using long smooth strokes, cut the fillet from the bone, keeping it as close to the bone as possible. It is easier to take the first fillet from the left side and then turn round and cut the right side in the same way.
3   Turn the fish over and complete the second side in the same way. The bone should be almost free of flesh.

Round fish

1   Cut along the centre of the back to the bone, using a sharp knife, and cut along the abdomen of the fish.
2   Working from head to tail and pressing the knife firmly down onto the bones, cut off the fillet from the bone, using short, sharp strokes.
3   Turn the fish over and remove the other fillet in the same way.

TO SKIN FISH

Whole flat fish (See step-by-step illustrations, page 99.)

1   Wash the fish and cut off the fins. Make an incision across the tail, slip the thumb between the skin and flesh and loosen the skin around the sides of the fish. A little salt on the fingers will help if it slips.
2   Holding the fish firmly on the surface with the other hand, strip the skin off the fish towards the head fairly sharply.
3   It is usually only the dark skin of flat fish that is removed although the white skin may also be stripped off in the same way if desired.

Fillets of fish

1   Lay the fillet of fish on a board or flat surface and hold the tail end of the skin very firmly with one hand.
2   Using a sharp filleting knife, place the knife at the tail end and, pressing the knife firmly and flatly against the skin, gradually work it towards the head with a sawing action. The fillet will gradually loosen from the skin. If the knife is at too sharp an angle to the skin, it will simply cut through the skin rather than slide along to loosen the fillet.

TO BONE A SMALL ROUND FISH

(See step-by-step illustrations, page 102).

1   Cut off the head, tail and fins. Split open by continuing the cut for gutting right down to the tail.
2   Put the fish onto a board, cut side downwards, and press at first lightly along the length of the backbone so the two sides of the fish splay out, one each side.
3   Press a little more firmly until you can feel the backbone loosening. Don't press too hard or the flesh will break up.
4   Turn the fish over and ease the backbone out with the fingers. Remove as many of the loose bones as possible, pulling out with a pair of tweezers if it helps.
5   If the fish contains a roe, this should be removed before taking out the backbone or it may well get squashed and spoilt.

POACHING FISH

This is a method sometimes referred to as boiling but that is incorrect for the water should only simmer very gently, or in fact 'shimmer'. Poaching can be done in a saucepan, frying pan or fish kettle on the hob or in a shallow covered container in a moderate oven (180°C/350°F/Gas Mark 4). The fish to be poached can be filleted, in steaks or cutlets or be small whole fish, including haddock and kippers, or larger pieces and whole fish that are traditionally poached, such as salmon and sea trout. The larger pieces and whole fish are usually cooked on the hob. The poaching liquid can be fish stock, milk, wine and water, etc., or a Court Bouillon, which is the traditional liquid used for poaching whole fish.

Heat the chosen liquid in a suitable-sized pan, gently lower in the fish – using strips of double foil to help manouevre it if a very large fish – and heat gently until it just returns to simmering. The liquid must cover the fish completely if it is a large whole fish. Cover the pan and simmer gently until just tender – allow 10–15 minutes per 450 g/1 lb. The thicker pieces will need the longer cooking time; a piece weighing say 675 g/1½ lb should only need 20–25 minutes. A knife can be gently inserted into the flesh to lift up a flake and ascertain if it is cooked. Do not overcook or the fish becomes dry and tasteless.

When ready, drain the fish thoroughly and place on a warmed serving dish. Serve with a sauce made including some of the cooking liquid or one of the sauces from the sauce chapter.

If cooking fillets of fish, they may be laid flat or folded or rolled up (known as *paupiettes*) and they need only be half covered with the cooking liquid. This cooking liquid should then be incorporated into the sauce, as it will contain a lot of the fish flavour.

Sole or Plaice Véronique   Serves 4

This is a classic fish dish of fillets cooked in a wine and cream sauce with green grapes. Flounder can also be cooked in this way.

---

8 fillets of sole or plaice
2–3 slices onion
1 carrot, peeled and sliced
½–1 bay leaf
a few sprigs of parsley
salt and pepper
150 ml/¼ pint/⅔ cup dry white wine
150 ml/¼ pint/⅔ cup water
100–175 g/4–6 oz green grapes
about 150 ml/¼ pint/⅔ cup milk
25 g/1 oz/2 tablespoons butter or margarine
15 g/½ oz/2 tablespoons flour
1 teaspoon lemon juice
3–4 tablespoons cream, double (heavy) or single (light)
sprigs of parsley to garnish

---

1   The fish may be skinned or not as preferred, but the dark skin of sole is usually removed. Either fold or roll up the fillets of fish with the skin inside and lay in a shallow ovenproof dish in a single layer.
2   Add the onion, carrot, bay leaf, parsley and seasonings

to the dish, combine the wine and water and pour over the top. Cover the dish with a lid or piece of foil.

3   Cook in a moderate oven (180°C/350°F/Gas Mark 4) for about 20–25 minutes or until the fish is tender.

4   Meanwhile, peel the grapes, cut in half and discard the pips.

5   Remove the fish to a serving dish and keep warm. Strain the liquid, measure and make up to 300 ml/ ½ pint/1¼ cups with more milk if necessary. Melt the fat in a pan, stir in the flour and cook for a minute or so to make a roux. Gradually add the cooking liquor and bring to the boil, stirring continuously.

6   Remove from the heat, stir in the grapes and lemon juice and adjust the seasonings. Simmer for 1–2 minutes longer, stir in the cream and pour back over the fish.

7   Garnish with the extra grapes and sprigs of parsley. Creamed potatoes and French beans or spinach make good accompaniments.

Halibut or Turbot with Prawns or Shrimp and Mushrooms   Serves 4

4 halibut or turbot steaks (about 175 g/6 oz each)
150 ml/¼ pint/⅔ cup dry white wine or cider
150 ml/¼ pint/⅔ cup water
salt and pepper
1 bay leaf
2 slices lemon
50 g/2 oz/¼ cup butter or margarine
25 g/1 oz/¼ cup flour
150 ml/¼ pint/⅔ cup milk
75 g/3 oz button mushrooms, sliced or chopped
50 g/2 oz peeled prawns or large shrimp
To garnish
4 whole prawns or large shrimp in shells
sprigs of parsley

1   Put the fish steaks in a frying pan. Add the wine and water, seasonings, bay leaf and lemon and bring to the boil. Cover the pan and poach for 10–15 minutes or until tender.

2   Remove the fish to a serving dish and keep warm. Boil the cooking liquor for a few minutes or until reduced to about 150 ml/¼ pint/⅔ cup in an open pan. Strain into a jug.

3   Melt 25 g/1 oz/2 tablespoons butter in a pan, stir in the flour and cook for a minute or so until bubbling. Remove from the heat.

4   Gradually add the cooking liquor and milk and bring to the boil. Simmer for a minute or so and season to taste.

5   Melt the remaining butter in a pan, toss in the mushrooms and cook for a minute or so, then add the prawns or shrimp and continue cooking until heated through.

6   Stir mushrooms and prawns and any liquor into the sauce, reheat gently and spoon over the fish.

7   Garnish with whole prawns or shrimp and parsley.

Court Bouillon (for poaching)

1.2 litres/2 pints/5 cups water or dry white wine and water mixed
1 carrot, peeled and sliced
1 onion, peeled and sliced
1 bay leaf
4–6 black peppercorns
1–2 slices lemon
2 tablespoons vinegar or lemon juice
1–2 teaspoons salt

1   Put all the ingredients into a saucepan and bring to the boil.

2   Cover and simmer for 20–30 minutes. Allow to cool if time allows.

3   Either use as it is or strain and use.

Poached Salmon   Serves 8–12

This method is good for poaching other fish too, such as sea trout, large fresh trout, bass, etc.

1.75–2.75 kg/4–6 lb salmon, cleaned
3 bay leaves
3.4 litres/6 pints/15 cups court bouillon (see above)
about 450 ml/¾ pint/scant 2 cups aspic jelly
To decorate
cucumber slices
stuffed green olives

1   Wipe the fish inside and out and lay the bay leaves along the inside of the fish.

2   Make the court bouillon (three times the recipe) in a fish kettle, preserving pan or the largest saucepan available. Do not strain. Have ready some extra boiling water.

3   Stand the fish on the tray from the fish kettle or strips of double foil. If to be curved, stand it upwards so the slit belly is flat on the table.

4   Carefully lower into the pan. Add extra boiling water so the fish is just covered. Bring back to the boil.

5   Cover the pan, turn down the heat and allow the water to just shimmer – fast boiling will break up the fish and toughen it. Cook, allowing 10 minutes per 450 g/1 lb.

6   Take off the heat and leave the fish in the water in a cool place until quite cold.

7   Remove the fish very carefully from the water and strip off the skin with the help of a small round-bladed knife. Put onto a serving dish and chill.

8   Make up the aspic jelly following the directions on the packet and leave until cold. Chill half of the jelly and when it begins to thicken brush it all over the fish.

9   Chill the fish and repeat the brushing with aspic twice more or until a glaze begins to form.

10   Dip slices of cucumber and stuffed olives into the liquid aspic and use to decorate the fish. When set, give a final coat of aspic all over and chill again.

11   Serve garnished with salad and accompany with boiled new potatoes and salads and either mayonnaise or Hollandaise sauce (see pages 35 and 36).

Boning a Round Fish (see page 100)

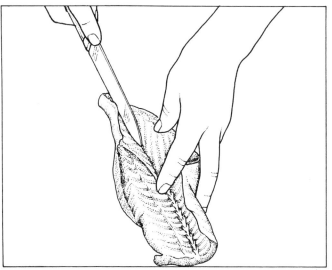

1 *Having cut off the head, tail and fins, make a slit along the abdomen right down to the tail.*

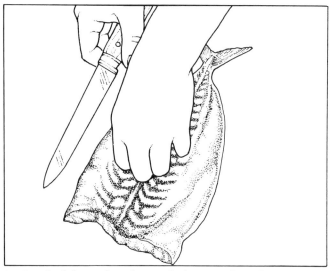

2 *Put the fish on a board, cut side downwards, and press along the length of the backbone so the two sides of the fish splay out.*

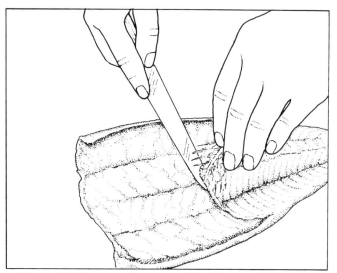

3 *Turn the fish over and ease out the backbone with your fingers.*

Fried Fish in Batter (see page 108)

1 *Make a well in the sifted flour and salt and add the egg and almost half the liquid.*

2 *Dip the fillets, one at a time, into the batter until evenly coated and slip straight into the hot oil.*

3 *Remove the fillets from the pan with a slotted spoon and drain on crumpled kitchen paper towel.*

OPPOSITE: *Orange and Watercress Salad and Chicory and Watercress Salad* (see page 145) *and Poached Salmon* (see page 101)

Bream Bonne Femme

Serves 4

This recipe can also be used for sole and plaice or flounder.

8 fillets of bream, skinned
1 small onion, peeled and finely chopped
100 g/4 oz button mushrooms
150 ml/¼ pint/⅔ cup dry white wine
150 ml/¼ pint/⅔ cup water
salt and pepper
1 bay leaf
a little milk
40 g/1½ oz/3 tablespoons butter or margarine
25 g/1 oz/¼ cup flour
2–3 tablespoons cream, double (heavy) or single (light)
To garnish
fried triangles of bread
sprigs of parsley

1 Wipe the fillets and either fold in three or roll up keeping the skin side inside.
2 Put the chopped onion into a large frying pan. Chop the mushrooms stalks and add to the pan. Put the pieces of fish on top.
3 Pour on the wine and water, season and add the bay leaf. Bring to the boil, cover the pan and simmer gently for about 15 minutes or until tender.
4 Remove the fish to a serving dish and keep warm. Boil the cooking liquor until reduced a little, then drain into a measuring jug and make up to 300 ml/½ pint/1¼ cups with milk.
5 Melt half the fat in a pan, add the mushrooms and fry gently for a few minutes. Keep warm.
6 Melt the remaining fat in another pan, stir in the flour and cook for a minute or until bubbling gently. Gradually add the liquid and bring to the boil, stirring continuously. Simmer for 2 minutes, then season to taste.
7 Stir the cream into the sauce, pour over the fish and garnish with the mushrooms and triangles of fried bread and sprigs of parsley.

GRILLING OR BROILING FISH

This is one of the more popular ways of cooking fish, especially steaks and cutlets and small whole fish. Trout, herrings, small plaice or flounder and sole, kippers, etc., all benefit from this method, but watch the lingering smell after grilling kippers! Filleted fish may also be grilled; it is probably best to line the grill tray or rack with foil and brush lightly with oil or melted butter before grilling. This will help prevent the fish sticking and mean at the end, the fishy smells can be folded up and discarded.

Wash and dry the fish and, if whole, remove the scales and cut off the fins. If it is a particularly plump whole fish (e.g. herring, mackerel), it is a good idea to make two or three diagonal cuts in the body flesh on each side to allow the heat to penetrate more quickly during cooking.

White fish such as plaice or flounder, sole, haddock, cod, halibut, etc. should be brushed with melted butter or oil to prevent drying out during cooking and placed in the grill pan; oily fish such as herrings, salmon and mackerel do not need extra fat. If on a diet, use lemon juice in place of oil and add extra during cooking. A little salt and pepper may also be added.

Thin fillets or steaks can be cooked on one side only but it is more usual to turn the fish halfway through cooking. Use a fish slice and/or palette knife or spatula and do so very carefully as fish are very fragile when cooked, especially flat fish.

Turn the grill or broiler on to moderate and allow about 5 minutes for thin fillets or 10–15 minutes for whole fish and steaks, turning these over halfway. Take care not to overbrown – burnt fish flesh is not very appetizing.

Serve hot topped with lemon wedges and a knob of butter or preferably herb butter (see below) or one of the sauces from the sauce chapter.

Herb Butter

50 g/2 oz/¼ cup butter
1 tablespoon freshly chopped parsley
grated rind of ½ small lemon
1 teaspoon dried thyme

1 Put the butter into a bowl and beat until soft.
2 Beat in the parsley, lemon rind and thyme until evenly blended.
3 Shape into a roll about 2.5 cm/1 inch in diameter, wrap in foil or plastic cling film and chill until firm.
4 Serve in slices laid on top of the fish or with grilled or broiled meats.

Note: Crushed garlic, ground black peppercorns and other available fresh herbs may be added for variation.

Grilled Halibut or Turbot Duglére

Serves 4

4 halibut or turbot steaks (about 175 g/6 oz each)
25 g/1 oz/2 tablespoons butter, melted
salt and pepper
Sauce Dugléré
25 g/1 oz/2 tablespoons butter or margarine
25 g/1 oz/¼ cup flour
150 ml/¼ pint/⅔ cup dry white wine or cider
150 ml/¼ pint/⅔ cup water
4 tomatoes
3–4 tablespoons cream, double (heavy) or single (light)
1 tablespoon freshly chopped parsley
sprigs of parsley to garnish

1 Trim the fish steaks, wash and dry. Place in a foil-lined grill pan, brush with melted butter and season lightly.
2 Cook under a moderate grill or broiler for about 15 minutes, turning the fish halfway and brushing again with melted butter.
3 Meanwhile, make the sauce. Melt the butter in a pan and stir in the flour. Cook for a minute or so until bubbling, then remove from the heat.
4 Stir in the wine and water and bring to the boil, stirring continuously. Remove from the heat.
5 Dip the tomatoes into boiling water for ½ minute and

then plunge into a bowl of cold water. Prick the skins which should split and peel off easily. Quarter the tomatoes, remove the seeds and chop the flesh roughly.

6   Add the tomatoes to the sauce along with seasonings and simmer for 2 minutes. Finally, stir in the cream and parsley and reheat gently without boiling.

7   Serve the fish on a warmed dish with the sauce spooned over and garnished with parsley. Courgettes (zucchini) or spinach and creamed potatoes are good with this.

Grilled Trout with Almonds   Serves 4

4 trout, cleaned (about 225–300 g/8–10 oz each)
25 g/1 oz/2 tablespoons butter, melted
salt and pepper
Sauce
40 g/1½ oz/3 tablespoons butter
50 g/2 oz/½ cup flaked almonds
2 tablespoons lemon juice
freshly chopped parsley to garnish

1   Wash and dry the fish and lay in a foil-lined grill pan, head to tail. Brush with melted butter and season.

2   Cook under a moderate grill or broiler for 7–10 minutes each side or until cooked through. Brush again with melted butter after turning the fish.

3   When ready, melt the butter for the sauce in a smallish saucepan. Add the almonds and fry slowly until the nuts turn a pale golden brown, stirring and/or shaking the pan frequently.

4   Remove from the heat, stir in the lemon juice and reheat gently. Season to taste.

5   Place the trout on a serving dish and spoon the almond sauce over the top. Sprinkle with parsley and serve.

BAKING FISH

This method is equally good for steaks, fillets and small whole fish as well as large fish, such as whole sea trout and salmon.

1   Wash and dry the fish and prepare as required. The fish may be stuffed if liked, either as a whole fish, with the bones removed, or wrapped up in fillets.

2   Put into an ovenproof dish with salt and pepper, a bay leaf or bouquet garni and about 4 tablespoons liquid (water, wine, milk, etc). Cover with a lid or foil.

3   Cook in a moderate oven (180°C/350°F/Gas Mark 4), unless otherwise directed in the recipe – large whole fish require a lower temperature – allowing about 10–20 minutes for fillets, 20–30 minutes for steaks, 25–40 minutes for small whole fish or until tender. Solid pieces of fish will need a little longer, but test after 30–40 minutes. The flakes should lift away easily when cooked if you insert a small palette knife or spatula.

4   Alternatively, wrap the prepared fish in buttered foil after adding seasonings, a squeeze of lemon juice and possibly a bay leaf and stand in a roasting tin or dish.

5   Bake at the same temperature, allowing about 25 minutes for steaks or 10–15 minutes per 450 g/1 lb for large pieces or according to the particular recipe.

6   Serve the fish with a sauce made using the juice that will have accumulated in the casserole or foil.

Salmon Steaks baked in Cream

Serves 4

4 salmon steaks (100–175 g/4–6 oz each)
1 onion, peeled and very finely sliced
1 tablespoon oil
1 tablespoon lemon juice
1 teaspoon Worcestershire sauce
salt and pepper
150 ml/¼ pint/⅔ cup single (light) cream
watercress to garnish

1   Wipe the salmon steaks and put into a lightly greased shallow casserole in a single layer.

2   Fry the onion gently in the oil until soft but not coloured. Stir in the lemon juice, Worcestershire sauce and seasonings and spread over the salmon.

3   Pour the cream over the steaks and cover the dish

4   Cook in a moderate oven (180°C/350°F/Gas Mark 4) for about 30 minutes or until the fish is tender.

Baked Stuffed Herrings   Serves 4

4 herrings or mackerel, cleaned and boned
1 onion, peeled and finely chopped
1 stick celery, finely chopped
2 tablespoons oil
1 dessert apple, peeled, cored and coarsely grated
grated rind of ½ lemon
good pinch of dried thyme
salt and pepper
50 g/2 oz/1 cup fresh breadcrumbs
1 egg yolk
150 ml/¼ pint/⅔ cup apple juice or cider
150 ml/¼ pint/⅔ cup milk
1½ tablespoons cornflour (cornstarch)
15 g/½ oz/1 tablespoon butter
lemon wedges to garnish

1   Wash and dry the fish and lay out flat, skin side downwards.

2   Fry the onion and celery gently in the heated oil until soft but not coloured. Add the apple and continue for a few minutes, stirring frequently. Remove from the heat. Stir in the lemon rind, thyme, seasonings, breadcrumbs and egg yolk and bind together.

3   Divide between the fish and spread over the flesh. Roll up the fillets from head to tail and secure with wooden cocktail sticks or tie loosely with thread.

4   Stand the fish in a casserole and pour the apple juice or cider over them. Season lightly.

5   Cook uncovered in a moderate oven (180°C/350°F/Gas Mark 4) for about 30 minutes or until cooked through.

6   Pour off the cooking liquor, make up to 150 ml/¼ pint/⅔ cup with water and put in a saucepan. Add all but 2 tablespoons of the milk and bring to the boil. Blend the cornflour with the remaining milk. Pour on the hot liquid and return to the pan. Bring to the boil, stirring continuously, and simmer for 2 minutes. Season to taste, add the butter and pour into a sauce boat.

8   Serve the sauce with the fish garnished with lemon.

Cidered Fish Casserole

Serves 4

675 g/1½ lb fillet of cod or haddock
2 tablespoons oil
1 large onion, peeled and thinly sliced
100 g/4 oz mushrooms, sliced
4 tomatoes, skinned and sliced (see page 17)
1 teaspoon dried thyme or oregano
salt and pepper
150 ml/¼ pint/⅔ cup cider (medium or dry)
Topping
3 tablespoons fresh breadcrumbs
25–40 g/1–1½ oz/⅓ cup grated Cheddar cheese

1 Wash the fish and remove the skin, if liked. Cut into four even-sized pieces and place in a lightly greased casserole.
2 Heat the oil in a pan and fry the onion gently for a few minutes until lightly browned, stirring occasionally. Add the mushrooms and continue cooking for a minute or so longer.
3 Spoon the onion mixture over the fish, cover with the sliced tomatoes and sprinkle with the herbs and seasonings.
4 Pour the cider into the casserole, cover and cook in a moderate oven (180°C/350°F/Gas Mark 4) for about 30 minutes or until the fish is tender. Remove the lid.
5 Combine the breadcrumbs and cheese and sprinkle over the fish. Put under a moderate grill or broiler until the topping is well browned. Serve at once.

SHALLOW-FRYING

This method is suitable for all types of filleted fish, steaks and cutlets and small whole fish that serve just one portion, such as sole, plaice, dabs, flounders, bream, cod, haddock, mackerel, herrings, trout, perch, pike, etc. Oil or lard is usually best, but to cook it 'à la meunière' (a special way of shallow-frying) the fat must be butter.

1 Prepare, wash and dry the fish and coat either in seasoned flour (add salt and pepper to about 50 g/ 2 oz/½ cup flour and roll the damp fish in it so it sticks) or in egg and breadcrumbs (beat an egg with 2 teaspoons water and seasonings and dip the fish first into this and then roll in bought golden breadcrumbs or freshly made white breadcrumbs, which may be made from stale bread, pressing them well in so they stick).
2 Put about 1 cm/½ inch oil or dripping into a frying pan and heat until fairly hot – not smoking hot, which will burn the fish without cooking it properly.
3 Put the fish in carefully so the side to be served facing upwards cooks first in the fat. Cook gently until the first side is browned – about 5 minutes, turn over very carefully using a fish slice and/or spatula and cook the other side for 5 minutes more or until cooked.
4 Remove from the pan with a fish slice or slotted spatula and drain on crumpled kitchen paper towel. Keep warm while frying the remainder.
5 Serve garnished with lemon wedges and parsley and with herb butter (see page 104).
6 To fry fish 'à la meunière', first shallow-fry it as above

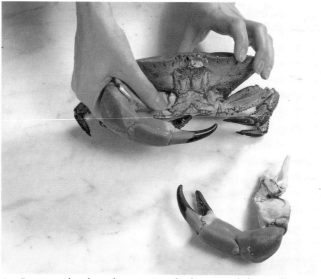

How to Dress a Crab (see page 113)

1 *Remove the claws by twisting clockwise and then pulling them free from the body.*

but using about 50 g/2 oz/¼ cup melted butter. Remove the fish to a serving dish and keep warm. Wipe the pan clean, add a further 25 g/1 oz/2 tablespoons butter to the pan and allow to melt. Add about 2 teaspoons lemon juice and pour over the fish. Sprinkle with freshly chopped parsley before serving.

Skate with Black Butter

Serves 4

Ask the fishmonger to prepare the skate by taking off the tough skin.

675–900 g/1½–2 lb prepared skate
1 recipe quantity court bouillon (see page 101)
about 3 tablespoons seasoned flour
1 egg, beaten
dried or fresh breadcrumbs
fat for shallow-frying
Black Butter
75 g/3 oz/⅓ cup butter
2 tablespoons wine vinegar
1 tablespoon capers
salt and pepper
1 tablespoon freshly chopped parsley

1 Put the pieces of skate into the court bouillon or salted water, bring to the boil, cover and simmer until tender – about 20 minutes. Drain and dry. Cut into pieces about 7.5 cm/3 inches wide.
2 Coat the fish first with seasoned flour, then dip into the beaten egg and finally coat in the breadcrumbs.
3 Heat about 1 cm/½ inch oil or lard in a frying pan and fry the pieces of fish for about 5 minutes each side or until golden brown. Drain on crumpled kitchen paper towel and keep warm.
4 Heat the butter in a small pan and cook gently until it turns a light golden brown. Quickly add the vinegar and capers and heat for a few minutes, shaking frequently. Season to taste and spoon over the fish. Sprinkle with parsley and serve at once.

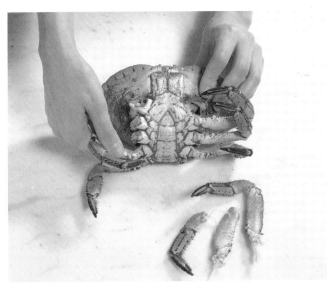

2   Tilt the crab until it is in a sitting position and then twist off the legs in the same way.

5   Having removed any white meat from the body shell, crack the legs and claws and ease out the white meat, then scoop out the dark meat from the main shell and put in a separate bowl.

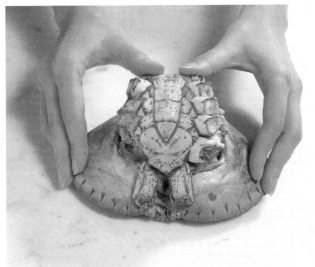

3   Holding the edge of the crab firmly with the fingers push up the centre part of the body.

6   Following the natural line, tap out the inside of the shell with a hammer.

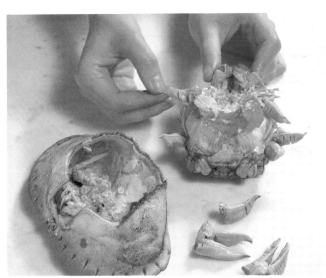

4   Discard the 'dead men's fingers' and remove the stomach sac.

7   Serve the prepared crab garnished with chopped hard-boiled egg white and sieved yolk, chopped parsley, cucumber and lemon.

DEEP-FRYING

The traditional British fish and chips are cooked by this method in a large pan of deep oil or fat. This method is easy to carry out at home provided you have a suitable pan for cooking. It should be a fairly large deep pan with a wire frying basket that fits inside or, alternatively, you can use one of the special electric deep-fryers, which are most efficient and very clean to use.

Cooking oil, lard or clarified dripping can all be used and the pan should be filled to half full – but no more for safety's sake. The fat must be free of moisture or it will spit during heating.

The oil should be heated to 177–188°C/350–370°F and the simplest way to test this is to fry a cube of bread which should take 50–60 seconds to brown evenly. Fat that is too hot will give an overcrispy brown outer coating with raw or partly cooked interior or, if too cool, the fish or whatever is to be fried will be soggy.

Coat the fish in egg and breadcrumbs or batter (see below) while the fat is heating. Do not cook battered fish in the basket, it will pull off during cooking; add carefully and lift out with a slotted spoon. It is most important to only cook a small amount at a time (e.g. 2 fish fillets) or the temperature of the oil will be lowered too quickly and not cook sufficiently. Electric fryers tell you when the oil temperature drops by a light coming on or off, provided you have set it at the correct temperature for what you are frying.

As soon as the fish (or whatever) is cooked, it should be removed from the oil with a slotted spoon or by lifting out the wire basket, allow the excess oil to drain back into the rest of the oil, then drain on crumpled kitchen paper towel. Serve as quickly as possible after cooking for the coating will become soggy if kept hot for long.

The oil can be cooled and strained into a clean bowl ready for future use. Oil will not keep indefinitely as it darkens with cooking and also becomes tainted with the food flavours, but straining after use will prolong its life.

Deep-frying can be used for all fillets coated with egg and breadcrumbs or batter as well as small whole fish, including sprats, sardines and whitebait, or for fish cakes, croquettes and aigrettes, etc.

Fried Fish in Batter   Serves 4

(See step-by-step illustrations, page 102.)

4 fillets of haddock, cod, whiting, plaice, skate, etc.
oil for deep-frying
Batter
100 g/4 oz/1 cup plain (all-purpose) flour
good pinch of salt
1 egg
150 ml/¼ pint/⅔ cup milk or milk and water mixed
lemon wedges to garnish

1   Wash and dry the fish. Put the oil on to heat to about 180°C/350°F or until a cube of bread will brown in 60 seconds.
2   For the batter, sift the flour and salt into a bowl and make a well in the centre (by pushing the flour up the sides of the bowl).

3   Add the egg to the well and almost half the liquid. Beat well, gradually incorporating the flour from the sides of the bowl, until smooth.
4   Gradually add the rest of the liquid, beating continuously until smooth.
5   When the oil is hot enough, dip the fillets, one at a time, into the batter until evenly coated and slip straight into the oil. Fry two at a time until golden brown and crisp. They should take 5–8 minutes and may need turning once.
6   Remove with a slotted spoon and drain on crumpled kitchen paper towel. Keep warm while frying the remainder.
7   Serve with wedges of lemon and tartare sauce.

Fish in Egg and Breadcrumbs

Serves 4

4 fillets of fish as above
oil or fat for deep-frying
a little flour
1 egg, beaten
golden breadcrumbs or fresh white breadcrumbs

1   Wash the fish and dry. Put the oil to heat as above.
2   Dip the fish first into the flour, shaking off any surplus. Next dip in beaten egg and finally coat evenly in golden or fresh breadcrumbs, making sure all the fish is covered – knock off any excess crumbs.
3   Put the coated fish in the wire cooking basket, lower into the fat and cook as above until golden brown and crispy.
4   Serve as above.

Note: The easiest way to coat fish in breadcrumbs is to either put the crumbs in a polythene bag, put in the fish and shake lightly until covered, or pour the crumbs onto a sheet of wax or greaseproof paper, foil or polythene and put the fish onto the crumbs, then turn over or flick the paper over again so the fish is evenly coated. Excess golden crumbs that are still dry can be put through a wire sieve and kept for future use.

Fried Whitebait   Serves 4 as a starter

450 g/1 lb whitebait, fresh or frozen
oil for deep-frying
flour
salt and pepper
To garnish
lemon wedges
sprigs of parsley

1   If using frozen whitebait, make sure they are completely thawed. Wash in cold water and drain very thoroughly. Put the oil on to heat until a cube of bread will brown in 60 seconds.
2   Put about 4 tablespoons flour into a polythene bag with a good shake of salt and pepper. Add a handful or so of the whitebait and toss around until evenly coated.

3 Shake off the excess flour (a sieve helps this process). Add to the hot oil, preferably in a wire basket, and fry for 2–3 minutes or until lightly browned.
4 Drain thoroughly on crumpled kitchen paper and keep warm while frying the remainder.
5 Sprinkle the whitebait lightly with salt and serve on individual plates garnished with lemon wedges and parsley and serve with thinly sliced brown bread and butter.

Note: For devilled whitebait, toss the fish in a mixture of 3 tablespoons flour, ½ teaspoon each of curry powder and dry mustard, ¼ teaspoon each of ground ginger and garlic salt, and a good shaking of black pepper.

Goujons of Sole   Serves 4

Goujons are strips of fillet of sole or plaice about 1 cm/½ inch wide and cut across the grain of the fillet. They are usually coated in egg and breadcrumbs (although it could be batter) and deep-fried. One or more flavoured mayonnaises are served as 'dips'.

4–6 fillets of sole or plaice or flounder (depending on size)
oil for deep-frying
a little flour
1–2 eggs, beaten
golden breadcrumbs or fresh white breadcrumbs
flavoured mayonnaises (see page 141)
lemon wedges to garnish

---

1 Cut the fillets into narrow strips. Put the oil on to heat.
2 Dip the goujons first in flour and then into beaten egg and finally coat in breadcrumbs.
3 Fry a few at a time for about 3–4 minutes or until golden brown and crispy. Drain on absorbent kitchen paper towel and keep warm while frying the remainder.
4 Serve with three or four mayonnaise dips, such as aurore, curry, horseradish and tartare, and garnish with lemon wedges.

COOKED FISH DISHES
There are numerous dishes that can be made using cooked fish in one way or another. These are just a few of the simple but popular ones. The fish for most of the dishes is cooked as follows: put the fish into a pan, barely cover with milk, water or a mixture of the two and a little salt and pepper. Bring to the boil, cover and simmer for 5–8 minutes until tender, then drain (reserving the liquor if needed). Skin the fish, flake roughly and remove any bones.

Fish Cakes   Serves 4

All types of fish can be used for fish cakes depending on your taste. Smoked fish gives a good flavour but white fish alone can be a little bland so it may be better to add a small amount of a well-flavoured fish too.

225–350 g/8–12 oz white fish (cod, haddock, etc.)
1 small fillet smoked mackerel (about 100 g/4 oz), or a
  90 g/3½ oz can tuna fish or salmon
450 g/1 lb potatoes
salt and pepper
25 g/1 oz/2 tablespoons butter or margarine
1 hard-boiled egg, finely chopped
1–2 tablespoons freshly chopped parsley
a little milk
1 egg, beaten
golden or dry breadcrumbs
oil or fat for frying

---

1 Cook the fish as above, then drain and flake, discarding the bones and skin.
2 Flake the mackerel, discarding the skin, or drain and flake the canned fish. Add to the white fish.
3 Peel the potatoes and boil in salted water until tender. Drain well and mash thoroughly adding seasonings to taste and the butter.
4 Add the fish, hard-boiled egg and parsley to the potato and work together. If on the dry side, add a tablespoon or so of milk.
5 Divide into eight and shape each piece into a round flattish cake on a floured surface. They should be about 7.5 cm/3 inches in diameter.
6 Dip in beaten egg and coat in breadcrumbs.
7 Heat either a frying pan with 1 cm/½ inch oil for shallow-frying or a pan of deep fat until a cube of bread browns in 60 seconds. Add the fish cakes a few at a time and cook until golden brown and crisp on the outside. Allow 3–4 minutes each side. Drain well on absorbent kitchen paper towel and serve with lemon wedges or with a sauce, such as tomato or parsley.

Note: If using all smoked fish, allow 350–450 g/¾–1 lb smoked fillet of haddock, cod or whiting and take care when adding extra salt.

ABOVE: *Baked Stuffed Herrings* (see page 105) *and Fried Whitebait* (see page 108)

OPPOSITE: *Coquilles St Jacques* (see page 115) *and Crab with Avocado* (see page 113)

Fish Pie

Serves 4

There are numerous ways of making a fish pie and the ingredients can vary widely. Here is a simple basic one to begin with; variations can easily be made as you go along.

450 g/1 lb any white fish fillets
150 ml/¼ pint/⅔ cup dry cider or water
a little water
salt and pepper
675–900 g/1½–2 lb potatoes
50 g/2 oz/¼ cup butter or margarine
150 ml/¼ pint/⅔ cup milk plus 3–4 tablespoons
50 g/2 oz mushrooms, chopped
3 tablespoons flour
2 tablespoons freshly chopped parsley
50 g/2 oz peeled prawns or large shrimp
40 g/1½ oz/⅓ cup grated Cheddar cheese

1   Cook the fish in a saucepan with the cider and sufficient water to barely cover and seasonings, as above.
2   Drain, reserving 150 ml/¼ pint/⅔ cup of the liquor, then flake the fish, discarding skin and bones.
3   Meanwhile, peel the potatoes and boil in salted water until tender. Drain well, mash thoroughly and beat in 15 g/½ oz/1 tablespoon butter and the 3–4 tablespoons milk to give a smooth spreading consistency.
4   Melt the remaining butter in a pan and fry the mushrooms briefly. Stir in the flour and cook for a minute or so. Gradually add the fish cooking liquor and milk and bring to the boil, stirring continuously.
5   Remove the sauce from the heat, season to taste and stir in the parsley, prawns or shrimp and flaked fish. Pour the mixture into an ovenproof dish.
6   Either spread the potato evenly over the top of the fish mixture or put into a piping bag fitted with a large vegetable nozzle and pipe all over the filling or in a wide border around the edge of the dish.
7   Sprinkle over the top with grated cheese and bake in a fairly hot oven (200°C/400°F/Gas Mark 6) for about 30 minutes or until piping hot and the top well browned. Serve hot.

Kedgeree

Serves 4

450 g/1 lb smoked haddock on the bone, or 350 g/12 oz
*   filleted smoked haddock, cod or whiting*
175 g/6 oz/1 cup long grain rice
salt and pepper
3 hard-boiled eggs
75 g/3 oz/⅓ cup butter or margarine
1 small onion, peeled and finely chopped
2–3 tablespoons freshly chopped parsley
3–4 tablespoons single (light) cream (optional)

1   Cook the fish in water or milk and water mixed for 5–8 minutes. Drain, discarding the liquor, and flake roughly, discarding skin and any bones.
2   Meanwhile, put the rice into a saucepan of boiling salted water, bring back to the boil, give a good stir, and simmer uncovered for 12–14 minutes or until just tender. Rice should be cooked until 'al dente', that is

just tender but still having a bit of a bite. Drain, rinse under hot running water and drain thoroughly.
3   Chop 2 eggs and slice the third.
4   Melt the fat in a pan and fry the onion gently until soft but not coloured. Toss in the flaked fish and heat through.
5   Add the chopped egg, seasonings and, finally, the cooked rice and toss over a low heat for a few minutes.
6   Either mix in the parsley and cream (if used) and turn into a warmed serving dish, or turn into the dish and sprinkle with parsley. Arrange slices of egg down the centre and serve.

SHELLFISH

Shellfish are popular with many people but are rather an expensive item. However, a little shellfish goes a long way and mixes well with other cheaper fish. Remember shellfish must be extremely fresh and, if bought frozen, should be consumed as soon as thawed, or cooked immediately.

CRAB
Available fresh, frozen or in cans. Crabs are usually sold ready boiled and most fishmongers will prepare and dress them ready for use. There are two very different edible parts of a crab: the white claw and leg meat and the brown body meat which consists of the liver and roe. Serve crab cold with salads or in cooked dishes.

LOBSTER
These are usually sold ready boiled when they turn a bright orange/red; they are black or grey when caught. Watch out for the claws if dealing with a live lobster! A very expensive shellfish but also available frozen and canned. Serve in one of the classic ways, e.g. Thermidor or Newburg, which involve removing the meat from the shell and claws, combining it with various sauces, etc., and returning it to the shell to complete cooking, often under the grill or broiler. A cold half lobster served with a good mayonnaise takes a lot of beating.

SHRIMP
These come in pink and brown varieties. Fresh shrimp are usually sold ready boiled but they are also popular when sold 'potted' in savoury butter to serve as a starter with toast. In Britain they are much smaller than prawns and far more tricky to peel, hence they are cheaper.

PRAWNS
Available fresh, ready peeled or in their shells, and also readily available frozen. They are more usually sold fresh ready boiled and still in the shells; if sold peeled, check whether they have already been frozen and thawed. Sizes vary widely depending on where they have been caught and from which country. Use cold in salad dishes or in many cooked dishes and sauces, but don't overcook as they have already been cooked once and they can become tough.

SCALLOPS
The scallop should look fresh with a whitish body and bright orange roe; do not buy those that look pale or greyish. They are sold on the flat shell or off – ask for the

rest of the shell too if you want it, although the fishmonger may make a small charge. They should come ready to cook with the black vein removed by the fishmonger. Poach, fry or grill or broil, after marinating.

MUSSELS

Take care if collecting mussels from around the local sea shores they may well be contaminated and will cause terrible tummy upsets. Available all year round, whether fresh, frozen without their shells or bottled. They must be alive when sold. A sharp tap on an open shell should make the mussel close; if it doesn't close tightly then discard as it is dead and consequently bad. Scrub thoroughly in several bowls of cold water to remove mud, sand and loose barnacles and pull off any weed. Use the same day they are bought if possible. If they have to be kept for 24 hours, put in a bucket of cold water with some oatmeal on top for food and keep in a cold place. Clean when ready to cook.

SCAMPI

Also called Norway Lobster, Dublin Bay Prawns, *langoustines* in France and *cigala* in Spain, this is a hard-shelled small crustacean related to the lobster. It is the peeled tail meat which we know as scampi. It is usually sold frozen.

COCKLES, WINKLES AND WHELKS

These are sold ready boiled. Cockles and whelks are already shelled but winkles may still be in the shell and will need a 'winkle-pin' to extract them. Usually served with vinegar. Also available frozen and bottled.

OYSTERS

Shells should be tightly closed when bought and the most popular way to serve is 'au naturel' or raw on the open shell. They must be alive when eaten or cooked or serious food poisoning will occur, so always buy from a reliable source. They can be cooked in various ways or added to other dishes such as Steak and Kidney Pie, New England Chicken or used in Angels on Horseback. Also available frozen and in cans, either plain or smoked.

CLAMS

Available all the year but best in the autumn. Sold live in the shell and eaten raw like oysters or cooked as for mussels. Can also be canned and smoked.

CRAWFISH OR SPINY LOBSTER

Similar to a lobster but it doesn't have the large fat claws. Prepared and eaten in the same way as lobster but there is much less flesh on it.

CRAYFISH

These look like miniature lobsters but come from fresh water. They vary in size from those small enough to use as garnishes to large enough to serve as lobster. They are simple to prepare: just remove the intestine tube from under the tail using a pointed knife, put into a pan of water, bring to the boil and simmer for 10–15 minutes.

HOW TO DRESS A CRAB
(See step-by-step illustrations, page 107.)
1   Lay the cooked crab on its back and remove the claws by twisting clockwise and pulling free from the body.

2   Tilt the crab until it is in a sitting position and then twist off the legs in the same way.
3   Put pressure on the back of the crab with the palm of the hand and at the same time pull out the pointed flap or 'apron' from the crab. (Or, holding the edge of the crab firmly with the fingers, push up the centre part of the body.)
4   The whole centre part of the body will then be free of the rest of the body. First discard the 'dead men's fingers', which are poisonous spongy cream-coloured sacs, and also take out the stomach sac from behind the head.
5   Using a skewer, remove any white meat from the body shell of the crab and put into a bowl.
6   Crack the legs and claws and ease out the white meat, then scoop out the dark meat from the main shell and put in a separate bowl. (If liked, following the natural line of the shell, tap out the inside of the shell with a hammer to give a larger opening.)
7   Wipe out the crab shell and brush the outside with oil if to be used for serving. Arrange the white meat on either side of the prepared shell.
8   Either mix the dark meat with 2 tablespoons white breadcrumbs or 2 tablespoons thick mayonnaise and spoon into the centre of the crab shell.
9   Garnish with chopped hard-boiled egg white and sieved egg yolk together with chopped parsley. Serve this prepared and dressed crab with salads. One crab will serve 1–2 people.

Note: The fishmonger will usually dress the crab for you at little extra cost.

Crab with Avocado   Serves 4

1 dressed crab
2 ripe avocados
lemon juice
4 spring onions (scallions), trimmed and chopped
2 tablespoons tomato ketchup
2 tablespoons thick mayonnaise
1–2 tablespoons cream or top of the milk
salt and pepper
To garnish
lettuce leaves
lemon slices
sprigs of parsley

1   Cut the avocados in half lengthwise and remove the stones.
2   Scoop out some of the avocado flesh, leaving a thickish layer all over the skin. Brush the interior of the avocado with lemon juice, then dice the flesh taken out and toss in lemon juice.
3   Mix the crab meat (white and brown) with the onions and avocado. Blend the ketchup and mayonnaise with cream and seasonings to taste and fold through the crab mixture.
4   Spoon back into the avocado shells, stand each on lettuce leaves on small plates and garnish with a slice of lemon and sprig of parsley.

How to Dress a Lobster

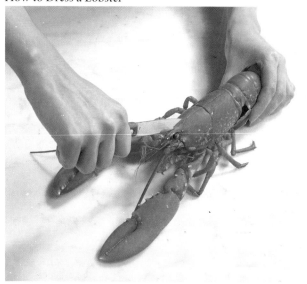

1   *Make a small cut between the eyes and shake out any excess liquid.*

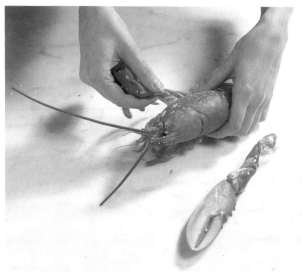

2   *Lift the head end and remove the claws by twisting them clockwise and pulling them away from the body. Twist off the legs in the same way.*

3   *Stretch out the lobster and cut right on down the central line of the tail to the end so it splits completely in two.*

4   *Remove the fine dark intestinal vein that runs towards the outer edge of the shell.*

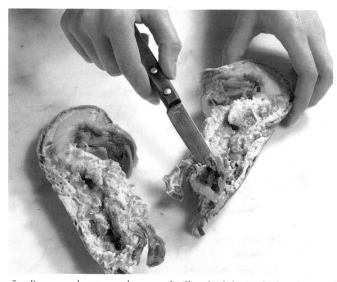

5   *Remove the stomach sac and gills which lie in the head part of the lobster.*

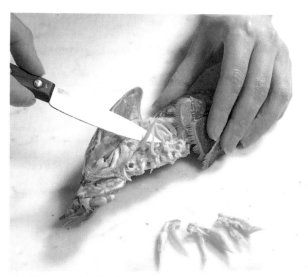

6   *Remove the 'dead men's fingers' from the upper part of the shell.*

7 Serve the prepared lobster garnished with lettuce, tomato, lemon and parsley and accompany by mayonnaise.

HOW TO DRESS A LOBSTER

Lobsters bought from fishmongers will be ready cooked.

1 Make a small cut between the eyes of the cooked lobster and shake out any excess liquid.
2 Lift the head end and remove the claws by twisting them clockwise and pulling them away from the body.
3 Lay the lobster down and twist off the legs in the same way.
4 Using a sharp knife cut into the body where it joins the tail and cut along the central line towards the head.
5 Stretch out the lobster and cut right on down the central line of the tail to the end so it splits in two.
6 Remove the fine dark intestinal vein that runs towards the outer edge of the shell.
7 Remove the stomach sac and gills which lie in the head part of the lobster. The green creamy part in the head is the liver and should be kept – it is a delicacy – and the spawn or red roe should also be kept.
8 If serving the lobster cold with mayonnaise, it is not necessary to remove the meat, but it should be loosened especially in the upper part of the shell so the 'dead men's fingers' can be discarded. Serve with lobster crackers for the claws and lobster picks to remove the flesh from the more fiddly parts. Alternatively, use a pair of nut crackers and a skewer.

Lobster Thermidor   Serves 2

1 large or 2 small cooked lobsters
50 g/2 oz/¹/₄ cup butter
1 tablespoon finely chopped onion
1 tablespoon freshly chopped parsley
1–2 tablespoons freshly chopped tarragon, or
  ³/₄–1 teaspoon dried tarragon
4 tablespoons dry white wine
300 ml/¹/₂ pint/1¹/₄ cups béchamel sauce (see page 33)
3 tablespoons grated Parmesan cheese
good pinch of dry mustard
salt and pepper

1 Split the lobsters in half and remove all the meat from the shells and claws, cutting the tail meat into slices.
2 Melt half the butter in a pan and fry the onion gently until soft. Add the parsley, tarragon and wine and simmer gently for 4–5 minutes.
3 Add the béchamel sauce, bring to the boil and simmer gently until thick and creamy. Add the lobster meat to the sauce with 2 tablespoons of the cheese, the remaining butter and mustard and seasonings to taste.
4 When piping hot, spoon the lobster mixture back into the shells, sprinkle with the remaining cheese and put under a moderate grill or broiler until golden brown. Serve at once with a salad or a selection of salads.

Coquilles St Jacques   Serves 4

8 large fresh scallops, or 225 g/8 oz frozen scallops,
  thawed
1 bouquet garni (see page 37)
150 ml/¹/₄ pint/²/₃ cup dry white wine
150 ml/¹/₄ pint/²/₃ cup water
salt and pepper
50 g/2 oz/¹/₄ cup butter
2 tablespoons finely chopped onion
100 g/4 oz button mushrooms, sliced
40 g/1¹/₂ oz/¹/₃ cup flour
2 tablespoons lemon juice
1 egg yolk
4 tablespoons single (light) cream
675 g/1¹/₂ lb creamed potatoes (see page 119)
2 tablespoons fresh white breadcrumbs
25 g/1 oz/¹/₄ cup Cheddar cheese, grated
To garnish
lemon wedges
watercress

1 Ask the fishmonger to open and prepare the scallops and to give you four deep shells.
2 Wash the scallops and put into a pan with the bouquet garni, wine, water and seasonings. Bring to the boil, cover the pan and simmer gently for 10 minutes until tender.
3 Drain the scallops, discard the bouquet garni and reserve the liquor. Cut each scallop into 1 cm/¹/₂ inch pieces.
4 Melt the butter in a pan and fry the onion gently for 2–3 minutes without allowing to brown, add the mushrooms and cook for a minute or so longer.
5 Stir in the flour, cook for a minute or two, then gradually add the cooking liquor and lemon juice and bring to the boil.
6 Simmer for 2–3 minutes, add the egg yolk blended with the cream and stir into the sauce with the scallops. Reheat gently and season to taste.
7 Meanwhile, pipe or spread the potato in a border around the edge of the scallop shells and put under a moderate grill or broiler until just beginning to colour.
8 Spoon the scallop mixture in the centre of the potato and sprinkle with breadcrumbs and cheese.
9 Replace under the grill and cook until a golden brown. Serve hot garnished with lemon and watercress.

Moules Marinières

Serves 4

Mussels are always sold fresh by the litre or pint, not in grammes or pounds. Frozen ones are sold by weight.

about 3.4 litres/6 pints/15 cups fresh mussels
50 g/2 oz/¼ cup butter or margarine
1 onion, peeled and finely chopped
½ bottle dry white wine
1 bay leaf
25 g/1 oz/¼ cup flour
150 ml/¼ pint/⅔ cup single (light) cream or milk
2–3 tablespoons finely chopped parsley
salt and pepper

1 Thoroughly wash and scrub the mussels, rinsing in several bowls of clean cold water and removing any barnacles, beards, mud and sand. Discard any muscles that are open and do not close when given a sharp tap.
2 Melt 25 g/1 oz/2 tablespoons butter in a large saucepan. Add the onion and fry very gently until soft but not coloured.
3 Add the wine and bring to the boil. Add the bay leaf and simmer for 2 minutes.
4 Add the mussels, cover the pan and simmer for about 10 minutes, shaking the pan frequently until the shells are all open.
5 Holding the mussels over the pan to catch the juices, break off the top shell of each and discard. Also discard any mussels that have not opened. Place the mussels on the lower shells in wide warm soup bowls and keep warm.
6 Discard the bay leaf from the cooking liquor and bring back to the boil. Cream the remaining butter with the flour and whisk it into the soup a small knob at a time. Simmer until thickened a little.
7 Add the cream and parsley and bring back to the boil. Season to taste, pour over the mussels and serve at once with plenty of hot crusty bread and a soup spoon.

Prawns or Shrimp Provençal

Serves 4

225–300 g/8–10 oz peeled prawns or large shrimp, thawed
*   if frozen*
3 tablespoons oil
1 onion, peeled and finely chopped
1 clove garlic, crushed
1 tablespoon tomato purée
2 teaspoons flour
425 g/15 oz can tomatoes, partly drained
4 tablespoons dry white wine
salt and pepper
pinch of sugar
dash of Worcestershire sauce
100 g/4 oz button mushrooms, sliced
225 g/8 oz/1⅓ cups long grain rice, boiled
freshly chopped parsley to garnish

1 Heat the oil gently in a saucepan, add the onion and garlic and fry gently until soft but not coloured, stirring frequently.
2 Add the tomato purée and flour and mix well.
3 Add the tomatoes, wine, seasonings, sugar, Worcestershire sauce and the mushrooms and simmer gently for 5 minutes, stirring frequently and breaking up the tomatoes.
4 Add the prawns or shrimp and heat through thoroughly, then adjust the seasonings.
5 Spoon the rice onto four plates making a well in the centre and spoon the prawn mixture into the well. Sprinkle with parsley and serve at once.

Note: Cook the rice in a large pan of boiling salted water for 12–14 minutes or until just tender, stirring occasionally, then drain, rinse under hot running water and drain again.

Scampi Risotto

Serves 4

225 g/8 oz scampi, thawed if frozen
175 g/6 oz/1 cup long grain rice
salt and pepper
1 tablespoon oil
25 g/1 oz/2 tablespoons butter
1 onion, peeled and thinly sliced
1 small green pepper, deseeded and chopped
100 g/4 oz mushrooms, sliced or chopped
200 g/7 oz can tomatoes
200 g/7 oz can sweetcorn kernels, drained
½ teaspoon dried basil
grated Parmesan cheese

1 Put a large saucepan of salted water on to boil. Add the rice and bring back to the boil, then simmer for 12–14 minutes, stirring occasionally, until tender.
2 Heat the oil and butter in a pan and fry the onion gently until soft. Add the pepper and mushrooms and continue cooking for 2–3 minutes.
3 Stir in the scampi, tomatoes, sweetcorn, basil and seasonings and simmer gently for about 10 minutes until most of the liquid has been absorbed.
4 Drain the rice, rinse under hot running water and drain again very thoroughly, then stir into the scampi mixture.
5 Stir until evenly mixed, heating gently all the time, and adjust seasonings.
6 Serve at once on warmed plates sprinkled with Parmesan cheese.

Note: Peeled prawns or large shrimp may be used in place of the scampi.

9 Vegetables

Although not strictly vegetables, beans and pulses, rice and pasta will be dealt with in this chapter as well as all the normal and more unusual varieties of vegetables.

Most vegetables are served as an accompaniment to the main dish but some are served in their own right as a starter (e.g. avocados, globe artichokes, asparagus, etc.) or as a light meal or supper dish (e.g. Cauliflower Cheese).

Vegetables play an important part in every diet for they are high in vitamins B and C as well as carotene and are good sources of iron and calcium. Another good point is the amount of fibre present, particularly when the vegetables are cooked and served with their skins still intact. Green leafy vegetables and potatoes are higher in vitamin C than other root vegetables.

It is important when preparing and cooking vegetables to remove as little of the valuable nutrients from just under the skin as possible, to cook them in the minimum of water, and to cook until only just tender so as to prevent losing all the nutrients. Overcooked vegetables tend to be flabby and uninteresting, pale in colour and spoilt in so many ways. No wonder many children dislike vegetables when all they know is the usually overcooked, stewed school cabbage. By cooking vegetables correctly we add a whole new dimension to eating, as is successfully pointed out by our vegetarian friends.

SELECTING AND STORING VEGETABLES

It doesn't matter whether you buy vegetables from a greengrocer or supermarket provided the produce is fresh and looks good. Do not be tempted to buy inferior produce because it is cheaper: the value is lost as is the flavour and it is not worth the extra effort required in preparation. Buy regularly and do not store any vegetable longer than necessary.

Root vegetables should stay fresh for 5–6 days if kept in a cool, dry well-ventilated place, preferably in a rack for this ensures air circulation. Green vegetables are best if used within 3 days, and spinach, in particular, is best used within 24 hours.

If vegetables are bought in polythene bags, either take them out or make large holes in the bag for ventilation. The same applies to vegetables covered with plastic cling film. Paper bags are best for storage of all vegetables (and fruit) for they are porous and do not cause sweating.

Vegetables should be prepared as near to the time of cooking as possible. Storing by soaking in water allows all the nutrients to seep out into the water which will be discarded even before cooking. Green vegetables can be wrapped in polythene to be chilled for several hours before cooking, but do not wash until just before cooking.

It is advisable to add boiling water to the vegetables for cooking or put the vegetables into boiling water, particularly green varieties. All frozen vegetables should be cooked in boiling water and not started off in cold.

Salt is added to most vegetables for flavour, but is by no means essential. However, if used, add about 1 teaspoon to 600 ml–1.2 litres/1–2 pints/2½–5 cups water. The exceptions to the salt rule are carrots and peas, which are better if the salt is added at the table.

SERVING VEGETABLES

1   Serve as soon as cooked: vegetables do not improve with keeping warm.
2   Do not overcook – they are better slightly underdone rather than overdone.
3   Always drain very thoroughly (reserving the liquor for gravy or a sauce if required) using a sieve or colander. With green vegetables, use a potato masher to squeeze out excess water. With very watery varieties, such as marrow (large zucchini), put a saucer upside down in the serving dish; this allows excess water to run to the bottom of the dish but keeps the vegetables out of it.
4   If frying vegetables, don't cover with a lid, as this will make them go soggy, and serve very hot.
5   Add a knob of butter to boiled and steamed vegetables just before serving.
6   Sprinkle with chopped parsley or other chopped fresh herbs both as a garnish and for extra flavour. Freshly ground black pepper and coarse sea salt can also be sprinkled over them, especially if they have been cooked without salt. Freshly ground coriander can also be used.
7   Some vegetables are enhanced by the addition of a white or cheese sauce just before serving. These are good with leeks, broad (lima) beans, celery, marrow (large zucchini), cauliflower, onions, carrots, small boiled potatoes, etc.

COOKING VEGETABLES

The main methods of cooking vegetables are as follows: boiling, steaming, roasting, baking, frying. Each vegetable is dealt with separately, with the main methods of cooking for each variety suggested along with several recipes. There are many other ways of cooking the vegetables but space restricts more ideas.

STEAMING VEGETABLES

Most vegetables are suitable for steaming, apart from those with a very high water content, such as tomatoes, cucumbers, mushrooms, etc., which are better cooked by other methods; red cabbage and peppers, which loose their texture and flavour; and root vegetables, which will take a very long time to cook this way unless chopped or sliced, when they are ideal. Any delicate vegetables, such as broccoli, leeks, chicory, cauliflower, asparagus, etc., are often better steamed than boiled for it is a much gentler method of cooking.

Below are a variety of steaming utensils available:

a) The simplest way to steam is to improvise with two soup plates put together to make a container which is then placed over a saucepan of gently simmering water.

b) Special steaming saucepans are available containing one or more saucepans with perforated bases which stand one on top of the other over the base saucepan with a lid on the top layer to keep in the steam; one or more of the layers can be used at a time.

c) A metal colander can be placed over a saucepan of water with a large lid or piece of foil over the contents.

d) The Chinese basket-work steamers build up into a tower and can be used with a wok or saucepan.

e) A double saucepan or boiler can be used for small amounts of vegetables provided some liquid is added; it will also double up for making sauces particularly the delicate ones, which are likely to curdle.

f) A plastic, glass or china basin covered with foil can be placed in a saucepan with boiling water coming half-way up the sides of the basin.

g) It is also possible to buy a custom-made metal steamer which is known as a flower and can be adjusted to fit in various-sized saucepans.

STEP-BY-STEP STEAMING

1 Put a saucepan on to boil with the steamer basket in position. Water should not come into contact with any steamer basket or the base of a saucepan, plate or container put on top of it. Only when steaming a basin (more often used for puddings) or using a closed steamer should water actually come up the side of it and then only halfway.

2 When boiling, put the prepared vegetables into the steamer, cover and bring back to the boil.

3 Turn the heat down immediately so that it is simmering gently, with steam still rising, but is not boiling madly.

4 Keep an eye on the water level and top up the pan with more boiling water as and when necessary.

5 If a large amount of vegetables are cooked at one time, it is a good idea to turn occasionally to ensure even cooking.

6 Prick the vegetables with a skewer or fork to test if they are tender in the centre – but do not leave until they are soggy.

7 Turn the vegetables into a warmed serving dish, top with a knob of butter and seasonings, if liked, and serve.

BOILING VEGETABLES

Use a pan of a size appropriate to the type of vegetables to be cooked. Take care to cook long enough but do not overcook or they will become soggy and uninteresting.

1 Put the desired amount of water into a saucepan with ½–1 teaspoon salt added if liked. Bring to a gentle boil.

2 Add prepared vegetables gradually and then bring back to the boil.

3 Cover the pan, reduce the heat so the water is just simmering and cook until the vegetable is just tender, testing with a skewer or fork.

4 Remove the pan from the heat and drain the vegetable into a colander or sieve over a bowl to catch the cooking juices. Use the juices to make a sauce or gravy, if liked.

5 If cooking a leafy vegetable, press out the excess water with a potato masher or the back of a spoon.

6 If still wet, return to a clean pan and stand briefly over a low heat, shaking continuously to dry off any remaining moisture.

7 Turn into a warmed serving dish, add butter and seasonings, toss gently and serve immediately.

Roasting, baking and frying will be dealt with under the individual vegetables.

ROOT VEGETABLES

POTATOES

This is the most versatile of all vegetables and can be cooked in numerous ways. There are various types of potatoes, roughly divided into whites and reds. Some varieties are said to be better for one method of cooking than others, and flavours do vary slightly, but in the end it is a matter of personal preference.

Potatoes bruise easily – buy in manageable amounts so they don't have to be stored for too long. Paper bags or sacks are best for storage; plastic bags cause sweating and they will soon go off and turn mouldy – always tip out of these bags and keep in a cool, dry dark place. Light causes them to turn green.

Peel potatoes as thinly as possible using a special potato peeler or a sharp, short-bladed knife. However, new potatoes and indeed small old potatoes can simply be scrubbed and cooked in their skins or with the skins peeled off (very easy) just before serving.

New potatoes are traditionally scraped – never peeled. Put straight into a pan or bowl of cold water to prevent discolouration. Potatoes may be cooked in cold water to start.

Allow 175–225 g/6–8 oz per portion.

Boiled – cut prepared potatoes into even-sized pieces, put into a saucepan with cold water to cover and ½ teaspoon salt per 450 g/1 lb potatoes. Bring to the boil, cover the pan, simmer gently until tender but unbroken. Allow 15–20 minutes for new potatoes and 20–30 minutes for old, depending on size. Drain well and turn into a serving dish. If liked, dot with butter and sprinkle with freshly chopped parsley or chives. Alternatively, coat in a parsley or cheese sauce.

Steamed – only suitable for small new potatoes or old potatoes cut into 5 cm/2 inch pieces. Allow about 30 minutes. Serve as for boiled.

Mashed – boil old potatoes in the usual way, drain and dry off in the saucepan over a gentle heat. Mash with a potato masher or fork.

Creamed – cook and mash as above and then beat in 25 g/ 1 oz/2 tablespoons butter and 3–4 tablespoons milk to each 675 g/1½ lb potatoes. Season well and beat until smooth and creamy. This process can be done in a food processor or with an electric hand whisk. Turn into a dish, mark the top with a knife or fork and sprinkle with chopped parsley.

Puréed – for piping potato it must be extra smooth. Either rub the boiled potatoes through a sieve or purée in a food processor until smooth and then beat in 50 g/2 oz/¼ cup butter to each 450 g/1 lb potatoes along with 1 egg yolk or whole egg or a little cream.

Baked Jacket – use even-sized potatoes. Scrub well and remove any 'eyes'. Either prick all over or cut a cross on one side. put in a fairly hot to hot oven (200–220°C/400– 425°F/Gas Mark 6–7) straight onto the shelves – no tin is necessary – and cook for ¾–1 hour for small potatoes or 1–1¼ hours for large ones or until soft when pinched. Either cut through the marked cross or cut a cross in each one and put in a knob of butter or a tablespoon of soured cream or mayonnaise.

Roast – use old potatoes – new ones do not roast in the same way – peel as usual and cut into even-sized pieces. Put into a saucepan of cold salted water, bring to the boil and simmer for 4–5 mintues. Drain well. Heat a roasting tin with about 100 g/4 oz/½ cup lard or dripping in it, add the potatoes and baste well. Bake in a hot oven (200–220°C/ 400–425°F/Gas Mark 6–7) for about 25 minutes or until beginning to brown. Turn over, baste again, and return to the oven for a further 20–30 minutes or until well browned and tender in the centres. Drain well and put into a serving dish. Potatoes may be roasted without parboiling, in which case increase the roasting time by about 10 minutes.They may also be roasted around the joint when little or no extra fat will be required.

Sauté – boil until barely tender and drain well. Cut into slices about 5 mm/¼ inch thick or dice. Melt about 5 mm/¼ inch butter, lard or oil in a frying pan and fry the potatoes until golden brown all over. Drain well and serve hot sprinkled with chopped parsley or chives.

French-fried or 'Chips' – use peeled old potatoes and cut into slices 5 mm/¼–½ inch thick and then again into strips the same width to give even-sized pieces. Soak in cold water for 30 minutes or longer (to remove excess starch). Drain well and dry thoroughly on a clean cloth (to prevent splattering in the oil). Heat a pan of deep deep fat or oil about half full to 190°C/375°F or until a chip dropped into the fat rises to the surface at once, surrounded by bubbles. Put prepared chips into the wire basket so it is only about a quarter full. Lower gently into the fat and cook for 6–7 minutes or until lightly coloured. Remove from the oil, drain off excess fat from the basket and turn the chips onto absorbent kitchen paper to drain. Cook the remainder of the chips in the same manner. Just before serving, reheat the fat as before and fry the chips for about 3–4 minutes or until crisp and golden brown. Turn onto absorbent paper towel to drain, then put in a dish, sprinkle lightly with salt and serve at once.

Game chips – prepare as above but cut into very thin slices. Fry as above but only for 3 minutes for the initial frying.

Duchesse Potatoes

Serves 4

450 g/1 lb potatoes
50 g/2 oz/¼ cup butter
1 egg
salt and pepper
grated or ground nutmeg

1   Peel, boil and drain the potatoes, then sieve, purée or mash very thoroughly.
2   Beat in the butter, egg, seasonings and a pinch of nutmeg until smooth.
3   Put into a piping bag fitted with a star vegetable nozzle and pipe out rosette shapes on a greased baking sheet, leaving about 2.5 cm/1 inch between each.
4   Bake in a hot oven (200–220°C/400–425°F/Gas Mark 6–7) for 25–30 minutes or until golden brown and crisp. Serve hot.

Note: Other shapes can be piped, including baskets, which can then be filled with cooked vegetables.

Almond Croquettes

Serves 4

450 g/1 lb potatoes, peeled and boiled
25 g/1 oz/2 tablespoons butter
1 egg
salt and pepper
1 egg, beaten for coating
25 g/1 oz/¼ cup flaked almonds, chopped
about 50 g/2 oz/1 cup fresh breadcrumbs
fat or oil for deep-frying

1   Sieve or smoothly mash the potatoes and beat in the butter, egg and seasonings.
2   Form into small rolls or balls and dip first into beaten egg and then roll in a mixture of chopped almonds mixed with the breadcrumbs.
3   Heat the oil or fat until a cube of bread browns in 40–50 seconds. Fry the croquettes a few at a time for 4–5 minutes until evenly golden brown. Drain on absorbent paper and serve at once.

Note: Croquettes may also be fried in hot shallow fat. They may also be cooked in a hot oven (220°C/425°F/Gas Mark 7) for about 30–45 minutes or until well browned.

Lyonnaise Potatoes

Serves 3–4

450 g/1 lb boiled potatoes, drained and thinly sliced
4 tablespoons oil
225 g/8 oz onions, peeled and thinly sliced
freshly chopped parsley

1   Heat 2 tablespoons oil in a frying pan and fry the onions gently until soft but barely coloured.
2   Add the rest of the oil to the pan and, when hot, add the potatoes. Fry gently, turning frequently, until the potatoes and the onions are golden brown and crisp.
3   Turn into a warmed dish and sprinkle with parsley.

JERUSALEM ARTICHOKES

Look for firm samples, not too knobbly or encased in mud. Store in a paper bag in a cool, dry place for up to a week. Scrub first, then peel carefully using a stainless steel knife or peeler, for they discolour easily. Plunge immediately into a bowl of cold water with the juice of a lemon added or 1 tablespoon vinegar. Do not leave to stand for longer than necessary before cooking. Cook in boiling salted water with a squeeze of lemon juice added for 15–20 minutes or until just tender. Drain well and serve either with a little melted butter and a sprinkling of parsley, or with a white or Hollandaise sauce (see pages 29 and 36).

Allow 175–225 g/6–8 oz per portion.

Scalloped Artichokes — Serves 4–6

675 g/1½ lb Jerusalem artichokes, boiled
1 small onion, peeled and sliced
1 tablespoon oil
300 ml/½ pint/1¼ cups cheese sauce (see page 31)
2 tablespoons fresh breadcrumbs
½ teaspoon dried mixed herbs
2 tablespoons grated Parmesan cheese

1 Slice the artichokes and lay in a fairly shallow ovenproof dish.
2 Fry the onion in the oil until soft and golden, stirring frequently. Add to the artichokes and mix lightly.
3 Bring the sauce almost to the boil and pour over the artichokes.
4 Combine the breadcrumbs, herbs and cheese and sprinkle over the top.
5 Either cook in a fairly hot oven (200°C/400°F/Gas Mark 6) for 20–30 minutes or until well browned, or put under a very moderate grill or broiler and cook slowly until browned.

PEPPERS

Peppers come in a variety of colours, the most common being green and red, but yellow, cream and dark purple are available during the late summer months. The flavour is strong and very distinct and can be rather overpowering, so they are more often used in conjunction with other ingredients or stuffed and baked. When buying, look for firm peppers without blemishes or bruises and store in a cool place or the salad drawer of the refrigerator for 3–5 days. Peppers should have the stalks cut off, then be cut in half lengthwise so all the bitter seeds can be discarded. The flesh is usually thinly sliced or chopped before use. Peppers can be fried in about 50 g/2 oz/¼ cup butter or margarine for about 10 minutes, stirring frequently until quite tender before serving. Some people prefer to skin the peppers before cooking. This is a bit tricky but the simplest way is to put the halved peppers under a moderate grill or broiler so the heat browns the outer skin until it turns black and cracks. This outer skin can then be peeled off leaving the flesh ready for use. Another way is to blanch the peppers in boiling water for 2 minutes and then drain. Plunge into cold running water until cold and drain again, then peel and cook as you like. Peppers can also be served raw or blanched in salads.

Allow ½–1 pepper per person.

Stuffed Peppers — Serves 4

4 peppers, red or green, or 2 of each
1 onion, peeled and chopped
225 g/8 oz streaky or fat bacon, derinded and chopped
100 g/4 oz/⅔ cup long grain rice, boiled
salt and pepper
½ teaspoon ground coriander
50 g/2 oz/¼ cup Cheddar cheese, grated
1 tablespoon grated Parmesan cheese
4 tablespoons fresh breadcrumbs
150 ml/¼ pint/⅔ cup stock

1 Cut the peppers in half lengthwise and discard the seeds. Lay in an ovenproof dish or roasting tin.
2 Fry the onion and bacon gently together in a frying pan with no extra fat added, stirring occasionally until soft.
3 Drain off any excess fat from the bacon mixture, then add the rice, seasonings, coriander and half the Cheddar and mix well.
4 Spoon the bacon mixture into the pepper cases. Combine the remaining Cheddar, Parmesan and breadcrumbs and sprinkle over the pepper fillings.
5 Pour the stock around the peppers, cover with a lid or greased foil and cook in a moderately hot oven (190°C/375°F/Gas Mark 5) for about 20 minutes or until the peppers are tender and the topping crisp and lightly browned.

BEAN SPROUTS

This traditional Chinese vegetable has become very popular and is simple to cook. It needs no preparation and adds plenty of new ideas to vegetable cooking and salads as well as Chinese dishes. Make sure you buy crisp, fresh looking punnets of the beansprouts and discard any brown sprouts. Store in a cool place or the salad drawer of the refrigerator and use within 48 hours, if possible. They are also available in cans.

Simply heat a couple of tablespoons of oil in a wide pan or wok, toss in the washed and drained bean sprouts and cook over a medium heat for several minutes until hot. Add a tablespoon of soy sauce if liked and serve.

Allow 75 g/3 oz per portion.

Bean Sprouts with Peppers and Mushrooms — Serves 4–6

175 g/6 oz bean sprouts
100 g/4 oz button mushrooms, sliced
3 tablespoons sherry
3 tablespoons oil
1 large onion, peeled and thinly sliced
1 red pepper, deseeded and thinly sliced
1 green pepper, deseeded and thinly sliced
½ teaspoon salt
1–2 tablespoons soy sauce
pinch of sugar

1 Soak the mushrooms in the sherry for at least 20 minutes.
2 Heat the oil in a frying pan or wok and fry the onion

gently until soft and lightly golden.

3 Toss in the peppers and continue cooking for about 3 minutes, stirring frequently.
4 Add the bean sprouts, the mushrooms and their soaking liquor, salt, soy sauce and sugar and cook for about a minute, stirring until well coated and hot.
5 Turn into a dish and serve at once.

OKRA OR LADIES FINGERS

This vegetable is grown in the Indies, America, India and Mediterranean countries and is probably best known for its inclusion in Gumbo's. It has a strange quality as it acts as a thickening agent when cooked. Okra should be young and fresh looking and a slightly murky pale green. They resemble small immature cucumbers of about 7.5–12.5 cm/3–5 inches long with the stalk end rounded and then tailing off to a point. Wash well and slice before adding to the chosen dish. The flavour is unique and an acquired taste.

Allow 75–100 g/3–4 oz per portion.

Okra Indian Style
Serves 4

450 g/1 lb okra, washed
2 large onions, peeled
75 g/3 oz/1/3 cup lard or margarine
3–4 cloves garlic, crushed
salt and pepper
2 teaspoons ground coriander
1/2 teaspoon turmeric
225 g/8 oz can peeled tomatoes
1 teaspoon freshly chopped mint, or
   1/2 teaspoon dried mint
1/2 teaspoon garam masala
freshly boiled rice (see page 134)

1 Slice one of the onions. Melt the fat in a pan and fry the sliced onion until soft.
2 Mince or purée the other onion in a blender or food processor and add to the pan with the garlic, plenty of salt and pepper, coriander and tumeric and cook gently for 5 minutes, stirring occasionally.
3 Cut the tops and tails from the okra and cut into 1 cm/1/2 inch slices. Add to the pan and mix gently. Cover the pan and simmer for 20 minutes.
4 Add the canned tomatoes and their juice, mint and garam masala and simmer for a further 10–15 minutes. Adjust the seasonings.
5 Serve with boiled rice and, if liked, poppadoms.
6 When serving as a vegetable, do not serve on the rice; the rice may be a separate accompaniment to dishes such as grills of meat or fried chicken or turkey pieces.

GARLIC

This is a bulb of the onion family and is, strictly speaking, more of a herb, but it is widely used in cooking and often put with vegetables and in salads. Each bulb is a collection of smaller ones which are called 'cloves'. It has a powerful acrid taste and pungent smell, so use sparingly; 1 clove garlic is usually sufficient for flavouring, although some special dishes, sauces and dressings call for more. A head of garlic should keep for up to a month in a cool dry place,

and cloves may be removed one at a time during this period without damaging the rest of the bulb. It will simply dry up when kept for too long or if stored in a warm atmosphere.

Peel the clove and then crush, either using a special garlic crusher or with the back of a heavy knife after slicing or roughly chopping; if it slips, sprinkle a little salt on the surface. Garlic may also be very finely chopped or finely grated. Always wipe the chopping surface quickly to prevent the smell from lingering. If the smell lingers on the breath, try chewing a sprig of fresh parsley – it helps remove the odour and any aftertaste from a heavily garlic-flavoured dish. Garlic is also available dried or minced or powdered or as garlic salt or pepper.

TOMATOES

Tomatoes are strictly a fruit but they are more usually found served as a vegetable or in a salad. They can be used for so many types of dishes, soups, sauces, casseroles, etc., as well as making a good vegetable accompaniment, requiring only a little cooking. The best flavoured ones are those freshly picked and eaten raw as a salad, but any type are suitable for cooking. Sizes vary enormously: there are the huge 'beef' tomatoes often weighing almost 450 g/1 lb each, which are good for baking and stuffing or slicing and frying. The normal tomato also varies in size and shape to some extent – often depending on the country where it was grown – and there are numerous varieties giving different flavours – some tomatoes are yellow when ripe, a very special variety. The increasingly popular tiny 'cherry' tomatoes, often from Holland, are very sweet and tasty and are good for garnishing many dishes as well as for using as a vegetable.

Raw tomatoes are widely used for garnishing dishes and they can be prepared in many ways (see Salads chapter). Many dishes call for peeled tomatoes. This is quickly and simply done by plunging the tomatoes into boiling water for a few seconds, then removing immediately to a bowl of cold water. When cool, the skins will split easily when pierced and can then be quickly peeled off. Another method is to impale the tomato on a fork and turn it gently over the flame from a gas cooker until the skin bursts and turns dark, then to peel it off with a knife.

Allow 1–2 per portion depending on size.

Grilled or Broiled – choose even-sized tomatoes and either cut in half or make a cross with a sharp knife just through the skin on the rounded end. Stand in a grill pan, cut side or cross end upwards, sprinkle lightly with salt and pepper and add a small knob of butter to each. Cook under a moderate heat for about 5 minutes, depending on size, or until soft. Do not overcook or they will become very soggy and sad-looking.

Baked – prepare as for grilling or broiling, although it is probably better to leave them whole. Stand in a shallow ovenproof dish and brush with melted butter, then season lightly, sprinkling with a few mixed herbs, if liked. Cover with buttered foil or wax or greaseproof paper or a lid and cook in a moderate oven (180°C/350°F/Gas Mark 4) for 15–20 minutes or until tender.

BEETROOT (BEET)

Look out for firm, heavy-feeling beet with few blemishes; don't buy flabby or soft specimens. Store raw in a paper bag or loose in a cool dry place for up to 5 days. Once cooked, keep unpeeled and unwrapped in the refrigerator for up to 4 days before use. Cut off the stalks at least 2.5 cm/1 inch from the root otherwise the beets will 'bleed' during cooking with all the colour ending up in the cooking water instead of in the vegetable. Wash thoroughly but take care not to damage the skins, or again they will 'bleed'. Cook in boiling water with salt added, if liked, until tender: the time depends on the size and age of the beetroot. Allow approximately 30 minutes for small early beets to 1½–2 hours for larger mature beets. If to serve hot, drain and peel at once – the skins just slide off – slice or dice and serve coated with white sauce. Baby beets can be served whole. To serve cold, leave in the water until cold then peel, slice or dice and place in a bowl with a little vinegar or French dressing (see page 140).

Allow 100–175 g/4–6 oz per portion.

CARROTS

Old and new carrots are dealt with in slightly different ways. They may be boiled or steamed. Store loose in a cool, dry place for up to a week.

New – trim off the leaves and either scrub or scrape lightly with a sharp knife. They are usually cooked whole by boiling. Carrots are sweet and some people prefer to cook without salt to keep the sweetness; if not, add a good pinch of both salt and sugar to the cooking water. Cook for about 15 minutes or until just tender – do not overcook. Serve tossed in melted butter, sprinkled with freshly chopped parsley.

Old – trim and pare off the skin very thinly. Cut into slices, dice or lengthwise strips. Cook as for new carrots but allowing 10–15 minutes for dice or strips of carrot and 8–15 minutes for sliced carrots depending on the thickness of the slices.

Carrots can also be served coated in parsley sauce.

Allow 100–175 g/4–6 oz per portion.

Glazed Carrots with Pineapple

Serves 4–6

450 g/1 lb carrots, peeled and cut into sticks
15 g/½ oz/1 tablespoon butter
200 g/7 oz can pineapple rings
salt and pepper
1 teaspoon sugar

1 Boil the carrots in unsalted water until just tender. Drain well.
2 Meanwhile, melt the butter in the pan, add 6 tablespoons of the pineapple juice, salt and pepper and sugar and bring to the boil. Boil until reduced by half.
3 Roughly chop the pineapple rings and add to the glaze. Heat through.
4 Toss in the carrots and shake about until evenly coated. Turn into a warmed dish and serve.

CELERY

Home-grown celery covered in soot has the best flavour of all, but it takes time to clean and prepare. Ready-cleaned celery and imported varieties (often quite a bright green) are much easier to deal with. Wrap unwashed and unbroken heads in newspaper and store in a cool, dark place for up to 5 days. If washed and dried, keep unwrapped in the refrigerator for up to 4 days. If cut apart, stand in a jug containing about 7.5 cm/3 inches of cold water. Celery can be cooked cut into 5 cm/2 inch lengths or sliced thinly, or cooked as trimmed hearts. Put into a pan of boiling salted water and simmer gently for 10–30 minutes, depending on the size of the pieces, until just tender. Small pieces of celery may be steamed, allowing about 15–20 minutes.

Drain the celery well and serve either tossed in melted butter with chopped parsley or fresh tarragon sprinkled over the top or coated in a white, parsley, cheese or Hollandaise sauce, or top with a mixture of fried breadcrumbs (see page 88) mixed with crisp fried and crumbled bacon rashers, or with 40 g/1½ oz/¼ cup roughly chopped walnuts or pecan nuts sautéed in 25 g/1 oz/2 tablespoons butter.

1 large head of celery will give 4–5 portions.

Celery and Carrots au Gratin

Serves 4–6

350 g/12 oz carrots
½ head celery
100 g/4 oz frozen peas (optional)
300 ml/½ pint/1¼ cups white sauce (see page 29)
½ teaspoon ground coriander
4 tablespoons fresh white breadcrumbs

1 Peel, trim and slice the carrots, cook in boiling water until tender.
2 At the same time, slice the celery and cook in boiling salted water until almost tender. Add the peas (if used) bring back to the boil and cook for a further 4–5 minutes.
3 Drain all the vegetables and mix together in a heatproof dish.
4 Bring the white sauce to the boil, add the coriander and pour over the vegetables.
5 Sprinkle with the breadcrumbs and put under a moderate grill or broiler until well browned and crispy.

CELERIAC

This is the root of the turnip-rooted celery and is an ugly knobbly ball but has a crunchy texture and slightly sweeter flavour than celery. It is a very underestimated vegetable. Store unwrapped in a cool, dry place for up to 2 weeks. Once cut, cover the cut surface only with plastic cling film or foil.

It needs to be peeled fairly thickly to get down to the true vegetable and small ones can be cooked whole, although they are more often diced or sliced. Boil or braise for the best results or serve raw (see Salads chapter).

Cook in boiling salted water or chicken or beef stock (using 1 stock cube) until quite tender – about 40 minutes to 1 hour. Either serve well drained and tossed in melted

Duchesse Potatoes (see page 119), Glazed Carrots with Pineapple and Crisply-fried Onion Rings (see page 125)

butter, or in a white sauce made using the cooking liquor, or with Hollandaise sauce, or puréed with 25 g/1 oz/ 2 tablespoons butter and plenty of black pepper beaten into it along with 2–3 tablespoons top of the milk or cream.

Allow 100–175 g/4–6 oz per portion.

Roast Celeriac
Serves 4–6

1 large head or 2 small heads celeriac
juice of ½–1 lemon
lard or dripping

1 Peel the celeriac and either cut into slices about 2 cm/ ¾ inch thick or cut into cubes of about 4 cm/1½ inches. Dip in lemon juice to prevent discolouration.
2 Either heat about 100 g/4 oz/½ cup lard or dripping in a roasting tin and add the pieces of celeriac, basting well, or arrange around the roasting joint and baste.
3 Cook in a moderate to fairly hot oven (180–200°C/ 350–400°F/Gas Mark 4–6) allowing about 45 minutes and basting at least once during this time.

FENNEL

Florence fennel is a light aniseed-flavoured bulb with solid white stems, a swollen base and feathery leaves. It is used as a vegetable and salad ingredient – the flavour of aniseed diminishes when cooked. It may be cooked in the same way as celery. Trim off the outer side skins and slice or dice together with the remainder of the bulb; alternatively, simply trim and either cut in half or into quarters and braise or poach ready to serve in a sauce. Reserve the feathery leaves to use as a garnish or chop and add to the sauce. Fennel makes a very good accompaniment to all fish dishes. Cook in salted water or a light stock, or braise in stock or milk with seasonings added to taste. A squeeze of lemon juice helps bring out the flavour.

Allow ½ head per portion unless very small then allow one each.

Braised Fennel with Olives
Serves 4

2 heads Florence fennel
300 ml/½ pint/1¼ cups chicken stock
salt and pepper
50 g/2 oz/¼ cup butter or margarine
finely grated rind of ½ small lemon
25 g/1 oz/¼ cup flour
12 black olives
chopped fennel leaves or parsley to garnish

1 Trim the fennel and cut each bulb in half or into quarters. Lay in a lightly-greased shallow ovenproof dish.
2 Bring the stock to the boil and pour over the fennel. Season, dot with half the butter and add the lemon rind.
3 Cover with a lid or foil and cook in a moderate oven (180°C/350°F/Gas Mark 4) for 45–60 minutes or until tender.

4 Drain off the cooking juices and make up to 300 ml/ ½ pint/1¼ cups again with stock, water or milk. Keep the fennel warm.
5 Melt the remaining fat in a small pan, stir in the flour and cook for a minute or so until bubbling.
6 Gradually add the cooking liquor and bring to the boil, stirring all the time. Add the olives and season to taste, then simmer for 2 minutes.
7 Pour the sauce and olives back over the fennel, sprinkle with chopped fennel leaves or parsley and serve.

KOHLRABI

This is a strange-looking vegetable with an enlarged stem resembling a turnip. It grows above the ground and has leaves on long stems that grow out of the vegetable at intervals on the top half of the vegetable only. The taste is similar to a mild turnip. It is green and purple and the leaves are curly. More often than not kohlrabi will be trimmed of stems and leaves before sale, otherwise they are rather unmanageable; look for young tender specimens. Peel quite thickly and cut into slices or cubes or, if very small, cook whole. Cook in boiling salted water for 30–40 minutes or until tender, depending on size, and serve simply tossed in melted butter and sprinkled with parsley or freshly ground coarse black pepper, or in a white sauce, or make into a purée or cream by mashing thoroughly by hand or in a food processor or mixer.

Allow 100–175 g/4–6 oz per portion.

Kohlrabi Fritters
Serves 4

225–350 g/8–12 oz kohlrabi
deep or shallow fat or oil for frying
Light fritter batter
125 g/4 oz/1 cup flour
pinch of salt
1 tablespoon oil
150 ml/¼ pint/⅔ cup cold water
2 egg whites

1 Peel the kohlrabi and cut into thin slices – about 5 mm/¼ inch or thinner.
2 If using deep fat or oil, put on to heat gently to 180°C/350°F.
3 For the batter, sift the flour and salt into a bowl and make a well in the centre of the flour. Add the oil and half the water and beat until very smooth.
4 Beat in the rest of the water gradually.
5 Just before required, whisk the egg whites in a clean, grease-free bowl until very stiff. Beat a tablespoon of the whites into the batter, then fold in the remainder evenly.
6 If using shallow fat, heat about 2 cm/¾ inch in a pan.
7 Dip the pieces of kohlrabi in the batter, one at a time, and add to the hot oil. Cook a few at a time until golden brown – about 3–5 minutes. It will be necessary to turn the fritters in shallow fat but may not be so in deep fat.
8 Drain on crumpled absorbent kitchen paper towel and keep warm in an uncovered dish while frying the remainder.

LEEKS

Leeks should look fresh and clean with dark green shanks and white bases. Keep in a cool atmosphere and use within 4–5 days of buying. They tend to be sandy and harbour mud between the layers. Remove coarse outer leaves and cut off all the tops and roots. Wash very thoroughly in cold water cutting through the centre to within 5 cm/2 inches of the base to ascertain all mud has been removed; alternatively slice thinly or into pieces about 2.5 cm/1 inch long, this makes washing much easier. Cook in boiling salted water for 10–20 minutes until tender, or steam thinly-sliced leeks, or sauté thinly-sliced leeks in butter.

Allow 1–2 leeks per portion depending on size.

Braised Leeks with Nutty Topping

Serves 4

6–8 leeks (depending on size)
25 g/1 oz/2 tablespoons butter or margarine
150 ml/¼ pint/⅔ cup stock
salt and pepper
a little ground coriander
Topping
25 g/1 oz/2 tablespoons butter
1 teaspoon oil
40 g/1½ oz/⅓ cup chopped walnuts, hazelnuts or almonds
3 tablespoons fresh breadcrumbs

1 Trim and thoroughly wash the leeks and lay side by side in a shallow ovenproof dish.
2 Dot with the butter, add the stock to the dish and season with salt, pepper and coriander.
3 Cover the dish and cook in a moderate oven (180°C/350°F/Gas Mark 4) for 40–50 minutes or until tender.
4 Meanwhile, make the topping. Melt the butter and oil in a pan, add the nuts and breadcrumbs and cook gently, stirring almost continuously, until evenly browned.
5 Spoon the nut topping over the leeks and serve.

ONIONS

Onions vary tremendously in size from tiny button to the huge Spanish onions; the flavours vary too from mild to very strong. The smallest onion is the 'cocktail' onion, often not much larger than a large pea, and it is used for cocktails and is sometimes violently coloured for use as a garnish or decoration. Shallots are smaller than the normal onion, have a stronger flavour than most onions and are widely used for pickling as well as for other dishes. The largest Spanish onions do in fact have a milder flavour than most English onions. Spring onions (scallions) are popular and are the bulb and leaves of a young onion, both of which are eaten; however, if the onions grow to maturity the green leaves are always discarded.

Peeling onions can cause a lot of tears. One theory is to peel them under water, another is to put sunglasses on, but whatever you do don't wipe onion-stained fingers near your eyes or you will surely need a handkerchief.

When buying onions, avoid any that are bruised or sprouting green shoots. They should be golden brown in colour with rustling skins, which show they have been well dried. Store in a cool dry dark place and use within a week.

There are numerous ways to cook onions to serve as a vegetable – for example, boiling, frying and baking – quite apart from all the main dishes that wouldn't be the same without the addition of onion.

Allow 100–175 g/4–6 oz per portion.

Agrodolce Onions

Serves 4–6

675 g/1½ lb button onions, peeled
3 tablespoons oil
6 tablespoons port
6 tablespoons red wine vinegar
2 tablespoons soft brown sugar
25 g/1 oz/¼ cup raisins
salt and cayenne pepper
freshly chopped parsley (optional)

1 Heat the oil gently in a frying pan and add the onions. Cook gently until they begin to brown, shaking the pan frequently or stirring them.
2 Add the port and vinegar and bring to the boil. Add the sugar, raisins, salt and a pinch of cayenne pepper and shake until dissolved and thoroughly mixed.
3 Cover the pan and simmer gently for 15–20 minutes or until the liquid is reduced to a syrupy glaze.
4 Turn into a serving dish and sprinkle with parsley.

Glazed Onions

Serves 4

450 g/1 lb button onions, peeled
salt and pepper
50 g/2 oz/¼ cup butter
2–3 teaspoons caster (superfine) sugar

1 Boil the onions in salted water until just tender – about 15–20 minutes – then drain well.
2 Melt the butter in a pan, add the onions and toss in the butter for 2–3 minutes.
3 Add the sugar and continue to toss in the mixture until evenly coated – about 2–3 minutes. Turn into a warmed dish and serve.

Crisply-fried Onion Rings

Serves 4

4 large onions, peeled
milk
flour
salt and pepper
fat or oil for deep-frying

1 Cut the onions into slices about 5 mm/¼ inch thick, then separate into rings.
2 Dip the onion rings in milk and then coat evenly in flour.
3 Heat the fat so that when an onion ring is dropped into the fat it immediately rises to the surface surrounded by bubbles. Gradually add some of the onion rings and fry until golden brown – 2–3 minutes. Drain on crumpled kitchen paper towel and keep warm in an uncovered dish while frying the remainder.

PARSNIPS

Parsnips should be firm and crisp and preferably not too encrusted in mud. Make sure there are no worm holes and store in a cool dry place either loose or in a paper bag – do not store in polythene unless dotted with numerous holes. Parsnips have the best flavour after the first frosts. Peel off the skin and cut off the top end. If small, leave whole or slice; if larger, quarter and remove the core if it is tough and then cut into dice or strips if you wish. Put into cold water until ready to cook. Boil and mash parsnips combined with potatoes for a delicious purée or topping to a Shepherd's Pie, or for special Duchesse Potatoes.

To boil, cook in boiling salted water for about 30 minutes or until tender. Drain thoroughly and serve tossed in butter with salt, pepper and a touch of nutmeg or ground coriander or coat in a white or parsley sauce (see pages 29 and 31).

Roast Parsnips   Serves 4

8 small or 4–6 large parsnips, peeled
salt

1   Cut the parsnips in half or quarters lengthwise and boil in salted water for 5 minutes.
2   Drain well and arrange around a roasting joint in the fat. Baste and cook for about an hour or until browned and tender. Baste when the meat is basted.
3   Alternatively, roast in a tin containing about 1 cm/½ inch hot oil or dripping in a hot oven (200–220°C/400–425°F/Gas Mark 6–7).

Parsnip Potato Purée   Serves 4–6

450 g/1 lb parsnips
450 g/1 lb potatoes
salt and pepper
50 g/2 oz/¼ cup butter or margarine
a little milk (optional)

1   Peel and dice the parsnips and potatoes and cook in separate pans in boiling salted water until tender. Allow about 20–30 minutes for parsnips and 15–20 minutes for potatoes. Drain thoroughly.
2   Combine the vegetables and mash very thoroughly until evenly mixed and smooth. Beat in the butter and seasonings to taste and, if a bit dry, add a little milk.
3   Turn into a serving dish and mark a design on the top with a fork or palette knife or spatula.
4   For piped parsnip potatoes, add the butter and an egg and beat well until smooth. If they are difficult to mash, first rub through a sieve before adding the butter, etc.
5   Cook as for Duchesse Potatoes (see page 119) or pipe on top of a meat or fish pie, etc.

TURNIPS

This is another good root vegetable which can be served in many ways. Buy firm heavy-feeling turnips and store in a cool, dry place for up to a week. Turnips tend to go mouldy inside if kept too long or if they are old. Peel fairly thickly to remove the tough skin and dice or slice – unless they are young turnips, which can be cooked whole. Boil in salted water for about 15 minutes or until tender – longer for whole ones. Toss in melted butter and serve sprinkled with parsley, or coat in a white, cheese or parsley sauce.

Allow 175 g/6 oz per portion.

SWEDES

This is a large root vegetable with a yellowish gold flesh and tough outer skin in shades of brown to almost purple. In Scotland swedes are called turnips or 'neeps'. Look for firm, crisp and heavy-looking swedes and store unwrapped in a cool, dry atmosphere.

Peel thickly and slice or dice before cooking in boiling salted water until tender, allowing 20–40 minutes depending on age. Drain and serve either tossed in butter or in a white sauce, or mashed well with salt, black pepper and nutmeg to taste. Alternatively, cut into a 4 cm/1½ inch cubes, parboil in salted water and roast in the fat around the roast for 45–60 minutes. Also good raw in salads.

Allow 100–175 g/4–6 oz per portion.

SWEET POTATOES

These are floury in texture and have a slightly sweet and perfumed taste. They are usually slightly elongated and the skins vary in colour from pale pink to deep purple. They are no relation to ordinary potatoes and originated in America where they are widely eaten in many ways including as a sweet when they are cooked with sugar and flavoured with spices. Look for firm potatoes; flabby ones will have been around for a long time. Peel and cut into cubes and cook in boiling salted water until tender – about 25–30 minutes. Serve as they are or tossed in butter, or mashed with butter, salt and pepper to taste. Sweet potatoes may be boiled for 5–10 minutes and then roasted around the joint for about an hour.

Allow about 225 g/8 oz per portion.

Glazed Sweet Potatoes   Serves 4

675 g/1½ lb sweet potatoes
salt
about 50 g/2 oz/¼ cup butter or margarine
2–3 tablespoons demerara sugar

1   Peel the potatoes and boil in salted water until almost tender, then drain thoroughly.
2   Cut into thick slices and lay in a greased roasting tin.
3   Brush with melted butter and sprinkle with sugar.
4   Bake in a hot oven (220°C/425°F/Gas Mark 7) for 15–20 minutes or until browned.

GREEN VEGETABLES

BEANS

There are many varieties of beans but the three main categories are broad (lima), runner (green) and French (snap). Each of these types has varieties that grow tall or stay as dwarf plants, and the beans, particularly the French varieties, vary in colour from the usual green to purple and yellow pods, which turn to green again when boiled.

BROAD (LIMA) BEANS

These beans should be crisp and strong; flabby ones are best avoided. Very young broad beans can be cooked in the pod either whole or sliced but are more usually shelled before cooking. Cook by boiling or steaming. Boil in salted water for 15–20 minutes or until tender and steam for about 20 minutes. When ready, drain and either serve tossed in butter or coated in a white or parsley sauce. They can also be served cooked and cold in salads. Store in newspaper in a cool, dry place for only a few days.

Allow 225–350 g/8–12 oz per portion.

Broad (Lima) Bean Gratiné

Serves 4–6

675 g/1½ lb broad (lima) beans, boiled
1 onion, peeled and sliced
1 tablespoon oil
6–8 rashers bacon, derinded and chopped
300 ml/½ pint/1¼ cups cheese sauce (see page 31)
25 g/1 oz/¼ cup grated Cheddar cheese
1 tablespoon grated Parmesan cheese
2 tablespoons fresh breadcrumbs

1 Fry the onion in the heated oil until soft but not coloured. Add the bacon and continue to fry until both the onion and bacon are golden brown, stirring from time to time. Drain off all the fat.
2 Toss the onion, bacon and beans together and add to the hot cheese sauce.
3 Turn into a heatproof dish and sprinkle with a mixture of the cheeses and breadcrumbs. Put under a moderate grill or broiler until an even golden brown.

FRENCH (SNAP) BEANS

These should be unblemished and crisp and snap easily; avoid flabby or limp beans. Store in the bottom of the refrigerator or a cool place for only a few days before use.

Top and tail the beans using a sharp knife or scissors and leave whole. Boil in salted water for 8–10 minutes or until barely tender or steam for 10–12 minutes. Drain well and serve topped with a knob of butter or herb butter (see page 104). They are also excellent served with a Hollandaise sauce (see page 36) and make a good salad ingredient. French beans may also be served hot topped with yogurt or soured cream or with French dressing spooned over them. Alternatively, fry some rashers of streaky bacon and crumble over the beans together with a finely-chopped hard-boiled egg.

Allow 100–175 g/4–6 oz per portion.

RUNNER (GREEN) BEANS

These should again be crisp and bright green; limp specimens are not good. Store in a cool place, preferably wrapped in newspaper, for only 2–3 days. Top and tail the beans and then 'string' by cutting the coarse strings from each side of the bean using a small sharp knife. Slice runner beans into thin slanting slices. Cook by boiling or steaming. Boil in salted water for 5–10 minutes or steam for 10–15 minutes. Drain and toss with salt and pepper and

butter. Fried almonds can be sprinkled over the beans before serving.

Allow 100–175 g/4–6 oz per portion.

BROCCOLI

There are three main types of broccoli, white, purple and green or calabrese. The white and purple varieties can be as small tight heads or small sprigs each with one or more tiny heads of white or purple. Most of the calabrese is imported and it is this type of broccoli that is available frozen.

Trim and cut away tough stalks, although with calabrese the stem should be quite tender and is cooked and eaten with the flowery head. Boil in salted water for about 10 minutes until still firm but tender; soggy overcooked broccoli is a waste. Broccoli can also be steamed, which preserves the very best of the flavour – allow 15–20 minutes. Reserve the cooking liquor for use in gravy, it is full of flavour and nutrients. White broccoli can be served as cauliflower with a white sauce or cheese sauce; the other varieties can be topped with butter or Hollandaise sauce.

Calabrese is sometimes called poor man's asparagus, it can be cooked and served as a starter in the same way as asparagus (see page 130).

Allow 175–225 g/6–8 oz broccoli per portion; 100–175 g/4–6 oz calabrese.

BRUSSELS SPROUTS

Buy bright green ones that are firm and tight. Discard yellowish ones. Remove wilted or 'wet' leaves before storing in a cool place in a paper bag, for 3–4 days.

Trim the sprouts, discarding discoloured leaves, and cut a cross in the stalks. Cook by boiling or steaming. If the sizes vary greatly, it is best to add the large ones first with the smaller ones put in 2–3 minutes later. Boil in salted water for 8–12 minutes depending on size, or steam (only the small tight sprouts) for 12–15 minutes. Drain thoroughly and serve tossed in butter with freshly ground black pepper or sprinkled with toasted or fried almonds.

Allow 100–175 g/4–6 oz per portion.

Brussels Sprouts with Chestnuts

Serves 4–6

450 g/1 lb sprouts, trimmed
225 g/8 oz chestnuts
about 300 ml/½ pint/1¼ cups stock
salt and pepper
40 g/1½ oz/3 tablespoons butter, melted

1 Either roast the chestnuts, after making a nick in each shell to prevent bursting, in the fire or on the solid hob of the cooker, then peel and keep warm, or put into a pan of cold water, bring to the boil for 5 minutes, then drain and peel the chestnuts removing both the tough outer skin and brown inner skin.
2 Put in a saucepan with stock to cover and seasonings and simmer in a covered pan until quite tender – about 30–40 minutes.
3 Cook the sprouts as usual in boiling salted water for 8–10 minutes or until tender. Drain well, mix the chesnuts and sprouts together and season.
4 Turn into a warmed dish and pour over melted butter.

CABBAGE

Several varieties are available: red, white, green and savoy. Cabbages should be plump and firm and always crisp, and feel heavy for their size. Make sure the outer leaves are not too badly bruised or damaged and that there are no deep cuts. Store in a cool place allowing only 2–3 days for green cabbage – the red and white varieties keep much longer, often up to 10 days. Cook by boiling or steaming or braising with other flavourings added. Red cabbage should be cooked as in recipe below.

Remove the coarse outer leaves, cut in half and remove the tough stem. Shred finely (or with some cabbages cut into wedges) and wash well. Cook rapidly in a small amount of boiling salted water in a covered pan for 5–10 minutes or until tender; crisp wedges will take 10–15 minutes. Alternatively, steam for 10–12 minutes. Drain well and serve topped with a knob of butter and a sprinkling of black pepper and/or grated nutmeg.

Allow 100–175 g/4–6 oz per portion.

Braised Red Cabbage   Serves 6

900 g/2 lb red cabbage
1 onion, peeled and thinly sliced
1 tablespoon oil
1 cooking apple, peeled and sliced
1 tablespoon brown sugar
salt and pepper
2 tablespoons vinegar
about 150 ml/¼ pint/⅔ cup water or stock

1 Fry the onion gently in the heated oil in a large saucepan until soft but not coloured.
2 Trim the cabbage, remove the stem and shred finely. Add to the saucepan with all the other ingredients.
3 Bring slowly to the boil, stirring well until evenly blended, then cover the pan and simmer gently for about 30 minutes.
4 Give the cabbage a good stir and add a little more boiling water if too dry. Cover the pan and simmer for a further 20–30 minutes or until very tender.
5 Alternatively, the cabbage mixture can be turned into a casserole and cooked in a moderate oven (180°C/350°F/Gas Mark 4) for 1–1¼ hours, stirring once or twice during cooking.

Note: This cabbage is excellent reheated so can be made earlier in the day or the day before.

CAULIFLOWER

Avoid limp leaves and florets or discoloured florets. Cauliflowers should always be crisp and brightly coloured, so don't buy bruised or sorry-looking examples. Store unwrapped in a cool place for 2–3 days.

Cauliflower is usually boiled, particularly if to be served whole, but when cut into florets it can also be steamed. Trim off the outer leaves and cut a deep cross in the stalk end. Cook stalk end downwards in fast boiling salted water which comes about halfway up the vegetable – for about 15–20 minutes, depending on size, or until tender. Florets of cauliflower will need only 8–10 minutes boiling

or about 15 minutes steaming. Drain and serve with a white, cheese or parsley sauce, or toss the florets in butter and sprinkle with chopped parsley and coarsely-ground black pepper. Florets may also be parboiled (see Kohlrabi Fritters, page 124) and fried.

A medium-sized cauliflower will serve 4.

Cauliflower Polonaise   Serves 4

1 medium-sized cauliflower
salt
6 tablespoons fresh breadcrumbs
40 g/1½ oz/3 tablespoons butter or margarine
1 hard-boiled egg
1–2 tablespoons freshly chopped parsley
paprika

1 Either cook the cauliflower whole or in florets in salted water until tender. Drain thoroughly and place in a serving dish.
2 Meanwhile, fry the breadcrumbs gently in the melted fat in a small pan until golden brown, stirring continuously.
3 Separate the egg and finely chop the white. Either rub the yolk through a fine sieve or grate finely.
4 Combine the breadcrumbs, egg yolk and white and parsley and sprinkle thickly over the cauliflower. Finally, sprinkle lightly with paprika and serve.

PEAS

Pea pods should be firm and plump and, as the season is so short for fresh peas, take advantage of them when they are around. Frozen peas are of course excellent and can be used and cooked in many ways to serve as a vegetable.

Split open fresh pea shells, remove the peas to a saucepan and discard the shells or use to make a delicious pea pod soup. Cover with boiling water, add about 1 teaspoon sugar and a sprig of fresh mint (if available) and cook until tender: young peas need 8–10 minutes, but larger and more mature ones may need 15–20 minutes; frozen peas need only 4–5 minutes. Peas are rarely cooked with salt, it is added after cooking if wanted; the sweetness of the peas is brought out by a touch of sugar, not salt. Drain peas well, discard the mint and toss with a knob of butter.

Allow about 225 g/8 oz peas in the shell per portion or 75 g/3 oz shelled, canned, bottled or frozen peas.

Peas à la Française   Serves 4–6

675 g/1½ lb peas, shelled
¼ lettuce, trimmed and finely shredded
6 spring onions (scallions), trimmed and sliced
sprig of fresh mint
150 ml/¼ pint/⅔ cup water
25 g/1 oz/2 tablespoons butter or margarine
2 teaspoons caster (superfine) sugar

1 Put all the ingredients into a saucepan and bring to the boil. Cover the pan and simmer very gently until the peas are tender – about 20 minutes.

2 Discard the mint and drain the peas thoroughly. Turn into a serving dish and add extra butter if liked.

MANGE-TOUT (SNOW PEAS)

These are pale delicate-green fleshy pods which are almost flat as the peas inside are not allowed to form much more than the size of a pinhead, and they are eaten whole. Simply top and tail and cook in the minimum of boiling salted water until just tender – about 5–10 minutes. They should still have a good 'bite' left in them. Mange-tout may also be steamed for about 10 minutes. Drain well, toss in melted butter and sprinkle with coarse sea salt and black pepper.

Allow 100–175 g/4–6 oz per portion.

SPINACH

There are various types of spinach, the main ones being the dark green variety with tough green stalks, which must be stripped off and discarded before cooking, and spinach beet or perpetual spinach, which has thick pale green or white stalks that are quite edible and are sliced up with the green leaves. Spinach harbours masses of mud and grit in its leaves and needs plenty of washing in clear cold water before cooking. Pack into a saucepan with a little salt and cook gently with only the water left clinging to the leaves after washing. Turn the leaves frequently until the water falls to the bottom of the pan and boils, then cover and simmer gently until tender – 5–10 minutes. Drain very thoroughly, using a potato masher to remove excess water, then toss with a knob of butter and add salt and pepper and a pinch of ground or grated nutmeg to taste. The spinach may be served left in leaves or be partly chopped or finely chopped according to taste.

Allow 175–225 g/6–8 oz spinach per portion.

CHINESE LEAVES OR CHINESE CABBAGE

These look like a cross between a very pale cos lettuce and a head of celery. They vary in size depending upon the country in which they are grown and some varieties have much curlier leaves than others, but they are all basically white-stemmed with pale green leaves growing from the stems. They are equally good cooked as a vegetable or in salads. The leaves keep well in a cool place or the salad drawer of the refrigerator for 7–10 days. Simply shred or slice the leaves and cook in the minimum of boiling salted water for about 5 minutes until tender. Drain thoroughly and toss with a knob of butter and freshly ground black pepper with a good sprinkling of freshly chopped parsley.

Allow 100–175 g/4–6 oz per portion.

SWISS CHARD

This is really two vegetables in one and is best cooked as such. The leaves are stripped off the broad rib-like stems and cooked and served as spinach. The stems, which are either white or purple, are trimmed with any stringy pieces stripped off and then cut into pieces 2.5–5 cm/1–2 inches long and cooked as for celery but with a little lemon juice added to the water to help keep the colour and add flavour. A cheese or parsley sauce may be added to the stems.

Allow about 175 g/6 oz leaves per portion and 2–3 stems per portion.

GREENS

This is a collective name given to all types of green vegetables, but also refers to a more loosely-packed type of cabbage with much smaller heads and a sweet nutty flavour. Spring or Cornish greens are most common but sprout tops and turnip tops, etc. are also known as greens. They should look fresh and crisp, with a good green colour and have tightly-packed heads. Store for only 1–2 days after purchase in a cool dry place wrapped in newspaper. Separate the leaves and cut off the tough base stem and any tough stems attached to the leaves. Wash thoroughly and shred roughly, then cook in the minimum of boiling salted water for about 10 minutes or until tender. Drain thoroughly, chop if liked and top with a knob of butter.

Allow 175–225 g/6–8 oz per portion.

OTHER VEGETABLES

AUBERGINES (EGGPLANT)

These are elongated smooth purple vegetables with a shiny skin. Choose firm, evenly-coloured samples without blemishes and store in a cool, dry place or the bottom of the refrigerator for up to a week. Aubergines are usually fried or stuffed and baked, or added to other mixtures of vegetables (such as for ratatouille) or casseroles. Aubergines are a watery vegetable and are better 'salted' before frying to extract excess moisture. To do this, trim the stem and any small leaves that surround it, wipe over and cut into slices. Layer in a colander or sieve with a generous sprinkling of salt between each layer and leave to stand with a weighted plate just touching the slices, for at least 30 minutes or until the moisture has come out. Rinse each slice under cold running water to remove the salt water and dry on absorbent kitchen paper towel. Aubergines are rarely peeled before cooking. Do not cut and leave to stand around before cooking as the slices or cubes will discolour.

Allow about 175 g/6 oz per portion.

Ratatouille   Serves 4–6

2 tablespoons oil
1 oz/25 g/2 tablespoons butter
2 onions, peeled and thinly sliced
1 clove garlic, crushed
1 small green pepper, deseeded and sliced
1 small red pepper, deseeded and sliced
1–2 aubergines (eggplant), diced
2 courgettes (zucchini), sliced
4 tomatoes, peeled and quartered
salt and pepper
freshly chopped parsley to garnish

1 Heat the oil and butter in a heatproof casserole and fry the onions and garlic until soft.
2 Add the peppers, aubergines, courgettes, tomatoes and seasonings and bring to the boil, stirring frequently.
3 Cover the pan and cook in a moderate oven (180°C/350°F/Gas Mark 4) for about an hour or until tender.
4 Stir well and serve sprinkled with parsley.

GLOBE ARTICHOKES

Artichokes should be a good green colour with tightly-clinging fleshy leaves and look fresh, not beginning to dry out, with the leaves beginning to open. They are usually served as a starter or first course but, if stuffed, make a good, light lunch meal. Serve hot with melted butter or Hollandaise sauce (see page 36); or cold with any type of dressing or mayonnaise, or stuffed with a delicate mixture of fish and/or shellfish, turkey or chicken, ham or tongue.

HOW TO PREPARE AN ARTICHOKE

1   Cut off the upper leaves of the artichoke and wash.
2   If liked, cut off a small amount of the tip off each leaf with kitchen scissors; this is not essential but makes the artichoke look marvellous when served.
3   Cut off the stem and trim it level with the base so that the artichoke will stand up firmly.
4   Cook in a large pan of boiling salted water, with the juice of ½ lemon added, for 40–45 minutes or until tender. Test for tenderness by inserting a skewer in the base of each artichoke.
5   Lift out of the water with a draining spoon and turn upside down so they drain thoroughly.
6   Serve hot with melted butter or Hollandaise sauce to dip the leaves in.
7   To eat the artichoke, pull off each leaf in turn with the fingers, dip the base of the leaf into the sauce or butter and put the base of the leaf between the teeth and pull of the edible fleshy part with the teeth.
8   Once all the leaves have been removed, cut off the central hairy 'choke' to expose the much prized artichoke heart. Use a knife and fork to eat the heart with the remaining dressing.

ASPARAGUS

Look for brightly-coloured, crisp-looking spears, don't buy limp flabby ones. Buy fresh to use within a day or two, store in a cool place or the bottom of the refrigerator. Take care not to damage the delicate heads of the spears.

HOW TO PREPARE ASPARAGUS

1   Cut off the woody ends of the spears and scrape the white part lightly, removing any coarse spines.
2   Tie the asparagus spears in bundles of serving portion size with fine string, keeping all the heads together.
3   Place the bundles upright in a deep saucepan of boiling salted water so the water almost reaches the tips. Cover the tips of asparagus with foil and simmer gently for 10–15 minutes until just tender.
4   Drain the asparagus thoroughly, untie the bundles and serve on a warmed dish each with a small bowl of melted butter or Hollandaise sauce (see page 36).
5   To eat, hold a spear by the stem end and dip the tip into the butter or sauce. Eat only as far down the stem as is tender. Discard the rest.

Asparagus may also be served cold with vinaigrette dressing or mayonnaise (see pages 140–1).

Note: Asparagus may be cooked lying flat in a saucepan but it is wiser to wrap the heads in foil first so they don't get damaged. Take care not to overcook as soggy or mushy asparagus heads spoil the dish.

Allow 8–12 spears per portion depending on size.

CHICORY

The chicory plant is grown in the dark to preserve the delicate flavour and prevent it from becoming too bitter. This keeps the heads almost white with a yellowish tinge to the tips of the leaves – if they are topped with bright green, the chicory is likely to be bitter. The heads should be crisp, firm and fresh looking. This vegetable is also used widely as a salad ingredient. To prepare for cooking, trim off the base and remove the core with a small sharp knife (this part may be bitter), remove any damaged outer leaves and wash but do not soak in water. Plunge into boiling salted water for 5 minutes to blanch, then remove from the water and drain. Return to a pan with the minimum of salted water, 25 g/1 oz/2 tablespoons butter or margarine, juice of ½ lemon and plenty of black pepper and simmer gently in a covered pan for about 20 minutes. Drain and serve sprinkled with chopped parsley or paprika.

Allow 1–2 heads per portion.

Braised Chicory   Serves 4–6

6–8 heads chicory, trimmed
salt and pepper
25 g/1 oz/2 tablespoons butter or margarine
good pinch of grated or ground nutmeg
3 tablespoons lemon juice
150 ml/¼ pint/⅔ cup chicken stock
1½ teaspoons cornflour (cornstarch)
2–3 tablespoons cream, double (heavy) or single (light)
freshly chopped parsley to garnish

1   Blanch the whole heads of chicory in salted water for 5 minutes and drain well.
2   If large heads, cut in half lengthwise, then lay in a well-greased shallow ovenproof dish and dot with the butter.
3   Combine nutmeg, seasonings and lemon juice with the stock and pour over the chicory. Cover with a lid or a piece of buttered foil.
4   Cook in a moderate oven (180°C/350°F/Gas Mark 4) for 1–1½ hours or until tender.
5   Blend the cornflour with 1 tablespoon water. Drain the cooking juices into a small pan, stir in the blended cornflour and bring to the boil for a minute or so. Add the cream, adjust the seasonings and reheat gently.
6   Serve the chicory with the sauce poured over and sprinkled with chopped parsley.

CORN ON THE COB

Choose the cobs when they are plump, well formed and have pale golden yellow kernels with pale watery green leaves. Cook while still fresh for they dry out quite quickly and loose their succulence and taste. To prepare, remove the outer green leaves and silky threads around the cob and trim the stalk. Put into a pan of boiling unsalted water (salt tends to toughen corn) and cook for 20–30 minutes, depending on size, or until tender. Drain well and serve with melted butter and plenty of freshly ground black pepper. Salt is best added to the butter.

Corn should be eaten with small fork-like holders that are stuck into either end of the cob, making it easy to lift the cob and dunk it in melted butter. Serve hot. The niblets may be cut off the cob for use in other dishes, but it is easier to buy frozen sweetcorn kernels or to use from cans.

Allow 1 cob per portion.

COURGETTES (ZUCCHINI)
Look for courgettes, with dark smooth skins, that are firm and unblemished; the smaller ones are better than those that have been allowed to grow on. Keep in a cool place or the salad drawer of the refrigerator and use within 3–4 days. They may be boiled, steamed, braised, sautéed and deep-fried. They are cooked with the skins still on, simply cut off tops and tails and wipe well. Either leave whole, if small, or cut into thin or thick slices or into sticks. Simmer in the minimum of salted water with a touch of lemon juice added for about 5 minutes, drain and toss in butter and chopped parsley.

Allow 100 g/4 oz per portion.

Buttered Courgettes (Zucchini) with Herbs
Serves 4

450 g/1 lb courgettes (zucchini), trimmed
salt and pepper
50 g/2 oz/¼ cup butter or margarine
2 tablespoons freshly chopped mixed herbs, or 1
    tablespoon dried mixed herbs
juice of ½ lemon

1 Slice the courgettes thinly and add to a saucepan of boiling salted water for 1 minute only. Drain very well.
2 Melt the butter in a pan, add the courgettes and toss in the butter for 2–3 minutes.
3 Add the herbs, lemon juice and a little seasoning and toss well until evenly cooked.
4 Turn into a serving dish and serve.

Courgette (Zucchini) and Tomato Bake
Serves 4

350 g/12 oz courgettes (zucchini)
4 tomatoes, skinned (see page 17)
1 onion, peeled and chopped
1 tablespoon oil
½ teaspoon dried basil
salt and pepper
40 g/1½ oz/⅓ cup grated cheese (optional)

1 Thinly slice the courgettes and tomatoes.
2 Fry the onion gently in the oil until soft but only lightly coloured. Add the herbs and seasonings.
3 Layer the courgettes, tomatoes and onion mixture in a greased ovenproof dish and cover with a piece of buttered foil.
4 Cook in a moderate oven (180°C/350°F/Gas Mark 4) for about 40 minutes or until tender. The dish may then be sprinkled with grated cheese and browned under a moderate grill or broiler.

Preparing a Globe Artichoke

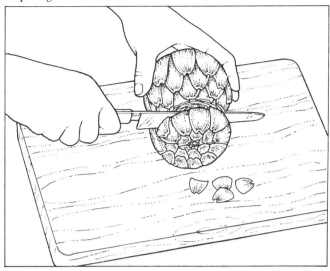

1 Cut off the upper leaves of the artichoke and wash it.

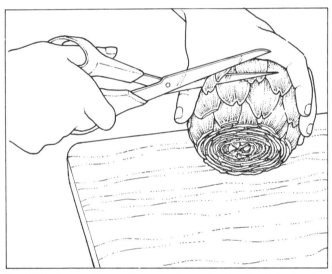

2 If liked, cut off a small amount from the tip of each leaf with kitchen scissors.

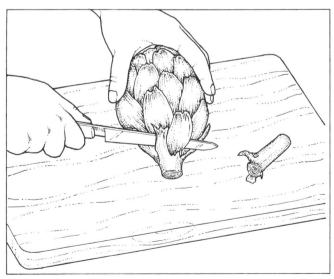

3 Cut off the stem and trim it level with the base so that the artichoke will stand up firmly.

MARROW (LARGE ZUCCHINI)

The skin should be smooth and unblemished and, when ripe, a fingernail should be able to pierce the skin easily. Store in a cool place and use within a week. Marrows should be peeled with the seeds discarded and the flesh cut into even-sized pieces. Cook in the minimum of boiling salted water until just tender – 10–20 minutes. Drain very thoroughly, putting an upturned saucer in the bottom of the serving dish if the marrow still seems wet. Serve as it is or coated with a white, cheese or parsley sauce. Marrow may also be steamed, when it will take 15–20 minutes to cook, or fried in about 25 g/1 oz/2 tablespoons butter or margarine, with no extra liquid added, in a covered pan on a low heat for 10–20 minutes, shaking frequently. Serve sprinkled with chopped parsley.

Allow about 175 g/6 oz per portion.

Stuffed Marrow (Large Zucchini)

Serves 4–5

1 marrow (large zucchini) (about 1 kg/2¼ lb)
350 g/12 oz raw minced or ground beef or pork
4 tablespoons fresh breadcrumbs
1–2 tablespoons dried mixed herbs
1 onion, peeled and finely chopped
salt and pepper
1 tablespoon capers
1 egg, beaten

1 Peel the marrow and cut in half lengthwise, then scoop out the seeds. Stand one half on a sheet of greased foil.
2 Combine the mince, breadcrumbs, herbs, onion, plenty of seasonings, capers and egg and put this stuffing into the two halves of the marrow.
3 Reassemble the marrow and wrap loosely but securely in the foil. Stand in a roasting tin.
4 Cook in a moderate oven (180°C/350°F/Gas Mark 4) for about an hour or until tender.
5 Remove from the foil and serve in slices with a mushroom sauce (see page 32).
6 Alternatively, cut the marrow into slices about 5 cm/2 inches thick and stand in a buttered ovenproof dish. Fill each with the stuffing, cover the dish and cook as above but for only 30–40 minutes until tender.

MUSHROOMS

There are several varieties of mushrooms: *Button* – buds that have not yet opened and are white; *Cup* – which are the large buds just beginning to open; *Flat* – these are the large open ones, full of flavour with the brown undersides.

Use button mushrooms whole or in slices in all types of dishes and sauces where no extra colour is wanted. Use cup mushrooms for general cooking, serving as vegetables and raw in salads either whole or sliced. The large flat mushrooms are ideal for grilling or broiling, frying and stuffing. Make sure mushrooms look white and fresh when selecting. Stale ones don't look appetizing and will not keep. All mushrooms dehydrate quickly so store in a covered container or a polythene bag in the refrigerator and use within 2–3 days. Fry or grill or broil or add to numerous dishes. Most mushrooms are cultivated and require only to be wiped and the stalks trimmed. If you can get hold of field mushrooms, the flavour is superior but they do need to be peeled and washed well before cooking.

Allow 50–75 g/2–3 oz per portion.

Grilled or Broiled Mushrooms

1 Wipe the mushrooms and cut the stalk level with the cup.
2 Melt about 50 g/2 oz/¼ cup butter for each 450 g/1 lb mushrooms to be cooked.
3 Dip the mushrooms into the melted fat or brush with it and stand in a foil-lined grill pan, cap upwards.
4 Cook under a moderate heat for about 2 minutes, then turn the mushrooms over and sprinkle lightly with salt, pepper and a touch of garlic powder (if liked) and grill for a further 2–3 minutes. Serve hot.

Fried Mushrooms

1 Trim the mushrooms and wipe thoroughly.
2 Heat 50 g/2 oz/¼ cup butter and 1 tablespoon oil for each 450 g/1 lb mushrooms to be fried and add salt and pepper and the juice of ½ lemon.
3 Add the mushrooms and cover the pan. Cook gently, shaking the pan frequently, for 4–5 minutes.
4 Serve hot sprinkled with parsley or fresh mixed herbs.

PUMPKIN

Traditional Halloween fare, this rather underestimated vegetable makes a tasty vegetable accompaniment as well as being the main ingredient of Pumpkin Pie and used in soup, jams and chutneys.

The best way to cook pumpkin is to peel and remove the seeds and cut it into cubes of about 5 cm/2 inches. It can then be roasted in the fat around the roast for about 40 minutes. Alternatively, cut into cubes and cook in boiling salted water or steam until tender – about 15–20 minutes. Drain well and serve as it is topped with butter and chopped parsley, or mash well and serve as a purée.

Allow about 225 g/8 oz per portion.

BEANS AND PULSES

These days, with the increasing interest in health foods and fibre in the diet, dried peas, beans and lentils have really come into their own. They are a valuable source of non-animal protein and B vitamins as well as providing a large amount of fibre or roughage.

The pulses should be fresh; after storage over 6 months they tend to become tough and even extended cooking will fail to soften them.

It used to be thought absolutely necessary to soak all dried peas, beans and other pulses at least overnight in cold water prior to cooking; this is not now quite so essential except for brown lentils and chick peas, although it does no harm. Instead, the pulses may be put into a pan, covered with cold water and brought to the boil, then removed from the heat and left to stand for 2–3 hours. Drain and they are ready to cook in the usual way. It is best to add salt for flavouring half to three-quarters of the way through cooking as the addition of salt at the start tends to slow down the softening process.

There has recently been some trouble with red kidney beans and the toxin they give off if not fast boiled for at least 20 minutes during their cooking. Gently simmering for a long time does not prevent the possibility of food poisoning, so, whichever method of cooking these beans is chosen, they MUST be boiled as well for at least 20 minutes before or during the cooking process.

LENTILS

There are two main types: *red* – which are the most common, and *brown* (or greenish-brown) – which are much larger.

Red lentils – cook quickly without soaking – about 15 minutes – to give a purée and make a delicious soup, especially if cooked with a ham bone. They are also good mixed with creamed potatoes for a rather different vegetable accompaniment.

Brown lentils – must be soaked overnight and then cooked for about 20–30 minutes, but they do keep their shape during cooking, making them good to add to casseroles and salads, as well as being useful as a vegetable.

Mix either type of lentils, after puréeing, into creamed potatoes and pipe into shapes to bake in the oven or pipe or spread on top of a meat or fish pie for a change.

DRIED PEAS

These are sold either whole or split, but without the wrinkled green skin. Bring to the boil, cool and soak for 2 hours and then boil gently in fresh water or stock for about 1½ hours or until tender. Mash or purée, add a knob of butter and seasoning to taste and serve as a vegetable.

Split peas are used for making the classic Pease Pudding to serve with boiled ham and smoked meats and are also an excellent addition to soups. After the initial soaking of 2 hours, boil in fresh water or stock for about 40 minutes.

Pease Pudding   Serves 4–6

225 g/8 oz/1¼ cups split peas
salt and pepper
1 ham bone or some bacon scraps
25 g/1 oz/2 tablespoons butter
1 egg, beaten
pinch of sugar

1   Put the peas in a pan, cover with cold water, bring to the boil and then leave to stand for 2 hours. Drain well.
2   Tie the peas in a cloth, place in a saucepan with a pinch of salt and with boiling water to cover and add the ham bone or bacon scraps.
3   Bring to the boil, cover and simmer for 2–2½ hours or until very soft. Lift out the bag of peas and drain.
4   Sieve or purée the peas in a food processor or blender and beat in the butter, egg, sugar and pepper to taste.
5   Tie up in a floured cloth or foil which is secured tightly at the top and boil for a further 30 minutes. Turn out and serve.

Note: The last boiling can be replaced by putting the pudding into a greased shallow ovenproof dish and cooking in a moderate oven (180°C/350°F/Gas Mark 4) for about 30–40 minutes or until set.

CHICK PEAS

These look like a pea with a groove down one side. They are very popular in Greece and Turkey as a 'nibble' with drinks and are simply boiled until tender (after at least 12 hours soaking in cold water – this is most essential with chick peas) and tossed in olive oil highly flavoured with garlic, lemon juice and seasonings. They take 20–40 minutes to cook depending on their age. Chick peas also form the base of the Greek hummus, served as a popular starter with pitta bread.

HARICOT (NAVY) BEANS

These are the traditional white beans used for the French Cassoulet and Boston Baked Beans. They are best soaked before cooking, although the quick method is fine, and should take about 1½ hours to cook, but for Boston Baked Beans and its variations need 6–8 hours very slow cooking in a cool oven. Haricot beans are also available in cans.

Allow 50–100 g/2–4 oz/¼–⅓ cups per portion

Boston Style Bean Casserole

Serves 4–6 as a main meal with a green salad, or 6–8 as a vegetable

350 g/12 oz haricot (navy) beans, soaked
2 onions, peeled and sliced
1 clove garlic, crushed
1 tablespoon black treacle
2 teaspoons dry mustard
1 teaspoon salt
1 tablespoon tomato purée
3 tablespoons wine vinegar
black pepper
450 ml/¾ pint/scant 2 cups stock or water
225 g/8 oz can tomatoes
225 g/8 oz button mushrooms, halved or quartered
freshly chopped parsley

1   Drain the beans and place in a heavy casserole. Add the onions, garlic, treacle, mustard, salt, tomato purée, vinegar and black pepper.
2   Bring the stock to the boil and pour into the casserole. Mix well and cover very tightly.
3   Cook in a cool oven (150°C/300°F/Gas Mark 2) for 4 hours.
4   Add the tomatoes and their juice and the mushrooms, give the casserole a good stir and re-cover. Return to the oven for 1–2 hours or until very tender. Serve sprinkled with parsley.

Note: This dish may be made earlier in the day and heated up when required – it will need about 40 minutes in a cool oven (150°C/300°F/Gas Mark 2) and may need a little boiling water or stock added to prevent it drying out.

FLAGEOLET BEANS

These are pale green thin elongated beans grown in France and Italy. They are more expensive than some varieties of bean but are well flavoured and add a good colour to any dish whether on their own or in combination with others. Also available in cans.

Herby Beans Serves 4

175 g/6–8 oz/1–1¼ cups flageolet beans, soaked
salt and pepper
4 tablespoons French dressing (see page 140)
1 tablespoon freshly chopped parsley
2 tablespoons chopped mixed fresh herbs
finely grated rind of 1 lemon

1 Drain the beans and cook in fresh water for 1–1½ hours or until tender, adding salt to taste after 1 hour.
2 When tender, drain the beans and keep warm.
3 Combine the dressing, herbs, lemon rind and plenty of black pepper and add to the beans. Toss thoroughly, turn into a dish and serve hot.

BUTTER BEANS

These are probably the best known and most used in cooking up until the last few years when all beans became popular. They are large creamy-white flat beans and are best if soaked for 2 hours and then boiled for about 1¼ hours. Drain thoroughly and either serve tossed in butter, sprinkled with parsley, coated in parsley or cheese sauce, or mixed with crisply-fried chopped onion and streaky bacon. This is a good vegetable to serve with boiled bacon and smoked meats, and can also be served cold in a salad.

Try a mixture of cooked butter beans, flageolet and red kidney beans or aduki beans in a parsley sauce as a vegetable accompaniment, or tossed in a garlic French dressing to serve hot as a vegetable or cold as a salad.

RED KIDNEY BEANS

These are very popular beans traditionally served cooked in Chili con Carne and added frequently to casseroles and cassoulet dishes. They give a good colour and are highly nutritious as well as blending well with many flavours and even more important having a good flavour of their own.

However, care must be taken to cook them properly. After soaking for about 2 hours, drain and place in a saucepan of clean water and bring to the boil. Boil hard for 20 minutes and then either lower the temperature and continue to cook for a further ¾–1 hour or until tender, or drain and add to a casserole or whatever to complete the cooking.

These beans are also very popular in cans and then are already cooked, so they can be simply stirred into the dish and thoroughly reheated, or drained and served as a salad in a dressing.

OTHER BEANS

There are many other varieties of beans available which are all dealt with in much the same way – cooking times vary with size and age of the bean. Experiment with mixtures of the beans. Here are a few other varieties:

Aduki Beans – tiny red beans similar to a very small red kidney bean but a duller colour with a distinctive white mark at the stem.
Black-eye – creamy coloured small beans with a distinct black 'eye'.
Mung – tiny moss-green-coloured beans which also sprout if not dried.

RICE AND PASTA

These are not vegetables of course but are widely used as vegetable accompaniments as well as forming the base of many a main dish. Both are easy to cook provided care is taken; on no account allow either to overcook, for, if soggy, they loose all taste and texture.

RICE

There are three main kinds of grains of rice – long, medium and short. The long slender grains are fluffy and they separate when cooked, so are ideal for using in made-up dishes as well as as an accompaniment. The medium or short grains are more moist and stickier when cooked so are better for sweet puddings and savoury dishes that need the rice to stick together, e.g. stuffings, rice rings, etc.

TYPES OF RICE

Long grain rice (Patna) – the hulls, germ and most of the bran is removed in processing, leaving a polished white grain. It stays white when cooked and has a mild and fairly bland taste.
Basmati rice – the traditional Indian rice used in Indian cookery. It has a distinct flavour and is a pale creamy-brown when cooked. It is a long grain rice, but the grains are slender, delicate and naturally perfumed. The best basmati rice is matured for a year before it is sold when its unusual nutty flavour and aroma have intensified. It must be washed thoroughly and picked over to remove impurities – such as small stones, etc. – before cooking.
Brown rice – this is whole unpolished grains with only the inedible husk and a small amount of bran removed. It is fawn-coloured when cooked and has a more chewy texture with much more flavour than ordinary long grain rice. It requires more water for cooking (as it has a higher absorption rate) and takes longer to cook – about 40 minutes.
Risotto rice – an Italian rice known as Arborio which is ideal for making risottos. It remains slightly firm in the centre and a little chewy, giving just the right texture to combine with the other ingredients.
Wild rice – this is not truly a rice but the seeds from a wild grass which are used for savoury dishes. It is expensive and not always easy to obtain but has a splendid taste for a special occasion.
Precooked and instant rices – these are widely available and are ideal for an emergency but are not a patch on properly-cooked rice. The rice is completely cooked and then dehydrated and packed into packets or cans. It really only needs reheating in boiling water or stock, taking only about 5 minutes to produce ready to eat. Follow the instructions carefully on the packet or can for cooking.

Boston Style Bean Casserole (see page 133) *and Fruit and Nut Rice* (see page 136)

PREPARING AND COOKING RICE

All rice should be washed in cold water until the water runs clear before cooking. This not only removes the excess starch from the grains but helps to keep it separate when cooked. It is more important to wash loose-packed rice and Basmati rice as there are always impurities packed in with the grains! For large parties, rice may be cooked 24 hours in advance, thoroughly rinsed and drained and stored in the refrigerator or a cool place in a covered container.

There are several ways of cooking rice that will give perfectly-cooked rice with separate grains. Everyone has their favourite way and, so long as the result is not a sticky soggy mess, then your method will be suitable. Many people worry about cooking rice, saying that it always sticks or turns soggy, but do not worry, it is really very simple if you follow one of the suggested methods.

Allow 40–50 g/1½–2 oz/¼–⅓ cup uncooked rice per portion.

'Plenty of Water' Method

1 Heat a large saucepan about three-quarters full with water and add 1 teaspoon salt.
2 When it boils, add the washed and drained rice, stir well and bring back to the boil.
3 Lower the heat and allow to simmer quite fast (not boil hard) for 12–14 minutes – stirring once during cooking – until the grains are just soft but not soggy. Test by removing a few grains and squeeze in your fingers – they should be tender but not too soft; the centre should still have a bit of 'bite' in it.
4 Drain the rice in a sieve and hold under a hot running tap to remove any more starch and separate the grains.
5 Shake off all excess moisture and turn into a serving dish. A knob of butter may be added and forked through the rice.

Absorption Method

1 Place 225 g/8 oz/1¼ cups long grain rice in a saucepan with 600 ml/1 pint/2½ cups water and 1 teaspoon salt. Bring to the boil and cover tightly with a well-fitting lid.
2 Reduce the heat and simmer gently for 14–15 minutes.
3 Remove from the heat, stir through the rice with a fork to separate the grains and turn into a serving dish. The rice should not need draining, but should separate when forked.
4 For a drier rice, simply leave to stand in a warm place in the covered pan for 5–10 minutes.

Note: When cooking rice by this method, it is important to observe the following points:
a) Don't increase the amount of water or the rice will be soggy.
b) Don't uncover the pan during cooking or the steam will escape prolonging the cooking time.
c) Don't stir during cooking, it will break up the grains and make them soggy.
d) Don't leave to stand for longer than 10 minutes before serving or the grains may stick together.

Oven-baked Rice

1 Place 225 g/8 oz/1¼ cups long grain rice in a greased shallow ovenproof dish.
2 Bring 600 ml/1 pint/2½ cups water to the boil with 1 teaspoon salt added. Pour over the rice and stir well.
3 Cover tightly with a lid or foil and cook in a moderate oven (180°C/350°F/Gas Mark 4) for 35–40 minutes or until the grains are tender and the liquid absorbed.

FLAVOURING RICE

Rice may have extra flavour added by using one of the liquids suggested below instead of salted water. Salt is still required, but not so much if using stock cubes.
a) Chicken, beef, game or vegetable stock.
b) Half orange juice and half water or stock.
c) Half canned tomato juice and half water or stock.
d) A quarter wine or cider and the rest stock or water.

SAVOURY RICE RECIPES

These can be used as a vegetable accompaniment or as the base of a risotto. Either cook the extra ingredients separately in a little oil or add to the oven-baked method with the liquid.

Savoury Rice

175 g/6 oz/1 cup long grain rice, cooked
1 large onion, peeled and chopped
1 clove garlic, crushed
2 tablespoons oil
½–1 red pepper, deseeded and chopped
½–1 green pepper, deseeded and chopped
salt and pepper

1 Fry the onion and garlic gently in the oil until soft, stirring occasionally.
2 Add the peppers and continue cooking for about 5 minutes, stirring frequently.
3 Stir into the rice, season to taste and serve hot.

Fruit and Nut Rice

175 g/6 oz/1 cup long grain rice, cooked in orange juice
  and water
grated rind of ½–1 orange
1 tablespoon oil
75 g/3 oz/½ cup raisins or sultanas (golden raisins)
2–3 rings canned pineapple, chopped
40 g/1½ oz/¼ cup whole blanched almonds, toasted and
  roughly chopped

1 Cook the rice in orange juice and water and keep warm, forking in the orange rind.
2 Heat the oil in a pan and toss in the raisins and pineapple, heat through for 2–3 minutes until really hot, then add the almonds.
3 Toss through the rice and serve.

Curried Rice

225 g/8 oz/1¼ cups long grain rice
1 large onion, peeled and chopped
1 tablespoon oil
½–1 teaspoon curry powder
good pinch of ground coriander
salt and pepper
600 ml/1 pint/2½ cups stock or water
40–50 g/1½–2 oz/¼–⅓ cup flaked almonds, toasted
(optional)

1 Fry the onion gently in the oil until soft, stirring frequently.
2 Add the rice, curry powder, coriander, seasonings and stock and bring to the boil. Stir well.
3 Cover the pan and simmer gently for 14–15 minutes or until tender and the liquid is absorbed.
4 Stir in the almonds, if used, and serve hot.

Saffron or Yellow Rice

Saffron grains are very expensive and not always easy to obtain; turmeric makes a good alternative, giving a good colour and mild flavour and is much more economical.

Cook 225 g/8 oz/1¼ cups long grain rice by any of the above methods but add ½–¾ teaspoon turmeric powder to the cooking liquid. If cooking the rice in plenty of boiling water, add 1½ teaspoons turmeric.

TO REHEAT COOKED RICE

Either boil about 2.5 cm/1 inch of water in a pan with a good knob of butter, toss in the rice, and heat through over a gentle heat, stirring nearly all the time until really hot, strain and serve. Or put in a lightly greased ovenproof dish, cover with buttered foil and heat in a moderate oven (160°C/325°F/Gas Mark 3) for about 30–45 minutes until piping hot. If you have a microwave oven, put the rice into a microwaveproof dish, cover with plastic cling film, make a few holes in it and heat on high for 1 minute, leave to stand for 2–3 minutes, give the rice a stir and then cook on medium for a further 1–1½ minutes or until really hot.

PASTA

Pasta is Italian in origin and made from a special hard wheat called durum. It is ground down to semolina and then mixed with water and other ingredients to make a dough. Colours are added with egg or spinach or by using a wholemeal semolina. It is then kneaded and shaped by passing it through special pasta making machines or moulds, which determine the shape and size to give us the pasta we know as macaroni, spaghetti, lasagne, vermicelli, etc. Machines can be obtained for shaping pasta, which fit onto some of the larger electric mixers. The shaped pasta is then dried and packed in boxes or cellophane, etc. Pasta is usually bought and sold dried in packets but fresh pasta has become very much more popular and is now quite widely available from the special pasta shops that have sprung up in many large towns and cities, Italian-orientated shops and many of the larger supermarkets.

Dried pasta will keep almost indefinitely but fresh pasta must be cooked the day it is made or bought. The main difference in the cooking is that fresh pasta requires only about 5 minutes cooking (instructions should be on the package or you should be told by the pasta shop) while the dry varieties require 10–15 minutes, depending on size.

TYPES OF PASTA

There are very many different shapes of pasta available, all of which have different names.

Long Spaghetti – is a solid rod of pasta in different thicknesses and lengths of either 25 cm/10 inch or 50 cm/20 inches. Simply lower into the boiling water pushing it lightly so it bends round the inside of the saucepan without breaking the rods.

Vermicelli – this is a much finer solid rod of pasta similar to spaghetti which can also be bought folded up in a bundle which resembles a bird's nest when cooked.

Lasagne – a flat sheet of pasta either plain or ribbed and usually either 5 cm/2 inches or 10 cm/4 inches wide and about 15–20 cm/6–8 inches long. It comes green (spinach flavoured), plain, or with added egg, or wholemeal.

Noodles – broad noodles are flat and called tagliatelle. They come folded or twisted into nests. The width varies from fine to quite thick. Available green, wholemeal and plain.

Spirals (Tortiglioni) – these resemble small corkscrews and are usually plain and unflavoured.

Shells (Conchiaglie) – these are pasta made into shells which look like winkles and come in various sizes.

Lumachine – tiny shells that are somewhat rounded. The translation is 'little snails' which is a good description.

Lumache – these are like shells of pasta.

Twistetti – these look like two strands of thick spaghetti twisted together and cut into short pieces.

Alphabetti – shaped pieces of flat pasta in the letters of the alphabet – often used in soups as a garnish.

Canelloni – these are large empty tubes of pasta about 10 cm/4 inches long. Cook and then stuff and serve in or with a sauce.

Rings – these are available from tiny up to quite large, and are cut from ribbed tubes of pasta.

Hoops – similar to rings but not ribbed.

Wagon wheels – varying sizes of cartwheel-shaped pasta.

Long macaroni – much thicker than spaghetti but with a hollow centre.

Elbow or short macaroni – much thicker than spaghetti, it varies in thickness from very thin up to the large 'drainpipes' but always has a hole through the centre and is curved and cut into short lengths.

Bucatini – this is a quick-cooking macaroni, similar to standard macaroni but thinner. It is available in long rods and short cut.

HOW TO COOK PASTA

As an alternative to a vegetable allow 50 g/2 oz/½ cup per portion whatever the shape. Pasta should double its weight at least when cooked. Pasta should be cooked until 'al dente' or so it still has a slight 'bite' to it. Do not allow it to become too soft and soggy.

1 Bring a large saucepan of water to the boil and add

1 teaspoon salt and 1 tablespoon oil (this helps keep it separate).
2 Add the pasta all at once and bring back to the boil, stirring with a wooden fork or spoon to make sure it does not stick to the base of the pan or itself.
3 Boil, uncovered, for 10–15 minutes or until 'al dente'. Wholemeal pasta takes a few minutes longer than other types; small cut shapes need a little less time – about 8–12 minutes.
4 Drain in a colander or sieve.
5 Melt a knob of butter in the saucepan and return the pasta to it. Shake well adding a good sprinkling of freshly ground pepper and a little grated nutmeg or coriander, if liked. Serve hot.

Note: With spaghetti, do not force it into the pan or it will break, just push it gently and as it softens it will curl around the inside of the pan.

Pasta is traditionally served sprinkled with grated Parmesan cheese. Bought dried ready-grated Parmesan cheese is available in cartons and packets but the best flavour is achieved by buying a piece of fresh Parmesan and grating it yourself as required. It is not much more costly, lasts a long time, goes a long way and the flavour is definitely superior. Finely grated Cheddar cheese may be used as an alternative.

Macaroni Cheese

Serves 4 as a snack or 6 as a vegetable

225 g/8 oz/2 cups short-cut macaroni
salt and pepper
1 tablespoon oil
40 g/1½ oz/3 tablespoons butter
4 tablespoons flour
568 ml/1 pint/2½ cups milk
1 teaspoon made English mustard
175 g/6 oz/1½ cups grated Cheddar cheese
2 tomatoes, sliced

1 Cook the macaroni in fast-boiling salted water, with the oil added for about 10 minutes only, then drain thoroughly.
2 Use the butter, flour and milk to make a white sauce (see page 29) season well, stir in the mustard and 100 g/4 oz/1 cup grated cheese until melted.
3 Stir the drained macaroni into the sauce and pour into an ovenproof dish.
4 Lay the sliced tomatoes over the macaroni and sprinkle with the rest of the cheese.
5 Stand on a baking sheet and cook in a fairly hot oven (200°C/400°F/Gas Mark 6) for 20–30 minutes or until bubbling and golden brown on top.

VARIATIONS

Mushroom macaroni – omit 100 g/4 oz/1 cup cheese from the sauce and the sliced tomatoes. Fry 100 g/4–6 oz/2–3 cups sliced or chopped mushrooms in 2 tablespoons oil until soft and add to the sauce with 1 teaspoon dried mixed herbs.

Bacon and Onion Macaroni – omit 50 g/2 oz/½ cup grated cheese from the sauce and the tomatoes. Fry 6 chopped derinded rashers streaky bacon and 1 finely chopped onion in the bacon fat, until crispy, then add to the sauce.

Tomato Spirals

Serves 3–4 as a snack or 4–6 as a vegetable

175 g/6–8 oz spirals or twistetti
3 tablespoons oil
1 onion, peeled and chopped
1 clove garlic, crushed
salt and pepper
1 red pepper, deseeded and chopped
1 tablespoon tomato purée
225 g/8 oz can peeled tomatoes
1 teaspoon Worcestershire sauce
pinch of sugar
½–1 teaspoon dried basil (optional)
chopped parsley to garnish

1 Heat 2 tablespoons of oil in a saucepan and fry the onion and garlic very gently until soft, stirring occasionally.
2 Put a saucepan of water to boil with the remaining oil and 1 teaspoon salt added. Add the pasta and cook until tender – about 10 minutes – stirring occasionally.
3 Add the pepper to the onion and fry gently for 2–3 minutes. Stir in the tomato purée, tomatoes, seasoning, Worcestershire sauce, sugar and basil if used. Bring to the boil, cover the pan and simmer gently for 10 minutes, giving an occasional stir.
4 Drain the spirals thoroughly and toss into the tomato sauce. Mix well, turn into a dish and serve sprinkled with parsley.

Tagliatelle with Bacon and Cream

Serves 3–4 as a snack or 4–6 as a vegetable

225 g/8 oz tagliatelle
salt and pepper
1 tablespoon oil
175 g/6 oz streaky bacon, derinded and chopped
6 tablespoons single (light) cream
a little Parmesan cheese (optional)

1 Cook the tagliatelle in a large pan of fast-boiling salted water with the oil added for about 10 minutes or until just tender.
2 Meanwhile, fry the bacon gently with no extra fat until the fat begins to run, then increase the heat and continue cooking until the bacon turns golden brown, stirring frequently.
3 Drain the tagliatelle thoroughly and return to the saucepan with the bacon, cream and plenty of freshly ground black pepper. Toss over a gentle heat without boiling. Turn into a warmed dish and serve sprinkled with Parmesan cheese, if liked.

Ratatouille (see page 129), *Macaroni Cheese* and (bottom) *Bacon and Onion Macaroni*

Salads form an important part of our diet, especially in these days of healthy eating. Their crispness and variety add a different dimension as an accompaniment to a main course and a salad is equally good as a meal on its own. Salads help achieve a well-balanced diet, for most salad ingredients supply a good proportion of the daily vitamin C requirement.

All salads require some type of dressing, usually added at the last minute or actually served at the table for guests to help themselves. Long soaking in dressings in most cases ruins the texture of the ingredients, especially ingredients such as lettuce, watercress, etc., although others benefit from a certain amount of marinating in place of cooking.

Salads to serve as accompaniments should be simple with only a few ingredients and a French or other light dressing in preference to a thick heavy one. Other salads, can be very hearty with a good selection of ingredients and may be tossed or served with a mayonnaise or thick rich dressing, but these salads are more likely to be served as a main meal or snack rather than as a side dish.

Many of the usual salad ingredients have already been described in the vegetable chapter and will only be mentioned briefly here with suggestions on how best to prepare them for inclusion in a salad.

STORING SALADS

Store salad ingredients in the salad drawer of the refrigerator or the warmest part of the refrigerator if possible. Keep them either in their original wrappings with holes made in it, if it is a polythene bag, or loosely wrapped in a polythene bag (again with perforations) and store in the coldest place possible if the refrigerator is too full. It is best to wash ingredients, especially lettuce and other greenery, just prior to serving for, if stored when wet, it will simply go mouldy and soggy and be unusable very quickly. Brown paper bags and newspaper are also good for wrapping ingredients as they are porous and allow them to breathe.

SALAD DRESSINGS

A salad is not at its best without a suitable dressing – however good the ingredients may be. Dressings vary widely from simple oil and vinegar mixtures to the classic mayonnaise and cooked salad dressings. This is only the beginning, for each type of dressing then has numerous variations – some specially made to blend with certain ingredients.

TYPE OF DRESSING INGREDIENTS

Oil – this can be of several types. Olive oil is the best oil but tends to be rather heavy and strong-flavoured and is too harsh for some palates. Try mixing it with one of the lighter oils to achieve the same excellent flavour but rather lighter and easier to digest.

Sunflower, ground nut, soya, corn and vegetable oils are all lighter in taste and can be used for all salad dressings. They all have their own flavour and it is up to you to pick your favourite. There are other special oils too that give wonderful flavours – such as walnut and almond oil – but they are much more expensive and not always easy to obtain. If you do have some, try adding just 2 or 3 tablespoons of one of these oils to one of the blander oils.

Vinegar – use a good quality wine vinegar for preference: white for mayonnaise and red or white for dressings. Cider and distilled vinegars are also good, as are the flavoured varieties, which usually have sprigs of fresh herbs floating in them. Very special vinegars such as raspberry or blackberry can also be used in small amounts – their colours give amazing results! Malt vinegar can be used but the colour is not so good and the flavour is, of course, much harsher.

Mustard – most dressings call for mustard. Use either dry English mustard, made English mustard, French or German varieties, Dijon or one of the flavoured varieties – such as thyme, tarragon, chive, etc. – or one of the whole grain or coarse grain ones. All types of mustard can be used, but decide on the flavouring to blend with your chosen salad ingredients.

Although the salad recipes given suggest one or other of the dressings, they can of course be varied and changed as you please to suit your own individual taste.

French Dressing

150 ml/¼ pint/⅔ cup salad oil
2 tablespoons vinegar (wine, cider, tarragon or white)
salt and freshly ground black pepper
1 clove garlic, crushed (optional)
½ teaspoon made English mustard
¼ teaspoon French mustard
1 tablespoon lemon juice
1 teaspoon caster (superfine) sugar

1 Place all the ingredients in a screw-top jar and shake until well blended.
2 Store the jar in a cool place. Shake well before use.

VARIATIONS

Garlic – add 2 crushed cloves garlic to the dressing.

Lemon – add the grated rind of 1 large lemon to the dressing and replace 2 tablespoons of the vinegar with lemon juice.

Herbs add 2 tablespoons freshly chopped parsley, 1 teaspoon grated onion, 1 teaspoon freshly chopped thyme, 1 tablespoon snipped chives and a good pinch of ground nutmeg to the dressing.

Chives – add 4 tablespoons freshly snipped chives.

Curry – add 1–2 teaspoons curry powder to the dressing depending on taste.

Anchovy – add ½ can well-drained and finely chopped anchovy fillets, but omit the salt.

Dried Mixed Herbs – add 1–2 tablespoons dried mixed herbs.

Blue Cheese – add 50 g/2 oz/¼ cup finely crumbled or grated blue cheese, e.g. Danish Blue, Stilton.

Soured Cream Dressing

150 ml/¼ pint/⅔ cup carton soured cream
salt and pepper
a little crushed garlic
good pinch of caster (superfine) sugar

Turn the soured cream into a bowl and season well with salt and pepper, garlic and sugar. Mix together thoroughly.

Note: This dressing can be used as it is for a salad or be added to.

VARIATIONS

Soured Mayonnaise – mix equal quantities of the above dressing with classic mayonnaise.

Piquant – add ½ teaspoon Worcestershire sauce, 1 tablespoon finely grated onion or chopped spring onions (scallions) and 1 tablespoon wine or cider vinegar.

Lemon or Orange – add the finely grated rind of ½–1 lemon or orange, or both.

Chive – add 2–3 tablespoons chopped chives and 1 tablespoon freshly chopped parsley.

Chunky – add 6 finely chopped gherkins, 2 tablespoons finely grated onion or finely chopped spring onions (scallions) and ½ small finely chopped red pepper.

Classic Mayonnaise

(See step-by-step illustrations, page 142.)

2 egg yolks (at room temperature)
½ teaspoon made English mustard
300 ml/½ pint/1¼ cups salad oil
1 tablespoon lemon juice
about 2 tablespoons vinegar (wine, cider or white)
1 teaspoon caster (superfine) sugar
salt and white pepper

1 Put the egg yolks and mustard into a warmed bowl and mix thoroughly.
2 Whisk in half the oil drop by drop, using a hand or electric hand-held whisk for preference, until thick. Do

not be tempted to hasten the adding of the oil or your mayonnaise will curdle.

3 Whisk in the lemon juice and then continue with the rest of the oil in the same way, although the process may be speeded up a little towards the end.
4 Add vinegar, sugar and salt and pepper to taste. Turn into a screw-top jar or plastic container with a tight-fitting lid and store for up to 3 weeks in the refrigerator.

Note: If the mayonnaise should curdle, it can be rectified as follows: put a fresh egg yolk in a clean warm bowl and gradually whisk in the curdled mixture, drop by drop, as before, then continue with the rest of the oil.

It is important to use eggs that have been kept at room temperature; if taken straight from the refrigerator, they will be much too cold and more likely to curdle.

VARIATIONS

Lemon – use all lemon juice in place of the vinegar and beat in the finely grated rind of 1 large lemon at the end.

Orange – use orange juice in place of the vinegar and beat in the finely grated rind of ½–1 orange at the end.

Green – beat in the very finely chopped leaves of a trimmed bunch of watercress and 2 tablespoons freshly chopped parsley.

Chive – beat in 3 tablespoons finely snipped chives or finely chopped spring onion (scallion) tops.

Curry – add 1–2 teaspoons curry powder, or according to taste.

Brandy or Whisky – add brandy or whisky in place of the vinegar.

Horseradish – add 2 tablespoons creamed horseradish or 1 tablespoon horseradish sauce.

Cocktail – add 2 tablespoons tomato ketchup or 1 tablespoon tomato purée and about ½ teaspoon Worcestershire sauce.

Cucumber – add about a quarter of an unpeeled cucumber, either very finely chopped or grated, and 1 tablespoon freshly chopped parsley.

Thousand Island Dressing

A thick creamy dressing full of flavour, good to serve with green or other root vegetable salads.

150 ml/¼ pint/⅔ cup mayonnaise
12 stuffed green olives, chopped
1 teaspoon finely chopped onion or spring onions (scallions)
1 hard-boiled egg, finely grated
2 tablespoons finely choped or minced green pepper
1 tablespoon freshly chopped parsley
1 teaspoon tomato purée
a little milk (optional)

Mix all the ingredients together until evenly blended, adding a little milk if it is too thick for the purpose for which it is required. Store in an airtight container in the refrigerator for up to 3 days.

Classic Mayonnaise (see page 141)

1   *Having mixed the egg yolks and mustard thoroughly, whisk in half the oil drop by drop.*

2   *Whisk in the lemon juice and then continue with the rest of the oil.*

3   *Stir in the vinegar, sugar and salt and pepper to taste.*

SALAD INGREDIENTS

PEPPERS

Any colour can be used. Wash, cut off the top and remove the seeds or cut in half and scoop out the seeds. Cut into thin slices or strips or chop. If the flavour is too strong, blanch by putting into a pan of cold water and bringing just to the boil. Drain and rinse immediately under cold running water until cold. Drain thoroughly and then dry before use.

BEAN SPROUTS

Simply look over and discard any discoloured ones, then wash and dry thoroughly and add to salads just as they are.

TOMATOES

One of the more versatile vegetables. Remove the stem and wash or wipe well. They may be used with the skins on or skinned if preferred. Some varieties have a very tough skin which is best removed first. However, other varieties lose a lot of their colour if the skins are removed. To skin them, dip in boiling water for about ½ minute, then put into a bowl of cold water. Make a small nick in the skin and it should peel off easily. Use whole, if very small; or sliced, quartered, cut into sixths or eighths; quartered with the seeds removed and then cut into narrow strips, or chopped or vandyked.
Vandyked Tomatoes – choose firm even-sized tomatoes and, using a small sharp-pointed knife, make a series of V-shaped cuts all round the centre of each tomato, cutting right through to the centre. Carefully pull the halves apart and use to garnish.

BEETROOT (BEET)

Peel the cooked beetroot carefully, removing any blemishes, and serve whole, if very small, or halved or quartered. Larger beet can be coarsely grated or diced, cut into sticks or slices. If to be served on its own as an accompaniment, it will keep better if covered with vinegar or a mixture of vinegar and water, seasoned with salt, pepper and a pinch of sugar. If to be added to a salad, it is best to do so at the very last minute for the colour is very bright and harsh and will seep into anything it touches. French dressing or a soured cream dressing blends well with beetroot, as does the flavouring of horseradish and mustard.

CARROTS

New carrots are best used in salads, but firm old varieties can be used too. Scrape or peel and top and tail and then either slice very thinly – for new ones – or coarsely or finely grate, finely dice or cut into thin sticks.

CELERY

Separate the sticks from the head and wash well in cold water, scrubbing to remove any dirt from the grooves. Strip off any strings from them and dry well. Slice thinly or cut into thicker pieces, dice or chop, or cut into thin sticks. They can also be made into curls for garnish.
Celery Curls – cut a celery stick into strips about 1 cm/½ inch wide and 5 cm/2 inches long. Make cuts along the length of each, close together and to within 1 cm/½ inch of one end. Leave the pieces in cold or iced water in a bowl (preferably in the refrigerator) for 1–2 hours or until the

cut strips curl up. Drain well and then leave on absorbent kitchen paper towel for the excess water to be absorbed before use.

CELERIAC
Peel this rather ugly root vegetable and cut into thin strips, dice or chunks and dip in cold water to which the juice of a lemon has been added. Drain well before use. Alternatively, coarsely grate and mix immediately with a French dressing, salad cream or mayonnaise. If left exposed to the air for too long, it is likely to discolour and will spoil the appearance of the salad.

FENNEL
Trim off the top stems and slice off the base of the root. Either slice thinly or chop the whole bulb as it is, or remove each piece and slice or chop individually. The slight aniseed flavour and crispness of fennel is an excellent addition to a salad. Reserve any feathery foliage on the bulb and use for garnish, or chop finely and add to the dressing.

SPRING ONIONS (SCALLIONS)
Simply trim off the top and tail, leaving a good amount of the green part, and if necessary peel off the outer layer of the onion. Wash and dry well and then use as they are, or sliced or chopped or trimmed down until there is only about 2.5 cm/1 inch of the green part left which can then be cut through lengthways in several places and soaked in iced water – as for celery curls – so the tops curl open to use for a garnish.

BEANS
Most beans can be used in salads but they are more often blanched or barely cooked first. Use broad (lima) beans whole and slice or cut long beans into manageable pieces. All beans benefit from marinating for an hour or so in a dressing before serving. They may be marinated separately before adding to the rest of the ingredients if the long time in the dressing is likely to spoil the other ingredients.

CAULIFLOWER
Cut into small florets, discarding all the green and tough stalks. Either use raw or blanch in boiling water for about ½ minute and then plunge into cold water and drain well. Cauliflower needs a dressing and is best mixed with other ingredients, but its crispness is ideal for salads.

PEAS
These add colour, texture and flavour to a salad, but they should be podded and cooked first. Use either fresh or frozen peas.

BRUSSELS SPROUTS
Trim tight clean sprouts of outer leaves and stems and then shred finely. The flavour is good and colour improves salads, especially when lettuces are at their poorest and very expensive. Do not use stale, yellowing sprouts as the flavour is not good enough for a salad – they must be perfectly fresh.

CHINESE LEAVES OR CABBAGE
One of the newest additions to salad ingredients and quite marvellous too. Simply trim the root end and remove any damaged outer leaves and shred finely. Some very tightly-packed leaves do not require washing, but if it is a loose head, it is best to remove the leaves one by one, wash, dry and then shred. Chinese leaves will keep in the refrigerator for at least a week in prime condition.

CHICORY
Trim off the root and any damaged outer leaves. Wash if necessary and dry, then either separate out the leaves to use as they are, or simply slice thinly straight across the head. Make sure that the top of the leaves are pale yellow and not green – greenness indicates that they may be bitter because they have been removed from the dark and their growing place for too long or too early.

COURGETTES (ZUCCHINI)
Trim and wipe well. Simply slice very thinly, chop or cut into narrow sticks and marinate in French dressing for at least an hour befor serving or adding to other ingredients.

MUSHROOMS
Use the white buttons for preference and trim the stem and wipe over. Do not peel the cultivated varieties. Slice thinly, chop or quarter, or, if very small, they may be left whole. Marinate in some type of dressing – not mayonnaise – for at least 30 minutes before serving.

ENDIVE
This is a type of lettuce with very curly leaves. It is large and tightly massed at the stem with the centre leaves a pale yellow gradually changing to bright green at the ends. Store wrapped in newspaper in a cool place or the bottom of the refrigerator and, when required, simply cut off the required number of leaves, wash and dry thoroughly. Pull apart and add to the salad. The leaves look a little like an unruly octopus, but the flavour is very good and they make an attractive addition to any salad. Endive keeps well, often remaining at peak condition for up to a week, provided it is kept in the cool.

WATERCRESS
Trim the coarse ends from the stalks and wash the watercress carefully, discarding any discoloured leaves. Drain and dry thoroughly and use on the day of purchase if possible. If you need to keep the cress, trim the bottoms of the stalks, wrap in newspaper and stand in a bowl of water in a cold place. Alternatively, after washing put the watercress in a polythene bag in the refrigerator, but it will be necessary to pick it over again before use, and it will only keep for 12 hours or so.

RADISHES
Trim off the root end and the leaves and wash well in cold water. Radishes are often sandy or gritty from the soil they were grown in. Serve whole, cut into slices or quarters or cut into roses for garnish.
Radish Roses – trim the radishes. Make four or eight small deep cuts in the centre at the root end. Leave the radishes in iced water for 1–2 hours, preferably in the refrigerator, until the cuts open out to form petals.

CUCUMBER

Wipe the skin thoroughly, or peel if preferred using a potato peeler. Slice the cucumber finely, or cut into cubes or sticks. If you like the cucumber softer rather than crisp, soak it in salt or vinegar for about an hour and then rinse and dry before serving. Cucumber is good to use as a garnish too.

Crimped Cucumber – run a fork down the unpeeled skin of the cucumber to remove narrow strips of the peel, then slice thinly to give an attractive edge to the slices.

Cucumber Cones – slice the unpeeled cucumber thinly, make a cut in each slice from the centre to the outer edge and then fold over to make a cone.

Cucumber Twists – slice the unpeeled cucumber quite thinly but not paper thin and make a cut from the centre out to the edge. Lift up the slice and put it down so one side of the cut faces forward and the other backwards, then press down as far as necessary to make the twist.

SPINACH

Use young fresh leaves after stripping out the stem. Wash well and dry and then tear up or shred to use with or in place of lettuce.

LETTUCE

Originally a salad wasn't a salad without lettuce. This is certainly not so nowadays, although lettuce is a very important salad ingredient, especially if prepared properly. There are many varieties of lettuce, all with different flavours and textures and keeping qualities. The usual round or cabbage lettuce is excellent in the summer when it is full of flavour and body, but its winter hothouse cousin still gives the colour and shape but lacks greatly in flavour. Store this type of lettuce in its perforated polythene bag or wrapped in newspaper at the bottom of the refrigerator or in the salad drawer and remove and wash and dry the leaves only as required. Chopping or slicing lettuce bruises the leaves and so it is much better to tear them into the required sized pieces. Other varieties include:

Cos (Romaine) – tall thin lettuce with dark green outer leaves and pale green ones in the centre. Crisp with crinkly leaves and a nutty almost sweet flavour. Ideal for adding to salads or using to serve the salad or other ingredients on. The tiny 'heart' leaves make good garnishes.

Little Gem or Density – miniature type of cos (Romaine) lettuce with much the same flavour and texture and colour too, but the leaves are tightly bunched together and do not open out loosely as with their cos relations. Keeps well.

Webbs Wonder (Boston) and Iceberg – tightly bunched crinkly leaves almost resembling a cabbage; the Webbs is a much darker green with the outer leaves loosening out a bit; the iceberg is almost white and tightly bunched throughout. Both keep well and have an excellent flavour and as they are so tightly bunched can be sliced.

A salad spinner is an ideal way of drying off washed lettuce leaves. Simply put the wet lettuce in it and spin until all the water has flown off into the base of it. Otherwise it is best to put the leaves into a clean cloth and shake fairly hard to remove the moisture.

To revive a 'limp' or withered lettuce, separate out the leaves and put into a bowl of cold or iced water. Leave to soak for about 15 minutes, then remove, drain and shake off the excess moisture and place in a bowl covered with a plate or in a loose polythene bag and leave in the refrigerator for 1–2 hours until crispy again. Use quickly.

AVOCADO

Make sure the avocado is just ripe when selecting: it should give very slightly when cradled in the hands and pressed very lightly at both the stem end and rounded end. If rock hard, it will require up to a week in a warm atmosphere to ripen; if very soft, don't buy it as the flesh is likely to be almost slimy and very discoloured when cut. There are several varieties of avocado, mostly coming from different countries. The taste is much the same but the size varies and the texture of the skin may vary from very smooth and green to thick, bumpy and brown. Some avocados that look very large will not be so when cut, it is simply that the avocado has a huge stone in the centre. Avocados discolour very quickly once cut. It is best to use a stainless steel knife and then dip in lemon juice immediately it is cut to halt the discolouration. Do not add the avocado to a salad until the last possible minute and then cut in half, remove the stone, peel and cut into slices, chunks, dice, etc. Dip first in lemon juice and then toss in the dressing before mixing with the other ingredients.

POTATOES

Use tiny cooked new potatoes whole or larger ones diced, or cut cooked old potatoes into dice. It is best to add the dressing or mayonnaise while the potatoes are still warm as they are easier to coat.

CABBAGE (WHITE AND RED)

Remove the outer leaves and the core and shred finely. This will keep in a polythene bag or airtight plastic container for 2–3 days in the refrigerator, if required, before use.

SIDE SALADS

A meal is often accompanied by a side salad, either instead of or as well as vegetables. This type of salad is simple, often comprising of only two or three ingredients that are usually dressed with a very ordinary type of French dressing. More elaborate salads are more often served as part of a buffet or with cold foods, and they are included further on in the chapter. Remember that for a side salad, the ingredients should blend well with the food to be served, although they can be quite variable in themselves. Do not add the dressing until the last minute or let each person help himself. The salads may be prepared on individual dishes or in one bowl, but if made in one bowl, there should be separate dishes on the table for each guest to put their salad on. The ingredients should be prepared as already described and then put together when required.

These salads will serve from 4–6 portions each.

Green Salad

Choose from two to five of the following ingredients and arrange on side plates or in one salad bowl. Either add a little French dressing just before serving and toss through the mixture, or allow each guest to help themselves first to the salad and then to the dressing: lettuce leaves, snipped mustard and cress, sprigs of watercress, sliced or diced cucumber (peeled or unpeeled), slices or spikes of chicory, shredded white cabbage, sliced Chinese leaves, thin strips of deseeded green pepper, spring onions (scallions), etc. A salad looks more professional if sprinkled with freshly chopped parsley, mixed herbs or snipped chives just before serving.

Endive, Onion and Egg Salad

1/3–1/2 endive
1/2 bunch spring onions (scallions), trimmed
1–2 hard-boiled eggs
about 6 tablespoons French dressing (see page 140)

1   Separate the endive, wash and dry well and then tear into manageable pieces. Put onto plates or into a bowl.
2   Either slice or chop the spring onions and sprinkle over the endive.
3   Separate the eggs and chop the whites, then finely grate the yolks and sprinkle both over the endive. Add the dressing just before serving.

Cucumber Salad

1/2 cucumber (peeled if preferred)
about 6 tablespoons French dressing (see page 140)
1 tablespoon chopped capers (optional)
freshly chopped parsley or mint

1   Thinly slice the cucumber or, if preferred, cut into small dice.
2   Put into four small bowls and add the dressing. Leave to stand for at least 30 minutes.
3   Just before serving, sprinkle with the capers (if used) and the parsley or mint.

Tomato and Onion Salad

4 tomatoes, sliced
2 medium onions, peeled and thinly sliced
about 4 tablespoons French dressing (see page 140)
salt (optional)

1   Combine the tomato slices and onions, layering alternately in a bowl or on four plates.
2   Spoon the dressing over the top and leave to stand for about 30 minutes before serving. Sprinkle with chopped parsley, if liked.

Note: If the flavour of raw onion is too strong, it can be made milder by soaking in salt. Simply put the onion slices in a bowl and sprinkle with about 1 tablespoon salt. Leave to stand for 1/2–1 hour, drain off the liquid and rinse thoroughly under cold running water. Drain again and dry before continuing as above.

Coleslaw

1/4 head white cabbage, finely shredded
2–4 sticks celery, thinly sliced or chopped
4 spring onions (scallions), trimmed and chopped
50 g/2 oz/1/4 cup sultanas (golden raisins)
2 carrots, peeled and coarsely grated
6–8 tablespoons mayonnaise or soured cream dressing (see page 141)
salt (optional)

1   Mix the cabbage, celery, onions, sultanas and carrots together in a bowl.
2   Add the mayonnaise or dressing and toss thoroughly. Leave to stand for about 30 minutes or so before serving on individual plates.

Chicory and Watercress Salad

3–4 heads chicory
1 bunch watercress, trimmed
about 6 tablespoons French dressing (see page 140)
salt (optional)

1   Cut off the bases of the chicory and slice most of the way up the head, but leave a few small spikes on each to use for decoration.
2   Discard the stalks and any tatty pieces of watercress, add the small sprigs to the sliced chicory and toss well.
3   Just before serving, add the dressing and arrange the salad on small plates, adding the spikes of chicory for garnish.

Orange and Watercress Salad

4–6 oranges
6 tablespoons French dressing (see page 140)
1 bunch watercress, trimmed
a few lettuce leaves

1   Finely grate the rind from 1/2–1 orange and add to the dressing.
2   Cut away the peel and white pith from the oranges, including the grated one.
3   Either slice the oranges thinly or ease out the segments from between the membranes of the oranges with a small knife and put into a bowl.
4   Arrange lettuce leaves on small plates or in a serving bowl. Add the dressing to the oranges and toss well. Spoon the oranges onto the lettuce leaves.
5   Use the watercress sprigs to dot in and around the oranges and serve at once.

Chinese Leaf Medley

about 1/3 head Chinese leaves, thinly sliced
1 green pepper, deseeded and very thinly sliced
1 carton mustard and cress, or bunch of watercress
about 6 tablespoons French dressing (see page 140)

1 Combine the Chinese leaves and pepper in a bowl and toss well.
2 Snip the cress from its carton with scissors, taking care not to remove any of the peat or black seeds, or separate the watercress into sprigs. Add the cress to the salad and mix.
3 Just before serving, add the dressing and toss well.

Grapefruit and Avocado Salad

2 grapefruits
1–2 ripe avocados
crisp lettuce leaves
4 tablespoons French dressing (see page 140)
freshly chopped mint or parsley

1 Cut away the peel and white pith from the grapefruit with a sharp knife. Ease out the segments from between the membranes, holding the fruit over a bowl to catch the juice. Put the segments into a bowl.
2 Halve, remove the stones and peel the avocados. Cut the flesh carefully into small cubes and add to the grapefruit juice.
3 Add the drained avocado to the grapefruit segments with the dressing, mix well and leave to stand for up to an hour.
4 To serve, arrange lettuce leaves or shredded lettuce on 4–6 plates, spoon the avocado mixture and its dressing on top, sprinkle with mint or parsley and serve.

Potato Salad

450–675 g/1–1 1/2 lb potatoes, peeled and boiled
150 ml/1/4 pint/2/3 cup mayonnaise (see page 141)
salt and pepper
1–2 tablespoons snipped chives or freshly chopped parsley

1 Boil the potatoes until only just tender; they must not be allowed to overcook and begin to break up. Drain very thoroughly and, while still warm, cut into dice. Put into a bowl.
2 Add plenty of seasonings to the mayonnaise and add to the still warm potatoes. Toss lightly and turn into a serving dish. Cover with foil or plastic cling film and leave until cold.
3 Sprinkle with chives or parsley before serving.

Carrot and Endive Salad

4 carrots, peeled and cut into very narrow sticks
1/4 endive, broken into small pieces
5 cm/2 inch piece cucumber, diced or thinly sliced
about 6 tablespoons French dressing (see page 140)

1 Combine the carrots, endive and cucumber and place in a bowl.
2 Add the dressing just before serving and toss well.

MORE SUBSTANTIAL SALADS

The following salads are more likely to be offered as a selection of two or more at a meal, or as part of a buffet meal, when probably four or more would be offered. The side salads can also be made up in larger quantities to mix with these ones.

Nutty Slaw   Serves 6

1/4–1/2 white cabbage, trimmed and finely shredded
2 carrots, peeled and coarsely grated or cut into thin sticks
2–4 spring onions (scallions) trimmed and sliced (optional)
2 tablespoons freshly chopped parsley
50 g/2 oz/1/3 cup shelled walnuts, roughly chopped
150 ml/1/4 cup/2/3 cup French dressing or mayonnaise (see pages 140–1)

1 Combine the cabbage, carrots, onions (if used), parsley and walnuts in a bowl.
2 Add the dressing or mayonnaise and toss thoroughly. Turn into a serving bowl, cover with plastic cling film and leave for at least 30 minutes and up to 4 hours before serving.

Red Cabbage Slaw   Serves 6

1/4–1/2 red cabbage, trimmed and finely shredded
2 eating apples, cored and sliced or chopped
1 tablespoon lemon juice
2 sticks celery, thinly sliced
1–2 tablespoons finely chopped raw onion
50 g/2 oz/1/3 cup salted peanuts
6 tablespoons French dressing (see page 140)
1 tablespoon brown sugar

1 Put the red cabbage in a bowl.
2 Toss the apples in the lemon juice until well coated to prevent discolouration and then add to the cabbage with the lemon juice.
3 Add the celery and onion to the salad followed by the peanuts and mix thoroughly.
4 Combine the dressing and sugar and pour over the salad. Turn into a bowl and serve. Do not make up more than about 30 minutes before required as the cabbage stains everything it touches.

Fennel and Seafood Salad (see page 150) and Liver and Bacon Pâté (see page 75)

Waldorf Salad

Serves 6

450 g/1 lb eating apples
juice of 1 lemon
1/2 head celery, sliced
50 g/2 oz/1/2 cup shelled walnuts, roughly chopped
150 ml/1/4 pint/2/3 cup mayonnaise or soured cream
  dressing (see page 141)
freshly chopped parsley

1   Wipe the apples, quarter, remove the cores and either
    slice or chop. Place immediately in a bowl with the
    lemon juice and toss so the flesh does not discolour.
2   Add the celery and walnuts and mix well. Drain off any
    excess lemon juice.
3   Add the dressing and toss thoroughly. Turn into a
    serving bowl and sprinkle with chopped parsley. This
    salad may be prepared up to 4 hours before required.

Fruity Salad

Serves 6–8

4 tomatoes, sliced
5 cm/2 inch piece cucumber, diced
2 sticks celery, sliced
2 red-skinned apples
2 green-skinned apples
juice of 1 lemon
2 kiwi fruit
150 ml/1/4 pint/2/3 cup French dressing (see page 140)
crisp lettuce leaves

1   Combine the tomatoes, cucumber and celery in a bowl.
2   Wipe the apples and quarter them. Remove the cores,
    dice the flesh and toss in the lemon juice, making sure
    they are completely coated.
3   Peel and slice the kiwi fruit and add to the other
    ingredients with the drained apples. Add the dressing
    and toss lightly.
4   Line a shallow bowl with lettuce leaves and spoon the
    salad on top. Do not assemble more than about 30
    minutes before required.

Mushrooms à la Grecque

Serves 6

450 g/1 lb button mushrooms, trimmed
1 onion, peeled and finely chopped
1 large carrot, peeled and diced
1 clove garlic, crushed
3 tablespoons oil
150 ml/1/4 pint/2/3 cup dry white wine
1 bay leaf
salt and pepper
4 tomatoes, skinned (see page 17)
freshly chopped parsley to garnish

1   Fry the onion, carrot and garlic in the oil very gently
    until soft, stirring frequently, but taking care that they
    do not brown.
2   Add the wine, bay leaf and plenty of salt and pepper
    and bring to the boil.

3   Wipe the mushrooms and, if large, halve or quarter.
    Add to the pan, cover and simmer gently for about 10
    minutes. Remove from the heat.
4   Quarter the tomatoes, remove the seeds and then cut
    each piece in half. Add to the mushroom mixture, pour
    into a bowl, cover and leave until quite cold. Sprinkle
    with parsley before serving.

Bean and Bacon Salad

Serves 4–6

225 g/8 oz prepared broad (lima) beans, boiled
4 rashers lean bacon, derinded and chopped
1 onion, peeled and finely chopped
2 tablespoons oil
4–6 tablespoons soured cream dressing (see page 141)
lettuce leaves

1   Put the beans in a bowl and leave until cold.
2   Fry the bacon and onion gently in the oil until soft, then
    continue until a pale golden brown. Add to the salad
    and leave to cool.
3   Add the dressing, toss thoroughly, cover and leave to
    stand for at least an hour.
4   Arrange lettuce leaves in a shallow bowl and spoon the
    bean mixture on top.

French (Snap) Bean and Artichoke Salad

Serves 6

450 g/1 lb French (snap) beans, cooked
425 g/15 oz can artichoke hearts, drained
1–2 tablespoons finely chopped raw onion
4 tomatoes, peeled, quartered and deseeded
a few black olives (optional)
150 ml/1/4 pint/2/3 cup French dressing (see page 140)

1   Cut the beans into pieces about 4 cm/1 1/2 inches long
    and place in a bowl.
2   Cut the artichoke hearts into quarters and add to the
    beans with the onion.
3   Cut the pieces of tomato into smaller pieces and add to
    the salad with a few black olives, if liked.
4   Pour the dressing over the salad and leave to stand for
    at least an hour before serving.

Kidney Bean and Celeriac Salad

Serves 6–8

425 g/15 oz can red kidney beans, drained, or 225 g/8 oz/
  1 1/2 cups red kidney beans, cooked (see pages 133–4)
1/2 celeriac, peeled and cut into fine sticks
juice of 1 lemon
225 g/8 oz carrots, peeled and cut into thin sticks
1 tablespoon finely chopped onion
200 g/7 oz can sweetcorn kernels, drained
6–8 tablespoons French dressing (see page 140)
lettuce leaves

1   Put the celeriac sticks immediately into a bowl with the lemon juice, mix well and leave to stand for 10 minutes.
2   Drain off the excess lemon juice from the celeriac and add the beans, carrots, onion and sweetcorn followed by the dressing. Mix thoroughly.
3   Arrange lettuce leaves on a shallow plate or dish and spoon the salad and dressing on top.

Note: This salad may be tossed in the soured cream dressing (see page 141) if preferred.

Sweetcorn and Bean Sprout Salad

Serves 8

300 g/11 oz can sweetcorn kernels, drained, or 350 g/12 oz frozen sweetcorn kernels, boiled
225 g/8 oz fresh bean sprouts, or a 300 g/11 oz can bean sprouts, drained
8 spring onions (scallions), trimmed and chopped
4 tablespoons French dressing (see page 140)
1 tablespoon soy sauce
fresh spinach leaves, trimmed

1   Combine the sweetcorn, bean sprouts and onions in a bowl and mix well.
2   Mix the dressing and soy sauce, stir through the salad and leave to stand for at least 30 minutes.
3   Tear up the spinach leaves and arrange a fairly thick layer over the base of a shallow serving dish. Spoon the salad on top and serve.

Cauliflower and Caper Salad

Serves 6

1 cauliflower, trimmed and cut into small florets
salt
150 ml/¼ pint/⅔ cup French dressing (see page 140)
2 tablespoons capers
2 medium-sized courgettes (zucchini), trimmed and thinly sliced
freshly chopped parsley or mixed herbs

1   Put the cauliflower into a saucepan of boiling salted water for 1 minute. Drain thoroughly and turn into a bowl.
2   Pour the dressing over the cauliflower and mix thoroughly. Add the capers and courgettes, mix again and then leave until quite cold.
3   Serve sprinkled liberally with parsley or mixed herbs.

Dressed Fennel

Serves 6–8

1–2 bulbs Florence fennel
1 tablespoon finely chopped onion
about 12 black olives, halved and stoned
6 tablespoons soured cream dressing (see page 141)
endive or lettuce leaves

1   Trim the fennel and chop, reserving any of the feathery leaves for garnish.
2   Put into a bowl with the onion, olives and dressing and mix well. Leave to stand for 30 minutes.
3   Arrange endive or lettuce in a bowl and add salad.

MAIN COURSE SALADS

Main course salads are a very quick and easy meal and provide plenty of nutrients as well as interesting flavours. All that is required as an accompaniment is crusty bread or rolls and butter. Remember salads are good for you in the winter as well as the summer and take a lot less preparation and cooking than many other meals.

Tuna Bean Salad

Serves 4

200 g/7 oz can tuna fish, drained and roughly flaked
225 g/8 oz prepared broad (lima) beans, cooked
425 g/15 oz can red kidney beans, drained
1 tablespoon finely chopped onion or chives
4 sticks celery, thinly sliced
5 cm/2 inch piece cucumber, diced
1–2 eating apples, cored and diced
1 tablespoon lemon juice
6 tablespoons French dressing (see page 140)
endive or lettuce
2 hard-boiled eggs, cut into wedges

1   Put the broad and red beans into a bowl with the onion or chives, celery and cucumber.
2   Toss the apples in the lemon juice, leave to stand for about 5 minutes, then drain and add to the salad with the dressing. Toss well.
3   Add the tuna fish and mix lightly. Turn onto a bed of endive or lettuce and serve garnished with wedges of hard-boiled egg.

Mortadella and Peanut Salad

Serves 4–6

225–350 g/8–12 oz mortadella sausage in a piece
100–175 g/4–6 oz salted peanuts
450 g/1 lb white cabbage, trimmed and finely shredded
4 spring onions (scallions), trimmed and sliced
200 g/7 oz can pineapple rings, drained and chopped
2 bunches watercress
3 hard-boiled eggs, cut into wedges
150 ml/¼ pint/⅔ cup French dressing (see page 140)

1   Put the peanuts, cabbage, onions and pineapple into a bowl and mix well.
2   Cut the mortadella into slices and then into narrow strips and add to the salad.
3   Trim the watercress and add about 1½ bunches to the salad. Toss lightly and arrange on a large serving dish. Garnish around the edge with the remaining watercress and wedges of egg.
4   Pour the dressing over the top, leave to stand for about 30 minutes and serve.

Spinach and Bacon Salad · Serves 4–6

about 300 g/10 oz fresh spinach leaves, trimmed and
  thoroughly washed
225 g/8 oz lean bacon rashers, derinded and chopped
1 tablespoon finely chopped onion
2 eating apples, cored and chopped
6 tablespoons French dressing (see page 140)
8 hard-boiled eggs
150 ml/¼ pint/⅔ cup mayonnaise
6 tomatoes, quartered
Croûtons
4 slices bread, crusts removed and diced
6 tablespoons oil
25 g/1 oz/2 tablespoons butter

1 To make the croûtons, fry the diced bread in a mixture
   of the oil and melted butter in a frying pan until golden
   brown all over. They will need to be turned over during
   cooking and watched very carefully as they suddenly
   burn!
2 Drain the croûtons on absorbent kitchen paper towel
   and leave until cold.
3 Dry the spinach leaves thoroughly, tear up and place in
   a salad bowl.
4 Fry the bacon gently in its own fat (no need to add
   extra oil) until brown and crispy. Drain on absorbent
   kitchen paper towel, cool and add to the spinach with
   the onion.
5 Put the apples immediately into the French dressing,
   leave to stand for 5 minutes and then add to the salad
   with the dressing. Toss well. Turn onto a shallow
   serving dish or plate.
6 Arrange the halved eggs around the edge of the salad or
   on it and coat each egg with the mayonnaise. Place the
   tomatoes in between the eggs. Sprinkle the croûtons
   over the salad.

Gruyère and Ham Salad · Serves 4

225 g/8 oz Gruyère cheese
225 g/8 oz cooked ham in a piece
6 tablespoons soured cream dressing (see page 141)
½ cucumber, diced
lettuce leaves

1 Cut the cheese and ham into thin strips and put
   together in a bowl.
2 Add the dressing and toss together. Add the cucumber
   and mix again.
3 Arrange the lettuce leaves on a plate and spoon the
   salad on top.

Fennel and Seafood Salad · Serves 4

2 bulbs fennel, chopped
1 tablespoon capers, chopped
100 g/4 oz cooked peas
150 ml/¼ pint/⅔ cup French dressing (see page 140)
100 g/4 oz peeled prawns or shrimp
200 g/7 oz can mussels in brine, drained
175 g/6 oz/1 cup long grain rice, boiled (see page 134)
½ can anchovy fillets, drained (optional)
sprigs of parsley to garnish

1 Put the fennel into a bowl with the capers, peas and
   dressing. Leave to stand for at least 30 minutes.
2 Add the prawns or shrimp and mussels and mix
   thoroughly.
3 Arrange the cold rice on a flat serving dish or plate and
   spoon the salad into the centre.
4 Cut the anchovy fillets in half lengthwise and use to
   make a lattice design over the salad. Fill in with sprigs
   of parsley for garnish.

Note: If anchovy fillets are too salty for you, simply soak
them in a little milk for 30 minutes, drain and dry before
using.

Curried Chicken Salad · Serves 4–5

350 g/12 oz cooked chicken meat, cut into narrow strips
150 ml/¼ pint/⅔ cup mayonnaise (see page 141)
2–3 tablespoons natural yogurt or soured cream
1–2 teaspoons curry powder (to taste)
2 tablespoons apricot jam
salt and pepper
grated rind of ½ lemon
4 spring onions (scallions), trimmed and chopped
100 g/4 oz cooked peas
100 g/4 oz green grapes, halved and depipped
100 g/4 oz black grapes, halved and depipped
175 g/6 oz/1 cup long grain rice, cooked
25 g/1 oz/¼ cup flaked almonds, toasted
watercress to garnish

1 Combine the mayonnaise, yogurt, curry powder, jam,
   seasonings, lemon rind and onions.
2 Add the chicken meat and peas, mix well, cover and
   leave to stand for at least an hour in a cool place.
3 Stir the grapes through the salad.
4 Arrange the rice around the edge of a flat plate and
   spoon the chicken mixture into the centre.
5 Sprinkle the almonds over the chicken and garnish
   around the edges with sprigs of watercress.

Kidney Bean and Celeriac Salad (see page 148) *and French Bean and Artichoke Salad* (see page 148)

11 Fruits

Fruit plays a very important part in every diet but, apart from being a necessity, it is a delicious and widely versatile food too. Many fruits are only served raw while others can be just as good when served raw or cooked. Fruits come from all over the world and are exported and imported widely so it is possible for a great many people to sample all types of foreign fruits as well as home-grown varieties. Seasons do of course vary and the imported fruits vary in cost depending on whether they are plentiful or scarce when exported. Some recipes will be given here but more will be found in the chapters on hot and cold puddings and in the pastry section.

APPLES
These are widely grown throughout the world in temperate regions. Varieties of apples are numerous and can be divided into eaters and cookers. Home-produced apples are ripe from late summer onwards and many will keep well into the following year, provided they have been expertly picked, packed and stored. One or two varieties of apples can double up as eaters and cookers, often mellowing as they age. Eating apples vary in size and skin colour, ranging from green through yellow and russet to red, and the flesh changing from crisp and tart to soft and sweet. Cookers tend to be larger and have skins ranging from green to partly red. Their flesh is crisp and often very tart, although this can sweeten up and some apples are quite sweet enough for some people to eat in spite of being labelled cookers. When peeled or cut, the flesh of all apples will discolour and turn brown very quickly. It is advisable to peel, core, slice and cook very quickly to prevent this or, if for garnish or decoration or to add to a salad or something that requires raw apple, the cut slices or pieces should be immediately dipped into lemon juice which will help counteract the tendency to discolour.

Popular varieties of apples that are available widely include: Cox's Orange Pippin, Golden Russet, Golden Delicious, etc. And popular cookers are Bramley's, Newton Wonder, etc.

It is more usual to only cook the cookers, but some dishes call for cooking one of the eating varieties, and very good they are too, but remember they are already sweet, so adjust the sweetness if for a sweet dish and add something to counteract the sweetness in a savoury dish.

APRICOTS
These are imported from warmer climes. They are about the size of a plum and yellowish-orange in colour with a velvety slightly rough skin and a stone like a plum in the middle. The flesh is the same colour as the skin. Apricots should be eaten when barely ripe for, when overripe, they become very soft, woolly and rather flavourless, while, if underripe, they are just hard and rather sour.

Use raw or cooked in puddings, pies, all types of cold desserts and preserves. The kernel of the apricot is very tasty and a few can be cracked open and added when stewing the fruit. Apricots are also available dried and in cans, and can be used in savoury dishes.

CHERRIES
The colour of these varies from almost all white with pink tinges through pink and red to almost black. Use raw or cooked, but take care not to swallow the stones. A special cherry stoner helps make the task of removing the stones easier. Use for pies and tarts, in fruit salads, sauces, fillings for cakes, etc. Cherries are excellent used in savoury recipes, and are also available in cans.

BLACKBERRIES
These are available wild and cultivated; the cultivated ones being much larger and juicier although not always as sweet. They are small and dark red to black with a mass of little pips all over. These pips can get into your teeth and in some recipes, after cooking to a purée, it is best to sieve the fruit. Use raw in fruit salads or cooked in pies, puddings and other desserts, and also use widely in preserving.

BILBERRIES
These do grow wild on bushes in some parts of Great Britain and can be found on moors and in hedgerows. However, most of them are imported and often sold in cans or frozen. The berries are very small, smaller than blackcurrants, and are dark blue to mauve in colour. They are sour, so they are best cooked before eating.

CRANBERRIES
These are small and round, bright crimson on the outside with sometimes a touch of yellow or cream, and full of tiny seeds inside. They are sour when eaten raw so should be cooked first and can be used for a wealth of ideas from compotes, soufflés, mousses, etc., to use in cakes and baking, and also in many savoury dishes.

AVOCADO
This is strictly termed a fruit, but I have decribed it in the chapter on salads. Use it raw in fruit salads, after dipping the flesh in lemon juice to prevent discolouration.

BANANAS

These are the fruit of a tropical tree, mainly grown in the tropics as well as the Canary Islands and Madeira, which have their own Canary or Dwarf banana – small, quite strongly-flavoured and sweet with a dark creamish-pink flesh. The larger Jamaican or plantain bananas are paler in colour and have a much less pronounced flavour. They are imported in huge bunches – called hands – and are often unripe and still green when they arrive. However, they ripen quickly in the warmth of special storage rooms. They are usually eaten raw or added to salads, compotes, etc., and are used for decoration but they must be dipped in lemon juice first to prevent discolouration. They may also be added to hot compotes and used in fritters, etc., and are sometimes served fried with some savoury dishes.

CRAB APPLE

This is really a wild species of very small apple, about the size of a walnut. There are several types of both Japanese and Siberian Crab apples – some are purely ornamental but can be used for cooking too. Most crab apples have a shiny red and/or yellow skin with firm flesh. They need to be cooked, as they are very sour, and are most often used in preserves and jams.

KIWI FRUIT

These used to be known as Chinese Gooseberries but, since their popularity in New Zealand and their subsequent export and popularity all over the place, this egg-shaped fruit with its brown rough and hairy skin and bright green flesh with black seeds in it has come to stay. The flavour is delicate but blends well with other fruits and can be used for decorations for both sweet and savoury dishes.

DAMSON

This is like a small plum with a skin of purple to dark blue and yellow flesh. It is again rather tart and best cooked to serve in pies, tarts and many other desserts. Once cooked, there are numerous stones and it is best to try and pick some of them out before serving. It is also widely used for preserves.

DATE

This fruit grows high up on date palms in warm climates. It is oval shaped and a rich shiny brown with a long cylindrical stone. Dates are available fresh, frozen and dried and poor quality fruit are stoned and packed into solid packs ready for cooking.

CURRANTS

There are three varieties of these: black, red and white. Blackcurrants are the most popular, being small black fruits about the size of a small pea and they grow in strings or clusters. They are rather tart in flavour so are more usually cooked, but they have a good rich taste ideal for puddings, pies, fruit compotes, etc., and are also used widely in preserves and fruit drinks.

The redcurrant is of course famous for redcurrant jelly. It is the same size as the black variety but bright crimson and almost translucent. Again, really too tart to eat raw, but lightly poached they are ideal for fruit salads, and are widely used in pies, puddings, soufflés, etc.

White currants are less common than the other two varieties but can be used in the same ways. They are a pinky white and again almost translucent.

ORANGES

These grow readily in any hot climate on an evergreen tree. There are two main types – sweet and bitter – but all are a good bright orange colour. A sweet orange eaten straight from the tree has an unbelievably good flavour – much richer and fresher than those that have had to be picked, packed and exported.

Sweet oranges are divided into several types:

Jaffa – these are the large oranges with thick, rough skins and bright orange in colour. The flesh is very juicy and very sweet.
Ovals – these are much smaller and almost oval in shape with a golden yellow-orange skin, which is much smoother than the Jaffas, and a light golden flesh.
Navel – these are given this name because of the small growth at one end of the orange. They are a good orange colour with very sweet and juicy flesh.
Blood – so called because the flesh is flecked with red, and the skins often have a red tinge. They are quite small and very sweet.

Sweet oranges are more often eaten raw or included in many types of cold sweets and desserts, but can be mixed with such fruit as apple for pies, etc. The grated rind and juice are widely used in both sweet and savoury dishes and the thinly pared rind (removed with a potato peeler) can be cut into strips and shapes to be cooked and used as a decoration or garnish.

Bitter oranges – known as Seville oranges – are used for marmalade making, wines, fruit juices and as a flavouring in savoury dishes. The flesh is far too bitter to eat raw, but it gives a certain piquancy to many savoury dishes and sauces, especially those incorporating domestic or wild duck and other game.

Different varieties of oranges are available all the year.

ORTANIQUE

This is a citrus fruit which is a cross between an orange and a tangerine. It has a bright orange colour and very sweet flesh with a slight tangerine flavour. It comes from Jamaica.

TANGERINE

There are several varieties of tangerines, which are all small types of orange with a thin easily-removed rind. Some have rather large pips and others have no pips at all, but are good to add to fruit salads, fillings for pies, etc., and the rind and juice is very good used in both sweet and savoury dishes and is also used widely in marmalade making.

CLEMENTINES

These are not quite so sweet as the tangerine, with a smoother skin, more the colour of an orange, and are usually almost pip-free.

SATSUMAS

These are a type of mandarin orange, similar to the mandarin in shape, colour and flavour, but seedless.

MANDARINS

These are rather flatter than a tangerine, almost looking as if they have been squashed. The skin is very loose around the fruit so comes off very easily. The skin is a deep rich orange and the flesh very sweet but often has pips.

UGLI FRUIT

This is also a citrus fruit and is a cross between a grapefruit and a tangerine. It is about the size of a smallish grapefruit with a slightly pointed end and rather loose skin which is very thick and a yellowish green. It has a sweetish very pleasant flavour and is usually served as a dessert fruit.

GRAPEFRUIT

This is the largest of the citrus fruits with a splendid but rather tart flesh. It is often eaten raw as it is, or with sugar to offset the tartness, and is also added to fruit salads, savoury salads, and cooked sweet and savoury dishes. It is most famous as a breakfast dish, served as it is, or as a starter to a meal, cold, or with sherry and sugar added and grilled or broiled or baked. The skin is smooth thick and yellow and the flesh too is usually yellow, although there are also 'pink' grapefruit which have a pretty pink-tinged flesh which tends to be a little sweeter than the yellow varieties. Also used widely in marmalade making and for fruit drinks.

LEMON

These, like oranges, are grown widely in any hot country and again come from an evergreen tree. There are many varieties which vary in size depending on which country they have come from. The skin is bright yellow, usually fairly thick and slightly rough, although some varieties are very smooth, but the flesh is very sharp and sour. It is probably the fruit most often used for flavouring, both in sweet and savoury dishes, either as juice or rind, and for both hot and cold dishes. Its acid juice is invaluable for coating fruits and vegetables that discolour easily when peeled or cut. Its uses are innumerable, but also include marmalade and all jam making, where its high protein content is useful, as well as cordials and sauces, etc.

LIMES

This citrus fruit is rather smaller than a lemon with a smooth green skin and yellow-green very tart flesh with a few pips. When ripe or overripe the skin becomes yellowish-green. Limes are rarely used raw in this country except as slices in drinks, but the peel and juice are often used for flavouring and the whole fruit is used for marmalades and cordials.

PEACHES

This is a round fruit with a soft velvet-like skin of yellow, red and orange and deep orange-yellow down to a creamy colour flesh, depending on variety and whether home-grown or imported. The stone is large, usually about the size of a damson or small plum, and is either a 'freestone', when it easily separates from the flesh, or clingstone, when it adheres firmly to the flesh and is often difficult to remove. Use raw in all types of sweet dishes and fruit salads or as a dessert fruit, or poach lightly to add to both sweet and savoury dishes, especially salads.

NECTARINES

This fruit is similar to a peach in flavour, colouring and appearance except it is usually a little smaller and the skin is smooth like a plum. Nectarines are usually eaten raw but can replace peaches in any recipe.

MELONS

Melons vary in colour, shape and type. They are usually slightly oval balls with a thick skin and rather watery flesh with seeds right in the centre of the fruit. Watermelon is the exception.

Ogen – small melons, sufficient for 1–2 portions with a smooth yellowish-orange skin with greenish stripes. The flesh is golden yellow, very sweet and has rather a scented flavour. Cut in half, discard the pips and serve.

Charentais – smaller than the Ogen usually with a similar skin and flesh almost a pink/orange colour. They smell and taste very sweet and scented. Halve, remove the seeds and serve.

Honeydew – an oval melon with dark green ridged skin or a pale greenish-white skin. The flesh is always a greenish-yellow, mellow flavoured and quite sweet. Serve in slices with the seeds discarded.

Canteloupe – this melon is almost rounded in shape but the skin is segmented and usually a dark green. The flesh is a pinkish-orange and quite sweet. Serve in slices.

Watermelon – this one is different from all the other melons as the pips are interspersed with the deep pink to red flesh. The flesh is very watery with a mild but very refreshing flavour. The skin is dark green and smooth, often with mottled black spots, and the size varies from that of a large grapefruit to larger than a football.

Melons are usually served as a starter or in fruit salads but can also be used in preserves and pickles.

RASPBERRIES

These soft juicy fruits are grown on canes. They are a deep pink-red with a central hull and a sweet but slightly sharp taste and numerous pips which do very little harm. They are usually eaten raw or added to all types of fruit desserts, but are also added to pies and other cooked dishes and make excellent preserves.

LOGANBERRIES

This soft fruit is similar to a raspberry but larger and a deep purplish-red colour with a hard central hull. Use fresh as raspberries or cook in pies, etc., and they make a wonderful jam.

MULBERRY

This fruit is similar to a blackberry in size but a little rounder. Mulberries are grown on large trees usually in an old garden and are becoming very rare. The colour is red which deepens to a deep maroon when really ripe and they then tend to fall off the tree. Use as raspberries and blackberries.

STRAWBERRIES

These are widely grown in many countries. They are bright red in colour and round with a pinkish flesh, a small central hull and tiny pips embedded in the outer skin. Sizes vary from that of a small cherry up to a large plum. They

Selection of Jams and Jellies (see pages 157–60)

are usuallly eaten raw, either on their own or in salads or desserts. Strawberry purée is also widely used in desserts.

RHUBARB

This is rather a strange fruit, as the edible part is the stem of a plant and the leaves are inedible. Early or 'forced' rhubarb is a bright pale to deep pink with very tender sticks. As it matures it becomes tougher and the colour changes to green tinged with pink and red. The flavour also increases and is rather sharp and acid. It cannot be eaten raw as it is too hard and sour. Poach in syrup to serve as it is or use widely in puddings and pies as well as in jams and preserves.

QUINCE

This fruit has a strange shape, a cross between an apple and pear, with a yellowish-green to russet-coloured skin which has a 'down' all over it. The flesh is creamy coloured and very hard with lots of black pips. The flavour is excellent and slightly perfumed and it is often cooked with apples to use in puddings and pies. It is always cooked, unless you like a hard rather strange-flavoured fruit to nibble. When cooked, the flesh turns a pink-orange and when made into preserves becomes a deep glowing orange-red. They are not always easy to find but are in season in the autumn.

POMEGRANATE

This strange fruit is about the size of an orange with a hard russet-coloured skin resembling a shell and masses of hard pips covered in soft, perfume-flavoured red flesh. It can be served as a dessert or added to fruit salads and the juice is often extracted to make into a drink or to add to fruit salads.

PLUMS

There are many different varieties of plums which vary in size, colour, shape and flavour. The skin ranges from yellow, through orange and pink to bright pink, red, purple and almost black, but the flesh is usually yellow often with a red tinge, especially in the darker-coloured ones. The stones can be freestone or clingstone and the flavour varies from deep and very sweet to really very tart; these tart plums are best kept for cooking. Many varieties are dessert plums and only eaten raw, but most types can be cooked and used in a wealth of puddings and pies, etc., and of course in preserves and pickles.

GREENGAGES

Also known as yellow gages, these are like small rather round plums with skins of green or greenish-yellow and a yellow flesh. The taste is often superior to plums and usually sweet. Use as for plums.

SHARON FRUIT

This is a new addition to the regular fruits. It looks like a rather flat large potato with a smooth deep orange skin – like a semi-ripe tomato – with a green calyx in the centre. It has a unique very pleasant flavour. Eat raw or add to fruit salads.

GUAVA

These are more often seen canned. The fruit is about the size of a pear and varies in shape from that of a pear to an apple or tomato. The flesh is a bright light pink which is fairly firm and there are many yellow hard seeds. Eat raw or put in fruit salads, or add to vegetable salads. They can also be added to a casserole.

LITCHIS OR LYCHEES

These strange fruits are grown on a tree and originated in China but are now grown elsewhere too. They are the size of a small plum with a hard reddish-brown scaly skin, rather like a thin shell, and translucent white flesh around a large shiny brownish-black stone. The flesh is very perfumed and sweet. They are eaten raw or added to fruit salads.

KUMQUAT

This is another fruit of a small tree originating in China and Japan. It is closely related to the orange but is the size of a small plum and an elongated oval in shape. Kumquats are eaten raw and added to fruit salads and desserts calling for fresh fruits. They are also used in preserves and crystallized.

GRAPES

Most grapes are imported. There are both black and white grapes. The black tend to be a dark purple, although at some times of year they are almost a deep red or murky light purple. White grapes tend to be a yellowish green and there are the tiny muscat grapes which are seedless and a bright pale green. The flesh is a translucent pale greenish-white in all varieties. They are usually eaten raw or added to fruit salads and fruit desserts and widely used as decoration, although some savoury dishes call for grapes, particularly fish and chicken dishes. Black grapes are usually halved and depipped, or left whole with the pips removed with the help of a hairpin; white grapes may be skinned or left unpeeled and prepared as for black grapes.

FIGS

There are two varieties, green and purple, and both have numerous small seeds inside. The green fig has a green skin and yellowish-green flesh, while the purple fig has a purple-brown outer skin and red to purple flesh. Eaten raw as a dessert or add to fruit salads. They are also widely available dried, when they are more often added to cooked puddings and sweets.

GOOSEBERRIES

These vary tremendously in size and shape. Some are round, others oval and others long, but apart from the large dessert gooseberries, which are green with purplish tinges or yellowish green, the gooseberry is green and either smooth or hairy. The inside is full of edible pips and they are very sour unless special dessert varieties. Add dessert gooseberries to all fruit salads and uncooked dishes, but the others must be cooked in some form with sugar added to counteract the tartness.

PINEAPPLE

This is a tropical fruit which is almost cylindrical in shape with a top of spiky greenish-grey leaves and a rough, hard, ridged skin of a yellowish-orange colour, sometimes tinged with green. The flesh is firm and juicy and, when ripe, very sweet and varies in colour from pale to deep yellow. The skin does contain numerous 'eyes' which must be cut out before serving. Pineapple is usually served fresh, cut into slices, and eaten as it is. Liqueurs may be poured over before serving or it may be sprinkled with sugar and grilled or broiled.

Plum Jam

For jam making, any white sugar can be used, whether granulated, caster (superfine), preserving or lump sugar. (See step-by-step illustrations, page 158.)

2.75 kg/6 lb plums (any variety but preferably freestone)
600 ml/1 pint/2½ cups water
2.75 kg/6 lb/12 cups any white sugar

1 Remove the stalks from the fruit and wash and drain well. Cut in half and, if possible, remove the stones. Crack some of the stones and remove the kernels. If the plums are not freestone, then leave them whole.
2 Put the plums and about a tablespoon or so of the kernels (if liked) into a preserving pan or very large saucepan. Add the water and bring slowly to the boil. Simmer gently, uncovered, until the fruit is very soft and the contents of the pan reduced by a third to a half. If using unstoned plums, remove the stones as they come to the surface with a slotted spoon.
3 Add the sugar all at once to the fruit, and stir continuously over a low heat until completely dissolved, then bring back to the boil.
4 If you have one, add a sugar thermometer to the pan and boil hard until the jam reaches setting point. Do not stir the jam once the sugar has begun to boil, but any excess scum can be removed from the surface with a slotted spoon. Setting point is reached in one of three ways. If using a sugar thermometer, boil until the jam reaches a temperature of 105°C/221°F – this should take 20–30 minutes. Or use the flake test – remove some of the jam on a wooden spoon and then let the jam drop off. If it has been boiled long enough, the drops will run together to form flakes which will then break off sharply. Or do the saucer test – which is very simple. Put a little jam on a cold saucer and leave it to cool. When you push your finger across the jam it should wrinkle. If not, boil for another 2 minutes and try again. Remember to remove the boiling jam from the heat while testing if it is set, otherwise, if it is ready, it will be overcooked and set too firmly.
5 Remove the jam from the heat and take off any scum with a slotted spoon and any stones that may still be there. A knob of butter stirred through the cooked jam will help disperse the scum.
6 Clean, sound jam jars should be put to warm in a cool oven when the sugar is added to the jam. Pour the jam carefully into the warmed jars (if not warmed, they will crack) and cover each with a waxed disc (wax side touching the surface of the jam). Cover with a dampened cellophane circle, stretch to cover the top of the jar smoothly and hold in place with a rubber band. Leave to cool.
7 When cold, wipe the jars so they are not sticky and label clearly with the type of jam and date made. Store in a cool, dry and preferably dark place. Keep for a couple of weeks before use. Jam stores well for up to a year and sometimes longer.
Makes about 4.5 kg/10 lb

VARIATIONS
Strawberry – use 1.6 kg/3½ lb strawberries, 3 tablespoons lemon juice and 1.4 kg/3 lb/6 cups white sugar – no extra liquid is required – and cook the fruit gently with the lemon juice for about 30 minutes. When ready, leave the jam to stand for 15 minutes before potting to prevent the fruit rising in the jars.
Raspberry – use 1.8 kg/4 lb each fresh raspberries and white sugar (8 cups). Cook with no added liquid for about 20 minutes, add the sugar and continue as for plum jam.
Blackcurrant – use 1.8 kg/4 lb blackcurrants, 1.7 litres/3 pints/7½ cups water and 2.75 kg/6 lb/12 cups white sugar. Make sure the blackcurrants are extra tender after the initial cooking in the water or a tough jam will result.
Gooseberry – use 1.8 kg/4 lb gooseberries, 750 ml/1¼ pints/3 cups water and 2.3 kg/5 lb/10 cups sugar. Top and tail the gooseberries before washing.

Redcurrant Jelly

Jellies are made in much the same way as jams except the cooked fruit must be allowed to drip through a scalded muslin bag into a bowl without being disturbed in any way if the finished jelly is to be completely clear.

1.4 kg/3 lb redcurrants
500 ml/scant pint/2½ cups water
sugar (allow 450 g/1 lb/2 cups to each 500 ml/scant pint/2½ cups strained juice)

1 Wash the fruit without removing the stalks and place in a saucepan with the water. Bring to the boil and simmer gently until very soft, stirring occasionally.
2 Mash the fruit well with a potato masher and then pour through a jelly bag. This bag can be a clean cloth or double thickness of muslin and it can be tied to the legs of an upturned stool with the bowl placed underneath it. Once the fruit mixture has been added to the bag, it must not be pressed or even touched or it will make the jelly turn cloudy. Leave to drip until nothing comes through – it is best left overnight.
3 Measure the juice – or extract as it is called – into a large saucepan and to each 500 ml/scant pint/2½ cups, add 450 g/1 lb/2 cups white sugar. Heat gently until the sugar dissolves, add a sugar thermometer, if available and boil until setting point is reached, 105°C/221°F. Test for setting as in Plum Jam.
4 Pour into warmed jars, cover with a waxed disc and cellophane paper top and, when cold, label. Store in a cool, dry, dark place.
It is difficult to say exactly how much jelly the recipe will make as it depends on how much it is boiled before straining, and how much liquid is strained out.
Makes about 2.3–2.75 kg/5–6 lb

Strawberry Jam (see page 157)

1 *Put the strawberries and lemon juice into a large saucepan or preserving pan. Cook the fruit gently for about 30 minutes before adding the sugar.*

3 *Take off any scum with a slotted spoon.*

2 *To test for setting point, put a little jam on a cold saucer and leave to cool. When you put your finger across the jam, it should wrinkle.*

4 *Put the jam carefully into warmed jars, cover and seal as in the method for Plum Jam.*

VARIATIONS

These are all made in the same way as redcurrant.

Blackberry and Apple – use 1.8 kg/4 lb blackberries, 900 g/2 lb cooking apples, washed and chopped up roughly including the skins and cores, 1.2 litres/2 pints/5 cups water and any white sugar as above.

Bramble – use 1.8 kg/4 lb blackberries, juice of 2 large lemons, 450 ml/³⁄₄ pint/scant 2 cups water and any white sugar.

Quince – use 1.8 kg/4 lb quinces, washed and cut up roughly with skins and cores, thinly pared rind and juice of

3 lemons, 1.7 litres/3 pints/7½ cups water and any white sugar. (Half quinces and half cooking apples can be used.)

Crab Apple – use 1.8 kg/4 lb crab apples, 1.4 litres/2½ pints/6¼ cups water, about 6 whole cloves or the thinly pared rind of 1 large orange (optional) and white sugar.

Apple and Orange – use 4 sweet oranges, 1.4 kg/3 lb cooking apples, both cut up roughly with peel, skin, pips and cores, 1.7 litres/3 pints/7½ cups water and any white sugar.

Damson – use 1.8 kg/4 lb damsons, 1.2 litres/2 pints/5 cups water and any white sugar.

OPPOSITE: *Winter Fruit Salad* (see page 162) *and Apples and Oranges Bristol* (see page 162)

Orange Marmalade

Marmalades are made in much the same way as jams but the thin slices of peel must be thoroughly cooked before adding the sugar or they will be hard and chewy and the pips and pith must be tied in a muslin bag and cooked with the fruit for the pectin is in this part of the fruit and without it the marmalade will not set.

1.4 kg/3 lb Seville oranges
juice of 2 lemons
2.75 litres/5 pints/12 cups water
2.75 kg/6 lb/12 cups white sugar

1 Wash the fruit thoroughly, scrubbing off any stubborn marks. Cut the fruit in half, squeeze out the juice and remove the pips and tough membrane. Set the pips and membrane aside and put the juice and lemon juice into a preserving or very large saucepan.
2 Cut the peel into thin shreds (or coarsely mince if preferred) and put into the preserving pan with the water. Tie the pips and membrane into a piece of muslin and add to the pan as well.
3 Bring slowly to the boil and then boil, uncovered, until tender and the contents of the pan are reduced by a third to a half. The peel must be really tender at this stage. This should take about 2 hours.
4 Remove the muslin bag and squeeze out as much juice as possible with the back of a wooden spoon.
5 Add the sugar and stir until completely dissolved and then bring to the boil. Add a sugar thermometer and boil until setting point is reached, 105°C/221°F. Test if set as for Plum Jam (see page 157).
6 Remove any scum from the surface and leave to stand for about 10 minutes to allow the peel to distribute itself evenly, then pour into warmed jars and cover with waxed discs and cellophane covers. When cold, wipe the jars, label clearly and store in a cool, dark place. Marmalade will keep for up to 18 months.
Makes about 4.5 kg/10 lb.

VARIATIONS

Mixed Fruit – use 4 lemons, 2 sweet oranges and 2 grapefruit, which should weigh in total 1.4 kg/3 lb, 2.75 litres/5 pints/12½ cups water and 2.75 kg/6 lb/12 cups white sugar.
Lemon or Lime – use 1.4 kg/3 lb thin-skinned lemons or limes, 2.75 litres/5 pints/12½ cups water and 2.75 kg/ 6 lb/12 cups white sugar.
Ginger – use 450 g/1 lb Seville oranges, 2.75 litres/ 5 pints/12½ cups water, 1.4 kg/3 lb cooking apples, 3 kg/6½ lb/13 cups white sugar, 225 g/8 oz preserved or stem ginger, finely chopped and 4 teaspoons ground ginger. Wash and peel the oranges and shred the peel finely. Cut up the flesh and tie the pips in a piece of muslin. Put the peel, flesh, juice, bag of pips and all but 150 ml/ ¼ pint/⅔ cup of the water into a preserving pan and simmer for 1½ hours until tender. Remove the pips. Peel, core and slice the apples, simmer in the remaining water until pulpy. Add to the oranges with the sugar, chopped and ground ginger and continue as above.

Peach Melba

Serves 4

4 fresh ripe peaches, or 6 nectarines
100 g/4 oz fresh or frozen raspberries
1 tablespoon caster (superfine) sugar
vanilla ice cream (see page 192)
a little whipped cream (optional)
2 tablespoons chopped shelled walnuts or pecan nuts

1 Cut the peaches in half and remove the stones, or if preferred cut into quarters or thick slices.
2 Rub the raspberries through a sieve and mix the sugar into the purée.
3 Put one or two scoops or several spoons of vanilla ice cream into four individual glasses or bowls. Add 2 peach halves or 3 nectarine halves to each dish and spoon the raspberry sauce over them.
4 Pipe a large whirl of whipped cream on top of the peaches, sprinkle with chopped nuts and serve.

Rhubarb Snow

Serves 4–6

450 g/1 lb rhubarb, trimmed
4 tablespoons water
juice of 1 large orange
50–100 g/2–4 oz/¼–½ cup any white sugar (or to taste)
2 eggs, separated
frosted mint leaves to decorate (see below)

1 Cut the rhubarb into 2.5 cm/1 inch pieces, wash and drain well.
2 Place in a saucepan with the water and orange juice. Bring to the boil, cover the pan and simmer very gently until the rhubarb is very soft and tender – about 5 minutes. Add sugar to taste and stir until dissolved.
3 Either beat the rhubarb until very smooth, rub through a sieve or purée in a liquidizer or food processor.
4 Turn the purée into a bowl and beat in the egg yolks until quite smooth. Cool.
5 Whisk the egg whites until very stiff and dry, beat 2 tablespoons into the rhubarb mixture and then fold the remainder quickly and evenly through the rhubarb.
6 Turn into individual glasses, chill and serve each decorated with a frosted mint leaf.

VARIATIONS

Apple – use 450 g/1 lb peeled, cored and sliced cooking apples and the grated rind of 1 small orange.
Blackberry and Apple – use 175 g/6 oz blackberries and 350 g/12 oz apples, and sieve to remove the pips.
Redcurrant and Apple – use 175 g/6 oz redcurrants (topped and tailed) and 350 g/12 oz apples.

Frosted Mint Leaves

Select 4 or 6 small sprigs of fresh mint and wash and dry thoroughly. Dip each into the egg white to be used for the snow and then immediately coat in caster (superfine) sugar. Leave on a plate to dry.

Stewed Fruits

Stewed fruit is called for in many recipes whether as a filling for a pie, or to serve hot or cold as it is. Most fruits can be stewed with various flavouring additions, but the sugar content does vary with all fruits and is in fact a matter of personal taste.

450 g/1 lb prepared fresh fruit
75–100 g/3–4 oz/¹/₃–¹/₂ cup any white sugar
150 ml/¹/₄ pint/²/₃ cup water

1 Make a syrup by dissolving the sugar in the water over a gentle heat. If you are cooking a hard fruit, increase the water to up to 300 ml/¹/₂ pint/1¹/₄ cups.
2 Add the fruit and simmer gently until it is soft but still keeps its shape. Do not allow to fast boil or the fruit will break up.
3 Some fruits are enhanced by the addition of certain flavourings; try one of the following:

To stewed pears, add 2 whole cloves, or a small piece of cinnamon stick, or the thinly pared rind of ¹/₂ orange.
To stewed apples, add the juice of ¹/₂ lemon, thinly pared rind of ¹/₂ lemon or orange, finely grated rind of ¹/₂ orange, 2–3 cloves or a small piece of cinnamon stick.
To stewed rhubarb, add a little grated orange rind or a piece of bruised root ginger.
To stewed plums, add the plum kernels or a few whole sweet blanched almonds.

All the following fruits are suitable for stewing and to serve hot or cold with cream, custard or ice cream. They can also be incorporated into other recipes.
Apples, blackberries and apples, rhubarb and apples, blackberries, blackcurrants, blueberries, cranberries, cherries, apricots, gooseberries, rhubarb, pears, red and white currants, plums, greengages, damsons, etc.
If you want to stew soft fruit, such as raspberries and strawberries, it is best to make the syrup as above and leave to cool. Put the fruit into a bowl, pour the syrup over and leave to stand for an hour or so. If stewed, they will just break up.

Stewed Dried Fruits   Serves 6–8

450 g/1 lb dried fruit (e.g. prunes, apricots, peaches, figs,
  apples, pears, etc., or a mixture of dried fruits)
600 ml/1 pint/2¹/₂ cups water
100–225 g/4–8 oz/¹/₂–1 cup demerara or any white sugar
piece of thinly pared lemon rind

1 Wash the fruits thoroughly and place in a bowl. Cover with the measured cold water and leave to soak for 8–12 hours.
2 Turn the soaked fruit and its liquor into a saucepan and add the sugar and lemon rind. Bring to the boil and simmer gently until the ingredients are tender – this will take from 15–30 minutes depending on type.
3 Turn the fruit into a bowl and serve hot or leave until cold and serve chilled with cream, custard or ice cream.

FRUIT SALADS

There are numerous types of fruit salad that can be made using all sorts of ingredients or keeping to just a few. Colours too can be used for a red, green or yellow salad. Make sure the fruit used is fresh and of good quality and allow a few hours for the flavours to marry together. Fruit salads are best served slightly chilled and with a pouring or whipped cream.

Fresh Fruit Salad   Serves 6–8

2 pears
2 red-skinned apples
2 large oranges
1 peach or nectarine (optional)
100 g/4 oz black grapes, halved and depipped
100 g/4 oz white grapes, halved and depipped
1–2 bananas (optional)
Syrup
100 g/4 oz/¹/₂ cup any white sugar
300 ml/¹/₂ pint/1¹/₄ cups water
juice of ¹/₂–1 lemon

1 For the syrup, put the sugar and water into a saucepan and heat gently until the sugar has dissolved, then bring to the boil and boil for 5 minutes. Allow to cool, add the lemon juice and pour into a bowl.
2 Peel, core and slice the pears and add immediately to the syrup.
3 Quarter, core and slice the apples, add to the syrup and mix well.
3 Cut off the top and bottom of the oranges. Stand them on a board and cut off the peel and pith together from top to bottom using a sharp knife. Either cut the oranges into thin slices or ease out the segments from between the membranes and add to the syrup.
4 Halve the peach or nectarine, remove the stone and either slice or chop and add to the salad with the grapes.
5 If using banana, peel and slice and dip in lemon juice to coat thoroughly before adding to the salad. Chill for up to 2 hours before serving.

Note: The syrup may be made using only half the water and, when cold, 150 ml/¹/₄ cup/²/₃ cup white wine may be added with the lemon juice.

Winter Fruit Salad
Serves 6

100 g/4 oz prunes, soaked
100 g/4 oz dried apricots, soaked
50 g/2 oz/¹/₃ cup raisins
3 oranges, peeled and segmented (see Fresh Fruit Salad)
1–2 bananas
2–4 tablespoons brandy (optional)
Syrup
100 g/4 oz/¹/₂ cup any white sugar
300 ml/¹/₂ pint/1¹/₄ cups water
pared rind and juice of 1 lemon

1   Make a syrup with the sugar, water, lemon rind and the juice of half the lemon, as above.
2   Stew the prunes and apricots together in their soaking liquor until tender – about 15 minutes. Add the raisins and leave to cool.
3   Drain the mixed prunes, apricots and raisins and add to the syrup with the orange segments.
4   Peel and slice the bananas and dip quickly in the remaining lemon juice. Add to the salad with the brandy if used, and mix well. Leave to stand for at least 2 hours before serving.

Note: On a very cold day this salad can be served hot. Simply transfer to a saucepan and heat very gently until really hot.

Red Fruit Salad
Serves 6–8

225 g/8 oz red cherries or blackcurrants
100 g/4 oz/¹/₂ cup any white sugar
300 ml/¹/₂ pint/1¹/₄ cups water
2 firm pears, peeled, cored and sliced
225 g/8 oz raspberries (fresh and frozen)
100 g/4 oz black grapes, halved and depipped
1–2 red-skinned apples (optional)

1   Put the cherries in a pan with the sugar and water. Heat gently until the sugar has dissolved, then bring to the boil and simmer gently for 3–4 minutes. Remove the cherries to a bowl with a slotted spoon.
2   Add the pears to the syrup and poach until barely tender – about 5 minutes. Cool a little, then add the pears and syrup to the cherries in the bowl.
3   Add the raspberries and any juice, followed by the grapes.
4   If using the apples, quarter, remove the cores and slice or chop. Dip in lemon juice and add to the salad. Mix thoroughly and cover with plastic cling film. Leave to stand for at least 6 hours before serving.

Apples and Oranges Bristol
Serves 6

6 dessert apples, or 4–5 cooking apples
3–4 oranges
175 g/6 oz/³/₄ cup white sugar
300 ml/¹/₂ pint/1¹/₄ cups water

1   First make the caramel. Put 50 g/2 oz/¹/₄ cup sugar into a small heavy-based saucepan and heat gently until it dissolves. Allow to cook gently until it becomes a light golden brown, without stirring. Pour quickly onto a greased baking sheet and leave to cool and set.
2   Use the remaining sugar and water to make a syrup and simmer for 2–3 minutes. Peel, core and slice the apples fairly thickly and add to the syrup.
3   Poach gently for about 5 minutes until the fruit is barely tender and in no way beginning to break up. If this happens, remove from the heat after 2–3 minutes. The apples should look almost transluscent.
4   Turn into a bowl and leave to cool.
5   Pare the rind from one of the oranges with a potato peeler, making sure none of the white pith is attached. Cut these strips into very narrow matchsticks, using a sharp knife. Put into a small saucepan with water to cover and simmer gently for 5 minutes or until tender. Drain.
6   Cut away the peel and pith from all the oranges and ease out the segments from between the membranes. Add to the apples and mix lightly.
7   Cover the salad and chill until almost ready to serve. Sprinkle first with the strips of orange rind, then break up the caramel into small pieces and sprinkle over the salad.

Note: Pears may be used in place of apples, or a mixture of apples and pears.

Baked Apples
Serves 4

4 medium-sized cooking apples
50 g/2 oz/¹/₃ cup raisins or sultanas (golden raisin)
¹/₂ teaspoon ground cinnamon or mixed spice
about 100 g/4 oz/¹/₂ cup demerara sugar
4 tablespoons water
25 g/1 oz/2 tablespoons butter

1   Wipe the apples and make a shallow cut through the skin around the middle of each one.
2   Using an apple corer (if possible), cut a hole through the centre of each apple to remove the core.
3   Stand the apples in an ovenproof dish, just large enough to hold them.
4   Mix the raisins, spice and about 25 g/1 oz/¹/₄ cup sugar together and use to fill the holes left by removing the cores.
5   Pour the water around the apples and sprinkle the rest of the sugar over and around the apples, pressing more into the holes, if possible.
6   Top each with a knob of butter and bake in a fairly hot oven (200°C/400°F/Gas Mark 6), uncovered, for ³/₄–1 hour until the apples are soft.

Note: Take care with some varieties of apples which cook quicker and then tend to explode!

FILLING VARIATIONS
Chopped dates, grated orange rind and brown sugar
Chopped stem ginger, glacé cherries and sugar
Chopped dried apricots and brown sugar

12 Pastry

Pastry making is an art said to be passed down from one generation to the next for as long as anyone can remember. It has simple rules which, if followed, will guarantee success. However, it is true that some people have an 'extra special' touch when it comes to making pastry – and this is something that cannot be taught.

Probably the most important thing to remember with pastry making is to keep everything cool – that is with the exception of choux and hot watercrust pastries (which require the water and fat to melt and come to the boil). The fat should be cool and firm but not too hard (unless specified to be so), so that it will easily cut into pieces to rub into the flour until the mixture resembles fine bread-crumbs, or will stay in flakes or cubes if being used for one of the flaked pastries. If the fat is too soft, a rubbed-in mixture will become greasy and not absorb the correct amount of liquid, thus giving a disappointing result.

Always use cold water and the coldest possible surface for rolling out – marble is best but is not always available. If when made the pastry becomes too soft to roll, simply wrap in foil or a polythene bag and chill for 30 minutes or so, when the rolling process will be much easier. When making flaked pastries, it is essential to allow them to rest and chill in the refrigerator between rollings or the flakes will not result.

Plain (all purpose) flour is normally used for pastry making, although there are some exceptions, and white flour makes a light pastry, although in these days of healthy eating, a wholemeal or granary flour can be used, either on its own or as a proportion of the white flour. Salt is always added when making pastry both for sweet and savoury dishes, without it the pastry does not taste right.

Fat is important too. For short and flaked pastries, an equal amount of butter or margarine and lard generally gives the best results. Using all lard gives a good short texture but lacks the flavour obtained by using a proportion of butter or margarine – butter of course giving the best flavour. However, if you use all butter or margarine with some of the short pastries, a very short-textured pastry results, making it difficult to roll out even after chilling. Rich flan pastries, pâte sucrée and choux pastry should all contain butter.

Take care when adding the liquid: too much gives a sticky unmanageable dough that bakes into a hard and brittle pastry, and the addition of extra flour does not help as it upsets the balance of ingredients, which again will spoil the texture. Keep the proportions correct and always weigh them accurately and, when adding the liquid, keep back a little at first: it can always be added if the mix is a little too dry. Take care also with the amount of flour dredged onto the rolling out surface. Only a little should be required otherwise again the proportions of the pastry will be affected and this spoils the finished result.

Pastry is fairly versatile and once made will freeze successfully for up to 3 months if wrapped securely in foil or thick polythene. Allow it to thaw out slowly and completely before attempting to roll it out. Ready-made pastry can also be kept in the refrigerator for up to 3 days before use. Allow to 'come to' a little before rolling as it will be too firm to use straight from the cold. The rubbed-in pastry ingredients can also be stored in the refrigerator in a polythene bag or airtight container and will keep well for 7–10 days. Simply remove and add the liquid when required.

A final note on pastry making: always roll out the pastry in one direction – straight in front of you. Turn it round gradually while continuing to roll to keep a good shape. Do not turn it over or overstretch during rolling or it will simply shrink back while baking. The rolling should always be light but firm, and do not roll out any more than necessary.

If you cannot find time to make the pastry yourself, then use a commercial fresh or frozen product in the same way.

HOW TO SHAPE AND USE PASTRY

TO LINE A FLAN TIN

1 Choose a plain or fluted flan ring of the required size, which should be placed on a flat baking sheet, or a loose-based flan or sandwich or layer cake tin, or a china flan dish, either round, square or oval.
2 Measure the depth of the tin, double this and add to the diameter of the tin. Roll out the pastry on a lightly floured surface to a little larger than the measurement, but do not cut to size.
3 Using a rolling pin to lift the pastry, carefully lower it into the tin or fold the pastry carefully in half and position it in the tin. Lift the edges carefully and mould to the inside of the tin taking care not to stretch the pastry but taking it right to the corners. With fluted flans, press your finger gently into each flute.
4 With a plain ring, trim or cut off the surplus pastry a little over the edge and crimp or flute the edge to decorate it; a fluted ring is trimmed by running the

rolling pin across the top of the tin or dish, when the surplus pastry will fall away.

AMOUNTS OF PASTRY TO LINE FLAN TINS OR RINGS

100 g/4 oz/1 cup flour, etc., fits a 15 cm/6 inch flan ring
125 g/5 oz/1¼ cups flour, etc., fits a 18 cm/7 inch flan ring
150 g/6 oz/1½ cups flour, etc., fits a 20 cm/8 inch flan ring
175 g/7 oz/1¾ cups flour, etc., fits a 23 cm/9 inch flan ring
200 g/8 oz/2 cups flour, etc., fits a 25 cm/10 inch flan ring

TO LINE TARTLET TINS

Arrange the shallow tins close together on a baking sheet. Roll out the pastry to a rectangle larger than the baking sheet then carefully lay it loosely over the tins (like a blanket) but take care not to stretch the pastry. Use a small knob of dough or a clean cloth to press the dough into each tin and then roll across the tins with a rolling pin and lift the surplus pastry carefully away. Reshape the pastry carefully into the tins using your fingers.

Deeper tartlet tins or sheets of patty or muffin tins have to be lined individually by cutting out circles or shapes of pastry a little larger than the tins and then lowering gently into the tins. The edges can be left as they are or be lightly crimped.

BAKING BLIND

This is a process often called for to part cook the pastry case before adding a cold or raw filling, or for complete cooking, or when the pastry case is to be stored for several days in an airtight container before use. It prevents the base rising up and the sides collapsing during cooking.

1　Line the flan tin as above and, if the pastry is to be completely cooked, prick all over the base with a fork. Cut a rough round of wax or greaseproof paper about 5 cm/2 inches larger than the tin. Non-stick baking paper and foil can also be used. Place the paper lightly in the pastry case.

2　Put a layer of uncooked beans (baking beans) or raw rice or pasta to cover the base evenly (and prevent it rising during cooking) and then bake for 15–20 minutes or until the pastry is set and almost cooked.

3　Carefully remove the paper and baking beans (retaining the beans for future use) and return the pastry case to the oven for about 5 minutes or long enough to complete the cooking and dry out the pastry.

4　If the pastry is to be part cooked before adding a liquid filling, it is best not to prick the base or the liquid will seep into the holes.

COVERING A PIE DISH

1　Roll out the pastry to the thickness required and cut out 5 cm/2 inches larger than the top of the dish, using the empty inverted dish as a guide.

2　Cut a 2.5 cm/1 inch strip off all round the edge.

3　Fill the pie dish up to the rim and so the filling is slightly rounded in the centre. With a very large dish, a very liquid filling or insufficient filling, it is best to place a pie funnel in the centre of the dish, which holds the pastry in position during cooking.

4　Damp the rim of the dish with water and position the pastry strip on this rim. Seal the join and brush the strip with water.

5　Lift the pastry lid with the help of the rolling pin and position it over the filling. Press the lid firmly onto the pastry rim to seal it and, if a pie funnel is used, press over the rim of the funnel to make a hole in the centre. Trim any excess pastry from the edge of the dish with a sharp knife held at an angle away from the dish.

6　The best way to really seal the edges of the pastry is to 'knock up' or 'flake'. This is done by holding a sharp knife horizontally to the cut edge and making a series of shallow cuts into the pastry so it resembles the pages of a closed book, all the way round. This must be done when using flaked pastries but is optional with short-crust, although it does give a much better finish. A finish is then given by 'scalloping' the edge. This is done simply by placing your thumb or two fingers gently onto the edge of the pastry and with the back of a knife pull the edge up vertically at regular intervals to form a scallop each side of your fingers; then move your fingers on and repeat. This ensures an even distance between each scallop. Traditionally it is said that sweet pies have small scallops while savoury pies have much wider ones.

7　Cut one or more slits in the top of the pastry to allow the steam to escape during baking and, if liked, roll out the pastry trimmings and cut out leaf shapes for decoration. These should be dampened with water before attaching and the whole pie should be glazed with beaten egg or milk before baking.

MAKING A DOUBLE CRUST PIE

As it sounds, this type of pie has a layer of pastry under and on top of the filling. The only difficulty here is to make sure the pastry underneath is sufficiently cooked and the best way to ensure this is to heat a baking sheet in the oven when you switch it on and then stand the pie directly on this sheet, so the underneath of the pie begins to cook at the same time as the top. This method can also be used for quiches with lots of liquid in them, which tend to have a soggy base.

Double crust pies are usually made from shortcrust pastry (or some type of short pastry) or from a shortcrust pastry base and one of the flaky pastries for the top crust.

1　Divide the pastry into two, one part being almost three-quarters of the dough. Use the larger portion first and roll out to about 5 cm/2 inches larger than the top of the pie dish or plate. Ease into it, pressing gently to fit the corners and up over the rim. Do not stretch or leave any air bubbles under the pastry and do not prick.

2　Add the cold filling (either cooked or raw); do not add hot fillings as they melt the pastry, making it difficult to shape, and spoil the texture.

3　Roll out the reserved pastry to a size large enough to cover the top of the pie. Brush the rim of the pastry in the tin with water, position the lid carefully and press the edges well together.

4　Trim the edges as for covering a pie (see above) and then either knock up and crimp or pinch the edges together between the thumb and forefinger all the way round.

5　Make one or two slits in the centre, decorate with pastry leaves made from the trimmings, if liked, and attach with water, then glaze with beaten egg or milk and bake.

PASTRY EDGINGS

There are several ways to decorate the edge of a pastry pie, flan or tart, some being very simple while others take a little more care. (See step-by-step illustrations, page 166.)

1 *Scallop* – place your thumb or forefinger on the pastry edge on the rim of the dish or tin, then with the back of a knife pull the pastry inwards to make an indentation. Move your thumb to the other side of the knife mark and repeat all the way round. The size of the scallops can be altered as you like.

  Can be used for any type of pastry – short or flaked.

2 *Pinched Crimp* – place the first finger of your right hand on the pastry edge on the rim of the dish or tin facing out from the filling. With the thumb and forefinger of the other hand, pinch the pastry around the finger into a point. Repeat all the way round.

  Not suitable for flaked pastries.

3 *Gable Edge* – use for an open tart, flan or pie. Cut the pastry edging all round the rim at 1–2.5 cm/½–1 inch intervals, then fold every alternate piece inward to lay over the filling or to fold over onto itself.

  Suitable for all pastries.

4 *Triangular Gable* – use for an open tart or flan, or pie. Cut the pastry edging all round the rim at 1–2.5 cm/½–1 inch intervals, then fold each cut section in over itself diagonally, taking the whole of the cut on the left side towards the centre of the pie and tapering it off to a point at the outer edge.

  Suitable for all pastries.

5 *Circular or Leaf* – cut a series of plain or fluted small circles of pastry (or small stars or other shapes) – about 1.25 cm/½–¾ inch in diameter – damp the pastry rim and lay the shapes evenly all round the rim just overlapping each one. An edging of leaves can also be made in the same way.

  Suitable for all pastries, but flaked pastries should be cut a little larger to allow for shrinkage during baking.

Shortcrust Pastry

This is probably the most used basic pastry for both sweet and savoury dishes. It is made by the rubbing-in method and the quantities are half the amount of fat to flour. Always use plain (all-purpose) flour for a true shortcrust. When made, take care not to overknead the pastry which will spoil its texture when baked. All the shortcrust pastries may be replaced with a wholemeal or granary pastry if preferred, and the savoury flans may also be made with a cheese shortcrust pastry. (See step-by-step illustrations, page 167.)

200 g/8 oz/2 cups plain (all-purpose) flour
good pinch of salt
50 g/2 oz/¼ cup butter or margarine
50 g/2 oz/¼ cup lard or white fat
about 4 tablespoons cold water to mix

1 Sift the flour and salt into a bowl.
2 Add the fats cut into small pieces and rub in with the fingertips until the mixture resembles fine breadcrumbs. This stage can be done in a food processor or large electric mixer fitted with a dough hook. If using a food processor, turn it on and off to give short bursts until the mixture looks like breadcrumbs.
3 Add sufficient water to mix to a pliable dough, using a round-bladed knife, palette knife or fork. Add 3 tablespoons first and then gradually the rest of the water as required.
4 Turn out onto a lightly floured flat surface and knead very lightly until evenly mixed. If time allows or you want to make the pastry in advance, wrap in foil or polythene and chill for 30 minutes or until required.
5 Roll out as required – see recipes – and bake in a fairly hot to hot oven (200–220°C/400–425°F/Gas Mark 6–7).

Note: Pastries are usually measured by their weight of flour, e.g. 200 g/8 oz shortcrust pastry is made from 200 g/8 oz/2 cups flour, *but* bought pastries are weighed ready made.

Wholemeal and Granary Shortcrust Pastries

For wholemeal pastry, use ingredients and method as above but either use all wholemeal flour or any proportion of white and brown flours to give the same weight. Brown flour requires a little more salt and the water content is usually increased by up to 1 tablespoon. Do not sift brown or granary flours.

  For granary pastry, make as wholemeal pastry, but there is no need to increase the salt content. This flour gives a very nutty pastry with pieces of whole grain baked in it.

Cheese Pastry

Make as for shortcrust pastry but stir about 50 g/2 oz/½ cup grated mature Cheddar cheese and 1–2 tablespoons grated Parmesan cheese into the breadcrumb mixture with a pinch of cayenne pepper or ½ teaspoon dry mustard. A little water may be required. Bake in a fairly hot oven (200°C/400°F/Gas Mark 6).

Pastry Edgings (see page 165)

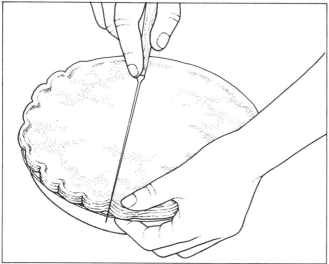

1   **Scallop** – *place your thumb on the pastry edge, then with the back of a knife pull the pastry inwards to make an indentation.*

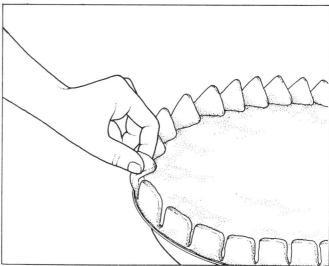

3   **Triangular Gable** – *cut the pastry edging all round the rim at 1–2.5 cm/½–1 inch intervals, then fold each cut section in over itself diagonally.*

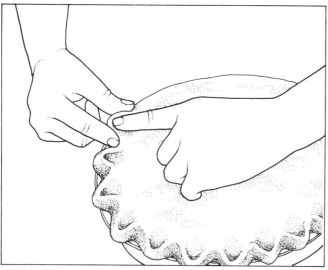

2   **Pinched Crimp** – *place your finger on the pastry edge facing out from the filling and with the thumb and finger of the other hand pinch around the finger into a point.*

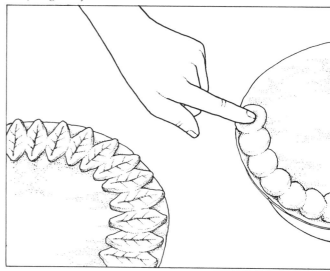

4   **Circular or Leaf** – *cut a series of plain or fluted circles or leaves of pastry, damp the pastry rim and lay the shapes evenly around the rim just overlapping each one.*

Lemon Meringue Pie   Serves 6

This firm family favourite is so much better when made properly with fresh lemons.

---

150 g/6 oz shortcrust pastry
finely grated rind and juice of 2 large lemons
3 tablespoons cornflour (cornstarch)
150 ml/¼ pint/⅔ cup water
50–75 g/2–3 oz/¼–⅓ cup caster sugar
2 egg yolks
a knob of butter
Meringue
2 egg whites
75 g/3 oz/⅓ cup (superfine) sugar

---

1   Roll out the pastry and use to line an 18–20 cm/ 7–8 inch shallow pie tin or flan ring, tin or dish and crimp the edge.

2   Bake blind (see page 164) in a fairly hot oven (200°C/ 400°F/Gas Mark 6) for 15–20 minutes. Remove the paper and beans and return to the oven for 5 minutes to dry out. Remove from the oven and leave to cool. Reduce the oven temperature to moderate (160°C/ 325°F/Gas Mark 3).

3   Put the lemon rind and juice into a measuring jug and make up to 125 ml/scant ¼ pint/good ½ cup with water, then blend in the cornflour and the 150 ml/ ¼ pint/⅔ cup water.

4   Put into a saucepan and bring slowly to the boil over a gently heat, stirring continuously. Boil for about 2 minutes or until thick and clear. Remove from the heat.

5   Stir in sugar to taste until dissolved and then beat in the egg yolks, followed by the butter. Pour the mixture into the pastry case.

6   Whisk the egg whites until stiff and dry and then whisk in the sugar a tablespoon at a time, making sure the meringue is stiff again before adding further sugar.

7   Either put the meringue into a piping bag fitted with a

large star vegetable nozzle and pipe attractively all over the lemon filling or simply spread it over, swirling with the back of a spoon.

8 Return to the oven for about 15 minutes or until the meringue is a pale golden brown. Serve hot or cold.

VARIATIONS

Orange – use the grated rind of 2 oranges and the juice of 2 oranges and 1 lemon.
Grapefruit – use the rind and juice of 1 grapefruit.
Lime – use the rind and juice of 2 limes and the juice of 1 lemon.

Apple and Blackberry Pie   Serves 5–6

Apple blends well with many other fruits for a pie; blackberry is one of the more popular.

200 g/8 oz shortcrust pastry
450–675 g/1–1½ lb cooking apples, peeled, cored and
  sliced
about 175 g/6 oz blackberries
100 g/4 oz/½ cup white sugar
beaten egg or milk to glaze

1 Roll out just under three-quarters of the pastry and use to line a pie dish as described for a double crust pie (see page 164).
2 Mix the apples, blackberries and sugar together and put into the pastry case, pressing down evenly.
3 Roll out the remaining pastry for the lid and position as described, decorate the top with the trimmings, make two slits in the top and glaze with beaten egg or milk.
4 Stand the pie on a hot baking sheet and bake in a hot oven (220°C/425°F/Gas Mark 7) for 20 minutes. Reduce the temperature to moderate (180°C/350°F/Gas Mark 4) and continue to cook for about 30–40 minutes or until the pastry is a light golden brown.
5 Serve hot or cold, sprinkled with sugar and accompanied by cream, custard or ice cream.

FILLING VARIATIONS

Use 675–900 g/1½–2 lb apples flavoured with ½ teaspoon ground cinnamon, mixed spice or ground ginger, or a few whole cloves or the grated rind of 1 orange.
Use 100 g/4 oz blackcurrants, redcurrants, cranberries or raspberries in place of the blackberries.
Use 350–450 g/¾–1 lb each of apple and rhubarb, apple and halved and stoned plums, apple and gooseberries, etc. Omit the apple and use about 675 g/1½ lb of rhubarb cut into 2.5 cm/1 inch lengths, blackcurrants or gooseberries, topped and tailed, plums or damsons, halved and stones removed if possible.

Shortcrust Pastry (see page 165)

1   Rub the fats into the flour and salt with the fingertips until the mixture resembles fine breadcrumbs.

2   Add sufficient water to mix to a pliable dough.

3   Turn out onto a lightly floured flat surface and knead very lightly until evenly mixed. Roll out as required.

Treacle Tart

Serves 4–5

This classic tart is made with golden syrup rather than treacle and is best flavoured with lemon to offset the sweetness.

150 g/6 oz shortcrust pastry
8 tablespoons golden syrup
finely grated rind of ½ lemon
50 g/2 oz/1 cup fresh white breadcrumbs
a few cornflakes, crushed (optional)

1 Roll out the pastry and use to line a shallow pie plate, tin or flan ring measuring about 18 cm/7 inches. Trim and crimp or decorate the edge. Reserve the pastry trimmings.
2 Warm the syrup slightly and pour into the flan case.
3 Sprinkle first with lemon rind and then with the breadcrumbs and leave to stand for a few minutes to allow the crumbs to begin to sink into the syrup. If you like a crunchy finish, sprinkle a few crushed cornflakes on top.
4 Bake in a fairly hot oven (200°C/400°F/Gas Mark 6) for about 25 minutes or until the pastry is a light golden brown and the filling firm and golden. Serve hot or cold.

Suitable to freeze for up to 3 months.

Note: To measure syrup easily, brush the spoon or scale pan all over with oil before dipping into the syrup or pouring in the syrup and it will simply slide off.

Mince Pies

Makes 18

Everybody's favourite around Christmas time and also at other times of the year.

200 g/8 oz shortcrust pastry
about 350 g/12 oz mincemeat
a little egg white, lightly beaten, or top of the milk
caster (superfine) sugar

1 Roll out almost two-thirds of the pastry on a lightly floured surface and cut into 18 plain or fluted rounds, about 7.5 cm/3 inches in diameter, using a special cutter or an upturned tumbler. Lightly grease or dampen 18 patty tins or muffin pans with water and place the circles in the tins.
2 Add about 2 teaspoons mincemeat to each pastry case.
3 Roll out the remaining pastry and use to make 18 lids, again either plain or fluted, about 6 cm/2½ inches in diameter or to fit the tops of the pies.
4 Damp the edges of the lids with water and position them over the mincemeat, pressing all edges well together to seal.
5 Brush the tops with egg white or milk and dredge with sugar. Make a small hole in the lid of each to allow the steam to escape.
6 Bake in a fairly hot oven (200°C/400°F/Gas Mark 6) for 20–25 minutes or until golden brown and the pastry is cooked through. When ready, the pies should

move around in the tins if given a sharp tap.
7 Remove carefully to a wire rack and leave to cool. They may, of course, be served hot or warm as well as cold and they are often accompanied by whipped cream or brandy or rum butter.

Suitable to freeze for up to 3 months, but they will also keep well in an airtight container in a cool place for up to 2 weeks. They can be warmed as required.

Quiche Lorraine

Serves 4–5

This is the bacon and cheese filled flan that began the popularity of the quiche. Nowadays, almost anything can be baked into a quiche, both to suit your taste and use up any leftovers. To ensure the base pastry is cooked through, it is wise to put a baking sheet into the oven when you turn it on, and then stand the quiche on this when it is put into the oven. The sizes of flan tins can be varied, see the chart of pastry amounts required for other sizes on page 164.

150 g/6 oz shortcrust pastry
225 g/8 oz lean bacon rashers, derinded and chopped
1 small onion, peeled and finely chopped (optional)
2 eggs beaten (large)
150 ml/¼ pint/⅔ cup single (light) cream or milk
150 ml/¼ pint/⅔ cup milk
salt and pepper
pinch of ground nutmeg
75 g/3 oz/¾ cup grated Emmenthal or Cheddar cheese

1 Roll out the pastry and use to line a 20 cm/8 inch flan ring, tin or dish.
2 Fry the bacon in its own fat in a small saucepan over a gentle heat until the fat begins to run, then increase the heat a little. Stir frequently. Add the onion, if used, and continue for 2–3 minutes.
3 Drain the bacon and onion thoroughly and put into the pastry case.
4 Beat the eggs thoroughly with the cream and milk and add plenty of seasonings – particularly pepper – and the nutmeg. Pour the mixture into the pastry case over the bacon.
5 Sprinkle the cheese into the flan so it is evenly distributed.
6 Stand the quiche on a hot baking sheet and bake in a hot oven (220°C/425°F/Gas Mark 7) for 15–20 minutes. Reduce the temperature to moderate (180°C/350°F/Gas Mark 4) and continue to cook for 30–35 minutes or until the filling is set and golden brown. Serve hot or cold.

Quiches are suitable to freeze for 1–2 months unless they contain a large proportion of tomatoes, mushrooms or courgettes (zucchini) which do not take kindly to freezing.

VARIATIONS

Mushroom and Herb – fry 175 g/6 oz sliced mushrooms in 2 tablespoons oil for 2–3 minutes and drain well. Use in place of the bacon and onions. Add 1 teaspoon dried mixed herbs or any one type of herb to the egg custard.

Stilton – fry 1 sliced or chopped onion in 1 tablespoon oil until golden brown. Add to the flan with 100 g/4 oz/1 cup crumbled Stilton cheese (or Danish Blue) and 50 g/2 oz/

½ cup grated Cheddar cheese in place of the bacon and onion. Add 1 tablespoon each chopped parsley and snipped chives to the egg custard.

Tuna Fish – fry 1 chopped onion in 1 tablespoon oil until soft. Add to the flan with a 200 g/7 oz can tuna fish, drained and flaked, in place of the bacon and onion. Add 1 teaspoon dried basil to the egg custard.

Salami and Tomato – roughly chop 175 g/6 oz sliced salami and lay in the flan case. Peel and slice 3–4 tomatoes and lay over the salami in place of the bacon and sprinkle with the cheese. Add ½ teaspoon dried mixed herbs to the egg custard, if liked.

Spinach – cook and thoroughly drain a 225 g/8 oz packet frozen leaf or chopped spinach and lay it in the flan case. Cover with 75 g/3 oz/¾ cup grated Cheddar cheese. Beat 2 eggs with 150 ml/¼ pint/⅔ cup single (light) cream, 4 tablespoons milk and plenty of seasonings and a good pinch of ground or grated nutmeg, pour into the flan case and bake.

Courgette (Zucchini) – trim and thinly slice 3 courgettes (zucchini) and fry gently in 50 g/2 oz/¼ cup butter or margarine until tender but crisp. Drain well and lay in the flan, in place of the bacon, onion and cheese. Add 2 tablespoons finely chopped spring onions (scallions) and 1 tablespoon grated Parmesan cheese to the custard and pour into the flan.

Cornish Pasties

In Cornwall, these pastry-encased mixtures of savoury meat originated as a packed lunch for the miners. Although now traditionally savoury, at one time they were savoury at one end and sweet at the other, thus providing a whole meal that was easy to transport. Every Cornish woman has her own traditional filling and many argue as to what is and what is not a true Cornish pasty. Perhaps these should be called Meat Pasties, but the filling is rather good.

---

200 g/8 oz shortcrust pastry
175 g/6 oz best raw minced or ground beef or finely
  chopped rump or flank steak
1 onion, peeled and very finely chopped
1 small carrot, peeled and very finely chopped
100 g/4 oz peeled potatoes, very finely chopped
salt and pepper
good pinch of ground nutmeg or coriander
1 teaspoon Worcestershire sauce
beaten egg or milk to glaze

---

1 Combine the meat, onion, carrot, potato, plenty of seasonings and the Worcestershire sauce.
2 Roll out the pastry and cut into four or five circles of 15–18 cm/6–7 inches in diameter. Divide the filling into portions and place one portion in the centre of each round.
3 Damp the edges of the pastry and bring together at the top. Press firmly together and crimp with the fingers and thumb. Stand on a lightly greased baking sheet.
4 Brush all over with beaten egg or milk and bake in a hot oven (220°C/425°F/Gas Mark 7) for about 30 minutes or until golden brown. Serve hot or cold.
Suitable to freeze for up to 2 months.

VARIATIONS

Leek and Bacon – thinly slice 2 leeks and blanch in boiling water for 2 minutes. Drain very well. Mix with 4–6 chopped lean bacon rashers, plenty of seasonings and 1 tablespoon top of the milk or cream. Continue as above.

Chicken and Mushroom – mince 175 g/6 oz raw lean chicken with 1 finely chopped onion and mix with 50–75 g/ 2–3 oz finely chopped button mushrooms, plenty of seasonings, 2 tablespoons thick mayonnaise and a good pinch of dried tarragon. Continue as above.

Cheese and Onion – mince 225 g/8 oz peeled onions and mix with 225 g/8 oz/2 cups grated Cheddar cheese, plenty of seasonings and 1 teaspoon Worcestershire sauce. Continue as above.

Note: Pasties may also be made using puff, flaky or rough puff pastry.

Sweet Flan Pastry

This is a richer pastry than shortcrust, having a higher proportion of fat, and is bound together with beaten egg. It will only freeze for up to 2 months.

---

100 g/4 oz/1 cup plain (all-purpose) flour
pinch of salt
50 g/2 oz/¼ cup butter or block margarine
25 g/1 oz/2 tablespoons lard or white fat
1–2 teaspoons caster (superfine) sugar
1 egg, beaten

---

1 Sift the flour and salt into a bowl.
2 Add the fats, cut into small pieces, and rub in carefully with the fingertips until the mixture resembles fine breadcrumbs (if using a food processor take extra care, for, as it is a rich pastry, it is very easy to overprocess).
3 Mix in the sugar, then add sufficient beaten egg and mix with a fork or round-bladed knife or a small palette knife until the ingredients come together.
4 Knead lightly, wrap and chill for 30 minutes before use.
5 Roll out and use as for shortcrust pastry – if for something savoury, simply omit the sugar – and bake in a fairly hot oven (200°C/400°F/Gas Mark 6).

Pâte Sucrée

1   Add the egg yolks to the flour, salt, sugar and butter.

3   Gradually pinch the mixture, using one hand only, until all the flour is incorporated.

2   Use a palette knife or spatula to tip the flour over the egg yolks and cover up well.

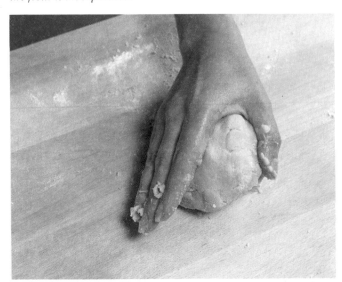

4   Work the dough quickly and lightly until smooth, using the palm of the hand, and form into a ball.

Pâte Sucrée

This is the famous French flan pastry, equivalent to our own enriched flan pastry. It is thin and crisp when baked and a favourite choice for all continental-style pastries and flans. It is made in a very special way. This quantity is sufficient to line an 18 cm/7 inch flan ring or 10–12 individual tartlet tings.

100 g/4 oz/1 cup plain (all-purpose) flour
pinch of salt
50 g/2 oz/¼ cup caster (superfine) sugar
50 g/2 oz/¼ cup butter
1½–2 egg yolks

1   Sift the flour and salt into a pile on a working surface and make a well or hole in the centre of the pile.
2   Put the sugar into the well.
3   Cut the butter into small pieces and add to the sugar with 1½ egg yolks.
4   Use a palette knife or a spatula to tip the flour over the egg yolks and cover up the well.
5   Gradually pinch the mixture, using one hand only, until all the flour is incorporated, then work the dough quickly and lightly until smooth, using the palm of the hand, and form into a ball. Add extra egg yolk as and if necessary.
6   Wrap the pastry in foil or polythene and chill for an hour.
7   Roll out thinly on a lightly floured surface or between two sheets of polythene and bake in a moderately hot oven (190°C/375°F/Gas Mark 5).

Puff Pastry (see page 173)

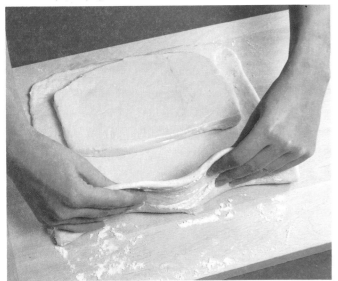

1 *Place the block of butter on one half of the rolled out pastry. Fold the pastry over to enclose the butter and seal the edges by pressing firmly together with a rolling pin.*

3 *Turn the pastry so the fold is to the right side and roll it out into a long strip that is three times long as it is wide.*

2 *Rub the pastry by pressing the rolling pin across the pastry at regular intervals.*

4 *Fold the bottom third of the pastry upwards and the top third downwards so that it is evenly folded.*

French Apple Flan

Serves 4–6

1 recipe quantity sweet flan pastry or pâte sucrée
550–675 g/1¼–1½ lb cooking apples
3 tablespoons water
sugar to taste
25 g/1 oz/2 tablespoons butter, melted
about 4 tablespoons apricot jam

1 Roll out the pastry, use to line an 18 cm/7 inch flan tin or ring, shallow pie tin or deep pie plate and crimp the edges.

2 Bake blind (see page 164) in a moderately hot oven (190°C/375°F/Gas Mark 5) for 15 minutes, remove the paper and beans and return the flan case to the oven for about 5 minutes to dry out and set.

3 Meanwhile, peel, core and slice all but two of the apples and stew gently in 2 tablespoons water until soft. Sweeten to taste, cool and then spoon into the pastry case.

4 Peel, core and thinly slice the remaining apples and arrange in overlapping circles over the cooked apples, beginning at the outside and working towards the centre. Brush with melted butter.

5 Protect the pastry edge with strips of foil, place the flan under a moderate grill or broiler and cook until the apples are just beginning to brown, turning the flan as necessary to brown evenly. Remove at once.

6 Heat the jam and remaining water together until melted and bring to the boil. Rub through a sieve and use to brush or spread all over the apple slices. Serve hot or cold with cream or ice cream.

Suitable to freeze for up to 3 months.

Note: For a larger flan, double all the ingredients and use a 25 cm/10 inch flan ring or dish.

Pecan Pie
Serves 6–8

1 recipe quantity sweet flan pastry or pâte sucrée
25 g/1 oz/2 tablespoons butter or soft tub margarine
175 g/6 oz/³⁄₄ cup light soft brown sugar
3 eggs, well beaten
175 g/6 oz/good ¹⁄₂ cup maple syrup
1 teaspoon vanilla essence
good pinch of salt
75–100 g/3–4 oz/³⁄₄ cup pecan halves

1 Roll out the pastry and use to line an 18–20 cm/ 7–8 inch fluted flan ring, tin or dish.
2 Bake blind (see page 164) in a fairly hot oven (200°C/ 400°F/Gas Mark 6) for 10 minutes. Remove the paper and beans and return to the oven for 5 minutes to partly dry out – it will not be completely cooked. Reduce the oven temperature to moderately hot (190°C/375°F/Gas Mark 5).
3 Combine the butter and sugar, then gradually beat in the eggs, followed by the maple syrup, vanilla essence and salt. The mixture will look a bit strange at this stage.
4 Arrange the pecans in the flan case, flat side downwards, then carefully pour in the filling.
5 Return to the oven for 35–40 mintues. The filling rises up rather dramatically but will fall again on cooling.
6 Leave to cool and either serve slightly warm or cold. Beware it is very rich, so serve only small portions at first!
Suitable to freeze for up to 2 months.

Grape Pastries
Serves 4–5

1 recipe quantity pâte sucrée
Filling
175 g/6 oz/³⁄₄ cup full fat soft cheese
grated rind of ¹⁄₂ lemon
25 g/1 oz/¹⁄₈ cup caster (superfine) sugar
2–3 tablespoons lemon juice
Topping
225 g/8 oz green grapes
3 tablespoons apricot jam
1 tablespoon water

1 Roll out the pastry and use to line four 11–12 cm/ 4¹⁄₂ inch individual flan or tartlet tins or 8–10 patty or muffin tins.
2 Prick the bases and bake blind (see page 164) in a moderately hot oven (190°C/375°F/Gas Mark 5) for about 15 minutes. Remove the paper and beans and return to the oven for about 5 minutes to dry out. Remove to a wire rack and leave until cold.
3 For the filling, cream the cheese, lemon rind and sugar together until smooth, then beat in sufficient lemon juice to taste and to give a spreading consistency.
4 Divide the filling between the tartlet cases, levelling the tops.
5 Peel the grapes, or leave as they are, if preferred, halve and depip and arrange over the cheese filling, in one or two layers.

6 Heat the jam and water gently in a small pan until melted, then bring to the boil. Rub through a sieve, leave to cool a little and carefully brush or spoon over the grapes. Chill before serving.
Not suitable to freeze.

Apricot Tart
Serves 8

1¹⁄₂ recipe quantity sweet flan pastry or pâte sucrée
1 recipe quantity crème pâtissière (see page 204)
450–675 g/1–1¹⁄₂ lb fresh apricots, or peaches or nectarines
juice of 1 lemon
6 tablespoons water or half water and half white wine
50 g/2 oz/¹⁄₄ cup caster (superfine) sugar
³⁄₄ teaspoon arrowroot
1–2 tablespoons flaked almonds, toasted

1 Roll out the pastry and use to line a 23 cm/9 inch loose-based flan tin, ring or dish.
2 Bake blind (see page 164) in a fairly hot oven (200°C/ 400°F/Gas Mark 6) for 15–20 minutes. Remove the paper and beans and return the pastry case to the oven for a few minutes to dry out. Cool in the tin or dish.
3 Meanwhile, make up the confectioner's custard and when cold spread into the flan case.
4 Halve the apricots, remove the stones and place the fruit in a frying pan, cut side downwards. If using peaches or nectarines, halve, remove the stones and slice thickly. Add the lemon juice, water, or water and wine mixed, and sprinkle the sugar over the top.
5 Cover the pan and bring the contents slowly to the boil, then simmer very gently for 5 minutes.
6 Using a slotted spoon, drain the apricots and lay them on top of the filling in the flan.
7 Blend the arrowroot with the minimum of cold water, add to the juices in the pan and bring back to the boil, stirring continuously until it becomes thick and clear.
8 Allow to cool slightly and then spoon over the apricots. When cold, remove the flan from the tin (but leave in a china dish) and sprinkle with the toasted almonds before serving.
Suitable to freeze for up to 2 months.

PUFF AND FLAKY PASTRIES
These pastries are made by a different method. Puff pastry is the richest of them, followed by flaky pastry (which is the most common one) and rough puff which, as the name suggests, is made in a much quicker way. However, the idea with all these pastries is to trap air between the layers of pastry each time it is rolled out, folded up and then chilled. Use butter for preference or a mixture of butter and block margarine (the soft tub margarine is not really suitable for any pastry and definitely not these ones). The first rolling gives the best and most even results, but the trimmings can be layered up and rerolled to use for smaller pastries. All these pastries take time and it is not worth attempting them if you cannot give the time required – and do not stint on the chilling times, they are essential.

Puff Pastry

(See step-by-step illustrations, page 171.)

450 g/1 lb/4 cups flour
1 teaspoon salt
450 g/1 lb/2 cups butter, firm but not too hard
300 ml/½ pint/1¼ cups iced water
squeeze of lemon juice

1 Sift the flour and salt into a bowl.
2 Take about 75 g/3 oz/⅓ cup butter and cut into pieces. Rub into the flour until the mixture resembles fine breadcrumbs.
3 Bind to a fairly soft dough with the iced water and lemon juice and then knead lightly in the bowl.
4 Roll out the pastry dough to a square measuring about 30 cm/12 inches on a lightly floured board and using a lightly floured rolling pin.
5 Soften the remaining butter a little using a palette knife or spatula to mix it and then form into an oblong block. Place the block on one half of the pastry, fold the pastry over to enclose the butter and seal the edges by pressing firmly together with the rolling pin. Next 'rib' the pastry by pressing the rolling pin across the pastry at regular intervals – this helps to distribute the air evenly.
6 Turn the pastry so the fold is to the right side and roll it out into a long strip that is three times as long as it is wide.
7 Fold the bottom third of the pastry upwards and the top third downwards so it is evenly folded, seal the edges and rib with the rolling pin as before. Place in a polythene bag and chill in the refrigerator for 30 minutes.
8 Repeat the rolling out, folding and chilling process five times more, giving the pastry a quarter turn each time so the fold is always on the right. Do not cut down on the chilling times.
9 Chill for at least an hour after the final rolling and preferably overnight. If more convenient, three rollings can be done one day, and the other three on the next day. The pastry is now ready for use.
10 Roll out as required and bake in a hot to very hot oven (220–230°C/425–450°F/Gas Mark 7–8).

Rough Puff Pastry

450 g/1 lb/4 cups plain (all-purpose) flour
1 teaspoon salt
350 g/12 oz/1½ cups firm butter (or butter/margarine and lard)
1 teaspoon lemon juice
about 300 ml/½ pint/1¼ cups iced water

1 Sift the flour and salt into a bowl. Cut the fat into neat pieces about 1 cm/½ inch square and toss into the flour without breaking up the pieces.
2 Add the lemon juice and sufficient water to mix to a fairly stiff dough – do not knead.

3 Turn the mixture onto a floured surface and roll out carefully with a floured rolling pin to a strip three times as long as it is wide.
4 Fold neatly into three as for the other flaked pastries, seal the edges and rib with the rolling pin (see Puff Pastry).
5 Give the pastry a quarter turn so the fold is to the right and repeat the rolling and folding process twice.
6 Wrap in polythene and chill for 30 minutes, then repeat the rolling and folding process twice.
7 Chill for 30–60 minutes and the pastry is ready for use.
8 Bake in a hot oven (220°C/425°F/Gas Mark 7).

Chicken and Pineapple Vol-au-vent Serves 4–5

½ recipe quantity puff pastry
beaten egg to glaze
Filling
150 ml/¼ pint/⅔ cup thick mayonnaise (see page 35)
1½ teaspoons curry powder
good dash of Worcestershire sauce
1 tablespoon apricot jam
salt and pepper
1–2 tablespoons lemon juice
4 spring onions (scallions), trimmed and chopped
2 tablespoons freshly chopped parsley
225 g/8 oz can pineapple rings, drained and chopped
225 g/8 oz cooked chicken or turkey meat, diced
a few toasted flaked almonds to garnish

1 Roll out the pastry to about 2.5 cm/1 inch thick and place on a lightly greased baking sheet. Cut out the largest possible circle or oval for the vol-au-vent.
2 With a small sharp knife mark a smaller oval or round to correspond with the shape leaving about a 2.5 cm/1 inch margin all round, then cut along this line to about halfway through the pastry for the lid.
3 Brush the top with beaten egg and chill for 10 minutes, then bake in a very hot oven (230°C/450°F/Gas Mark 8) for about 30 minutes or until well risen, well browned and firm. Cover with a sheet of wax or greaseproof paper if overbrowning.
4 When cooked, carefully remove the lid and scoop out any soft pastry inside. Return to the oven for about 5 minutes to dry out the inside. Cool on a wire rack.
5 Combine the mayonnaise, curry powder, Worcestershire sauce, jam, plenty of seasonings and sufficient lemon juice to give a thick coating consistency, then add the onions, parsley, pineapple and chicken. Mix well and leave to stand for at least 20 minutes.
6 To serve, stand the vol-au-vent on a serving dish, spoon the filling into it and sprinkle with almonds. Replace the lid and serve with salads.

The baked pastry case may be stored in the freezer in a rigid container for up to 3 months.

Poacher's Roll

Serves 6–8

1/2 recipe quantity puff pastry
450 g/1 lb sausagemeat
225 g/8 oz lean bacon rashers, derinded and chopped
1 small onion, peeled and finely chopped
100 g/4 oz button mushrooms, chopped
salt and pepper
1 teaspoon dried sage
beaten egg to glaze

1 Combine the sausagemeat, bacon, onion, mushrooms, seasonings and sage and form into a brick shape.
2 Roll out the pastry and trim to a square of about 30 cm/12 inches.
3 Lay the sausagemeat down the centre of the pastry. Brush the edges with beaten egg and fold the pastry over to enclose the filling.
4 Trim off any surplus pastry from the ends, brush with egg and fold up to enclose the filling completely.
5 Turn the roll over so the pastry join is underneath and place on a greased baking sheet. Decorate the top with leaves made from the pastry trimmings and attach with beaten egg. Make two or three slits in the top of the roll.
6 Glaze with beaten egg and bake in a hot oven (220°C/ 425°F/Gas Mark 7) for 20 minutes. Reduce the temperature to moderately hot (190°C/375°F/Gas Mark 5) and continue to cook for 30–40 minutes until well browned. Lay a sheet of wax or greaseproof paper over the roll if it seems to be overbrowning.
7 This roll can be served hot, but is best if left until cold and then served in slices with salads.

Jalousie

Serves 6

1/2 recipe quantity puff pastry
175 g/6 oz chunky thick marmalade or mincemeat
450 g/1 lb apples, peeled, cored and sliced
milk or egg white to glaze
1–2 tablespoons caster (superfine) sugar

1 Roll out the pastry and trim to a 30 cm/12 inch square. Cut in half and place one piece on a dampened or lightly greased baking sheet.
2 Roll out the second piece until it measures 33 × 20 cm/ 13 × 8 inches, then fold in half lengthwise.
3 Using a sharp knife, cut into the fold at 1 cm/1/2 inch intervals to within 2.5 cm/1 inch of the edges and ends.
4 Spread the marmalade or mincemeat over the pastry on the baking sheet leaving a 2.5 cm/1 inch margin all round. Cover with the slices of apple, forming into a brick shape.
5 Brush the pastry margin with milk or water and position the lid on top, carefully unfolding it to completely enclose the filling and so that the margins fit neatly together.
6 Press the margins very firmly together, flake all round the sides with a sharp knife and then scallop with the back of a knife.
7 Brush all the pastry with milk or egg white and dredge with caster sugar to give an even covering. Bake in a hot oven (220°C/425°F/Gas Mark 7) for 25–30 minutes until the pastry is well risen and golden brown. Serve hot or cold in slices with cream or ice cream.

Flaky Pastry

450 g/1 lb/4 cups flour
1 teaspoon salt
350 g/12 oz/1 1/2 cups firm butter (or butter/margarine and lard mixed)
1 teaspoon lemon juice
about 300 ml/1/2 pint/1 1/4 cups iced water

1 Sift the flour and salt into a bowl and rub in 75 g/ 3 oz/1/3 cup of the fat until the mixture resembles fine breadcrumbs.
2 Add the lemon juice and sufficient water to the dry ingredients to mix to a fairly soft elastic dough.
3 Knead lightly on a floured surface, then roll out to a strip three times as long as it is wide.
4 Divide the remaining fat into three equal portions and use one part to cut into small flakes which should be laid evenly over the top two-thirds of the pastry.
5 Fold the bottom third of the pastry upwards and top third downwards, seal the edges and 'rib' with the rolling pin (see Puff Pastry). Put into a polythene bag and chill in the refrigerator for 20 minutes.
6 Remove the pastry from the refrigerator and, with the folded side of the pastry to the right, roll out again to a strip three times as long as it is wide. Repeat the 'flaking' process with the second portion of fat, fold up as before and wrap and chill again for 20 minutes.
7 Repeat step 6 using the final portion of fat and chill for 15 minutes.
8 A final rolling and folding process may be carried out without adding any fat. Chill the pastry for an hour and it is then ready for use.
9 Bake in a hot oven (220°C/425°F/Gas Mark 7).

Chicken and Mushroom Pasties (see page 169) and Poacher's Roll

Cream Horns

½ recipe quantity flaky pastry
1 egg, beaten, or 1 egg white, lightly beaten
a little caster (superfine) sugar (optional)
lemon cheese or curd, raspberry jam or bramble jelly
250 ml/8 fl oz/1 cup whipping cream, whipped

1 Lightly grease 16 metal cream horn tins (or eight and repeat when the first batch are cooked).
2 Roll out half the pastry thinly to a strip measuring about 63 × 11 cm/25 × 4½ inches. Cut into eight long strips about 1 cm/½ inch wide.
3 Brush the strips with either beaten egg or egg white and then wind one strip of pastry carefully around the outside of each horn tin, beginning at the tip, keeping the glazed side outwards and overlapping the pastry as you wind.
4 Place the horns on a greased baking sheet keeping the pastry join underneath. Glaze again and sprinkle the horns with caster sugar (if used).
5 Bake in a hot oven (220°C/425°F/Gas Mark 7) for about 10 minutes or until well puffed up and golden brown. Cool for a few minutes, when the pastry should begin to shrink slightly and allow the horn tins to slip out easily. Cool the pastries on a wire rack. Repeat with the remaining pastry to make eight more.
6 When cold put about 1 teaspoon lemon cheese or curd or jam in the tip of each horn and then fill up with whipped cream.
   Makes 16
The unfilled pastry horns can be frozen in a rigid container for up to 3 months.

Note: For savoury horns, do not sprinkle the pastry with sugar before baking; they may be left plain or be sprinkled with sesame or poppy seeds before baking. Fill with a savoury white sauce filling of fish or cooked meat to serve hot, or with a mayonnaise or white sauce based filling to serve cold.

Palmiers

½ recipe quantity flaky pastry
a little caster (superfine) sugar
mixed spice or ground cinnamon
Filling *(optional)*
whipped cream
raspberry or apricot jam

1 Roll half the pastry out thinly and evenly to a rectangle measuring about 30 × 25 cm/12 × 10 inches.
2 Sprinkle liberally with caster sugar and then with a little spice.
3 Fold the long sides halfway to the centre, dredge again with sugar and spice.
4 Fold the folded sides right to the centre and dredge with sugar and spice again.
5 Fold in half lengthwise to hide all the other folds and press lightly together.
6 Cut through the roll to give 12 even-sized slices, then

place the *palmiers* on greased baking sheets, keeping them well apart.
7 Open the top of each out a little and flatten slightly with a round-bladed knife, then dredge with a little more sugar.
8 Bake in a hot oven (220°C/425°F/Gas Mark 7) for about 7 minutes or until golden brown. Turn over carefully and continue baking for a further 4–5 minutes or until golden brown. Cool the *palmiers* on a wire rack. Repeat with the other half of the pastry.
9 To fill (if liked), spread whipped cream over half of them and jam over the other half and then sandwich together.
   Makes 24, or 12 filled pairs

Sausage Rolls

½ recipe quantity flaky pastry
450 g/1 lb sausagemeat
1 small onion, peeled and very finely chopped or minced
salt and pepper
beaten egg to glaze

1 Combine the sausagemeat, onion and seasonings. Divide the sausagemeat into four and roll each into a long sausage about 25 cm/5 inches long.
2 Roll out the pastry thinly and cut into two squares of about 25 cm/10 inches, then cut each square into two strips of 25 × 12.5 cm/10 × 5 inches.
3 Lay one roll of sausagemeat on each piece of pastry keeping it to one side of the centre.
4 Damp the edges of pastry and fold over to enclose the filling. Press the edges firmly together and flake with a sharp knife.
5 Cut into the required size – about 4 cm/1½ inches for cocktails, 5–7.5 cm/2–3 inches for normal rolls, or up to 12.5 cm/5 inches for really big ones. Place on lightly greased or dampened baking sheets.
6 Glaze each one with beaten egg and make two or three cuts along the top, depending on size. Bake in a hot oven (220°C/425°F/Gas Mark 7), allowing about 20 minutes for the small rolls and 25–30 minutes for the large ones, or until well puffed up and golden brown. Remove to a rack to cool. Serve hot, warm or cold.
   Makes 8 to about 48 depending on size
Suitable to freeze for up to 2 months.

Note: Sausage rolls can also be made using puff, rough puff or shortcrust pastry. If using shortcrust, bake in a fairly hot oven (200°C/400°F/Gas Mark 6).

Choux Pastry

Although called a pastry, it is more of a paste because it needs to be piped or spooned into shape before baking – there is no way it could be rolled out. It is used for both sweet and savoury dishes and can be baked or in some cases deep-fried. The success lies in the amount of air that is beaten into it with the eggs and it is also important to add the flour all at once and cook the paste until it forms a ball, leaving the sides of the pan clean. Also take care when baking, as a sudden draught caused by peeping in the oven can cause the buns to sink rather dramatically. (See step-by-step illustrations, page 178.)

65 g/2¹/₂ oz/¹/₂ cup plus 2 tablespoons plain (all-purpose) flour
pinch of salt
50 g/2 oz/¹/₄ cup butter
150 ml/¹/₄ pint/²/₃ cup water
2 eggs, beaten

1   Sift the flour and salt into a bowl.
2   Put the fat and water into a saucepan and heat gently until the fat melts, then bring quickly to the boil.
3   Add the flour to the pan all at once and beat with a wooden spoon (over a gentle heat) until smooth and the mixture forms a ball, leaving the sides of the pan clean.
4   Remove from the heat, spread the paste out over the base of the saucepan and leave to cool for about 10 minutes.
5   Beat the eggs vigorously into the paste, about a tablespoon at a time, to give a smooth and glossy mixture. A hand-held electric mixer is best for this as it helps incorporate the maximum amount of air required for a good rise. The pastry is now ready for use.
6   Bake in a hot oven (220°C/425°F/Gas Mark 7).

Note: Choux balls can be piped and then frozen before baking (thaw completely when required to bake) or can be baked, cooled and then frozen for up to 3 months. Cooked choux balls are best refreshed in a warm oven after thawing and before filling.

Chocolate Eclairs

1 recipe quantity choux pastry
250 ml/8 fl oz/1 cup whipping or double (heavy) cream
100 g/4 oz plain chocolate
25 g/1 oz/2 tablespoons butter

1   Put the choux pastry into a piping bag fitted with a plain 1 cm/¹/₂ inch nozzle. Pipe the mixture onto greased baking sheets keeping a straight line and cutting the mixture off sharply with a knife to give lengths of about 6 cm/2¹/₂ inches. Keep well apart.
2   Bake in a hot oven (220°C/425°F/Gas Mark 7) for 20–25 minutes or until well risen, firm and pale golden brown. Make a slit in the side of each one for the steam to escape and return to the oven for a few minutes to dry out the inside. Remove to a wire rack and leave until cold.
3   Just before serving, whip the cream until stiff and use to fill the éclairs either by spreading or piping it in through the slit.
4   Melt the chocolate in a heatproof bowl over a pan of hot water, or in a microwave set on cool, until smooth, then stir in the butter until melted.
5   Cool until the chocolate begins to thicken, then carefully dip the top of each éclair into the chocolate until well coated or spread with a small spatula. Leave to set.
    Makes 12–14 éclairs

The baked éclairs can be frozen in a rigid container for up to 3 months, but they need to be refreshed in a warm oven for a few minutes and cooled before filling to serve.

Note: Eclairs can be made whatever size you like from the tiny petit fours, which are piped out to about 2.5 cm/1 inch long, up to the giants of about 15 cm/6 inches.

VARIATION
Coffee – Top with coffee glacé icing made by mixing 100 g/4 oz/1 cup sifted icing (confectioners') sugar with 1–2 teaspoons coffee essence or strong black coffee and sufficient warm water to give a consistency that will coat the back of a spoon.

Profiteroles   Serves 6

These little choux buns can also be filled with cream and topped with chocolate or coffee icing as for the éclairs. However, this must be one of the most popular desserts.

1 recipe quantity choux pastry
450 ml/³/₄ pint/scant 2 cups whipping cream
a little icing (confectioners') sugar
Chocolate sauce
175 g/6 oz plain chocolate
1 small can evaporated milk
1 tablespoon rum (optional)

1   Put the choux pastry into a piping bag fitted with a 2 cm/³/₄ inch plain nozzle and pipe out walnut-sized balls onto greased baking sheets. Alternatively, spoon teaspoons of the mixture onto the baking sheets.
2   Bake in a hot oven (220°C/425°F/Gas Mark 7) for about 25 minutes or until well puffed up, golden brown and firm to the touch. Remove from the oven, pierce each with a skewer to allow the steam to escape and cool on a wire rack.
3   For the sauce, break up the chocolate and melt it gently in the top of a double saucepan or heatproof bowl over a pan of gently simmering water, or in a microwave set on cool. Stir until quite smooth and then add the evaporated milk a little at a time, stirring continuously and reheating gently as necessary. The chocolate will stiffen at first but then comes smooth. Stir in the rum, if used, and put into a serving jug.
4   Whip the cream until stiff and put into a piping bag fitted with a 5 mm/¹/₄ inch plain nozzle. Use to fill the choux buns by inserting the nozzle into the hole pierced to allow the steam to escape. Alternatively, split the buns, fill with cream and reassemble.
5   Arrange the buns carefully on a plate or in individual bowls building up into a pyramid shape. Dredge fairly thickly with icing sugar and serve with the chocolate sauce.
    Suitable to freeze as for eclairs.

Note: Do not be tempted to fill the profiteroles too far in advance or they will go soggy; a couple of hours is plenty.

Choux Pastry (see page 176)

1   *Put the fat and water into a saucepan. Have the sifted flour and salt ready for when the mixture boils.*

2   *Add the flour all at once and beat until smooth and the mixture forms a ball.*

3   *Beat the eggs vigorously into the cooled paste, about a tablespoon at a time.*

Cheese Aigrettes

1 recipe quantity choux pastry
2 tablespoons grated Parmesan cheese
50 g/2 oz/½ cup grated mature Cheddar cheese
oil or fat for deep-frying

1   Make the choux pastry as usual and beat in the Parmesan and Cheddar cheeses.
2   Put the choux mixture into a piping bag fitted with a 1 cm/½ inch plain nozzle or large star vegetable nozzle.
3   Heat the oil or fat until a cube of bread browns in about 30 seconds – to about 180°C/350°F.
4   Pipe small balls of the mixture – about 1 cm/½ inch in diameter – or drop small teaspoons of it into the hot fat, a few at a time and fry for a few minutes until well puffed up and golden brown all over, turning over during frying, if necessary.
5   Drain on absorbent kitchen paper towel and keep warm, uncovered, while frying the remainder. Serve warm or hot.
Makes 30–40

VARIATIONS
These are best served with a flavoured mayonnaise (see page 141).
Cheese and Prawn or Shrimp – add 100 g/4 oz finely chopped peeled prawns or shrimp to the above mixture before frying.
Cheese and Bacon – fry or grill or broil 175–225 g/6–8 oz streaky bacon rashers until quite crisp, then drain and crumble. Add to the mixture when cold with a good pinch of mixed herbs, if liked.
Smoked Mackerel – add about 100 g/4 oz finely flaked or chopped smoked mackerel fillet to the above mixture.

Cream Horns (see page 176),
Grape Pastries (see page 172)
and Profiteroles with Chocolate Sauce (see page 177)

13 Hot Puddings

Nothing is better to come home to on a cold winter's day than a piping-hot steamed pudding. This is only one of numerous types of hot puddings that can be made simply and will cook with little attention: others include baked puddings, some with crumble tops or scone toppings; pies and flans, some with meringue tops, some mainly fruit and others custard-based; light airy soufflés to eat straight from the oven before they sink; and pancakes served in a variety of ways, including the delicious Crêpes Suzettes in their syrupy sauce of fruit juices, sugar and liqueurs.

In spite of the calorie counters in the family, you can always find an excuse once in a while for serving something that might err on the fattening side. Children need to eat plenty of fruit and not just stodge but a good mix of the two is ideal and none of these puddings are oversweet; extra sugar can easily be handed round at the table if really necessary.

MILK PUDDINGS

Most of these can be cooked in the top of a double saucepan, but baked puddings are so easy to prepare and need no attention at all during baking.

Rice Pudding   Serves 4

It is preferable to use one of the short grain pudding rices for puddings as they absorb more liquid and produce a better finished dish.

---

3 tablespoons short grain rice
2 tablespoons caster (superfine) sugar
568 ml/1 pint/2½ cups milk
a large knob of butter
freshly grated nutmeg, or 1 bay leaf (preferably fresh)

---

1 Wash the rice in a sieve under cold running water, drain thoroughly and put into a well-buttered 900 ml/ 1½ pint/3¾ cup ovenproof dish.
2 Add the sugar, pour on the milk and mix lightly. Top with small pieces of the butter and sprinkle with grated nutmeg, or sink the bay leaf in the milk.
3 Bake in a cool oven (150°C/300°F/Gas Mark 2) for about 2 hours. After cooking for 30 minutes the pudding may be stirred to give a slightly creamier finished dish. Serve hot as it is or with demerara sugar.

VARIATIONS
Spicy – omit the nutmeg or bay leaf and add 1 teaspoon ground cinnamon or mixed spice.
Fruit – add 50 g/2 oz/⅓ cup dried fruit and 1 tablespoon cut mixed peel to the ingredients, and it is essential to stir this one after 30 minutes.
Apricot – put 50–75 g/2–3 oz/½ cup chopped dried apricots into a pan of water and bring to the boil. Drain and add to the pudding with 2 extra tablespoons milk.

Semolina Pudding   Serves 4

This pudding can either be made in a saucepan by gentle simmering or be baked in the oven for a short while. 'Quick' semolina only needs about 10 minutes simmering.

---

4 tablespoons semolina
568 ml/1 pint/2½ cups milk
about 40 g/1½ oz/¼ cup caster (superfine) sugar

---

1 Heat the milk and butter together in a saucepan and sprinkle on the semolina.
2 Bring slowly up to the boil, stirring continuously until the mixture begins to thicken. Cook for 2–3 minutes until the grain looks clear.
3 Remove from the heat and stir in the sugar until dissolved. Pour the mixture into a greased 900 ml/ 1½ pint/3¾ cup ovenproof dish and bake in a moderately hot oven (200°C/400°F/Gas Mark 6) for about 30 minutes, or until lightly browned.
4 Alternatively, leave the semolina in the saucepan and simmer very gently for about 15 minutes, stirring frequently.

Semolina is often served with a jam such as raspberry, strawberry, blackcurrant, bramble, etc., or ginger preserve is stirred through it for extra flavour.

VARIATIONS
Chocolate – add 2 tablespoons sifted cocoa to the milk in the saucepan before adding the semolina.
Fruit – add the finely grated rind of an orange or lemon to the milk.

CUSTARD PUDDINGS

Baked Custard
Serves 4

568 ml/1 pint/2½ cups milk
3 eggs, or 2 eggs and 2 egg yolks
2 tablespoons caster (superfine) sugar
a few drops of vanilla essence (optional)
freshly grated nutmeg

1 Warm the milk in a saucepan until really quite hot but in no way boiling. Whisk in the eggs and sugar until well blended.
2 Strain the custard into a lightly greased 900 ml/ 1½ pint/3¾ cup ovenproof dish and stand on a baking sheet or preferably in a roasting tin containing about 2.5 cm/1 inch of warm water.
3 Add the essence (if used) and sprinkle lightly with grated nutmeg.
4 Bake in a moderate oven (160°C/325°F/Gas Mark 3) for 45–60 minutes or until the custard is set and firm. To test, slip a knife straight downwards into the custard and pull it slightly sideways – if the cut is clean, the custard is ready; if not, return to the oven for about 10 minutes. Serve hot or cold.

Note: The custard may be baked in 4–5 individual dishes if preferred, when 35–45 minutes will be ample cooking time.

Bread and Butter Pudding
Serves 4–6

This is an old favourite and one that not only uses up bits and pieces always found in a kitchen but it can have many extra ingredients added to it to give extra interest.

4–5 slices bread, brown or white
about 50 g/2 oz/¼ cup butter
100 g/4 oz/⅔ cup raisins
50 g/2 oz/⅓ cup cut mixed peel
grated rind of 1 small orange or 1 lemon
about 6 tablespoons demerara sugar
a little mixed spice or ground cinnamon
2 eggs (large)
450 ml/¾ pint/scant 2 cups milk

1 Spread the bread with most of the butter and cut into strips or squares. Use the remaining butter to grease a 1.2 litre/2 pint/5 cup ovenproof dish.
2 Arrange the bread, buttered side upwards, in layers in the dish alternating with the raisins, peel, fruit rind and about three-quarters of the sugar. Sprinkle with the spice.
3 Beat the eggs and milk together and strain into the dish over the bread. Leave to stand for 15 minutes, then sprinkle with the rest of the sugar.
4 Bake in a moderately hot oven (190°C/375°F/Gas Mark 5) for 45–60 minutes or until well risen and golden brown. Serve hot with custard or cream.

VARIATIONS
Bread, Butter and Apple – peel, core and slice 450 g/1 lb cooking apples and lay half in the base of an ovenproof dish. Cover with half the bread and dried fruit, etc., then with the rest of the apples and the remainder of the bread pudding ingredients. Strain the custard over, leave to stand, sprinkle with the remaining sugar and bake as above.
Bread, Butter and Marmalade – after spreading each slice of bread with butter, add a good spreading of marmalade – either a good chunky orange marmalade or ginger preserve. Cut down a little on the sugar content and continue as above.

Queen of Puddings
Serves 4–5

450 ml/¾ pint/scant 2 cups milk
25 g/1 oz/2 tablespoons butter
grated rind of 1 lemon
2 eggs, separated
65 g/2½ oz/⅓ cup caster (superfine) sugar
75 g/3 oz/1½ cups fresh white breadcrumbs
3 tablespoons red jam or marmalade

1 Warm the milk in a saucepan but do not bring to the boil. Remove from the heat and stir in the butter, lemon rind and 25 g/1 oz/¼ cup sugar until dissolved.
2 Place the breadcrumbs in a 1.2 litre/2 pint/5 cup greased ovenproof dish. Beat the egg yolks into the milk and pour over the breadcrumbs. Leave to stand for 15 minutes, undisturbed.
3 Bake in a moderate oven (180°C/350°F/Gas Mark 4) for 25–30 minutes or until lightly set. Remove from the oven.
4 Warm the jam or marmalade gently and spread over the breadcrumbs.
5 Whisk the egg whites until very stiff and dry, then whisk in the rest of the sugar, a little at a time, making sure the meringue is stiff again before adding further sugar. Either put the meringue into a piping bag fitted with a large star nozzle and pipe over the jam, or spread it using a palette knife or the back of a spoon.
6 Return the pudding to the oven for about 15 minutes or until the meringue is a light golden brown. Serve hot.

STEAMED PUDDINGS

GENERAL RULES

1   Put a steamer, with the base portion half-filled with water, or a large saucepan with sufficient water to come about halfway up the side of the basin, on to boil.
2   Grease the pudding basin well inside, put a disc of wax or greaseproof paper in the bottom and grease, or use non-stick baking paper.
3   Cut a double piece of wax or greaseproof paper about 12.5 cm/5 inches larger than the top of the basin and grease this well. Also cut a piece of foil a little larger still. If the pudding is likely to rise above the top of the basin during cooking, then a pleat should be made in the paper to allow for this, in which case cut the circle larger accordingly.
4   Fill the basin about two-thirds full and definitely no more than three-quarters full with the mixture.
5   Cover the basin tightly with the wax or greaseproof paper, folding the edges so they tuck under the rim of the basin, then cover again with the foil and tie string around it securely so it is airtight. A piece of string tied over the top of the basin for a handle makes it much easier to remove the pudding.
6   Keep the water in the steamer boiling rapidly and keep a kettle of water near the boil so it can be topped up with boiling water as necessary. If using a saucepan, it is often better to put a couple of old skewers in the base to keep the basin off the bottom for, if by accident the pan should boil dry, the basin will break if touching the bottom. Keep the water in the saucepan only gently simmering around the basin and top up with more boiling water as necessary.
7   When ready, remove the basin carefully with the string handle and leave to stand for 4–5 minutes before opening, this will allow the pudding to shrink slightly from the sides and turn out more easily.

Plain Sponge Pudding   Serves 4–6

100 g/4 oz/½ cup butter or margarine
100 g/4 oz/good ½ cup caster (superfine) sugar
2 eggs, beaten
175 g/6 oz/1½ cups self-raising flour
a few drops of vanilla essence
a little milk or lemon juice to mix

1   Put the steamer or saucepan with water in on to boil. Grease a 900 ml/1½ pint/3¾ cup basin with butter or margarine.
2   Cream the fat and sugar together until light and fluffy and very pale in colour, using a wooden spoon or a hand held electric mixer, or in a large electric mixer.
3   Beat in the eggs one at a time, following each with a spoonful of flour. Beat in the vanilla essence.
4   Sift the remaining flour and gradually fold into the creamed mixture alternating with 1–2 tablespoons lemon juice or milk to give a consistency that will drop easily off the wooden spoon.
5   Turn the mixture into the basin and level the top. Cover with greased wax or greaseproof paper and foil as above and secure with string.

6   Steam for 1½ hours. Turn out and serve with a jam sauce made by heating 225 g/8 oz red jam with 4 tablespoons water. If liked, thicken this by blending 1 teaspoon arrowroot with a little cold water, adding this to the jam and bringing back to the boil until clear.

VARIATIONS

Golden or Maple Syrup – put 3–4 tablespoons golden or maple syrup into the bottom of the greased basin before adding the sponge mixture. The grated rind of 1 orange or 1 lemon may be added to the sponge mixture which blends well with the syrup flavour. Extra heated syrup may be served in a jug.

Jam – put 3–4 tablespoons of any red or black jam into the base of the basin before adding the sponge mixture. Serve with custard or a jam sauce as above.

Ginger – sift 1½ teaspoons ground ginger with the flour and fold in 50–100 g/2–4 oz/¼–⅓ cup chopped stem or crystallized ginger before putting the pudding into the basin.

Spotted Dick – fold in 100–175 g/4–6 oz/¼–⅓ cup mixed dried fruit or just sultanas (golden raisins), currants or raisins and the grated rind of 1 lemon, if liked, before putting into the basin. Serve with custard.

Mincemeat Surprise – use about 225 g/8 oz mincemeat to line the base and halfway up the sides of the greased basin. Add the pudding mixture and steam. When turned out, carefully respread the mincemeat over the pudding, if necessary. Serve with custard or cream.

Chocolate – blend 4 tablespoons powdered cocoa with 1–2 tablespoons very hot water until smooth. Beat into the creamed mixture after the eggs. Alternatively, sift the cocoa with the flour and fold in, adding a little extra milk, if necessary. Do not use lemon juice. Serve with custard or chocolate sauce (see page 32) with a tablespoon of rum added, if liked.

Orange or Lemon – add the finely grated rind of 1–2 oranges or lemons with the appropriate juice used instead of milk. Serve with a marmalade sauce made in a similar way to the jam sauce.

Apple and Apricot Pudding   Serves 6

1 recipe quantity basic sponge pudding
100 g/4 oz/⅔ cup dried apricots, soaked overnight in cold water
350 g/12 oz cooking apples, peeled, cored and sliced
2 tablespoons granulated or demerara sugar

1   Make up the sponge mixture as before. Grease a 1.2 litre/2 pint/5 cup pudding basin or bowl.
2   Drain the apricots and chop fairly small. Mix with the apples and sugar.
3   Put about one-third of the sponge mixture in the base of the basin. Cover with almost half the fruit mixture.
4   Add another layer of sponge, the rest of the fruit and then the remainder of the sponge mixture.
5   Cover the basin and steam for 2 hours.
6   Turn out and serve with cream or custard.

Steamed Suet Pudding

Serves 4–6

Instead of a sponge pudding, a suet pudding is sometimes steamed in a basin or bowl to serve with syrup or jam or to be cooked with a centre of stewed fruit.

175 g/6 oz/1½ cups self-raising flour
pinch of salt
75 g/3 oz/¾ cup shredded suet
50 g/2 oz/good ¼ cup caster (superfine) sugar
about 150 ml/¼ pint/⅔ cup milk

1 Prepare the steamer or saucepan and grease a 900 ml/1½ pint/3¾ cup basin or bowl.
2 Sift the flour and salt into a bowl and mix in the shredded suet and sugar.
3 Make a well in the centre and add sufficient milk to mix to a dough with a soft dropping consistency. It must not be hard or kneaded.
4 Put into the basin, cover and steam for 1¾–2 hours. Turn out and serve with a jam or syrup sauce, or marmalade sauce, or with stewed fruit.

Cranberry Christmas Pudding

Serves 6–8

This is an almost instant Christmas pudding, much lighter in texture than the traditional one, and only needs to be prepared the night before cooking and serving. Cranberries are always available fresh around Christmas and frozen all the year, so it is a pudding to serve at any time of the year.

225 g/8 oz/2 cups plain (all-purpose) flour
225 g/8 oz/good cup light soft brown sugar
175 g/6 oz/1 cup sultanas (golden raisins)
225 g/8 oz/1⅓ cups seedless raisins
175 g/6 oz/1½ cups cranberries, roughly chopped
50 g/2 oz/⅓ cup cut mixed peel
grated rind of 1 lemon
½ teaspoon mixed spice
100 g/4 oz/½ cup butter, softened
2 teaspoons bicarbonate of soda
350 ml/12 fl oz/1½ cups boiling water
2 eggs, beaten

1 Sift the flour into a bowl and add the sugar, dried fruits, cranberries, mixed peel, lemon rind and the spice and mix very well. Cut the butter into small pieces and place all over the surface of the ingredients.
2 Dissolve the bicarbonate of soda in the boiling water and pour over the mixture. Mix lightly together with a wooden spoon or flat whisk, then cover with a clean cloth and leave to stand overnight in a cool place.
3 Next day add the beaten eggs and beat thoroughly.
4 Grease a 1.7 litre/3 pint/7½ cup pudding basin and spoon in the mixture. Cover as for a steamed pudding.
5 Steam, as above, for 3 hours, topping up the saucepan with more boiling water as necessary.
6 To serve, turn the pudding out carefully onto a warmed plate and top with a sprig of holly. Serve with brandy butter or cream.

Steaming a Pudding

1   *Before adding the sponge mixture put the golden syrup or other flavouring in the bottom of the greased basin or bowl.*

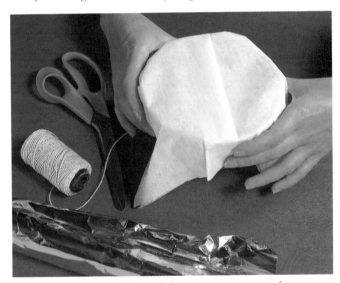

2   *Cover the basin tightly with the wax or greaseproof paper, folding the edges so they tuck under the rim of the basin.*

3   *Having covered with foil, tie string around it securely so it is airtight, then tie more string over the top to make a handle.*

Christmas Pudding

Serves 8–12

This particular pudding recipe has been in my family for many years and differs from some puddings as it contains no flour – only breadcrumbs, which give a much lighter finished pudding. A Christmas pudding should be made at least 2 months before required to allow it to mature.

100 g/4 oz/²⁄₃ cup sultanas (golden raisins)
100 g/4 oz/²⁄₃ cup currants
100 g/4 oz/²⁄₃ cup seedless raisins
100 g/4 oz/²⁄₃ cup stoned raisins, chopped
50 g/2 oz/¹⁄₃ cup cut mixed peel
50 g/2 oz/¹⁄₃ cup glacé cherries, chopped, washed and dried
50 g/2 oz/¹⁄₃ cup blanched almonds, chopped
50 g/2 oz/¹⁄₂ cup ground almonds
100 g/4 oz/2 cups fresh white breadcrumbs
1 small carrot, peeled and finely grated
1 small cooking apple, peeled, cored and grated
100 g/4 oz/scant 1 cup shredded suet
¹⁄₂ teaspoon mixed spice
pinch of ground nutmeg or allspice
¹⁄₄ teaspoon ground cinnamon
grated rind and juice of 1 lemon
grated rind and juice of ¹⁄₂ orange
100 g/4 oz/¹⁄₃ cup golden syrup
2 eggs, beaten
2 tablespoons brandy (optional)
4 tablespoons brown ale or sherry

1   Place all the ingredients in a large mixing bowl, adding them in the order they are listed and mixing in each one as added.
2   Grease a 1.5 litre/2¹⁄₂ pint/6¹⁄₄ cup basin or bowl liberally with lard (for preference) and spoon the mixture into the basin, filling to no more than three-quarters full. Cover as for steamed pudding (see page 182).
3   Place the pudding in a saucepan with boiling water coming halfway up the sides of the basin and simmer gently for 7–8 hours, topping up the pan as necessary with more boiling water. The long cooking is essential for the traditional flavour and appearance of this type of pudding.
4   Remove the pudding from the pan and leave until quite cold. Remove the covering, add 1–2 tablespoons brandy, if liked, and cover again as before with fresh wax or greaseproof paper and foil. Store in a cool, dry place away from direct sunlight for at least 2 months and up to a year.
5   When ready to serve, reboil the pudding for 3–4 hours as before. Turn out onto a warmed dish and serve with cream or brandy butter and sugar. To ignite the pudding, warm 3–4 tablespoons brandy, pour over the pudding carefully and set alight. A sprig of holly with its stem wrapped in foil may be placed in the top of the pudding.

Brandy Butter

100 g/4 oz/¹⁄₄ cup unsalted butter
225 g/8 oz/2 cups icing (confectioners') sugar, sifted, or
*   175 g/6 oz/1¹⁄₂ cups icing (confectioners) sugar and*
*   50 g/2 oz/¹⁄₄ cup light soft brown sugar*
3–4 tablespoons brandy

1   Beat the butter until soft, then gradually beat in the sugar alternating with the brandy. A little extra sugar may be needed; it depends on how firm you want the butter to be.
2   Turn into a bowl, cover with plastic cling film and chill until required.

BAKED PUDDINGS

There are a great many puddings that are baked and served both in winter and summer. The basic baked sponge is most versatile as it can be added to many different types of fruit as a topping, or have the ingredients baked into it.

Basic Baked Sponge

Serves 4–5

75 g/3 oz/¹⁄₃ cup butter or margarine
75 g/3 oz/scant ¹⁄₂ cup caster (superfine) sugar
1 egg, beaten
150 g/5 oz/1¹⁄₄ cups self-raising flour
a few drops of vanilla essence
milk to mix

1   Grease a 600–900 ml/1–1¹⁄₂ pint/2¹⁄₂–3³⁄₄ cup oven-proof pie dish with butter or margarine.
2   Cream the fat and sugar until very pale and fluffy. Beat in the egg until thoroughly incorporated.
3   Sift the flour and fold into the mixture with the essence and alternating with a little milk to give a dropping consistency.
4   Put into the greased dish, level the top and bake in a moderate oven (180°C/350°F/Gas Mark 4) for 30–40 minutes or until well risen, firm to the touch and golden brown.
5   Serve the pudding from the dish with custard, jam sauce or syrup.

VARIATIONS

Lemon or Orange – add the finely grated rind of 1 orange or lemon to the mixture after the flour and replace the milk with fruit juice.

Spicy Fruit – sift ¹⁄₂ teaspoon ground cinnamon, mixed spice or ground ginger with the flour and add 75–100 g/3–4 oz/¹⁄₂–²⁄₃ cup dried mixed fruit and 25–50 g/1–2 oz/¹⁄₄–¹⁄₃ cup cut mixed peel or chopped glacé cherries to the mixture after the flour. Serve with custard.

Chocolate – add 3 tablespoons cocoa sifted with the flour or stir 50 g/2 oz/¹⁄₃ cup chocolate dots or coarsely grated chocolate into the mixture before turning into the dish. Serve with chocolate sauce.

Pineapple Upside Down Pudding

Serves 4–6

This is another favourite baked pudding. The pineapple can easily be replaced by apricots, peaches, cherries, pears or other fruit if preferred.

1 recipe quantity basic baked sponge pudding
50 g/2 oz/¼ cup butter or margarine
50 g/2 oz/¼ cup soft brown sugar
225 g/8 oz can pineapple rings
a little cornflour (cornstarch) (optional)

1 Grease a 20 cm/8 inch round cake tin and line the base with greased wax or greaseproof paper or non-stick baking paper.
2 Cream the butter and sugar together until well blended, then spread over the base of the tin.
3 Drain the pineapple rings (reserve the juice) and arrange these over the sugar mixture in the tin. A halved glacé cherry may be placed in the centre of each pineapple ring if liked.
4 Spread the sponge mixture evenly over the pineapple rings, without moving them at all.
5 Bake in a moderate oven (180°C/350°F/Gas Mark 4) for about 45 minutes or until well risen, golden brown and firm to the touch.
6 Thicken the pineapple juice by adding 2 teaspoons cornflour blended in a little cold water, turn into a saucepan and bring to the boil. Boil for a minute or so until clear and slightly thickened.
7 Carefully turn out the pudding onto a warmed serving dish, so the pineapple slices make an attractive pattern on top. Serve hot with the pineapple juice or cream or custard, if preferred.

Lemon Surprise Pudding

Serves 4–6

This is another delicious baked pudding with the surprise being a layer of a lemony custard which forms under the sponge during baking.

50 g/2 oz/¼ cup butter or margarine
100 g/4 oz/good ½ cup caster (superfine) sugar
grated rind and juice of 1 large lemon
2 eggs, separated
300 ml/½ pint/1¼ cups milk
50 g/2 oz/½ cup self-raising flour

1 Cream the fat and sugar together until light and fluffy and pale in colour and then beat in the lemon rind.
2 Add the egg yolks and the flour and beat well. Stir in the milk and 2–3 tablespoons lemon juice (depending on the size of the lemon) until quite smooth.
3 Grease a large ovenproof dish – about 1.3 litres/2¼ pints/5½ cups – with butter. Whisk the egg whites until very stiff and fold quickly and evenly through the mixture. Pour into the dish.
4 Stand the dish in a roasting tin containing about 2.5 cm/1 inch of water and bake in a fairly hot oven (200°C/400°F/Gas Mark 6) for about 45 minutes or

until the top is set and feels spongy and springy when pressed. Serve hot.

VARIATIONS
Orange – use grated orange rind in place of the lemon rind and 1 tablespoon orange juice and 1–2 tablespoons lemon juice in place of just lemon juice.
Chocolate – omit the lemon rind, replace the fruit juice with milk or rum and sift 1½ tablespoons cocoa with the self-raising flour.

Rhubarb and Apple Crumble

Serves 4–6

A crumble mixture is begun in the same way as pastry by rubbing the fat into the flour and then stirring in sugar and any flavourings. It is then spooned as it is over the fruit – not made into a dough as with pastry. The quantities are half fat and sugar to flour and the sugar may be brown or white and the flour, brown or white or a combination. Use a spice to compliment the fruit to be used.

450 g/1 lb trimmed rhubarb
2 cooking apples
about 100 g/4 oz/good ½ cup granulated or any white sugar
175 g/6 oz/1½ cups plain (all-purpose) flour
pinch of salt
½ teaspoon ground ginger or mixed spice
75 g/3 oz/⅓ cup butter or margarine
75 g/3 oz/scant ½ cup caster (superfine), soft brown or demerara sugar

1 Wipe the rhubarb over and cut into 2.5 cm/1 inch pieces. Peel, core and slice the apples and layer up in a 1.2 litre/2 pint/5 cup ovenproof dish with the granulated sugar.
2 Sift the flour into a bowl with the salt and ginger. Cut the fat into small pieces and rub into the flour until the mixture resembles fine breadcrumbs, then stir in the sugar.
3 Sprinkle the crumble mixture over the fruit to give an even layer and so there is no fruit showing through.
4 Bake in a fairly hot oven (200°C/400°F/Gas Mark 6) for about 40 minutes or until the crumble is well browned and the fruit underneath appears to be tender. Serve with cream or custard.

Note: If preferred, the fruit may be stewed or part-stewed in the minimum of water before adding the crumble. It is best to cool the fruit first or the fat in the crumble will melt before it has a chance to cook. If cooking by this method, it should take only about 30 minutes to cook.

VARIATIONS
Use any type of fruit you like either on its own or combined with another.

Basic Pancakes (see page 188)

1   *Add the egg and half the liquid to the sifted flour and salt.*

3   *Using a very flexible palette knife or spatula, loosen the pancake and turn it over carefully.*

2   *Pour about 2 tablespoons of the batter into the pan and twist the pan around until the batter forms a thin skin over the base.*

4   *As they cook, layer the pancakes with a small piece of wax or greaseproof paper between each one.*

Spiced Apple Charlotte   Serves 4–6

A charlotte is a mixture of dry stewed fruit encased in a tin or ovenproof dish with slices of white bread that have been dipped in melted butter. Traditionally, it should be turned out to serve with the bread slices golden and crispy, but it is often baked in a pie dish and served straight from the dish. The fruit mixtures can be varied, but if it is to be turned out it must not be too juicy or the charlotte will collapse.

900 g/2 lb cooking apples
4 tablespoons raisins
1 teaspoon mixed spice
25 g/1 oz/¼ cup chopped walnuts
6 slices white bread
about 50 g/2 oz/¼ cup butter or margarine, melted
about 175 g/6 oz/¾ cup sugar or to taste
2 tablespoons fresh breadcrumbs or stale cake crumbs

1   Peel, core and slice the apples and stew in the minimum of water (about 2 tablespoons) until tender. Remove from the heat and stir in the raisins, spice and walnuts and leave to cool.
2   Remove the crusts from the bread. Grease a round cake tin about 12.5 cm/5 inches in diameter or a 1.2 litre/ 2 pint/5 cup pie dish. Cut 1 slice bread to fit the base of the tin or dish, dip in melted butter and position in the base. Dip the rest of the slices (keeping one or one and a half for the lid) in the butter and arrange around the sides of the dish.
3   Add sufficient sugar to the fruit to sweeten and stir in the crumbs, then spoon into the lined tin or dish. Cover with the last piece of bread, dipped in butter and, if liked, sprinkle with a little sugar.
4   Bake in a moderately hot oven (190°C/375°F/Gas Mark 5) for about an hour or until set and the bread top is crusty and firm. Turn out or spoon from the dish and serve with cream or custard.

OPPOSITE: *Apple and Apricot Pudding* (see page 182) *and Bread and Butter Pudding* (see page 181)

PANCAKES

These are a very popular hot pudding. In Britain, they are traditionally served on Shrove Tuesday with lemon and sugar, but they are also served in many more ways, both sweet and savoury, all through the year. (See step-by-step illustrations, page 186.)

Basic Pancakes
Serves 4

100 g/4 oz/1 cup plain (all-purpose) flour
pinch of salt
1–2 eggs
275 ml/scant 1/2 pint/1 1/4 cups milk
lard for frying
2 lemons, quartered
caster (superfine) sugar

1   Sift the flour and salt into a bowl and make a well in the middle.
2   Break an egg into the well (or 2 eggs for thinner, richer crêpes) and add about half of the liquid.
3   Gradually work the flour into the liquid using a wooden spoon, spatula or flat hand whisk. Beat until it is quite smooth.
4   Add the rest of the liquid, a little at a time, again beating until quite smooth. If the lumps persist, either purée in a blender or food processor or pour through a sieve.
5   At this stage, the batter may be left to stand for several hours in a cool place before use. Beat well again before use and if it seems rather thick add another tablespoon or two of milk.
6   To make the pancakes, heat a knob of lard in a small frying pan (18–20 cm/7–8 inch base) until it is really hot and swirl it around the sides and base of the pan so it is completely coated.
7   Pour about 2 tablespoons of batter into the pan and twist the pan around until the batter forms a thin skin all over the base of the pan. Cook over a moderate heat for 1–2 minutes or until the underside of the pancake is golden brown.
8   Using a very flexible palette knife or spatula, loosen the pancake if it is stuck in any place and then turn it over carefully. Alternatively, if you are brave enough, it can be 'tossed'! Cook the second side for a minute or so until lightly browned.
9   Turn out onto a piece of wax or greaseproof paper sprinkled with sugar and keep warm. Cook the rest of the pancakes in the same way, adding a knob of lard to the pan to cook each one. Arrange in layers with a small piece of paper between each one.
10   To serve, sprinkle the pancakes with lemon juice and sugar, roll up or fold into quarters and serve on warmed plates. Or offer sugar and lemon separately.
     Makes 8 pancakes to serve 4

VARIATIONS

Orange – add the grated rind of 1 orange to the pancake batter. Make the pancakes in the usual way and serve with a marmalade sauce made by heating 5–6 tablespoons marmalade in a saucepan with 2–3 tablespoons water plus 1 tablespoon orange liqueur, if liked.
Fruit – fill the pancakes with any type of stewed fruit, roll up, sprinkle with sugar flavoured with ground cinnamon and serve with cream or ice cream.

Fried Blackberry and Apple Pancakes
Serves 4

8 pancakes made from the basic batter recipe
225 g/8 oz cooking apples
100 g/4 oz blackberries
sugar to taste
50 g/2 oz/1/4 cup butter or margarine
a little caster (superfine) sugar for dredging

1   Make the pancakes as usual, adding the grated rind of 1 orange or lemon to the batter, if liked.
2   Peel, core and slice the apples and stew with the blackberries (or blackcurrants, redcurrants, cranberries, raspberries, etc.) in the minimum of water until soft. Sweeten to taste with sugar and leave to cool.
3   Divide the filling between the pancakes, placing it in the centre of each and folding in the sides and then rolling up to completely enclose the filling.
4   Melt half the fat in a frying pan and fry half of the parcels, two at a time, until golden brown and crisp on both sides. Drain on absorbent paper towel and keep warm. Melt the remaining butter and fry the remainder in the same way.
5   Sprinkle with caster sugar or sugar and a good pinch of ground cinnamon and serve with cream or ice cream.

Crêpes Suzettes
Serves 4

These are a real speciality, ideal to serve for a special occasion. Use a large frying pan or two smaller ones to ensure the pancakes are well soaked in the delicious juices.

8 pancakes made from the enriched pancake batter using 2 eggs
50 g/2 oz/good 1/3 cup caster (superfine) sugar
50 g/2 oz/1/4 cup butter
grated rind of 2 oranges and 1 lemon
juice of 2 oranges
1 tablespoon lemon juice
4–6 tablespoons brandy

1   The pancakes may be made earlier in the day and stacked up on a plate with a disc of wax or greaseproof paper, non-stick baking paper or foil between each. Cover with plastic cling film or foil and keep in the refrigerator or a cool place.
2   For the sauce, put the sugar into a frying pan and heat gently until it melts, then continue slowly until it begins to brown.
3   Add the butter, orange and lemon rinds and juices and heat until the caramel dissolves.
4   Fold each pancake into four and add to the pan. Spoon the sauce over each one as it is added. Simmer gently for 2–3 minutes or until piping hot, spooning the sauce frequently over them.

5   Just before serving, warm the brandy and pour into the pan over the pancakes. Set alight and serve at once on warmed plates, with the brandy sauce spooned over.

HOT SOUFFLÉS

Remember when cooking and serving a hot soufflé for a pudding, it is essential to get the timing right. It is better to keep the guests waiting for the soufflé, as it *will not* wait for you and must be served directly from the oven to the table or it will sink dramatically and the whole effect and pudding will be spoilt.

Vanilla Soufflé   Serves 4–6

50 g/2 oz/good ¼ cup caster (superfine) sugar
4 eggs
4 tablespoons plain (all-purpose) flour
300 ml/½ pint/1¼ cups milk
½ teaspoon vanilla essence
icing (confectioners') sugar for dredging

1   Grease a 18 cm/7 inch soufflé dish.
2   Cream the sugar with 1 whole egg and 1 egg yolk until pale in colour. Stir in the flour, then gradually add the milk and mix to give a smooth consistency.
3   Transfer to a saucepan and bring slowly to boiling point, stirring all the time, to give a thick smooth sauce, then simmer for 2 minutes. Remove from the heat and allow to cool slightly.
4   Separate the other 2 eggs and beat the yolks into the sauce with the vanilla essence.
5   Put the 3 egg whites into a clean grease-free bowl and whisk until very stiff and standing in peaks. Fold the egg white evenly through the sauce and pour at once into the preapred dish.
6   Bake in a moderate oven (180°C/350°F/Gas Mark 4) for about 45 minutes until well risen, firm to the touch and golden brown. Do not look in the oven for the first 35 minutes, unless you have a glass door.
7   Remove immediately from the oven, dredge lightly with sifted icing sugar and serve at once.

VARIATIONS
Fruit – arrange sliced soft or canned fruits in the base of the soufflé dish before adding the soufflé mixture. Try sliced strawberries and/or peaches, bananas, chopped pineapple, raspberries or orange segments, spooning 2 tablespoons liqueur over the fruit, if liked. Continue as above.

Hot Fruit Soufflé   Serves 4–6

425 g/15 oz can raspberries, apricots, peaches, pears, etc., drained
40 g/1½ oz/3 tablespoons butter
4 tablespoons flour
150 ml/¼ pint/⅔ cup milk
50 g/2 oz/good ¼ cup caster (superfine) sugar
4 eggs, separated
1 tablespoon brandy or other liqueur

1   Butter a soufflé dish of 18 cm/7 inches in diameter or 1.7 litres/3 pints/7½ cups.
2   Purée the chosen fruit and, if full of pips, sieve to remove them.
3   Melt the butter in a saucepan, stir in the flour and cook for a minute or so until bubbling. Gradually add the milk and stir until smooth, then add the fruit purée, and bring slowly to the boil, stirring continuously. Allow to simmer for 2 minutes, then remove from the heat.
4   Beat in the sugar until dissolved, followed by the egg yolks and liqueur.
5   Whisk the egg whites until very stiff and standing in peaks. Beat 2 tablespoons into the sauce and then fold in the remainder evenly.
6   Pour into the prepared dish and bake in a moderate oven (180°C/350°F/Gas Mark 4) until well risen, golden brown and firm to the touch.
7   Serve immediately with pouring cream or a sauce made from the fruit juice which should be thickened with 1–1½ teaspoons arrowroot, blended with a tablespoon of cold water, and brought to the boil until thick and clear.

Baked Chocolate Soufflé   Serves 4–6

100 g/4 oz/1 cup chocolate dots or plain chocolate
2 tablespoons rum or water
400 ml/¾ pint/scant 2 cups milk
50 g/2 oz/good ¼ cup caster (superfine) sugar
4 tablespoons flour
15 g/½ oz/1 tablespoon butter
4 eggs, separated
icing (confectioners') sugar to dredge

1   Grease a soufflé dish of 18 cm/7 inches in diameter or 1.7 litres/3 pints/7½ cups with butter.
2   Melt the chocolate with the rum or water in a bowl over a pan of gently simmering water, or in a microwave set on cool. Stir until smooth.
3   Heat most of the milk to just below boiling. Stir in the sugar until dissolved, then pour onto the chocolate and stir until well blended.
4   Blend the flour with the remaining milk until smooth then gradually add the chocolate mixture. Return to the saucepan and bring to the boil, stirring frequently. Simmer for 2 minutes.
5   Add the butter and stir until melted, then leave the sauce until warm.
6   Beat in the egg yolks until evenly mixed. Whisk the egg whites until stiff and standing in peaks. Beat 2 tablespoons into the chocolate mixture, then fold in the remainder.
7   Pour the mixture into the prepared dish and bake in a moderate oven (180°C/350°F/Gas Mark 4) for about 45 minutes or until well risen and firm to the touch.
8   Remove from the oven, dredge the top with sifted icing sugar and serve immediately.

14 Cold Desserts

This section covers a large number of different types of cold desserts far too numerous to include in this book, so I will pick on a few of the favourites and elaborate on and around these. Ice cream and sorbets (sherbets) immediately spring to mind for both are very popular and most versatile; cold soufflés and mousses are ideal for everyday to very elegant eating and are not as complicated as you are often led to believe; and there are many custard-based desserts including crème caramels, creams and, of course, the ever popular trifle in its many guises.

Cream plays an important part in making cold desserts. A word of advice here on which type to use. For whipping, use only double (heavy) or whipping cream; single (light) and other thinner types of cream do not contain enough fat to whip satisfactorily so should be used just for pouring. However, double (heavy) cream can be 'watered down' or extended with milk or wine (as in syllabub) and it will still whip satisfactorily – add up to 2 tablespoons to each 150 ml/¼ pint/⅔ cup double (heavy) cream, or use 2 parts double (heavy) cream mixed with 1 part single (light) cream – i.e. 300 ml/½ pint/1¼ cups double (heavy) and 150 ml/¼ pint/⅔ cup single (light) – and whip as usual. Take care not to overwhip cream, it is very easily done. Do not whip it too hastily and stop fairly frequently to check on the consistency. The cream should be thick enough to stand in soft peaks which just flop over at the top and not a solid mass which suddenly curdles and is then no more use. Soft whipped cream is much easier to fold into a dessert; if too stiff, it will not incorporate either as smoothly or easily. For piping, carry out the last part of whipping with great care. Use a rotary whisk or hand-held electric mixer for preference, or use a fork or small balloon whisk for very small quantities. In warmer weather, the cream will whip quicker and is more likely to curdle than in cold weather. Always take cream straight from the refrigerator to whip, do not leave it around in a warm atmosphere.

This leads on to cream cheese and cottage cheese desserts, namely cheesecakes, which suddenly arrived and are here to stay in a big way. And we mustn't forget meringues and the many ways they can be prepared for desserts, from serving simply with whipped cream or spread over the top of a sponge or fruit pudding to using to mask ice cream for a spectacular Baked Alaska or the many types of luscious gâteaux or cakes that are based on meringue. Again care is called for with meringue making: remember to always use a clean grease-free bowl; do not overwhisk either before or after adding the sugar; and do add the sugar in small amounts. And talking of gâteaux, there are also the many types of cake-based ones with a wide variety of fillings,

toppings and flavours that make wonderful desserts.

Cold desserts are ideal to serve when entertaining for they can be made a while in advance. This allows much more time for preparing other things and being with your guests.

ICE CREAMS

Ice creams are rarely made of cream alone, although they should have a good proportion of it. Egg custard, cream, fruit purées and egg whites are the usual ingredients, which are mixed in varying proportions to give richer or more delicate creams. Once you have mastered the method of making ice cream, numerous flavours can be prepared to suit your tastes. Fresh fruit flavours are much better than using too many artificial flavourings and they keep better in the freezer. Once made, the ice cream can be incorporated into ice cream cakes or gâteaux, either just using ice cream or combining with layers of sponge and/or meringue, and when formed into a *bombe* (often combined with a sorbet) it makes a spectacular dessert.

Home-made ice creams will store for up to 3 months in a home freezer, but can be made in a refrigerator and stored in the ice compartment for 2–3 weeks depending on the star rating.

The best methods are achieved by using a special ice cream churn. This involves a hand-operated or electric churn which turns the ice cream making it extra smooth while freezing it. However, excellent ice cream is made everyday without one of these 'extras'.

MAKING ICE CREAM
1   Whatever method of ice cream making you choose, always set the freezer or refrigerator to its coldest setting in plenty of time before beginning. It is also essential to use everything cold, which means ingredients, utensils and bowls, etc.
2   The process of freezing reduces the sweetness and flavour, so allow for this when sweetening and flavouring, but take care not to overdo it.
3   For best results, stir the mixture every 30 minutes until it is half frozen and mushy, then beat thoroughly, return to the freezer and leave undisturbed until thoroughly frozen.
4   Ice cream will freeze quicker in a shallow container or ice cube tray. If it is to be used for spooning, do the first freezing in the shallow container, then after the thorough beating, turn into a deeper bowl or basin to complete the freezing.

Rhubarb and Apple Crumble (see page 185) *and Lemon Surprise Pudding* (see page 185)

5   When the ice cream is ready it is *essential* to remember to return the refrigerator or deep freeze to its normal setting. If left on fast freeze or the coldest setting, it will not only cost much more to run, but will spoil much of the food kept in the actual refrigerator.

6   When serving ice cream, it is a good idea to transfer the container to the refrigerator from the freezer for about 30 minutes before serving to allow it to 'come to' slightly and make serving easier.

7   Serve ice cream in dishes or bowls that have been chilled first. To serve, dip the spoon or ice cream scoop into cold water first and between each spooning.

Rich Vanilla Ice Cream   Serves 6–8

(See step-by-step illustrations, page 194.)

300 g/½ pint/1¼ cups milk
75–100 g/3–4 oz/about ½ cup caster (superfine) sugar
2 eggs, beaten, or 4 egg yolks
1 teaspoon vanilla essence (or use sugar that has been infused with a vanilla pod)
300 ml/½ pint/1¼ cups double (heavy) cream, half whipped

1   For the custard base, heat the milk and sugar until hot but not boiling. Pour onto the beaten eggs, stirring all the time. Return to the saucepan.

2   Heat gently and bring slowly almost to the boil, stirring continuously until thick enough to coat the back of the spoon. Do not allow to boil or the custard will curdle. It may be easier to make the custard in a double saucepan or a bowl standing over a saucepan of gently simmering water as it is less likely that the custard will curdle, although it does take a little longer.

3   Strain the custard into a bowl and stir in the essence. Cover with plastic cling film and leave until cold.

4   When cold, whip the cream until thick but in no way stiff. It should just be rather floppy and only form soft peaks. Fold evenly into the custard and turn into a shallow freezing container or ice cube tray with the dividers taken out.

5   Freeze until the ice cream is half frozen, that is firm around the outside and mushy in the middle. Turn the mixture out into a cold bowl.

6   Break down with a fork or whisk and then beat until smooth and the ice crystals have been broken down. Return to the freezing container.

7   Replace in the freezer and freeze until completely firm. When ready, if not to be used at once, cover the bowl or container with foil.

VARIATIONS

Coffee – add 1½–2 tablespoons instant coffee powder to the milk before making the custard. Omit the vanilla.
Chocolate – stir 100 g/4 oz plain chocolate, which has been melted, into the custard before adding the cream, or, alternatively, stir the same amount of grated chocolate into the mixture with the cream.
Orange or Lemon – add the grated rind of 1–2 oranges or lemons to the custard before adding the cream. Omit the vanilla.

Vanilla Ice Cream (cream-based)   Serves 4–5

300 ml/½ pint/1¼ cups double (heavy) cream
3 tablespoons milk
75 g/3 oz/about ⅔ cup icing (confectioners') sugar, sifted
½ teaspoon vanilla essence
1 egg white

1   Put the cream and milk into a cold bowl and whip until thick and standing in peaks, but not too stiff.

2   Fold in the icing sugar and vanilla essence and pour into a freezing tray or dish.

3   Freeze until the mixture is just firm, but not hard.

4   Turn out into a cold bowl, break down with a fork and then beat hard until smooth and all the ice crystals have been broken down.

5   Whisk the egg white until very stiff and fold evenly into the ice cream.

6   Return to the freezing container and freeze until hard.

VARIATIONS

Tutti Fruitti – stir in 25 g/1 oz/¼ cup chopped toasted almonds, 40 g/1½ oz/¼ cup chopped glacé cherries, 50 g/2 oz/⅓ cup chopped sultanas (golden raisins) or raisins and a little grated orange or lemon rind after the first freezing.
Chocolate Flake – stir in 50–100 g/2–4 oz plain or milk chocolate, coarsely grated, after the first freezing.
Liqueur – replace 2 or 3 tablespoons of the milk with any liqueur – brandy, Tia Maria, Crème de Menthe, etc.
Coffee –replace 2 tablespoons of the milk with coffee essence or very black sweet coffee.
Coffee Walnut – make as coffee ice cream but stir 50 g/2 oz/½ cup chopped walnuts into the mixture after the first freezing.
Fruit – fold 150 ml/¼ pint/⅓ cup thick fruit purée (e.g. raspberry, strawberry, blackcurrant, redcurrant, apricot, etc.) into the whipped cream before the first freezing.

Brown Bread Ice Cream   Serves 6

100 g/4 oz wholemeal slices of bread, crusts removed
450 ml/¾ pint/scant 2 cups double (heavy) cream
100 g/4 oz/about 1 cup icing (confectioners') sugar
½ teaspoon vanilla essence
50 g/2 oz/good ¼ cup granulated sugar
50 ml/2 fl oz/¼ cup water

1   Place the sliced bread on a baking tray in a slow oven (140°C/275°F/Gas Mark 1) for about an hour or until crisp and dry. Crush in a blender or food processor, or place between two sheets of wax or greaseproof paper and crush with a rolling pin to give fine breadcrumbs.

2   Whisk the cream until just standing in soft peaks and stir in the icing sugar and vanilla essence.

3   Turn into a shallow container or ice tray and freeze for about an hour or so or until the cream is firm around the edges and mushy in the centre.

4   Meanwhile, place the granulated sugar and water in a small saucepan and stir over a low heat until the sugar

has dissolved. Increase the heat and boil the syrup for 2 minutes without further stirring. Remove from the heat, stir in the breadcrumbs and leave until cold.

5   Turn the ice cream into a cold bowl and beat until smooth and creamy, then stir in the breadcrumb mixture until evenly blended. Return to the freezing container and replace in the freezer until hard.

WATER ICES, SORBETS (SHERBETS) AND GRANITA

The basis of a water ice is a syrup made from sugar and water to which a fruit juice or fruit purée and a small amount of egg white is added. Sorbets (sherbets) are similar and made in much the same way but a larger proportion of whisked egg whites are added to give a much softer finished texture. A granita is a flavoured syrup which is frozen and stirred frequently as it freezes to give a slushy but frozen mixture.

Lemon Water Ice   Serves 4–6

225 g/8 oz good cup caster (superfine) sugar
600 ml/1 pint/2½ cups water
3 lemons
1 egg white

1   Put the sugar and water into a saucepan and heat gently until the sugar has dissolved, stirring frequently.
2   Pare the rind thinly from the lemons using a potato peeler and add to the syrup. Simmer gently for 10 minutes.
3   Leave the syrup to cool, then add the juice of the 3 lemons.
4   Strain the cold mixture into a shallow freezing container and freeze until very mushy and half frozen.
5   Turn the mixture into a cold bowl and mix until even. Whisk the egg white until stiff and fold through the mixture.
6   Return to the freezing container and freeze until firm.

VARIATIONS
Fruit – use 300 ml/½ pint/1¼ cups of the syrup as above and mix with 300 ml/½ pint/1¼ cups fruit purée (e.g. raspberry, strawberry, blackcurrant, blackberry, gooseberry, apricot, etc.) and the juice of ½ lemon.

Blackcurrant Sorbet (Sherbet)

Serves 5–6

300 ml/½ pint/1¼ cups water
100 g/4 oz/good ½ cup caster (superfine) sugar
225 g/8 oz blackcurrants, frozen or fresh
juice of ½ lemon
2 egg whites

1   Put the water and sugar into a saucepan. Bring to the boil and boil gently for 10 minutes. Cool.
2   Meanwhile, stew the blackcurrants in the minimum of

water in a covered pan until tender – about 15 minutes. Cool a little, then rub through a sieve or purée in a blender or food processor.
3   Combine the sugar syrup, blackcurrant purée and lemon juice and pour onto an ice tray. Freeze until almost firm.
4   Turn the mixture into a cold bowl, break down and beat until mushy. Whisk the egg whites until very stiff and fold through the mixture.
5   Return to the freezing container and freeze until firm. Serve it slightly on the soft side rather than rock hard.

Coffee Granita   Serves 6

100 g/4 oz/good ½ cup caster (superfine) sugar
1.2 litres/2 pints/5 cups water
100 g/4 oz/1 cup coarsely ground coffee
2 tablespoons brandy or Tia Maria (optional)
lightly whipped cream (optional)

1   Put the sugar and water into a saucepan and heat gently until dissolved. Bring to the boil and boil hard for 3 minutes, then remove from the heat.
2   Stir in the ground coffee and leave to stand for 15 minutes, stirring occasionally.
3   Strain the mixture through a fine sieve or muslin-lined sieve, cool and chill.
4   Add the brandy or Tia Maria (if used) and pour into one or two shallow ice cube trays. Freeze for about an hour or until just beginning to solidify.
5   Stir the mixture until slushy and then return to the freezing container and freeze for a further 30 minutes.
6   Repeat the stirring and freezing process at 30 minute intervals until thick and slushy, and firm but granular.
7   To serve, spoon into tall glasses and decorate each with a whirl of whipped cream, if liked.

Ice Cream Bombe   Serves 8–10

1 recipe quantity rich chocolate ice cream, half frozen
½ recipe quantity blackcurrant or raspberry sorbet, half frozen
½ recipe quantity cream-based vanilla or coffee walnut ice cream, half frozen
To decorate
whipped cream, toasted almonds and glacé cherries

1   Grease a pudding basin or bowl or ice cream bombe mould (about 1.5 litre/2½ pint/6½ cup capacity).
2   Line the container with the half-frozen chocolate ice cream so it is an even thickness all over.
3   Spoon the blackcurrant or raspberry sorbet into the ice-cream-lined basin and then cover with the vanilla or coffee walnut ice cream.
4   Freeze until all the ice cream is quite firm.
5   To serve, unmould the *bombe* on a cold dish and decorate it with whipped cream, nuts and glacé cherries, if liked. Leave in the refrigerator for about 30 minutes or so to 'come to' before serving. It may be necessary to use a knife dipped in hot water to cut the *bombe* evenly.

Coffee Ice Cream (see page 192)

1 *Heat the custard in a bowl over a pan of gently simmering water until it is thick enough to coat the back of a spoon.*

3 *When the ice cream is half frozen, turn the mixture into a cold bowl and beat until smooth with a fork.*

2 *Fold the softly whipped cream into the cold custard.*

4 *Spoon into serving dishes and decorate with grated chocolate and biscuits or wafers.*

Iced Meringue Gâteau   Serves 10–12

2 baked meringue discs, 20–23 cm/8–9 inch diameter (see page 204)
1 recipe quantity orange cream-based ice cream, half frozen (see page 192)
1 recipe quantity apricot cream-based ice cream, half frozen (see page 192)
To decorate
a little whipped cream
a few apricot halves and/or slices of kiwi fruit

1 Thoroughly grease a 23 cm/9 inch round cake tin, preferably loose-based.
2 Place one of the meringue discs in the bottom. Cover with the orange ice cream and level.
3 Add the other layer of meringue and the apricot ice cream. Level the top and freeze until firm.
4 To serve, remove the gâteau carefully from the tin and place it on a plate. Put the whipped cream into a piping bag fitted with a star nozzle and use to decorate the top of the gâteau with the apricot halves and/or slices of kiwi fruit. Leave to 'come to' in the refrigerator for about 30 minutes before serving.

Ice Cream Bombe (see page 193) *and Chocolate Orange Cheesecake* (see page 206)

CUSTARD-AND CREAM-BASED DESSERTS

There are several varieties of these, ranging from baked egg custards with caramel to trifles, charlottes and the basic creams set in moulds.

Crème Caramel   Serves 8

2 tablespoons cold water
150 g/5 oz/scant ⅔ cup caster (superfine) sugar
3 tablespoons boiling water
Custard
568 ml/1 pint/2½ cups milk
1 vanilla pod, or a few drops of vanilla essence
4 eggs (large)
2 egg yolks
40 g/1½ oz/scant ¼ cup caster (superfine) sugar

1   Put the cold water and sugar into a small heavy-based saucepan and heat gently until the sugar has completely dissolved, stirring occasionally.
2   When the sugar has dissolved, boil the syrup, without further stirring, until it turns a rich golden brown. Remove from the heat at once and slowly spoon in the boiling water, stirring if necessary to loosen the caramel.
3   Lightly oil eight 150 ml/¼ pint/⅔ cup dariole moulds or small cups. Divide the caramel between these, and leave in a cool place until set.
4   For the custard, pour the milk into a saucepan, add the vanilla pod (or essence) and bring barely to the boil. Remove from the heat and leave to stand for 10 minutes for the flavour of the vanilla pod to infuse with the milk.
5   Put the eggs and egg yolks into a bowl with the sugar and beat together until pale and fluffy.
6   Remove the vanilla pod from the milk and pour onto the eggs, stirring all the time. Strain into a jug.
7   Stand the dariole moulds in a roasting tin and pour in the custard so they are all equally full.
8   Add about 2.5 cm/1 inch of warm water to the roasting tin and bake in a cool oven (160°C/325°F/Gas Mark 3) for about 45 minutes or until set. To test if cooked through, insert a fine skewer in the centre and if it comes out clean, they are ready.
9   Remove the moulds from the water bath and while still warm ease away from the sides of the moulds with a small knife. Shake once and invert onto a serving plate or into a glass dish. Ease the mould away, let all the caramel pour out, and leave until cold before serving.
10 The caramels can be cooled and chilled, after loosening from the sides and then turned out as and when required.

Note: The mixture may be baked in one large ovenproof dish. Prepare and cook as above but increase the cooking time to 1–1¼ hours. Chill before turning out.

Olde Englishe Trifle   Serves 6

This is traditionally flavoured with sherry and layered with sponge, raspberries and peaches, but the fruit can be varied to suit.

8 trifle sponge cakes
about 75 g/3 oz/4 tablespoons raspberry jam
225 g/8 oz can raspberries, or 175 g/6 oz fresh raspberries
4 tablespoons sherry
225 g/8 oz can peach slices, drained
450 ml/¾ pint/scant 2 cups thick custard (see page 32)
300 ml/½ pint/1¼ cups whipping cream
whole blanched almonds, toasted, or pistachio nuts,
    blanched, to decorate

1   Split the sponge cakes in half, spread with jam and reassemble. Cut each into cubes and place in a glass serving bowl.
2   Drain the raspberries and sprinkle over the sponge cake. Mix the juice with the sherry and pour over the top. If using fresh raspberries, reserve the juice from the peaches and mix with the sherry.
3   Add the peach slices to the bowl and leave to stand for 15 minutes.
4   Make up the custard and, when cool, pour over the trifle ingredients and leave until set and cold.
5   Whip the cream until stiff, put about a quarter into a piping bag fitted with a star nozzle. Spread the remainder over the custard, marking an attractive design with a round-bladed knife.
6   Use the rest of the cream to pipe a shell border or whirls around the outside of the trifle. Decorate with toasted almonds or small clusters of pistachio nuts, or chop about 2 tablespoons of the nuts and sprinkle over the centre of the trifle. Chill before serving.

Ginger and Apricot Trifle   Serves 6

8 trifle sponge cakes
about 75 g/3 oz/4 tablespoons raspberry jam or ginger
    preserve
425 g/15 oz can apricot halves
5–6 pieces stem ginger
3–4 tablespoons ginger syrup (from the ginger jar)
3–4 tablespoons ginger wine or whisky
450 ml/¾ pint/1⅓ cups thick custard (see page 32)
300 ml/½ pint/1¼ cups whipping cream
a few flaked almonds, toasted
strips of angelica

1   Use the sponge cakes and jam as for Olde Englishe Trifle.
2   Drain the apricots and reserve 2–3 tablespoons of the syrup. Halve the apricots and lay over the cake.
3   Slice 1–2 pieces of ginger for decoration, chop the rest and sprinkle over the apricots. Mix the reserved syrup, ginger syrup and ginger wine or whisky and pour over the fruit and sponge.
4   Make the custard and, when cool, pour over the trifle. Leave to set and cool.

5 Whip the cream until stiff and put into a piping bag fitted with a large star nozzle. Use to pipe a lattice all over the surface of the custard.
6 Use ginger, almonds and angelica to decorate.

Custard Cream

Serves 4

3 egg yolks
3 tablespoons caster (superfine) sugar
300 ml/½ pint/1¼ cups milk
a few strips of thinly pared lemon rind, or ½ vanilla pod or 1 teaspoon vanilla essence
3 teaspoons powdered gelatine
2 tablespoons water
300 ml/½ pint/1¼ cups double (heavy) cream

1 To make the custard, whisk the eggs and sugar together lightly.
2 Warm the milk and lemon rind or vanilla pod or essence and leave to infuse for 10 minutes, then remove the lemon rind or pod.
3 Pour the milk on to the eggs and mix thoroughly. Strain the mixture into the top of a double saucepan or boiler, or a basin standing over a pan of gently simmering water.
4 Stir over a very gentle heat until the sauce thickens and will coat the back of a spoon. Do not allow to boil or it will curdle. Remove from the heat and allow to cool, covered with plastic cling film.
5 Use a 900 ml/1½ pint/3¾ cup jelly mould or bowl and rinse out with cold water.
6 Put the gelatine and water into a small basin and stand over the saucepan of simmering water until dissolved, or dissolve in a microwave oven set on cool. Cool a little and then pour into the custard stirring all the time.
7 Whip the cream until thick and floppy and fold into the custard mixture until evenly blended. Chill until on the point of setting and then pour quickly into the wetted mould or basin. Chill until quite firm.
8 To serve, unmould the cream. First fill a bowl with very hot water and wet the serving plate with cold water. Draw the tip of a knife or finger around the rim of the mould and immerse the mould for 1–2 seconds in the water. Place the plate in position, quickly upturn so it is the correct way up and give one or two sharp shakes and the cream should be felt to slide out onto the plate. If it resists, then repeat the dipping in hot water and try again. If it is not centrally positioned on the plate, it can be moved on the wet plate as necessary.
9 The cream may be surrounded with fresh or canned fruit before serving.

VARIATIONS

Orange or Lemon – omit the vanilla and add the grated rind of 1 orange or lemon to the mixture just before pouring into the mould.
Liqueur – omit the vanilla and add 1–2 tablespoons orange or coffee liqueur, brandy, or whisky to the custard.
Chocolate – dissolve 2 tablespoons sifted cocoa powder in the milk before making the custard.
Coffee – replace 1–2 tablespoons of the milk with coffee essence.

Charlotte Russe

Serves 6–8

1 tablet lemon jelly
juice of 1 lemon, strained
300 ml/½ pint/1¼ cups milk
3 tablespoons water
3 teaspoons powdered gelatine
3 egg yolks
2 tablespoons caster (superfine) sugar
2 tablespoons brandy, Grand Marnier, Orange Curaçao or sherry
about 12 soft sponge fingers or a packet of Boudoir biscuits
150 ml/¼ pint/⅔ pint double (heavy) cream
To decorate
a little whipped cream
1 kiwi fruit, peeled and sliced

1 Make up the jelly by placing in a 600 ml/1 pint/2½ cup jug with the lemon juice and sufficient boiling water to fill the jug. Stir until dissolved and then leave until cold.
2 Pour a little jelly into a 900 ml/1½ pint/3¾ cup sloping-sided charlotte tin and leave to set. The layer should be about 2 cm/¾ inch deep. Leave the rest of the jelly to set.
3 Heat the milk in a saucepan until fairly hot but not boiling. Blend the water with the gelatine in a small basin and stand over a pan of gently simmering water until dissolved.
4 Beat the egg yolks and sugar together, pour on the warm milk and stand the bowl over the pan of simmering water. Cook gently until thickened sufficiently to coat the back of a spoon.
5 Stir the gelatine and brandy into the custard and cool until beginning to thicken.
6 Arrange the sponge fingers side by side all around the tin resting on the jelly.
7 Whip the cream until thick and fold into the custard mixture. Pour quickly into the tin and chill until set.
8 Trim the sponge fingers level with the top of the mousse and then carefully unmould the russe on a serving dish.
9 Chop the jelly and spoon around the base of it and decorate the top and around the base with whipped cream and slices of kiwi fruit.

Fruit Brûlée

Serves 6

475–675 g/1–1½ lb any type of stewed fruit, sweetened
300 ml ½ pint/1¼ cups soured cream or natural yogurt
caster (superfine) sugar for topping

1 Put the stewed fruit into a heatproof dish and level the top.
2 Spread a layer of soured cream or yogurt over the fruit and chill thoroughly.
3 Spoon an even layer of sugar over the surface and brown under a moderate grill or broiler as for Crème Brûlée. Don't worry if some of the cream bubbles through. Chill before serving.

Crème Brûlée

Serves 4–6

Traditionally this should be made with all double (heavy) cream, but this tends to be very rich and can curdle. I think the following recipe is just as good and causes a lot less bother.

600 ml/1 pint/2½ cups whipping or single (light) cream
1 egg
4 egg yolks
a few drops of vanilla essence
1½ tablespoons caster (superfine) sugar
caster (superfine) sugar for topping

1   Pour the cream into a bowl.
2   Beat the egg, egg yolks, essence and sugar together and add to the cream. Beat gently until evenly blended.
3   Strain the custard into a fairly shallow heatproof dish of about 900 ml/1½ pint/3¾ cup capacity or individual dishes. A china flan dish is good.
4   Stand the dish in a roasting tin with about 2.5 cm/1 inch of warm water added and bake in a cool oven (150°C/300°F/Gas Mark 2) for about an hour or until set. Remove from the water bath, leave to cool and then chill thoroughly.
5   Spoon a thin even layer of caster sugar over the surface of the custard so no custard is showing. Place under a moderate grill or broiler and cook until the sugar turns an even golden brown all over. Turn the dish around as necessary and, if overbrowning in one place, tilt the dish so the caramel runs out evenly. Chill for 2–3 hours before serving.
6   To serve, break the caramel with the back of a serving spoon and serve the custard with a portion of caramel.

Chocolate Pots

Serves 4

100 g/4 oz plain chocolate or chocolate dots
25 g/1 oz/2 tablespoons butter
4 egg yolks
2 tablespoons rum
4 tablespoons double (heavy) cream
2 egg whites
To decorate
a little whipped cream
a few pistachio nuts or chocolate matchsticks

1   Break up the chocolate and put into a heatproof bowl over a pan of hot water or in the top of a double saucepan. Add the butter and heat until melted. Stir until smooth.
2   Beat in the egg yolks and rum. Whip the cream until floppy and stir into the mixture.
3   Whip the egg whites until stiff and fold evenly through the chocolate mixture.
4   Divide between four individuals 'pots' or glasses and chill until set.
5   Just before serving, top each with a whirl of whipped cream and a few chopped pistachio nuts or 2 chocolate matchsticks impaled in each.

Marron Crèmes

Serves 6

1 can sweetened chestnut spread (about 240 g/8½ oz)
2–3 tablespoons coffee liqueur or brandy
300 ml/½ pint/1¼ cups double (heavy) or whipping cream
about 6 marrons glacés
2 egg whites

1   Turn the chestnut spread into a bowl, add the liqueur or brandy and beat until smooth.
2   Whip the cream until very thick but not too stiff and fold three-quarters into the chestnut mixture.
3   Chop 4 marrons glacés finely and add to the mixture.
4   Just before serving, whisk the egg whites until stiff and fold through the mixture evenly.
5   Divide between six glasses and top each with a whirl of the remaining cream and a piece of the remaining marrons glacés.

SYLLABUBS

These are yet another cream-based dessert; they are very quick to make and serve and quite delicious for those who like cream. There are several types of syllabub, some of which separate out leaving the lemony wine mixture beneath the creamy top.

Lemon Syllabub

Serves 4

2 egg whites
100 g/4 oz/good ½ cup caster (superfine) sugar
finely grated rind of 1 lemon
2 tablespoons lemon juice
300 ml/½ pint/1¼ cups double (heavy) cream
150 ml/¼ pint/⅔ cup dry white wine or cider
lemon slices to decorate

1   Whisk the egg whites until stiff and standing in peaks.
2   Fold in the sugar, lemon rind and lemon juice.
3   Whip the cream with the wine until thick and floppy.
4   Fold into the egg white mixture and divide between four glasses.
5   Leave to stand in a cool place or the refrigerator for several hours to allow the syllabub to separate slightly.
6   Decorate each serving with a twist of lemon and serve with sponge fingers or langue-de-chat biscuits.

Sherry Syllabub

Serves 4

finely grated rind and juice of 1 large lemon
75 g/3 oz/scant ½ cup caster (superfine) sugar
2 tablespoons brandy
2 tablespoons sherry
300 ml/½ pint/1¼ cups double (heavy) cream
a few ratafia biscuits
lemon jelly slices to decorate

1   Put the lemon rind and juice, sugar, brandy and sherry into a bowl and leave to stand for at least an hour.
2   Add the cream to the mixture and whip until thick.

3 Crumble about 4 ratafia biscuits into the base of four glasses. Pour the syllabub mixture on top and add one or two jelly slices to decorate. Serve at once.

Pink Syllabub   Serves 4

grated rind and juice of 1 lemon
2 tablespoons caster (superfine) sugar
150 ml/¼ pint/⅔ cup rosé wine
300 ml/½ pint/1¼ cups double (heavy) cream
a few drops of cochineal or pink food colouring (optional)
crystallized rose petals to decorate

1 Put the lemon rind and juice, sugar and half the rosé wine in a bowl with the cream. Whisk until the mixture holds it shape.
2 Add the rest of the wine and whisk a little more.
3 Add a few drops of pink colouring, if liked, then turn into four glasses and chill for at least an hour.
4 Serve each glass decorated with crystallized rose petals.

SOUFFLÉS AND MOUSSES

A mousse is a light creamy dessert that usually has a base of a custard type sauce or fruit purée to which eggs and whipped cream are often added. Gelatine is usually used to set the mousse, although sometimes it is partly frozen and no gelatine is necessary. A mousse is served in a bowl or individual dishes and not very often turned out.

A soufflé is a fluffy dish that is lightened by the addition of stiffly beaten egg whites and it is very important to add them evenly and lightly to achieve the correct consistency. Soufflés are also set with gelatine and the base is is usually egg yolks and sugar beaten together over heat until thick and creamy. The flavouring or fruit purée is then added, followed by cream and egg whites. It is usual for a soufflé to have the mixture standing at least 2.5 cm/1 inch above the rim of the dish and this is achieved by adding a paper collar to the dish before filling (see page 200).

Raspberry Mousse   Serves 6–8

450 g/1 lb raspberries, fresh or frozen
caster (superfine) sugar to taste
4 teaspoons powdered gelatine
3 tablespoons water
150 ml/¼ pint/⅔ cup double (heavy), whipping or soured
    cream
2 egg whites
whipped cream for decoration

1 Reserve a few whole raspberries for decoration and sieve or purée the rest of the fruit in a blender or food processor. (Sieving will remove all the pips.)
2 Sweeten the raspberry purée to taste with caster sugar.
3 Put the gelatine and water into a small basin and stand over a pan of gently simmering water for a few minutes until the gelatine has dissolved and become clear. Cool a little.
4 Stir the gelatine through the raspberry mixture.

5 Whip the cream until thick and floppy and fold into the raspberry mixture, or fold in the unwhipped soured cream. Leave until starting to thicken.
6 Finally, whisk the egg whites until stiff and standing in peaks and fold quickly and evenly through the mousse.
7 Pour into a serving bowl or six individual dishes and chill until set.
8 To serve, top each portion or the bowl with whirls or spoonfuls of cream and decorate with the reserved raspberries.

VARIATIONS
Use strawberries or loganberries in place of the raspberries. Use 425 g/15 oz cans raspberries, strawberries, gooseberries, blackcurrants, apricots, etc., in place of the fresh fruit, drain the contents reserving 3 tablespoons of the juice to use in place of water to dissolve the gelatine, and then sieve the fruit to give 300 ml/½ pint/1¼ cups fruit purée.

Pineapple Mousse   Serves 6–8

425 g/15 oz can pineapple rings
2 eggs, separated
50 g/2 oz/good ¼ cup caster (superfine) sugar
3 teaspoons powdered gelatine
2 tablespoons lemon juice
150 ml/¼ pint/⅔ cup double (heavy) or whipping cream
toasted flaked almonds to decorate

1 Reserve 2 pineapple rings for decoration. Blend or purée the remainder of the pineapple with half the pineapple juice.
2 Put the pineapple purée, egg yolks and sugar into a basin standing over a saucepan of gently simmering water and cook gently, stirring frequently, until the mixture thickens sufficiently to coat the back of a spoon. Remove from the heat.
3 Put the gelatine and lemon juice in a small basin and stand over the simmering water until dissolved. Stir through the pineapple mixture and leave to cool.
4 Whip the cream until thick and floppy and fold into the mixture and then whisk the egg whites until very stiff and standing in peaks and fold these through the mousse.
5 Turn into a bowl or individual glasses and chill until set.
6 To serve, cut the remaining pieces of pineapple into small pieces and use to decorate the mousses together with a sprinkling of toasted almonds.

Note: Do not use raw pineapple with gelatine mixtures, the pineapple must be canned or cooked first otherwise the gelatine will not set it.

VARIATIONS
Use any other type of canned fruit, keeping to the same size of can, to replace the pineapple.

Coffee Cloud Mousse Serves 4–6

400 ml/14 fl oz/1¾ cups very strong black coffee
3 teaspoons powdered gelatine
100 g/4 oz/good ½ cup light soft brown or caster
*   (superfine) sugar*
2 tablespoons Kahlua or Tia Maria or rum
about 50 g/2 oz ratafia biscuits or macaroons, crumbled
300 ml/½ pint/1¼ cups double (heavy) cream
To decorate
ratafia biscuits or toasted almonds

1 Put about 4 tablespoons of the coffee into a basin with the gelatine and stand over a saucepan of gently simmering water until dissolved. Stir in the sugar until dissolved, then remove from the heat.
2 Add the gelatine syrup mixture to the rest of the coffee and chill until beginning to thicken.
3 Lightly fold the crushed biscuits into the coffee mixture.
4 Whip the cream until thick but still floppy and fold about three-quarters of it into the coffee mousse.
5 Turn into a bowl or individual glasses and chill until set.
6 To serve, spoon a dollop of floppy cream onto each mousse or around the edge of the bowl and decorate with ratafia biscuits or toasted almonds.

PREPARING A SOUFFLÉ DISH

1 Cut a strip of double wax or greaseproof paper or single non-stick baking paper long enough to reach right round the outside of the soufflé dish with the ends overlapping and deep enough to reach from the bottom of the dish to about 6.5 cm/2½ inches above the top of the dish.
2 Tie the paper round the outside of the dish with string or stick with adhesive tape or use pins and paper clips to keep it fitting tightly to the sides of the dish. It must be close fitting or it will not prevent the mixture from running down between the paper and the dish.
3 If using wax or greaseproof paper, grease the paper on the inside very lightly.
4 When set, the soufflé mixture should stand about 2.5 cm/1 inch above the top of the rim of the dish and have been held in place with the paper.
5 To remove the paper collar, first remove the string, sticky tape or pins and then ease the paper away from the soufflé with the help of a knife dipped in hot water.
6 The sides of the soufflé may be left as they are or be coated with chopped nuts, toasted coconut, grated chocolate, etc.

  It is very important to use the correct size of dish for a soufflé if it is to come above the rim of the dish sufficiently. The mixtures will vary depending on how much air has been incorporated at all the different stages but the following are a rough guide to capacity:
16 cm/6½ inch dish (1.5 litre/2½ pint/6¼ cup) requires a 9 egg quantity and should serve 8–10 portions.
15 cm/6 inch dish (1.2 litre/2 pint/5 cup) requires a 6 egg quantity and should serve 6–8 portions.
12.5 cm/5 inch dish (600 ml/1 pint/2½ cup) requires a 3–4 egg quantity and should serve 4–6 portions.

Lemon Soufflé Serves 4–6

3 eggs, separated
225 g/8 oz/good cup caster (superfine) sugar
2 large lemons, or 3 small ones
3 teaspoons powdered gelatine
about 250 ml/8 fl oz/1 cup whipping cream
To decorate
lemon jelly slices or mimosa balls
angelica strips cut into leaves

1 Prepare a 12.5 cm/5 inch soufflé dish (see above). Put the egg yolks and sugar into a large bowl standing over a saucepan of gently simmering water.
2 Grate the rind from all the lemons and add to the bowl with the strained squeezed juice of 1 lemon.
3 Whisk the mixture over the heat until thick, pale in colour and the whisk leaves a heavy trail when lifted. Remove from the heat and continue to whisk until cool.
4 Put the gelatine into a small basin with the squeezed juice of the remaining lemon(s) and 1 tablespoon water and place over the simmering water until dissolved. Cool a little and then stir into the lemon mixture.
5 Whip the cream until floppy and standing in soft peaks and fold about two-thirds into the soufflé mixture. Leave until thick and on the point of setting.
6 Whisk the egg whites until very stiff and standing in peaks and then fold quickly and evenly through the lemon mixture. Pour quickly into the prepared dish and chill until set.
7 To serve, carefully peel off the paper from around the soufflé. Whip the cream a little more until stiff enough to pipe and then put into a piping bag fitted with a star nozzle. Pipe 6 or 8 whirls on top of the soufflé and top each one with a lemon slice or 3 mimosa balls and 1 or 2 angelica 'leaves'.

Note: This mixture may be doubled and turned into a large glass bowl or into a 15 cm/6 inch (1.2 litre/2 pint/5 cup) soufflé dish.

VARIATIONS
Orange – use the grated rind of 2 oranges and the juice of 2 lemons.
Lemon and Lime – use the grated rind of 1 large lemon and 2 small limes and the juice of 1 lemon and 1½ limes.

Chocolate Soufflé Serves 8

6 eggs, separated
6 tablespoons water
175 g/6 oz/good ¾ cup caster (superfine) sugar
175 g/6 oz plain chocolate or chocolate dots
2 tablespoons powdered gelatine
3 tablespoons rum
300 ml/½ pint/1¼ cups whipping cream
To decorate
a little grated chocolate
glacé or maraschino cherries

1 Prepare a 15 cm/6 inch (1.2 litre/2 pint/5 cup) soufflé dish in the usual way.
2 Put the egg yolks in a large heatproof bowl with 4 tablespoons of the water and the sugar. Whisk over a pan of gently simmering water until thick, pale in colour and the whisk leaves a heavy trail when lifted. A hand-held electric mixer is best for this task. Remove from the heat and whisk until cool.
3 Melt the chocolate in a heatproof basin over the simmering water and stir until smooth. Take care not to get any water into the chocolate or it will turn firm and spoil the texture.
4 Dissolve the gelatine in a basin with the remaining water and rum over the simmering water.
5 Stir first the chocolate and then the dissolved gelatine into the whisked mixture until evenly blended. Leave until beginning to thicken.
6 Whip the cream until thick and floppy and fold three-quarters of it into the mixture.
7 Finally, whisk the egg whites until very stiff and standing in peaks and fold quickly and evenly through the mixture.
8 Pour quickly into the prepared dish and chill until set.
9 To serve, carefully peel off the paper collar from around the soufflé and use the grated chocolate to coat the sides of it. Whip the cream until stiff enough to pipe, put into a piping bag fitted with a star nozzle and pipe about 8–10 stars on top of the soufflé. Use halved glacé or maraschino cherries to place between the cream.

Vanilla Soufflé

Serves 5–6

4 eggs, separated
5 tablespoons water
100 g/4 oz/good ½ cup caster (superfine) sugar
½ teaspoon vanilla essence
4 teaspoons powdered gelatine
200 ml/7 fl oz/scant cup whipping cream
To decorate
a little whipped cream
1 chocolate flake bar, or a few pistachio nuts, blanched

1 Prepare a 12.5 cm/5 inch (600 ml/1 pint/2½ cup) soufflé dish.
2 Put the egg yolks, 3 tablespoons of the water, the sugar and vanilla essence into a heatproof bowl and whisk over a pan of gently simmering water until thick, pale in colour and the whisk leaves a heavy trail when lifted. Remove from the heat and whisk until cool.
3 Dissolve the gelatine in the remaining water as above and cool a little, then stir into the mixture.
4 Whip the cream until thick and floppy and fold evenly through the mixture and leave until starting to thicken.
5 Whisk the egg whites until stiff and standing in peaks and fold quickly and evenly through the mixture.
6 Pour into the prepared dish and chill until set.
7 To serve, carefully remove the collar from around the soufflé. Pipe a border of whipped cream, using a star nozzle, all around the top edge of the soufflé and decorate with pieces of chocolate flake or clusters of pistachio nuts.

VARIATIONS

Coffee – omit the vanilla essence and stir 1–2 tablespoons coffee essence into the mixture with the gelatine.
Fruit – omit the vanilla and stir 150 ml/¼ pint/⅔ cup thick fruit purée into the mixture with the gelatine. Reduce the cream to 150 ml/¼ pint/⅔ cup.
Chocolate Flake – stir 2–3 crumbled milk flake chocolate bars into the mixture after adding the gelatine.

MERINGUES

There are basically three types of meringue. The most often used and traditional meringue is called Meringue Suisse and is made by whisking the egg whites until very stiff and then whisking in the sugar (allowing 50 g/2 oz/good ¼ cup sugar to each egg white) about 2 teaspoons at a time. This meringue can be piped or spread as required for all tea-time meringues as well as for discs and shells and other shapes. A rather more complicated meringue called Meringue Cuite is a cooked meringue (made by whisking the egg whites and icing (confectioners') sugar over a gentle heat before piping into shapes to cook) and is used mainly for meringue baskets and shell shapes. The third type of meringue is American Meringue and it has a marshmallow consistency which is achieved by adding a higher proportion of sugar than normal plus the addition of vinegar and usually cornflour (cornstarch) – this is used for   Pavlova.

Meringue Suisse

With all meringues it is essential to use scrupulously clean and dry bowls and implements. The slightest trace of grease will reduce the volume and stiffness of the egg white and cause a failure. The ingredients must be weighed accurately too, for an excess of sugar will unbalance the meringue and will usually result in a soggy sticky mass. Once you have mastered the art using caster (superfine) sugar, you can experiment with 'brown sugar' meringues by using a proportion of up to two-thirds light soft brown sugar sifted with caster (superfine) sugar. This gives a delicious nutty taste and a delicate coffee-coloured result. (See step-by-step illustrations, page 202.)

4 eggs (large)
225 g/8 oz/good cup caster (superfine) sugar

1 First separate the eggs, placing the whites in a large grease-free bowl. Put the yolks into a covered container, chill and use for something else.
2 Whisk the whites, using a rotary whisk, balloon whisk or hand-held electric whisk, until the mixture is thick and white and stands in stiff peaks. Take care not to overwhisk or the egg whites will begin to turn watery.
3 Whisk in about two-thirds of the sugar, a level tablespoon at a time until completely incorporated and the meringue is stiff again before adding further sugar.
4 Fold in the rest of the sugar a little at a time, using a metal spoon and a figure of eight folding movement.
5 The meringue is now ready to spread or pipe.
6 Put the meringue onto baking sheets lined with non-stick baking paper.

Meringues (see page 201)

1   *Whisk the egg whites until standing in stiff peaks.*

3   *Either, using two tablespoons fill one with meringue and use the other to scoop the meringue onto the paper keeping a good oval shape.*

2   *Having whisked in two-thirds of the sugar, fold in the remainder, using a metal spoon and a figure of eight movement.*

4   *Or, fit a large piping bag with a large plain vegetable nozzle or a large star nozzle and pipe out shell shapes (see method).*

MERINGUE SHELLS, STARS AND BARS

1   Line two baking sheets with non-stick baking paper or greased wax or greaseproof paper.

2   Take two tablespoons and fill one with meringue. Use the other one to scoop the meringue onto the paper, keeping a good oval shape; if necessary, use a palette knife or spatula dipped in cold water to smooth out the shapes. Keep each one a little away from the next.

3   Alternatively, fit a large piping bag with a large plain vegetable nozzle (about 2 cm/¾ inch) or a large star nozzle and pipe out shell shapes. To do this put the nozzle onto the paper firmly. Squeeze out some of the meringue and at the same time lift the nozzle off the paper and move it a little away, touch the nozzle onto the surface again and quickly lift the piping bag away. This should give a nice shell shape, but will take a little practice to perfect.

4   Bake the meringues in a cool oven (110°C/225°F/Gas Mark ¼) for about 2 hours. It is a good idea to reverse the baking sheets in the oven after an hour. The meringues should be crisp and dry and peel off the paper easily. If they still stick, bake for a further 30 minutes.

5   Leave the meringues to cool on the paper and then peel off and store in an airtight container with non-stick or wax or greaseproof paper between the layers.

6   Serve as they are or sandwich together with cream, and sprinkle with nuts or grated chocolate, if liked.

7   For stars, use the piping bag and star nozzle, pipe out rosettes of meringue by putting the nozzle onto the paper and pressing out a quantity the size required and then removing the nozzle sharply with a down-up movement. Cook as for shells.

8   For bars, use the same piping nozzle and pipe out straight lines of mixture about 10–12.5 cm/4–5 inches long, or squiggle the piping bag to give zig-zag bars, or pipe in a continuous twisted line to give a very elegant and professional-shaped bar. Cook as for shells.

OPPOSITE: *Ginger and Apricot Trifle* (see page 196) *and Hazelnut Meringues with strawberries and cream* (see page 205)

MERINGUE DISCS

1 Cover two baking sheets with non-stick baking paper and draw a circle of the required size on each: 20–23 cm/8–9 inch is the usual size unless you require an extra large disc for a party. Another way is to make three discs and draw each circle 2.5 cm/1 inch smaller than the last to give a graduated finished result.
2 Fill a piping bag fitted with a plain nozzle 1–2 cm/ ½–¾ inch in diameter or a large star vegetable nozzle and, starting in the middle of the circle, pipe a continuous line to fill the drawn circle. Repeat with the second circle. A 4 egg white meringue mixture will be sufficient for two circles.
3 Bake in a cool oven (110°C/225°F/Gas Mark ¼) for 2½–3 hours, again reversing the trays in the oven after an hour.
4 Cool on the paper, then peel off and store in an airtight container.

Note: Once made and cooked, meringue discs and shapes will keep well for at least a week before use.

Apricot Meringue Cream   Serves 6

4 egg white meringue mixture
Crème Pâtissière
300 ml/½ pint/1¼ cups milk
50 g/2 oz/good ¼ cup caster (superfine) sugar
20 g/¾ oz/scant ¼ cup flour
15 g/½ oz/1 tablespoon cornflour (cornstarch)
1 egg
1 egg yolk
a few drops of vanilla essence
a large knob of butter
Filling
425 g/15 oz can apricot halves, drained
a few strips of angelica

1 Use the meringue to make a 20–23 cm/8–9 inch round disc and the remainder to pipe into stars, both on non-stick baking paper. Bake as above.
2 For the crème pâtissière, put the milk into a saucepan and heat gently. Put the sugar, flour, cornflour, egg and egg yolk into a bowl and beat together with a fork or small hand whisk until smooth. Add 3–4 tablespoons of the hot milk gradually, beating all the time.
3 Add the rest of the milk, and return everything to the saucepan. Cook very gently until the mixture thickens and comes up to the boil, stirring all the time. Continue to cook for at least a minute, still stirring, then remove from the heat.
4 Beat in the vanilla and butter, turn into a bowl, cover with plastic cling film and leave until quite cold.
5 To assemble, put the meringue disc onto a serving dish. Beat the crème pâtissière until smooth and spread all over the meringue.
6 Arrange the stars of meringue all around the edge of the meringue, sticking them on to the cream, then arrange a circle of upturned apricot halves inside the meringue stars. Pile the rest of the stars in the centre.
7 Complete the decoration by adding strips of angelica made into leaves between the apricots.

Meringue Fruit Gâteau   Serves 6–8

4 egg white meringue mixture
300 ml/½ pint/1¼ cups double (heavy) cream
1–2 tablespoons liqueur or brandy
225 g/8 oz raspberries or strawberries
2–3 tablespoons grated chocolate

1 Use the meringue mixture to make two meringue discs of 20–23 cm/8–9 inches as above.
2 To assemble, whip the cream and liqueur or brandy together until thick but not too stiff. Mix just over half of it with just over half the raspberries or sliced strawberries.
3 Stand one meringue disc on a serving plate and spread with the fruit cream. Cover with the second disc.
4 Spread the rest of the cream over the meringue taking it almost to the edges.
5 Arrange the raspberries or halved strawberries around the outside of the cream and sprinkle the chocolate over the centre of the cream.
6 Chill for up to an hour before serving.

Brown Sugar Meringues

Makes about 6–8 pairs

3 egg whites
75 g/3 oz/scant ½ cup caster (superfine) sugar
75 g/3 oz/scant ½ cup light soft brown sugar
150 ml/¼ pint/⅔ cup whipped cream
25 g/1 oz/¼ cup chopped hazelnuts, toasted

1 Whisk the egg whites in a clean grease-free bowl until stiff and standing in peaks.
2 Sift the caster and soft brown sugar together twice until thoroughly mixed.
3 Whisk two-thirds of the sugar into the egg whites, a spoonful at a time, making sure the meringue is stiff again before adding further sugar.
4 Fold in the rest of the sugar, using a metal spoon.
5 Line two baking sheets with non-stick baking paper.
6 Put the meringue into a piping bag fitted with a large star nozzle and pipe out twisted bars about 10 cm/ 4 inches long.
7 Bake in a cool oven (110°C/225°F/Gas Mark ¼) for about 2 hours, reversing the trays in the oven after an hour. Leave to cool.
8 To assemble, whip the cream until stiff and fold in the chopped nuts. Use to sandwich the meringues together in pairs.

Meringue Cuite

Use for making meringue nests and shells and for baking into 'nutty' meringues.

250 g/9 oz/scant 1¼ cups icing (confectioners') sugar
4 egg whites
a few drops of vanilla essence (optional)

1 Sift the icing sugar once or twice.
2 Put the egg whites into a fairly large heatproof bowl and whisk until frothy.
3 Add the icing sugar and whisk until blended. Stand the bowl over a saucepan of gently simmering water and whisk the mixture until it becomes thick and white and stands in peaks. Whisk in the essence if used. The meringue is now ready for use.

Meringue Nests   Makes about 8

1 recipe quantity meringue cuite
½ recipe quantity rich vanilla ice cream (see page 192)
about 225 g/8 oz fresh fruit

1 Put the meringue into a piping bag fitted with a 1 cm/½ inch plain nozzle or a large star nozzle.
2 Line one or two baking sheets with non-stick baking paper and draw circles of 10–12.5 cm/4–5 inches.
3 Use the meringue to fill in these circles, beginning in the centre of each, then pipe another line on top of the outside edge of the meringue to form a basket. Instead of a line, a series of rosettes or dots may be piped. Alternatively, put spoonfuls of the meringue onto the paper and press out with the back of a spoon to shape a basket with a hollow in the centre.
4 Bake in a cool oven (110°C/225°F/Gas Mark ¼) for about 2 hours, reversing the trays in the oven after an hour. Cool.
5 To serve, peel the cases off the paper and stand on a serving dish. Add 2–3 tablespoons of ice cream (any flavour) and top with fresh fruit (e.g. cherries, raspberries, strawberries, kiwi fruit, mangoes, apricots, etc.)

Meringue Basket   Serves 10

This is quite a complicated dessert and takes a little time to complete. Make up one quantity of meringue cuite and bake the outline, then make up a second batch to complete the basket. The mixture of fruit can be altered to suit your choice and availability.

2 recipe quantities meringue cuite (made up separately)
about 150 ml/¼ pint/⅔ cup double (heavy) cream
2 tablespoons milk or liqueur
Filling
425 g/15 oz can lychees
½ Ogen melon, peeled, deseeded and diced
2 oranges, peeled and cut into segments
100–175 g/4–6 oz strawberries or raspberries
25 g/1 oz/good ¼ cup whole blanched almonds

1 Make up 1 recipe quantity meringue cuite.
2 Line two large baking sheets with non-stick baking paper and draw two 18 cm/7 inch circles on each.
3 Put the meringue into a piping bag fitted with a plain 1 cm/½ inch nozzle and use to outline three of the circles and completely cover the last one.
4 Bake in a cool oven (110°C/225°F/Gas Mark ¼) for about an hour or until firm and will peel off the paper.
5 Make up the second batch of meringue and put into a piping bag fitted with a large star vegetable nozzle.
6 Leave the meringue disc on the non-stick paper on a baking sheet, peel off the other three rings and place one on top of the other on the disc.
7 Using the piping bag, carefully pipe vertical lines all round the outside of the basket, then use the remainder of the meringue to pipe an attractive border around the top and base of the basket.
8 Bake in the same cool oven for about an hour or until the outside meringue is cooked. Cool and peel off the paper.
9 To assemble, stand the basket on a serving dish. Whip the cream with the milk or liqueur until stiff and spread most of it in the base of the basket.
10 Combine the lychees, melon, orange segments, slices of strawberry or raspberries and the nuts and spoon into the basket, piling the mixture up in the centre.
11 Put the remaining cream into a piping bag fitted with a star nozzle and complete the decoration with stars or rosettes of cream.

Hazelnut Meringues   Serves 6

2 egg whites
150 g/5 oz/1¼ cups icing (confectioners') sugar, sifted
50 g/2 oz/½ cup hazelnuts, toasted and finely chopped
Topping
150 ml/¼ pint/⅔ cup whipping cream
6 large strawberries, or about 175 g/6 oz small strawberries

1 Line a baking sheet with non-stick paper.
2 Use the egg whites and sifted icing sugar to make meringue cuite.
3 Remove from the heat and fold in the chopped nuts.
4 Spoon the mixture onto the paper into 6 even-sized and shaped rounds.
5 Bake in a cool oven (150°C/300°F/Gas Mark 2) for about 40 minutes or until pale cream in colour and easy to remove from the sheet. (They may be cooked in a cooler oven as for meringue cuite for 1–1½ hours when the colour will be much whiter.)
6 To serve, peel the meringues off the paper and stand on a serving dish. Whip the cream until stiff and spread over the top of each one. Top with a large strawberry each or decorate with smaller strawberries left whole, cut in half or sliced.

Pavlova
Serves 6

3 egg whites
175 g/6 oz/scant cup caster (superfine) sugar
1/2 teaspoon vanilla essence
1/2 teaspoon vinegar
1 teaspoon cornflour (cornstarch)
250 ml/8 fl oz/1 cup double (heavy) cream
2 tablespoons milk or white wine
2–3 kiwi fruit, peeled and sliced
3 oranges, peeled and sliced

1 Use the egg whites and caster sugar to make a meringue in the same way as meringue cuite.
2 Remove from the heat and beat in the vanilla essence, vinegar and cornflour.
3 Draw an 18 cm/7 inch circle on a piece of non-stick baking paper and put on a baking sheet. Spread the meringue out over the circle making a dip in the centre.
4 Bake in a cool oven (150°C/300°F/Gas Mark 2) for an hour or until firm. Leave on the paper until cold.
5 To serve, peel the meringue off the paper and stand on a serving plate. Whip the cream and milk or wine together until stiff and use to spread over the meringue.
6 Use the fruits to decorate the pavlova over the cream. Serve within an hour of assembling.

CHEESECAKES

There are quite a few ways to make these rather delicious desserts based on cream, cottage and curd cheeses. Some need to be baked; others simply consist of a biscuit crumb base with a cheese layer set with gelatine and fresh fruit or a fruit sauce over the top.

Lemon Cheesecake
Serves 6–8

50 g/2 oz/1/4 cup butter
150 g/5 oz digestive biscuits, crushed
350 g/12 oz/about 1 cup cottage cheese
75 g/3 oz packet full fat soft cheese, softened
grated rind of 1 large lemon
50 g/2 oz/good 1/4 cup caster (superfine) sugar
2 tablespoons lemon juice
2 tablespoons top of the milk
2 teaspoons powdered gelatine
2 tablespoons water
225 g/8 oz green or green and black grapes, halved and depipped
2 tablespoons apricot jam, sieved

1 Grease an 18–19 cm/7–7½ inch loose-bottomed cake tin or flan ring on a baking sheet.
2 Melt the butter in a pan and stir in the biscuit crumbs until evenly blended. Turn into the tin and press to evenly cover the base. Chill until set.
3 Sieve or purée or blend the cottage cheese until smooth. Beat in the cream cheese followed by the lemon rind, sugar, lemon juice and milk.
4 Put the gelatine and water into a small basin and stand over a pan of gently simmering water until dissolved.

Leave to cool a little and then stir through the cheese mixture.
5 Quickly pour over the biscuit base in the tin and chill until set.
6 To serve, remove the cheesecake carefully from the tin or ring and stand on a serving dish.
7 Arrange the grapes attractively over the top of the cheesecake. Heat the jam with 2 teaspoons water and use to brush over the grapes. Chill until required.

VARIATIONS
Use crushed gingernuts in place of the digestive biscuits. Replace the grapes with a fruit purée made by stewing 225 g/8 oz blackcurrants, blackberries, apricots, etc., in about 6 tablespoons water until very tender and thick. Sweeten to taste and then leave until quite cold. Just before serving spoon the purée over the top of the cheesecake.

Chocolate Orange Cheesecake
Serves 8–10

40 g/1½ oz plain chocolate or chocolate dots
40 g/1½ oz/3 tablespoons butter
175 g/6 oz digestive biscuits, crushed
Filling
225 g/8 oz packet full fat soft cheese
75 g/3 oz/scant ½ cup caster (superfine) sugar
grated rind of 1 orange
4 tablespoons orange juice
3 teaspoons powdered gelatine
1 tablespoon lemon juice
1 large can evaporated milk, chilled overnight
To decorate
150 ml/¼ pint/⅔ cup whipping cream
1½–2 packets plain chocolate finger biscuits (optional)
orange jelly slices

1 Grease a 19–20 cm/7½–8 inch loose-based round cake tin.
2 Melt the chocolate and butter over a gentle heat. Stir in the crushed biscuits, until well blended.
3 Turn into the tin and press evenly over the base. Chill until set.
4 For the filling, beat the cheese and sugar together until very light and smooth. Gradually beat in the orange rind and juice.
5 Dissolve the gelatine with the lemon juice and 1 tablespoon water in a basin over a pan of gently simmering water. Cool a little, then mix evenly into the cheese mixture.
6 Whisk the evaporated milk (preferably using an electric mixer) until thick and standing in soft peaks, then fold quickly and evenly into the cheese mixture.
7 Pour into the tin over the biscuit base and chill until quite set – preferably overnight.
8 To serve, remove the cheesecake from the tin and put on a serving dish. Whip the cream until stiff and spread a thin layer all round the outside of the cheesecake. Stick chocolate finger biscuits (cut to size) all round the sides. Decorate the top with whirls of whipped cream and orange jelly slices.

15 Baking

When it comes to baking it is easy to write a whole book on the subject but rather more difficult to condense it all into a single chapter. However, I have given instructions on the basic methods of cake making, including creaming, whisking, rubbing in, etc., and provided with each method a basic cake and variations, plus some further recipes for cakes made in the same way or a very similar way. This should give a fairly wide aspect of the subject and plenty of ideas to keep both you and the family occupied for quite a while.

With cake making, it is essential to follow a recipe exactly, measure the ingredients accurately and add them in the correct order. Do not open the oven door any more than necessary during cooking or the cake is likely to sink, and always close the door and move the cake gently – sudden movements or jolts or bursts of cold air are death to all cakes.

It is also important to grease and line the cake tin properly before you begin to ensure the cake will turn out cleanly when baked; there is nothing more annoying than to find your beautifully baked cake will not come out of its tin. Remember, too, to turn the oven on at the required temperature when you begin to make the cake. This should ensure the oven has reached the correct cooking temperature by the time the cake is ready to go into the oven. Very few cakes benefit from standing around for long once made and many of them, especially those that are whisked or have whisked egg white folded into them, will flop before they are even baked if made to wait. Do not put the cake into the oven until it has reached the required temperature.

Most cakes are suitable to freeze for up to 3 months, more often without the filling or icing, although butter cream takes to freezing very well. Wrap the cake in foil or thick polythene or put into a rigid plastic container and, if a layered cake, put a piece of wax or greaseproof or non-stick paper or foil between the layers before packing; this makes them easy to separate when thawed. Thaw out the cake completely before adding the filling and any decoration.

In fact, most cakes keep well for a few days in an airtight container, so it may not be necessary to freeze them; a whisked sponge stales quickest and is best eaten within 24 hours or up to 48 hours. Creamed mixtures keep well for 7–10 days; rubbed-in cakes for up to a week (scones being the exception and best eaten within 2 days). The richer the mixture the better the cake will keep – rich fruit cakes improve with keeping and are often better when kept for 2–3 weeks before use, especially if dosed with brandy (as for the Christmas cake) before wrapping in foil!

When a baked cake is ready, it should be well risen and firm to the touch, but it is also wise to check with a clean straight skewer which is pressed right down into the centre of the cake. It should come out clean and, if it comes out at all sticky, it means the cake is not yet ready, so cook it for 10 minutes longer and test again. Sometimes a cake looks ready but when turned onto a wire rack simply sinks rapidly, so do take the trouble to test it. Allow the cake to stand in the cake tin for half a minute or so before turning out; this allows the cake to shrink slightly from the sides of the tin and it will then come out more easily. However, a rich fruit cake, such as the Christmas cake, is best left in the tin until cold. Just follow the recipes; each will tell you the best time for turning out of the tin.

LINING CAKE TINS

If using special non-stick coated tins, follow the manufacturer's instructions for preparation. However, if baking a rich fruit cake, it is still best to line the tin because the cake needs protection during the long cooking necessary. With all other tins it is necessary either to grease and flour, or grease, line with wax or greaseproof paper and grease again. Use oil, melted lard or melted margarine for greasing; melted butter sometimes tends to make cakes stick. If you prefer, use non-stick silicone baking paper for lining and then there is no need to grease at all. Rich cakes need the tins lining with a double thickness of paper, all others only require a single thickness.

TO LINE A DEEP ROUND TIN

1   For rich mixtures that require long cooking, you should use a double thickness of wax or greaseproof paper and line both the sides and base of the tin. For a less rich mixture, use only a single thickness. Both are lined in almost the same way.

2   Cut one or two strips of double wax or greaseproof long enough to reach round the outside of the tin with sufficient to overlap and wide enough to come 2.5 cm/ 1 inch above the rim of the tin.

3   Fold the bottom edge up about 2 cm/¾ inch and crease it firmly. Open out and make slanting cuts into the folded strip with scissors at 2 cm/¾ inch intervals.

4   Place the tin on a double thickness of wax or greaseproof and draw round the base. Cut out the circles a little inside the pencil line.

5   Grease the inside of the tin and place one circle in the base then grease just around the edge of the paper.

6   Place the long strips in the tin, pressing them against

the sides with the cut edges spread out over the base. Grease all over the side paper.

7   Finally, position the second circle in the base and grease again. With single thickness lining, put first the sides and then the base in to the tin.

TO LINE A DEEP SQUARE TIN

Follow the instructions for the deep round tin but it is not necessary to make the slanted cuts into the folded piece. Instead make folds at the corners and cuts into the folds only at these corners so the paper fits neatly.

TO BASE LINE ROUND OR SQUARE TINS

This method is used to prevent the cake bottom falling out or sticking and is used for sponge and sandwich mixtures and light fruit cakes, but not for rich mixtures or heavily fruited cakes.

1   Cut a single piece of wax or greaseproof paper to fit the bottom of the tin by standing the tin on the paper and drawing around it. Cut it out a little smaller than the pencil line.

2   First grease the inside of the tin completely, then position the paper in the base and grease the paper.

TO LINE A SHALLOW RECTANGULAR TIN

For Swiss rolls and other cakes baked in rectangular tins it is always wise to line completely before baking.

1   Cut a piece of wax or greaseproof paper about 7.5 cm/3 inches larger than the tin (and larger still if the sides of the tin are deeper than 2.5 cm/1 inch).

2   Place the tin on the paper and make a cut from the corners of the paper to the corners of the tin.

3   Grease inside the tin, put in the paper so that it fits neatly, overlapping the paper at the corners to give sharp angles, and then grease the paper.

TO LINE A LOAF TIN

Use the same method as for lining a shallow rectangular tin but cut the paper at least 15 cm/6 inches larger than the top of the tin. Grease the tin, position the paper, folding the corners neatly, and grease the paper.

QUICK MIX CAKES

This is a method where all the ingredients are put into a bowl and beaten well until thoroughly mixed. The cake rises because it contains both self-raising flour and baking powder and you must use a soft tub margarine. This gives a rather close-textured cake which will keep for up to a week. It is ideal if you are in a hurry but does not have the light and airy texture of a properly-creamed mixture.

Vanilla Quick Mix Cake

175 g/6 oz/scant cup caster (superfine) sugar
175 g/6 oz/³⁄₄ cup soft tub margarine
3 eggs
175 g/6 oz/1¹⁄₂ cups self-raising flour
1¹⁄₂ teaspoons baking powder
a few drops of vanilla essence

1   Grease, base line and grease two 20 cm/8 inch round sandwich or layer cake tins.

2   Put the sugar, margarine and eggs into a large mixing bowl. Sift in the flour and baking powder and add the vanilla essence.

3   Mix together with a wooden spoon or hand-held electric mixer, then beat hard until smooth and glossy – about 1–2 minutes.

4   Turn into the prepared tins, dividing the mixture evenly, and spread the tops lightly until even.

5   Bake in a moderate oven (160°C/325°F/Gas Mark 3) for 30–35 mintues or until well risen, just firm to the touch and the sides of the cake are beginning to shrink away from the sides of the tin.

6   Leave in the tin for about half a minute, then loosen if necessary and turn out onto a wire rack. Remove the paper from the cake and invert onto another wire rack so the top of the cake is not spoilt. Leave to cool.

7   Sandwich the cakes together with jam (using about 175 g/6 oz) or with butter cream of your chosen flavour (see page 223) and sprinkle the top with caster sugar.

VARIATIONS

Chocolate Quick Mix – add 1¹⁄₂ tablespoons cocoa powder sifted with the flour to the 3 egg mixture, or 1 tablespoon to the 2 egg.

Coffee Quick Mix – omit the vanilla essence and add 3 teaspoons instant coffee powder sifted with the flour or 1¹⁄₂ tablespoons coffee essence to the 3 egg mixture, or 2 teaspoons coffee powder or 1 tablespoon coffee essence to the 2 egg mixture.

Orange or Lemon Quick Mix – omit the vanilla and add the finely grated rind of 1 orange or lemon to the mixture.

QUICK MIX CAKES OF DIFFERENT SIZES

This amount of mixture may also be baked in a greased and lined rectangular tin measuring 28 × 18 × 4 cm/ 11 × 7 × 1¹⁄₂ inches allowing 35–40 minutes, or in a 1.2 litre/2 pint/5 cup basin or bowl, greased and dredged with flour and the excess shaken out, and 25 g/1 oz/¹⁄₄ cup cornflour (cornstarch) sifted with the flour into the mixture and baked for about an hour.

A smaller cake may be made using two-thirds of the mixture, e.g. 100 g/4 oz/good ¹⁄₂ cup caster (superfine) sugar, etc., and can be baked in two 18 cm/7 inch greased and base-lined sandwich or layer cake tins for 25–30 minutes, or in 18 paper cake cases standing in patty or muffin tins for about 15–20 minutes, or in a 20 cm/8 inch greased and base-lined deep sandwich or layer cake tin, a 20 cm/8 inch greased and flour-dredged ring mould or an 18 cm/7 inch deep square tin, all for 35–40 minutes.

All these cakes can be decorated in many ways with various types of icing. See next chapter for more ideas.

Butterscotch Quick Mix Cake

100 g/4 oz/1 cup self-raising flour
1 teaspoon baking powder
75 g/3 oz/¹/₃ cup soft tub margarine
100 g/4 oz/good ¹/₂ cup light soft brown sugar
2 eggs
1 tablespoon water
a few crushed butterscotch sweets for decoration
Icing
50 g/2 oz/¹/₄ cup butter or soft margarine
100 g/4 oz/about 1 cup icing (confectioners') sugar, sifted
1 tablespoon golden syrup

1 Grease a 20 cm/8 inch square cake tin and line the base with greased wax or greaseproof paper.
2 Sift the flour and baking powder into a bowl.
3 Add the margarine, sugar, eggs and water and mix until well incorporated and then beat for about 2 minutes until smooth and pale in colour.
4 Turn into the prepared tin, level the top and bake in a moderate oven (160°C/325°F/Gas Mark 3) for about 45 minutes or until well risen and firm to the touch. Turn out into a wire rack and leave to cool.
5 For the icing, cream the fat until soft and creamy, then gradually beat in half the icing sugar. Beat in the syrup and then the rest of the sugar to give a smooth and even icing.
6 Spread the icing over the top of the cake, mark an attractive pattern with the prongs of a fork and sprinkle with the crushed butterscotch. Leave for about 2 hours to set before cutting.

Marble Cake

100 g/4 oz/¹/₂ cup soft tub margarine
100 g/4 oz/good ¹/₂ cup caster (superfine) sugar
2 eggs
175 g/6 oz/1¹/₂ cups self-raising flour
1¹/₂ teaspoons baking powder
2 tablespoons milk
a few drops of vanilla essence
a few drops of pink liquid food colouring
2 teaspoons cocoa powder, sifted
Mocha Icing
50 g/2 oz/¹/₄ cup butter or margarine
75 g/3 oz/³/₄ cup icing (confectioners') sugar, sifted
25 g/1 oz/¹/₄ cup cocoa powder, sifted
2 teaspoons coffee essence or very strong black coffee
1 chocolate flake bar (optional)

1 Grease an 18 cm/7 inch deep round cake tin and line the base with greased paper.
2 Put the margarine, sugar and eggs into a bowl. Sift in the flour and baking powder and add the milk. Mix until well incorporated and then beat until smooth – about 2 minutes.
3 Divide the mixture into three portions. Add the vanilla essence to one, a few drops of pink colouring to the second, and the cocoa powder to the last. Mix until all are evenly blended.

4 Put alternate teaspoons of the mixtures into the prepared tin, arranging the colours so they overlap and make some sort of pattern. Level the top.
5 Bake in a moderate oven (160°C/325°F/Gas Mark 3) for about an hour or until well risen and firm to the touch. Turn out onto a wire rack and leave until cold.
6 For the icing, beat the fat and icing sugar together until creamy then beat in the cocoa powder alternately with the coffee essence. Spread over the top of the cake, swirling it around with a round-bladed knife. Sprinkle with flaked chocolate, if liked, and leave to set.

Cherry Walnut Loaf

150 g/6 oz/³/₄ cup soft tub margarine
160 g/6 oz/scant cup caster (superfine) sugar
3 eggs
75 g/3 oz/scant ¹/₂ cup glacé cherries, quartered, washed and well dried
200 g/8 oz/ 2 cups self-raising flour
1¹/₂ teaspoons baking powder
40 g/1¹/₂ oz/¹/₃ cup shelled walnuts, roughly chopped
Topping
75 g/3 oz/scant ¹/₂ cup glacé cherries, halved
3 tablespoons apricot jam, sieved

1 Line a 23 × 12.5 × 7.5 cm/9 × 5 × 3 inch loaf tin with greased wax or greaseproof paper.
2 Put all the ingredients for the cake together in a mixing bowl and beat well until smooth – about 4 minutes by hand or 2 minutes with a hand-held electric mixer.
3 Turn into the prepared tin and level the top. Arrange the halved cherries over the top of the cake.
4 Bake in a moderate oven (160°C/325°F/Gas Mark 3) for 1¹/₂–1³/₄ hours or until well risen and firm to the touch.
5 Cool in the tin for 5 minutes, then turn out onto a wire rack. Strip off the paper and turn the loaf the right way up. Heat the jam a little and brush over the cherry topping. Leave to cool.

CREAMED CAKES

The most famous of these is the Victoria sandwich cake, which uses equal quantities of fat, sugar, flour and eggs to give a light and airy sponge cake that keeps well and tastes extremely good. It is very versatile and can be flavoured in numerous ways. It will also take additions of fruit and nuts, etc., without spoiling its texture. Other creamed mixtures are made in much the same way but are not so rich, having a greater proportion of flour and usually some sort of liquid. Self-raising flour is used for most of these cakes, although some do have a proportion of plain (all-purpose) flour added. They may be filled and decorated in numerous ways and baked in a variety of sizes and different-shaped tins. This cake is ideal as a basic birthday cake for those who don't like fruit cake.

Victoria Sandwich Cake

1   Cream the fat and sugar together until light and fluffy and pale in colour.

3   Fold in the remaining flour, alternating with the essence and water.

2   Beat in the eggs, one at a time, until completely incorporated and follow each egg with a tablespoon of flour.

4   Serve filled with jam and whipped cream or butter cream. Lay a doyle on top of the cake and sift icing (confectioners') sugar over the top. Carefully remove the doyle to leave a pattern.

Victoria Sandwich Cake

150 g/6 oz/³⁄₄ cup butter or soft margarine
150 g/6 oz/scant cup caster (superfine) sugar
3 eggs (large)
150 g/6 oz/1¹⁄₂ cups self-raising flour
a few drops of vanilla essence
1 tablespoon cold water

1   Grease two 20 cm/8 inch round sandwich or layer cake tins and line the bases with greased wax or greaseproof paper.
2   Put the fat and sugar in a bowl and cream together using a wooden spoon or hand-held electric mixer until the mixture is very light and fluffy and pale in colour. It is very important to cream sufficiently at this stage or the mixture will not accept the rest of the ingredients as it should.

3   Beat in the eggs, one at a time, until completely incorporated and follow each with a tablespoon of the flour.
4   Sift the remaining flour and fold into the creamed mixture, using a metal spoon for preference, alternating with the essence and water. The mixture should be a soft dropping consistency.
5   Divide between the tins and level the tops, spreading out from the centre with a round-bladed knife, but only very lightly; do not push out all the air that has been incorporated.
6   Bake in a moderately hot oven (190°C/375°F/Gas Mark 5) for about 20–25 minutes or until well risen and firm to the touch.
7   Cool in the tin briefly until the sides of the cakes begin to shrink slightly from the tin and then turn out onto a wire rack. Invert onto another wire rack so they are the right way up and leave until cold.

Swiss Roll (see page 213)

1   *Whisk the eggs and sugar in a bowl over a saucepan of gently simmering water until the mixture is thick enough to leave a trail when the whisk is lifted out.*

3   *Trim the edges and make a shallow cut across the cake about 1 cm/½ inch from the end and then roll up the cake quickly and neatly with the paper still inside.*

2   *Having whisked until cool, fold the sifted flour and the runny butter evenly through the mixture, using a metal spoon.*

4   *Once rolled, peel off the paper from the top surface of the roll – this prevents it sticking as it cools.*

8   Sandwich together with jam or butter cream as for quick mix cakes. Sprinkle the top with caster (superfine) sugar or cover with butter cream.

Note: This mixture may also be baked in a rectangular tin (28 × 18 × 4 cm/11 × 7 × 4 inches) lined with greased wax or greaseproof paper for about 25 minutes, or in about 26 paper cake cases placed in patty or muffin tins for about 15 minutes.

A smaller cake using 100 g/4 oz/½ cup fat, etc., and 2 eggs can be baked in two 18 cm/7 inch sandwich or layer cake tins for about 20 minutes at the same temperature.

VARIATIONS

Chocolate – replace 25 g/1 oz/¼ cup of the flour with cocoa and add ½ teaspoon baking powder, both sifted with the flour.

Coffee – omit the vanilla essence and replace the water with coffee essence or dissolve 2 tablespoons instant coffee in 1 tablespoon boiling water, cool and use.
Orange or Lemon – omit the vanilla essence and add the finely grated rind of 1 orange or lemon to the mixture after the flour.
Mocha – replace 1 tablespoon flour with sifted cocoa and use 2 teaspoons coffee essence and 1 teaspoon water in place of the water.
Almond – omit the vanilla essence and add ½ teaspoon almond essence in its place.
Walnut or Hazelnut – add 40–50 g/1½–2 oz/⅓–½ cup finely chopped walnuts or toasted hazelnuts to the mixture after the flour.

Coffee Fudge Cake

150 g/6 oz/³/₄ cup butter or soft margarine
160 g/6 oz/scant cup dark soft brown sugar
3 eggs, beaten
150 g/6 oz/1¹/₂ cups self-raising flour
1 tablespoon strong black coffee
2 teaspoons black treacle
6 tablespoons apricot jam
¹/₂ recipe quantity coffee butter cream (see page 223)
40 g/1¹/₂ oz/¹/₃ cup finely chopped walnuts
icing (confectioners') sugar for dredging

1 Grease two 20 cm/8 inch round sandwich or layer cake tins and line the base with greased wax or greaseproof paper.
2 Use the fat, sugar, eggs, flour and coffee and treacle (in place of the water) to make a cake in the same way as the Victoria Sandwich Cake.
3 Divide the mixture between the tins and level the tops. Bake in a moderately hot oven (190°C/375°F/Gas Mark 5) for about 25 minutes or until well risen, golden brown and firm to the touch.
4 Turn out onto a wire rack and leave to cool.
5 When cold, sandwich the cakes together with the apricot jam.
6 Make up the butter cream and use a little of it to spread around the sides of the cake.
7 Put the chopped nuts onto a sheet of wax or grease-proof paper or foil and, holding the cake carefully in both hands, roll the sides in the nuts so the cake is evenly coated. Add extra nuts where required with a palette knife or spatula. Stand the cake on a serving plate.
8 Dredge the top of the cake fairly heavily with sifted icing sugar, so it looks white.
9 Put the remainder of the butter cream into a piping bag fitted with a small star nozzle. Mark the cake into eight wedges with a knife and then pipe a line of shells from the centre of the cake along each line to give a wheel design.
10 Use the rest of the butter cream to pipe a shell edge all round the top of the cake. Leave to set.

VARIATION
This cake may be made by replacing 25 g/1 oz/¹/₄ cup flour with cocoa and ¹/₂ teaspoon baking powder and using chocolate icing (see page 224) in place of the coffee.

Almond Cake

100 g/4 oz/¹/₂ cup butter or soft margarine
150 g/5 oz/²/₃ cup caster (superfine) sugar
3 eggs
75 g/3 oz/³/₄ cup ground amonds
40 g/1¹/₂ oz/scant ¹/₃ cup plain (all-purpose) flour
a few drops of almond essence
caster (superfine) sugar for dredging

1 Grease an 18 cm/7 inch deep round cake tin and line with greased wax or greaseproof paper.
2 Cream the fat and sugar, as for Victoria Sandwich Cake, and then beat in the eggs, one at a time, following each with a little of the ground almonds.
3 Add the rest of the almonds and the sifted flour and fold in quickly and evenly with a few drops of almond essence.
4 Turn the mixture into the prepared tin and level the top.
5 Bake in a moderate oven (180°C/350°F/Gas Mark 4) for about 50 minutes or until golden brown and firm to the touch – a skewer inserted in the centre should come out clean.
6 Cool in the tin for a minute or so and then turn out carefully onto a wire rack. Turn the right way up and sprinkle the top of the cake with about 2 tablespoons caster sugar. Leave to cool.
7 Store in an airtight container for up to a week.

Note: This cake is very moist and is best eaten within 4–5 days. Keep in a cool place.

Battenburg

150 g/6 oz/³/₄ cup butter or margarine
150 g/6 oz/scant cup caster (superfine) sugar
3 eggs
150 g/6 oz/1¹/₂ cups self-raising flour
1 tablespoon water
a few drops of vanilla essence
a few drops of pink liquid food colouring
raspberry flavouring (optional)
4–5 tablespoons apricot jam
225 g/8 oz marzipan
caster (superfine) sugar for dredging

1 Grease a rectangular cake tin (about 28 × 18 × 4 cm/ 11 × 7 × 1¹/₂ inches) and line with greased wax or greaseproof paper.
2 Make a division across the centre of the tin with a piece of greased double thickness foil to give two equal-sized tins.
3 Use the fat, sugar, eggs, flour and water to make a Victoria Sandwich Cake and then divide the mixture in two.

4 Beat the vanilla essence into one portion and spread it evenly into one part of the tin.

5 Add a few drops of pink colouring and raspberry flavouring, if liked, to the other portion and mix until evenly blended and a good pale pink. Spread into the other part of the tin.

6 Bake in a moderately hot oven (190°C/375°F/Gas Mark 5) for about 30 minutes or until well risen and firm to the touch.

7 Turn the cake carefully onto a wire rack, peel off the paper and take out the foil divider to give two cakes. Leave until cold.

8 Trim the cakes to an even size and cut in half lengthwise. Spread the top of one white and one pink piece of cake with jam and top with alternate coloured pieces. Spread the sides of one double layer with jam and stick the two pieces together to give a chequered effect.

9 Trim the cake again, if necessary so it is square. Use the remaining jam to brush all around the outside of the cake.

10 Roll out the marzipan on a surface sprinkled lightly with caster sugar or between two sheets of polythene until large enough to enclose the whole cake (about 35 × 25 cm/14 × 10 inches).

11 Place the cake in the centre and wrap the marzipan around the cake to cover it completely, but leaving the ends open, and trim off at the ends. Mark a pinched 'finger and thumb' decoration all along the top edges to give a neat finish to the cake and mark a criss-cross pattern on the top with a sharp knife. Sprinkle a little sugar over the marzipan and leave to set. Serve cut in slices.

WHISKED SPONGE CAKES

These can either be made with or without butter. The addition of melted butter (which must be cool but still runny before folding in) keeps the cake fresh for a little longer; otherwise fatless whisked sponge cakes should be baked and eaten on the same day, if possible. Whisked sponges depend greatly on the amount of air whisked into the mixture of eggs and sugar at the initial stage and then the gentle folding in of the flour. Heavy-handedness will simply produce a heavy and rather unpleasant-textured cake. It is almost essential to use an electric mixer for making these cakes and, if using a hand-held one, the mixture must be put into a heatproof bowl over a saucepan of very gently simmering water. If you use a large electric mixer, no heat is required, although it is a good idea to warm the bowl before you begin and to use all ingredients at room temperature – do not use eggs taken straight from the refrigerator.

Swiss Roll

(See step-by-step illustrations, page 211.)

4 eggs
100 g/4 oz/good ½ cup caster (superfine) sugar
100 g/4 oz/1 cup plain (all-purpose) flour, sifted twice
25 g/1 oz/2 tablespoons butter, melted and cooled
about 225 g/8 oz/⅔ cup jam for filling
icing (confectioners') or caster (superfine) sugar

1 Grease a Swiss roll or shallow rectangular tin of about 30 × 25 cm/12 × 10 inches with greased wax or greaseproof paper. Lightly dredge with flour and shake out the excess.

2 Put the eggs and sugar into a large heatproof bowl. Stand the bowl over a saucepan of gently simmering water and whisk until the mixture is thick and pale in colour and at least doubled in bulk and the whisk leaves a thick trail when lifted. Remove from the heat and continue to whisk until cool. If using a large electric mixer, no heat is required.

3 Sift the flour onto the mixture and then fold in very quickly and evenly using a metal spoon.

4 Add the cooled but still runny butter and mix evenly through the mixture.

5 Pour into the prepared tin and spread out evenly so there is plenty of mixture in the corners of the tin.

6 Bake in a moderately hot oven (190°C/375°F/Gas Mark 5) for about 15–20 minutes or until the mixture is a pale golden brown and just firm to the touch.

7 Lay a sheet of wax or greaseproof paper or non-stick paper on a flat surface and dredge lightly with sugar. Turn the cake straightaway onto this and strip off the lining paper. Immediately take a large sharp knife and cut off all the edges of the cake neatly.

8 Make a shallow cut across the cake about 1 cm/½ inch from the end and roll up the cake quickly and neatly with the paper still inside. (It is a good idea at this stage to peel off the paper from the top surface of the roll to prevent sticking.) Leave to cool on a wire rack.

9 Unroll the cake carefully and remove the paper. Beat the jam until smooth and then spread quickly over the cake. Reroll carefully and trim the ends. Dredge with sifted icing sugar or caster sugar and the cake is ready to serve.

VARIATIONS

Spicy – sift ½ teaspoon ground cinnamon or mixed spice with the flour.

Ginger – sift ½–1 teaspoon ground ginger with the flour.

Coffee – sift 2–3 teaspoons instant coffee powder with the flour.

Chocolate – replace 1 tablespoon of the flour with sifted cocoa.

Lemon or Orange – add the grated rind of 1 small orange or 1 lemon with the melted butter

Nutty – add 40 g/1½ oz/⅓ cup very finely chopped walnuts, hazelnuts or toasted almonds with the melted butter.

Crystallized Ginger Cake (see page 216)

1 *Rub the fat into the sifted flour and spice with the fingers until the mixture resembles fine breadcrumbs.*

3 *Turn into the prepared tin and level the top. Sprinkle with the sugar crystals.*

2 *Add the eggs and milk to form a soft dropping consistency.*

4 *Test the cooked cake with a skewer, which should come out clean.*

Walnut and Raspberry Roll

1 walnut-flavoured Swiss roll
about 100 g/4 oz/¹⁄₃ cup raspberry jam
150 ml/¹⁄₄ pint/²⁄₃ cup double (heavy) cream
1–2 tablespoons milk
good pinch of ground cinnamon
icing (confectioners') sugar for dredging
8 walnut halves for decoration

1 Make the Swiss roll and leave to cool on a wire rack with the paper still inside.
2 Unroll the cake and remove the paper, then spread evenly with raspberry jam.
3 Whip the cream with the milk and cinnamon until thick and just stiff. Use about three-quarters of it to spread over the jam and then reroll the cake carefully.
4 Dredge the top of the cake heavily with sifted icing sugar.
5 Put the remaining cream into a piping bag fitted with a star nozzle and pipe a line of stars or shells along the top of the cake. Use the walnuts to decorate it.

Note: 100–175 g/4–6 oz fresh or frozen and thawed raspberries may be used in place of the jam; simply spread with cream, lay the raspberries over the cream and roll up.

OPPOSITE: *Gingerbread* (see page 217), *Walnut and Raspberry Roll and Battenburg* (see page 212)

RUBBED-IN CAKES

This method of mixing a cake is for a plainer, coarser-textured cake but makes a really good type of 'cut and come again' cake, plus teabreads and buns. The proportions of fat to flour vary from a quarter fat to flour for scones and working upwards to half to two-thirds.

Rub in the dry ingredients, stir in flavourings and fruits or whatever is to be added and mix to a soft dropping consistency with beaten egg and milk or fruit juice – or sometimes no egg is used at all. When making scones, the most important thing to remember is to handle the dough as little as possible. Just bring the ingredients together into a ball and mix until barely smooth and then pat out with your hand on a lightly floured surface for the best results.

Crystallized Ginger Cake

(See step-by-step illustrations, page 214.)

250 g/10 oz/2½ cups self-raising flour
1 teaspoon ground ginger or mixed spice
100 g/4 oz/½ cup butter or margarine
100 g/4 oz/good ½ cup light soft brown or caster
  (superfine) sugar
50 g/2 oz/¼ cup crystallized or stem ginger, finely chopped
100 g/4 oz/⅔ cup raisins
2 eggs, beaten
3 tablespoons milk
1 tablespoon coffee sugar crystals or crushed sugar lumps

1   Grease a 15 cm/6 inch deep round cake tin with single greased wax or greaseproof paper.
2   Sift the flour and ginger or spice into a bowl. Add the fat cut into small pieces and rub into the flour with the fingers until the mixture resembles fine breadcrumbs. The rubbing-in can be done in a food processor, but take care not to overprocess and turn it on in short bursts only.
3   Stir in the sugar, ginger and raisins and mix well.
4   Add the eggs and milk and mix to form a soft dropping consistency.
5   Turn into the prepared tin and level the top. Sprinkle with the sugar crystals.
6   Bake in a moderately hot oven (190°C/375°F/Gas Mark 5) for about 1 hour or until well risen, firm to the touch and browned. Test with a skewer, which should come out clear.
7   Cool in the tin for a minute or so, then turn out onto a wire rack and leave to cool. Store wrapped in foil or in an airtight container for up to 10 days.

VARIATION
Omit the ginger and chopped ginger and add chopped glacé cherries instead.

Scones

225 g/8 oz/2 cups self-raising flour
pinch of salt
50 g/2 oz/¼ cup butter or margarine
1½ tablespoons caster (superfine) sugar
1 egg
about 5 tablespoons milk or sour milk
beaten egg or milk to glaze

1   Either grease a baking sheet or dredge it liberally with flour.
2   Sift the flour and salt into a bowl. Add the butter, cut into small pieces, and rub in until the mixture resembles fine breadcrumbs. This process may be carried out in a food processor, turning it on in short bursts.
3   Stir in the sugar. Add the egg and sufficient milk to mix to a fairly soft dough using a palette knife or spatula.
4   Turn out onto a lightly floured surface and gently flatten the dough out to about 2–2.5 cm/¾–1 inch thick.
5   Using a well-floured plain or fluted cutter of about 4–5 cm/1½–2 inches or an upturned glass, stamp out the scones. Reroll the remaining pastry lightly and cut out more scones.
6   Place on the baking sheet, keeping fairly close so they will just touch as they bake (this gives good soft sides). Either brush with beaten egg or milk or dredge the tops with sifted flour.
7   Bake in a hot oven (230°C/450°F/Gas Mark 8) for 12–15 minutes or until well risen, golden brown and just firm. Slide the scones onto a wire rack and leave to cool.
8   Scones are best eaten on the day they are made, either warm or cold and split and spread with butter and jam or with jam and whipped cream. They can be kept in an airtight container for a few days, but they should be refreshed in a warm oven before serving. Scones will freeze well in a polythene bag for up to 3 months.
Makes 8–10 scones

VARIATIONS
Fruit – add 50 g/2 oz/⅓ cup currants, sultanas (golden raisins), raisins or cut mixed peel to the dry ingredients.
Lemon or Orange – add the finely grated rind of 1 lemon or orange to the dry ingredients.
Walnut – add 40 g/1½ oz/¼ cup chopped walnuts to the dry ingredients.
Cheese – omit the sugar and add a pinch of dry mustard and 40–50 g/1½–2 oz/¼–⅓ cup finely grated mature Cheddar cheese or 1–2 tablespoons grated Parmesan cheese to the dry ingredients.
Herb – omit the sugar and add 2 teaspoons freshly chopped herbs or 1½ teaspoons dried herbs to the dry ingredients.

Rock Buns

200 g/8 oz/2 cups self-raising flour
$^1\!/_2$ teaspoon mixed spice
$^1\!/_2$ teaspoon ground cinnamon
100 g/4 oz/$^1\!/_2$ cup butter or margarine
50 g/2 oz/$^1\!/_3$ cup currants
50 g/2 oz/$^1\!/_3$ cup sultanas (golden raisins) or raisins
50 g/2 oz/$^1\!/_3$ cup mixed peel
100 g/4 oz/good $^1\!/_2$ cup demerara sugar
grated rind of $^1\!/_2$ lemon or orange
1 egg, beaten
2–3 tablespoons milk

1 Grease two baking sheets or 16–18 patty or muffin tins.
2 Sift the flour and spices into a bowl and add the butter cut into small pieces.
3 Rub in the fat until the mixture resembles fine breadcrumbs using either the fingers or a food processor.
4 Stir in the currants, sultanas or raisins, peel, sugar and lemon or orange rind until evenly mixed.
5 Add the egg and sufficient milk to mix to a stiff dough using a palette knife or spatula.
6 Put the mixture into 12–16 rough heaps on the baking sheets or divide between the patty tins. Do not smooth the mixture, it must be left rough.
7 Bake in a fairly hot oven (200°C/400°F/Gas Mark 6) for about 20 minutes or until lightly browned and firm to the touch. Remove carefully to a wire rack and leave to cool. Store in an airtight container for up to 10 days. Makes 12–18 buns

VARIATION

Ginger – replace the spices with 1 teaspoon ground ginger and replace the cut mixed peel with finely chopped crystallized or stem ginger.

Cranberry Teabread

225 g/8 oz/2 cups plain (all-purpose) flour
$1^1\!/_2$ teaspoons baking powder
$^1\!/_2$ teaspoon bicarbonate of soda
50 g/2 oz/$^1\!/_4$ cup butter or margarine
150 g/6 oz/scant cup light soft brown or caster (superfine) sugar
grated rind of 1 orange
75 g/3 oz/$^3\!/_4$ cup shelled walnuts, chopped
50 g/2 oz/$^1\!/_3$ cup raisins
4 tablespoons bottled cranberry sauce
4 tablespoons orange juice (not squash)
1 egg, beaten

1 Grease a loaf tin of about 23 × 12.5 × 7.5 cm/9 × 5 × 3 inches with greased wax or greaseproof paper.
2 Sift the flour, baking powder and soda into a bowl and add the butter cut into small pieces.
3 Rub in the fat until the mixture resembles fine breadcrumbs, either using the fingers or a food processor.
4 Stir in the sugar, orange rind, walnuts and raisins. Beat the cranberry sauce, orange juice and egg together. Add

to the dry ingredients and mix lightly until evenly mixed.
5 Turn into the prepared tin and bake in a moderate oven (180°C/350°F/Gas Mark 4) for 1–1$^1\!/_4$ hours or until well risen, golden brown and firm to the touch. Test with a skewer, which should come out clean.
6 Turn out onto a wire rack and leave until cold. Wrap in foil or store in an airtight container for up to 10 days.
7 Serve in slices either plain or spread with butter.

MELTED CAKES

Gingerbreads in particular are made in a different way by melting the fat and sugar and possibly treacle and, when cool, beating eggs and the dry ingredients into the liquid. The mixture is then turned into the tin and baked.

Gingerbread

225 g/8 oz/2 cups plain (all-purpose) flour
1 teaspoon mixed spice
2 teaspoons ground ginger
1 teaspoon bicarbonate of soda
100 g/4 oz/$^1\!/_2$ cup butter or margarine
50 g/2 oz/good $^1\!/_4$ cup dark soft brown sugar
50 g/2 oz/2 tablespoons black treacle or molasses
150 g/6 oz/scant $^1\!/_2$ cup golden or corn syrup
2 eggs, beaten
150 ml/$^1\!/_4$ pint/$^2\!/_3$ cup milk or sour milk
a few lemon jelly slices to decorate
Lemon icing (optional)
100 g/4 oz/1 cup icing (confectioners') sugar, sifted
1–2 tablespoons lemon juice

1 Grease and line an 18 cm/7 inch deep square cake tin with greased wax or greaseproof paper.
2 Sift the flour, spice, ginger and bicarbonate of soda together into a bowl.
3 Put the butter, sugar, treacle and syrup into a small saucepan and heat gently until melted. Take care not to overheat or let it reach anywhere near boiling point, then allow to cool until lukewarm.
4 Add the melted mixture, eggs and milk to the dry ingredients and beat well until smooth and bubbly.
5 Pour into the prepared tin and bake in a cool oven (150°C/300°F/Gas Mark 2) for 1$^1\!/_4$–1$^1\!/_2$ hours or until firm to the touch and a skewer inserted in the centre comes out clean.
6 Cool in the tin and then turn out onto a wire rack.
7 The cake may be left as it is or topped with a lemon glacé icing.
8 For the icing, put the sifted icing sugar into a small bowl and beat in sufficient strained lemon juice to give a thick spreading consistency.
9 Spread over the top of the gingerbread and, just before it sets, arrange lemon jelly slices around the edge. Leave until quite set. Store in an airtight container for up to 3 months.

Note: Gingerbreads tend to improve with keeping so it is often a good idea to make the cake 2–3 days before required and add the icing when necessary.

Bread (see page 221)

1   *Knead the dough by punching down and pushing away from you with the palm of your hand. Fold it over towards you, give a quarter turn and repeat.*

3 and 4 *Shape into loaves or rolls according to your requirements.*

2   *Place in an oiled polythene bag and put in a warm place until doubled in size and it springs back when pressed with a finger.*

Brownies

These are more of a chewy chocolate and nut bar than a cake but are made by the melting method and are very more-ish indeed!

50 g/2 oz plain chocolate or chocolate dots
65 g/2½ oz/scant ⅓ cup butter or margarine
150 g/6 oz/scant cup caster (superfine) sugar
½ teaspoon vanilla essence
65 g/2½ oz/good ⅔ cup self-raising flour
pinch of salt
50 g/2 oz/½ cup chopped walnuts
40 g/1½ oz/¼ cup raisins, chopped
2 eggs, beaten

1   Grease a shallow 20 cm/8 inch square cake tin and line with greased wax or greaseproof paper.

2   Break up the chocolate and put into a heatproof bowl with the butter. Stand over a saucepan of gently simmering water and stir until melted and thoroughly mixed.

3   Beat in the sugar and vanilla essence and remove from the heat.

4   Sift the flour and salt into a bowl and mix in the walnuts and raisins.

5   Make a well in the centre and add the beaten eggs and melted mixture. Beat until smooth and even, then pour into the prepared tin.

6   Bake in a moderate oven (180°C/350°F/Gas Mark 4) for about 40 minutes or until well risen and just beginning to shrink away from the sides of the tin. There will be a hard crust formed on the top.

7   Leave to cool in the tin and then, when cold, cut into squares or fingers. Store wrapped in foil or in an airtight container.
Makes about 12

OPPOSITE: *Rock Buns* (see page 217), *Cranberry Teabread* (see page 217) *and Scones* (see page 216)

RICH FRUIT CAKES

These are made by the creaming method as for Victoria Sandwich cakes but the quantities vary and they are heavily fruited in one way or another. All rich cakes must have the tin lined with double wax or greaseproof paper to protect the sides and base of the cake from becoming too brown. Also it is wise to wrap a band of newspaper or brown paper of about 3–4 thicknesses around the outside of the tin, securing it with a piece of string, before baking.

Simnel Cake

This is a traditional Easter cake with a layer of marzipan baked through the centre of the cake.

200 g/8 oz/2 cups plain (all-purpose) flour
1 teaspoon baking powder
1 teaspoon ground cinnamon
1/4 teaspoon ground nutmeg or allspice
150 g/6 oz/3/4 cup butter or margarine
150 g/6 oz/scant cup light soft brown or caster (superfine)
    sugar
3 eggs
2 tablespoons milk
100 g/4 oz/2/3 cup raisins
150 g/6 oz/1 cup currants
100 g/4 oz/2/3 cup sultanas (golden raisins)
50 g/2 oz/1/3 cup cut mixed peel
50 g/2 oz/1/3 cup glacé cherries, quartered, washed and
    dried
grated rind of 1 orange
450 g/1 lb marzipan
a little apricot jam
about 1 metre/1 yard yellow ribbon, 2.5 cm/1 inch wide

1 Grease and line an 18 cm/7 inch deep round cake tin with greased double wax or greaseproof paper.
2 Sift together the flour, baking powder and spices.
3 Put the fat into a bowl and cream until soft, then add the sugar and cream together until light and fluffy and very pale in colour.
4 Beat in the eggs, one at a time, following each with a spoonful of flour.
5 Fold in the remainder of the flour, alternating with the milk.
6 Combine all the dried fruits, peel, cherries and orange rind and stir evenly through the mixture.
7 Spread half of the cake mixture into the prepared tin and level the top.
8 Roll out one-third of the marzipan on a lightly sugared surface or between two sheets of polythene and trim to a circle to fit the tin; then lay it carefully on the cake mixture. Level it but do not press down firmly.
9 Spread the rest of the cake mixture over the marzipan and level the top. Tie a thick band of paper around the outside of the tin and bake in a moderate oven (160°C/325°F/Gas Mark 3) for about 2 hours or until cooked through and the sides of the cake have shrunk slightly from the tin. Test with a skewer, but remember the marzipan will be sticky while hot.
10 Cool in the tin for 15–30 minutes, then turn out on to a wire rack and leave until cold.
11 Roll out half of the remaining marzipan in the same way to a circle to fit the top of the cake, trimming neatly. Brush the top of the cake lightly with jam and position the lid, pressing down evenly. Mark a criss-cross design all over the marzipan using a sharp knife and then make a decorative edging all round the edge of the marzipan with a fork or finger and thumb.
12 Roll the rest of the marzipan into 11 even-sized balls and arrange around the edge of the marzipan top, attaching each with a dab of jam. Tie the ribbon round the sides of the cake over a strip of wax or greaseproof paper to prevent the grease seeping through.

Christmas Cake

200 g/8 oz/1 1/3 cups raisins
200 g/8 oz/1 1/3 cups currants
200 g/8 oz/1 1/3 cups sultanas (golden raisins)
100 g/4 oz/2/3 cup cut mixed peel
50 g/2 oz/1/2 cup ground or finely chopped blanched
    almonds
50 g/2 oz/1/3 cup glacé cherries, quartered, washed and
    dried
200 g/8 oz/1 cup butter
150 g/6 oz/scant cup light or dark soft brown sugar
4 eggs
200 g/8 oz/2 cups plain (all-purpose) flour
1 teaspoon mixed spice
1 tablespoon lemon juice
about 4 tablespoons brandy or rum (optional)

1 Grease a 20 cm/8 inch deep round cake tin and line with greased double wax or greaseproof paper.
2 Put all the dried fruits, peel, almonds and cherries into a bowl and mix well.
3 Put the butter into a bowl and cream it until soft. Add the sugar and continue to cream either by hand, using a wooden spoon, or with an electric mixer until light and fluffy and very pale in colour.
4 Beat in the eggs, one at a time, following each one with a spoonful of the flour.
5 Sift the remaining flour with the mixed spice and fold into the creamed mixture followed by the lemon juice.
6 Add the fruit mixture and stir until evenly blended. Turn into the prepared tin and level the top. Tie a thick strip of newspaper or brown paper around the outside of the tin.
7 Bake in a cool oven (150°C/300°F/Gas Mark 2) for about 3 1/2 hours or until a skewer inserted into the centre of the cake comes out clean.
8 Leave in the tin until cold. If to keep the cake for more than about a week, prick all over the cake with a thin skewer and spoon the brandy or rum (if used) over the surface so it sinks into the cake. Wrap in foil or put into an airtight container and leave for a few days, or up to a month before use, or cover with marzipan and royal icing (see pages 222–3 and 225–6).

BREAD

No baking chapter would be complete without a recipe for making bread. Bread making itself is an art and needs a little practice to perfect but it is a most satisfying and relaxing occupation, well recommended when time allows both for the delicious bread it provides and the therapy for the cook. Special strong white or brown bread flour is recommended for bread making. (See step-by-step illustrations, page 218.)

White Bread

675 g/1½ lb/6 cups strong white or bread flour
2 teaspoons salt
15 g/½ oz/½ tablespoon lard
15 g/½ oz fresh yeast, or 1½ teaspoons dried yeast and
*   1 teaspoon caster (superfine) sugar*
450 ml/¾ pint/scant 2 cups warm water (about 43°C/
*   110°F)*
beaten egg or milk to glaze (optional)
poppy or sesame seeds (optional)

1   Sift the flour and salt into a bowl. Add the lard and rub in finely with the fingers.
2   If using fresh yeast, dissolve it in the warm water using a fork to mix it or, for dried yeast, dissolve the sugar in the water and sprinkle the yeast on top. Leave in a warm place for about 10 minutes or until a thick frothy layer has formed on the top.
3   Add the yeast liquid to the dry ingredients and mix to a firm elastic dough, using a palette knife or spatula.
4   Turn onto a lightly floured surface and knead the dough for about 10 minutes or until smooth and no longer sticky. To do this, you punch the dough down and away from you using the palm of your hand, then fold it over towards you, give a quarter turn and repeat.
    (The dough can also be mixed and kneaded in a large electric mixer fitted with a dough hook, following the manufacturer's instructions – about 3–4 minutes.)
5   Shape the dough into a ball, place in a large oiled polythene bag and tie loosely at the top or put into a floured bowl and cover with a damp cloth or piece of plastic cling film. Put to rise in a warm place for about an hour or until the dough springs back when lightly pressed with a floured finger.
6   Remove the dough from the bag, turn out onto a lightly floured surface and 'knock back' by kneading until it is smooth and even again and the air bubbles have been knocked out.
7   The dough is now ready for shaping. Grease two loaf tins, one 900 g/2 lb and the other 450 g/1 lb, or three of the smaller loaf tins.
8   Divide the dough into two portions – two-thirds and one-third. Shape each piece to fit a tin by kneading and rolling to give a shape as wide as the tin and a little longer. Tuck the ends under and place evenly in the tin.
9   Lay a sheet of oiled polythene lightly over the loaves and put to rise in a warm place until the dough reaches the tops of the tins.
10 The loaves may be brushed with beaten egg or milk and sprinkled with poppy or sesame seeds, if liked, or simply dredged lightly with flour. Bake in a very hot oven (230°C/450°F/Gas Mark 8) allowing 35–40 minutes for the large loaf and about 30 minutes for the smaller one. When ready, the loaves should be well risen and golden brown and sound hollow when the base of the loaf is tapped.
11 Turn out onto a wire rack and leave to cool. Home-baked bread freezes well for up to 3 months, simply wrap in polythene or foil.

VARIATIONS

Brown – make as above but use strong wholemeal flour and increase the yeast content to 25 g/1 oz of fresh yeast or 1 tablespoon dried yeast and the water by 2 tablespoons.
Light Brown – make as above but replace a third to a half of the white flour with a strong wholemeal flour.

Quick Brown Bread

This is really a cheating way of making bread as the dough only has one rising. The flavour is still very good, but the keeping quality is cut quite severely. However, it will keep well for a couple of days and will freeze.

225 g/8 oz/2 cups strong plain (all purpose) white flour
225 g/8 oz/2 cups wholemeal flour
1½ teaspoons salt
2 teaspoons sugar
15 g/½ oz/½ tablespoon lard
15 g/½ oz fresh yeast, or 2 teaspoons dried yeast and
*   1 teaspoon caster (superfine) sugar*
300 ml/½ pint/1¼ cups warm water (43°C/110°C)
salted water to glaze
oatmeal (optional)

1   Sift the white flour into a bowl. Add the wholemeal flour, salt and sugar and mix well.
2   Add the lard and rub in finely with the fingertips.
3   If using fresh yeast, dissolve it in the warm water or, for dried yeast, dissolve the sugar in the water and sprinkle the yeast on top. Leave in a warm place for about 10 minutes or until frothy.
4   Add the yeast liquid to the dry ingredients and mix to form a fairly firm dough. Turn onto a floured surface and knead for about 10 minutes or until smooth and no longer sticky.
5   Divide the dough in half (or use it all together) and shape each half into a baton by rolling backwards and forwards with the palms of the hands.
6   Place on a greased baking sheet and brush the tops with salted water. Sprinkle with oatmeal (if used) and cover lightly with oiled polythene. Put to rise in a warm place until doubled in size.
7   Remove the polythene and bake in a very hot oven (230°C/450°F/Gas Mark 8) for 15 minutes, then reduce the temperature to fairly hot (200°C/400°F/Gas Mark 6) and continue baking for about 10 minutes for the smaller loaves or about 20 minutes for a large loaf. The bases should sound hollow as soon as the loaves are cooked. Cool on a wire rack.

— 16 Icing and Decorating —

Many cakes are best when simply iced and decorated; it is an art to ice an elaborate wedding or other celebration cake, something that takes time to learn and requires plenty of practice. However, simple cake decoration is easy and needs only a little time and patience to complete with very pleasing results.

Sponge cakes are usually iced with butter cream or glacé icing or a frosting. Rich cakes need a layer of marzipan and then royal icing or bought fondant icing which is rolled out and used to cover cakes. The marzipan acts as a barrier between the cake and icing, which would otherwise be stained by the richness and colour of the cake. Marzipan should be added to the cake and allowed to set for 2–7 days before adding the top icing. Rolled out fondant icing needs about 48 hours to dry, while royal icing needs about 24 hours – longer if icing tiered cakes with several coats of icing. Sponge cakes can also have a thin layer of marzipan added if preferred; it certainly makes adding the icing an easier task but not everyone likes the taste of marzipan. Where a sponge cake has a crumbly surface, it is a good idea to brush the whole cake with apricot glaze before adding the icing. This will prevent crumbs appearing on the surface of the cake as it mixes into the butter cream.

This chapter will give basic icings with directions for use, plus some traditional Christmas cake designs and other designs for birthday and everyday cakes. Once you can make the cakes and the icings, you can then quickly devise your own colour schemes and designs.

Marzipan and fondant icing can be used to make flowers, leaves and other shapes and are really much nicer than bought decorations.

Icing Cakes
Apricot Glaze

Once made, this can be stored in an airtight container in the refrigerator for up to a week, but it should be boiled and cooled again before applying to a cake.

175–225 g/6–8 oz/¹/₂–²/₃ cup apricot jam
2–3 tablespoons water

1 Put the jam and water into a saucepan and heat gently until the jam has melted, stirring occasionally. Bring to the boil.
2 Rub through a sieve into a bowl and leave until cold.
3 Use straightaway or store in an airtight container.

Marzipan (or Almond Paste)

You can make your own marzipan very simply with ground almonds, sugar and egg yolks or buy a good quality marzipan, not the cheapest variety, which is ready to use. Bought marzipan is available in the traditional bright yellow and also white, which is ideal for using for colouring marzipan to get good true colours for moulding. If bought marzipan becomes very hard, it can be warmed gently and then kneaded until smooth and pliable or, if you have a microwave oven, wrap it in polythene and heat for a few seconds on medium heat, when it is just right to use again. Trimmings of marzipan can be wrapped securely in polythene and put in an airtight container to use as required. Home-made marzipan must be used as it is made.

Rich cakes must be completely covered in marzipan, as must any to be covered in royal icing, but sponge and quick mix cakes and any others may have just the top covered. Make sure the marzipan is added as smoothly as possible (filling any dents in the cake with scraps of marzipan), as this makes it much easier to add a smooth layer of icing.

100 g/4 oz/good ¹/₂ cup caster (superfine) sugar
100 g/4 oz/1 cup icing (confectioners') sugar, sifted
200 g/8 oz/2 cups ground almonds
1 teaspoon lemon juice
a few drops of almond essence
1 egg or 2 egg yolks (or 1 ¹/₂–2 egg whites for a whiter marzipan)

1 Combine the sugars and ground almonds in a bowl and make a well in the centre.
2 Add the lemon juice, almond essence and most of the egg or yolks. Gradually work together to give a firm but manageable dough adding more egg as required.
3 Turn out onto a lightly sugared surface and knead until just smooth. Wrap in polythene and/or foil and then overwrap with more polythene and use within 2 days, or, preferably, straightaway.
Makes 450 g/1 lb marzipan

HOW TO MARZIPAN A CAKE
Make up the amount of marzipan required or use a commercial marzipan following the chart below. (See step-by-step illustrations, page 226.)

Square		15 cm/6 in	18 cm/7 in	20 cm/8 in
Round	15 cm/6 in	18 cm/7 in	20 cm/8 in	23 cm/9 in
Marzipan	350 g/12 oz	450 g/1 lb	575 g/1¹/₄ lb	800 g/1³/₄ lb

1 Place just over half the marizpan on a working surface dredged with icing (confectioners') sugar or between two sheets of polythene. Roll out evenly to a strip that is twice the depth of the cake. Take a piece of string and cut it exactly the circumference of the cake and cut another piece the depth of the cake.

2 With the string as a guide, cut into two strips which are both the same depth as the cake and together are the length of the string.

3 Stand the cake on a cake board and brush all round the outside with apricot glaze. Loosely roll the marzipan strips into a coil and unroll around the sides of the cake, moulding it to the sides as you unroll it. Make sure the marzipan touches the cake board.

4 Use trimmings to fill any indents on top of the cake, then brush the top with apricot glaze.

5 Roll out the remaining mazipan to a round to fit the top of the cake (use a plate as a guide), cut out and position on the cake. Press the edges together with a round-bladed knife and smooth over the joins on the sides of the cake.

6 If the marzipan seems unduly moist, rub all over with sifted icing (confectioners') sugar.

7 Store the cake, uncovered, in a warm dry place for at least 24 hours and preferably longer before applying the icing.

TO MARZIPAN THE TOP OF A CAKE

Use just under half the recommended amount for a whole cake and roll out a little larger than the top of the cake. Brush the cake top with apricot glaze and then invert the cake onto the marzipan and cut round the edge neatly. Remove trimmings, turn the cake up the right way again and leave to set.

Butter Cream

This is the standard soft icing used on so many cakes. It can be flavoured and coloured in many ways to suit all types of cakes. It can also be used as a filling and is suitable for piping as well. For the best flavour, it is essential to use butter. It will keep in an airtight container in the refrigerator for about a week – remember to allow it to return to room temperature before use – and will also freeze for up to 3 months, either as it is or on the cake.

This recipe makes sufficient butter cream to coat the top and sides of an 18 cm/7 inch sandwich or layer cake or to cover the top and fill the cake.

100 g/4 oz/½ cup butter (or soft tub margarine)
175–225 g/6–8 oz/1½–2 cups icing (confectioners') sugar, sifted
a few drops of vanilla essence
1–2 tablespoons top of the milk, milk or lemon juice

1 Cream the butter until very soft with a wooden spoon or a hand-held electric mixer.

2 Beat in the sugar, a little at at time, adding the essence and sufficient milk or lemon juice to give a fairly firm but spreading consistency.

The butter cream is now ready for use and can be flavoured as below.

VARIATIONS

Coffee – omit the vanilla essence and replace 1 tablespoon of the milk with coffee essence or very strong black coffee, or beat in 2–3 teaspoons coffee powder with the sugar.

Chocolate – add 25–40 g/1–1½ oz melted plain chocolate, or dissolve 1–2 tablespoons cocoa powder in a little very hot water to give a paste and, when cool, beat into the icing.

Orange or Lemon – omit the vanilla essence, replace the milk with orange or lemon juice and add the finely grated rind of 1 orange or lemon.

Mocha – dissolve 1–2 teaspoons cocoa powder in 2 teaspoons coffee essence or strong black coffee and add in place of part of the milk.

Brandy and Rum – omit the vanilla essence and replace the milk with brandy, rum, whisky, sherry or any other liqueur. A few drops of an appropriate-coloured liquid food colouring may also be added.

Almond – omit the vanilla essence and beat in a few drops of almond essence and, if liked, 2 tablespoons very finely chopped toasted almonds.

Apricot – omit the vanilla essence and milk and beat in 3 tablespoons sieved apricot jam, a pinch of grated lemon rind and just a squeeze of lemon juice.

TO COVER A CAKE WITH BUTTER CREAM

1 Stand the cake on a plate or cake board and make sure there are no loose crumbs on the cake. If it appears to be very crumbly, then it is wise to brush the cake with apricot glaze first.

2 Using a small round-bladed or palette knife, spread an even layer of butter cream all round the sides of the cake. If you have an icing turntable, it makes it much easier to manoeuvre the cake, but it is not essential. Once you have got the cake evenly covered and the sides reasonably smooth it can be decorated in one of the following ways:

a) Take a fork and run around the sides of the cake in a wavy line starting at the top and working down to the base. The lines can be altered as you like to give an interesting effect.

b) Take an icing comb with a serrated edge (a piece of plastic specially formulated for this purpose and available from cake icing stores) and run this around the cake either keeping it straight or waving it.

c) Add only a thin layer of butter cream and then roll the sides of the cake in either chopped nuts, toasted coconut, toasted flaked almonds, grated chocolate or chocolate vermicelli. This is done by tipping the chosen coating onto a sheet of wax or greaseproof paper and then, holding the cake in two hands, simply rolling it round in the coating until it is evenly covered. Any gaps can be filled in using a palette knife or spatula.

3 To cover the top of the cake, put the butter cream in the centre of the cake and, using a round-bladed knife or small palette knife, spread it out gradually from the centre to the sides of the cake. Do not press too hard or the surface of the cake may lift off and spoil the look of the butter cream. When reasonably smooth, use one of the following ways to decorate it:

a) Starting at one side of the cake, run a small round-bladed knife or palette knife backwards and forwards across the top of the cake to give a smooth row of lines.

b) Do the same as above and then, with the same knife, run lines at right angles to the first lines at about 2.5 cm/1 inch intervals.

c) Take a fork or palette knife and 'rough up' the surface of the icing.

d) Spread the icing out over the cake and then swirl it unevenly all over the surface.

4   The top of the cake may then be sprinkled with chopped nuts, grated chocolate or vermicelli, toasted coconut, etc., and left to set; or have whirls of butter cream piped around the top edge which are then in turn topped with a piece of decoration; or a continuous line of stars or shells around the edge of the cake or a little way in from the edge; or a lattice of piping; or many more variations. If you are going to add further decoration to the top of the cake, it is wise to make up 1½–2 quantities of the basic recipe of butter cream. For a 20 cm/8 inch round sandwich or layer cake you will require this amount to fill and cover the top and add a few piped decorations.

Glacé Icing

This is the quickest of icings to make and useful for icing sponge and sandwich or layer cakes. It does tend to set rather quickly, so it is advisable to stand the bowl of made icing over another bowl, containing hot water. The icing is also smoother if you blend the icing (confectioners') sugar with hot or warm liquid rather than using cold. Glacé icing may be coloured and flavoured as you like. When trying to smooth the icing out, always use a palette knife or spatula dipped into hot water; keep a jug of hot water beside the cake while adding the icing.

   This recipe makes sufficient icing to cover the top of a 20 cm/8 inch round cake.

225 g/8 oz/2 cups icing (confectioners') sugar
2–4 tablespoons hot water
food colouring and/or flavouring (optional)

1   Sift the icing sugar into a bowl.
2   Gradually beat in sufficient water to give a smooth icing, thick enough to coat the back of the spoon. Use a wooden spoon for preference and not an electric mixer as that will incorporate too many air bubbles, which are difficult to disperse. Extra water or sugar can be added to achieve the correct consistency.
3   Add a few drops of food colouring or flavouring, if using. Take special care when adding the colouring to add only a minute amount at a time; the best way is to dip a skewer into the colouring and then dip this into the icing and beat in until evenly distributed. Extra colouring can be added but it is impossible to remove when too much has been added.
4   Use the icing at once or place the bowl over another bowl of hot water for a short time.
5   Another way to make the icing is to put all the ingredients into a saucepan and heat gently, stirring all the time until well mixed and smooth. Take care not to overheat or the icing will crystallize.

VARIATIONS

Lemon or Orange – use strained fruit juice instead of water and add a few drops of yellow or orange colouring.

Coffee – use a little coffee essence or strong black coffee in place of part of the water.

Chocolate – dissolve 2–3 teaspoons cocoa powder in the water and add to the icing sugar.

Mocha – dissolve 1 teaspoon cocoa powder and 2 teaspoons instant coffee powder in the water and add to the icing sugar.

Coloured – simply add colouring, a little at a time, using the tip of a skewer, and a suitably-flavoured essence too, if liked.

TO TOP A CAKE WITH GLACÉ ICING

1   Fill the cake and assemble, then stand on a plate or cake board.
2   Cut a strip of single or double thickness non-stick baking paper the circumference of the cake plus a little for overlapping and which stands at least 2.5 cm/1 inch above the top of the cake. Position around the cake and secure with pins, paper clips and/or string.
3   Make up the icing and pour into the centre of the cake. Either tilt the cake so the icing runs evenly to cover it, or spread it out with the help of a palette knife or spatula. Leave to set.
4   When ready to serve and the icing is quite dry, carefully undo the paper and peel off gently from around the sides of the cake. Add other decorations as required.

Note: Small cakes can be topped with glacé icing either by dipping the cake itself into the runny icing or spreading a little onto each one with a palette knife or spatula. Leave to set. The decoration is best set into the icing.

Quick Frosting

This is a much quicker and simpler to make frosting than the true American frosting, as it does not require a sugar thermometer. However, once ready, it does set almost immediately so must be spread or swirled onto the cake with haste. This quantity is sufficient to fill and cover an 18 cm/7 inch sandwich or layer cake, or cover a 20 cm/ 8 inch cake or ring mould. Again, no glaze or marzipan is required and it can be used on all cakes except rich fruit cakes.

1 egg white
150 g/6 oz/scant cup caster (superfine) sugar
pinch of salt
2 tablespoons water
pinch of cream of tartar

1   Put all the ingredients into a large heatproof bowl and mix lightly.
2   Stand the bowl over a saucepan of gently simmering water and beat hard, using a hand-held electric mixer, for preference, or a rotary whisk, until the mixture is thick and stiff enough to stand in peaks.
3   Remove from the heat and pour over the cake. Spread the frosting at once to cover all over the cake and swirl

it with a round-bladed knife, pulling up into peaks, if liked. Leave to set.

Note: A few drops of colouring may be beaten into the mixture, but it is best to add near the end as the whisking makes the colour paler as it thickens. Sifted soft brown sugar may be used in place of caster (superfine) sugar to give a butterscotch frosting.

Royal Icing

This is the true white firm icing used for wedding cakes and other celebration cakes which can be modestly or highly decorated. The icing can be made up in any quantity so long as you allow 1 egg white to every 225 g/8 oz/2 cups sifted icing (confectioners') sugar. However, it is best not to make up more than a 4 egg white quantity at a time because, although it will keep well for 2–3 days in a covered airtight container, it is better to make in fairly small quantities. However, for a really flat surface, especially on the last layer, it is wise to make the icing 24 hours before required to give plenty of time for the air bubbles to subside before the icing is put onto the cake.

Glycerine is added to royal icing to help soften the icing and make cutting easier; without it, if the cake is iced too long before required, it can be like carving through concrete.

Royal icing is an art and to get a smoothly iced cake does take practice. It is advisable to add several thin coats of icing rather than one thick one and to invest in an icing ruler to help get the top smooth and an icing comb to assist with the sides. A turntable does also help with getting good smooth and even sides to the cake.

If you are a real beginner, it is a good idea to just make the icing on top of the cake smooth and then to put rough icing round the sides. This is particularly effective for a Christmas cake but can be used for other occasions too. Remember to allow the layers of icing to dry completely before adding the next one or you may pull off the previous layer and give yourself a real problem in trying to smooth it all out again.

3 egg whites
about 675 g/1½ lb/6 cups icing (confectioners') sugar, sifted
3 tablespoons strained lemon juice
1–1½ teaspoons glycerine

1 Beat the egg whites until frothy in a large grease-free bowl, but do not allow them to begin to stiffen.
2 Gradually beat in about half of the sugar using a wooden spoon for preference – a hand-held electric mixer can be used but it incorporates much more air in the form of air bubbles and these are very difficult to disperse and will spoil the appearance of the icing.
3 Beat in the lemon juice and glycerine and half of the remaining icing sugar.
4 Gradually beat in enough of the remaining icing sugar to give a smooth consistency which will just stand in soft peaks.
5 Put the icing into an airtight plastic container or into a bowl covered with a damp cloth and leave to stand for

a while to encourage the air bubbles to come to the surface and burst.
6 The icing is now ready for coating a cake or it can be thickened for piping decorations or for rough icing.

Use the following chart as a rough guide for the quantity of icing required to smoothly ice cakes – enough for two thin coats. Extra icing is required for decoration.

Square Round	15 cm/6 in	18 cm/7 in	20 cm/8 in	23 cm/9 in
15 cm/6 in Icing sugar	18 cm/7 in	20 cm/8 in	23 cm/9 in	25 cm/10 in
450 g/1 lb	575 g/1¼ lb	675 g/1½ lb	900 g/2 lb	1 kg/2¼ lb

HOW TO ICE A CAKE SMOOTHLY
Some people prefer to ice the top of the cake first and then the sides; others do it the other way round. It doesn't really matter so long as you add several thin coats of icing instead of one thick uneven coat.

A normal cake requires two coats on the top and sides with perhaps a third coat on top. Wedding cakes require several further coats, particularly if they are tiered cakes. Don't loose patience the first time you attempt to ice a cake, it is a little difficult at first but quite easy when you know how. (See step-by-step illustrations, page 227.)

TO ICE THE TOP OF THE CAKE
1 Place the cake on a cake board which should be 2.5–5 cm/1–2 inches larger than the tin the cake was baked in and attach it with icing, making sure it is quite central.
2 Put a quantity of icing in the centre of the cake and with a palette knife or spatula smooth it out using a paddling movement and pressing alternately firmly and lightly yet keeping the icing fairly even – this helps to expel any more air bubbles. Remove any excess icing that has slipped over the edge of the cake.
3 Take an icing ruler or a long palette knife and draw it across the cake towards you, keeping the ruler at an angle of about 30 degrees and pressing just firmly enough to keep the icing smooth and even. Do not press too lightly or the icing will not level, or too heavily, when it will bite into the marzipan and give a very uneven surface. This process does take a little practice but, if it doesn't seem smooth enough after the first run (and that is rather unlikely even for me), then put a little more icing onto the cake and repeat. You can go on doing this for quite a while both for practice and until you are satisfied the layer is even enough. Do remember to keep the icing bowl covered with a damp cloth or plastic cling film all the time except when taking out the icing or a crust will form on the icing as it begins to set and then the little pieces in the icing will make it impossible to get a smooth top.
4 Remove the surplus icing by running the palette knife or spatula around the top edge of the cake holding it at right angles to the cake. Wipe the knife and do the same a second time so the sides are clean. Leave to dry.

Marzipanning a Cake (see pages 222–3)

1   With the string as a guide, cut the rolled out marzipan into two strips that are both the same depth as the cake and together are the length of the string.

3   Using a plate as a guide, cut a round of marzipan to fit the top of the cake and place in position.

2   Brush the cake with apricot glaze and unroll the coil of marzipan round the cake, moulding it to the sides as you unroll it.

4   Press the edges together and smooth over the joins with a round-bladed knife.

TO ICE THE SIDES OF A ROUND CAKE

If possible, place the cake on its board on an icing turntable, otherwise put on an upturned plate.

1   Spread a thin but covering layer of icing all round the sides of the cake. Again, use a paddling action to push out as much air as possible and then make the icing fairly smooth with the palette knife or spatula.
2   Hold an icing comb or scraper or a palette knife at an angle of about 45 degrees to the cake and starting at the back of the cake, with your free hand slowly rotate the cake and at the same time move the comb slowly and evenly around the sides of the cake. Remove the comb at an angle and rather swiftly so the join is hardly noticeable.
3   If the layer is uneven or has bare patches in it, add more icing where necessary and repeat the process. With the first layer it doesn't matter if you have more than one join, as the top layer will cover these. With a round cake care must be taken that the base of the comb doesn't tilt outwards giving a rather strange shaped

cake with sides that are much wider at the base than the top. This is rectified by holding the comb a little firmer and slightly towards the bottom and remembering all the time not to let the base come outwards.
4   Lift any excess icing off the top of the cake using a palette knife or spatula, again rotating the turntable at the same time. When sufficiently smooth, leave to dry. Also remove any excess icing from around the base.

TO ICE THE SIDES OF A SQUARE CAKE

1   The best way to achieve good even square corners is to ice the two opposite sides of the cake and, when dry, ice the remaining two sides. Spread some icing on one side in the same way as above and, keeping it fairly even with plenty of icing at each end of the side, draw the comb or palette knife towards you, keeping the cake still (not on a turntable) to give an even side.
2   Cut off the icing down the corners with a palette knife or spatula to give a sharp angle and remove the excess

Icing a Cake (see pages 225)

1   *Put a quantity of icing on top of the cake and, with a palette knife or spatula, smooth it out using a paddling movement.*

3   *Smooth the icing on the sides of the cake using a scraper held at an angle of about 45 degrees to the cake and turning the cake at the same time.*

2   *Take an icing ruler and draw it across the cake towards you, keeping the ruler at an angle of about 30 degrees.*

4   *Lift any excess icing off the top of the cake using a palette knife or spatula. When dry, add further coats as required.*

from both the top and the base of the cake with a palette knife.
3   Repeat with the opposite side and leave to dry.
4   Do exactly the same with the other two sides and leave to dry. Cut off the corners to give sharp neat angles.

ADDING A SECOND OR THIRD COAT
1   Make sure the cake is dry. Using a serrated-edged knife or piece of fine sandpaper, pare down any lumps or bumps that shouldn't be on the cake and brush away any icing with a dry pastry brush.
2   Repeat the methods for icing the top and sides of the cake but take care that the cake is really dry before adding more icing. Icing usually takes about 4 hours to be dry enough to add the next coat from sides to top, but it needs longer before adding another coat to the same place. The temperature of the room and atmosphere make the drying times vary.
3   Once the cake is completely iced, it is wise to leave it for 24 hours before adding any decoration.

Ready-to-roll Fondant Icing

This icing is available in packets and is ready to roll out and put onto the cake. It usually comes in white but is simple to colour by kneading in a few drops of liquid food colouring until evenly blended and of the shade you want. Remember the icing is likely to dry a shade darker than you make it. It is again a little tricky the first time you try to use it but is very obliging so you can reroll several times without harming the icing until you get the result you want. This type of icing can be used for any type of cake, whether sponge or rich fruit cake. It can be used over marzipan, when the marzipan should be brushed with a little beaten egg white to attach, or straight onto a sponge cake, when the cake should be brushed with apricot glaze.

1   Roll out the icing on a surface dredged with icing (confectioners') sugar or a mixture of icing (confection-

ers') sugar and cornflour (cornstarch), or between two sheets of polythene, to a round or square about 10 cm/4 inches larger than the top of the cake.
2 Lay the icing over the rolling pin and place evenly over the top of the cake.
3 Press the icing onto the sides of the cake, working the icing evenly to the back of the cake. Dip your hands in cornflour (cornstarch) and/or icing (confectioners') sugar and rub the surface in a circular movement to give an even covering. When neatly covered, cut off the surplus icing from around the base and press evenly into the side of the cake.
4 For square cakes, cut a piece of icing at each corner and mould carefully to give even-shaped corners. Leave to dry.

CHRISTMAS CAKES

There are three ways to ice a Christmas cake: completely rough-iced, smooth top and rough-iced sides and completely smooth. All these methods can be used for a round or square cake and the decorations adapted very simply. Red and green ribbons make a cake look very festive and the Christmas ornaments are easy to buy around Christmas time. If you feel a little more ambitious, you can make your own marzipan holly leaves, Christmas trees, etc., and also try to make the Christmas roses, but it doesn't matter, they still look good if you use bought ones.

Holly and Ivy Cake

20 cm/8 inch round or square Christmas cake covered with marzipan
royal icing made with 4 egg whites (see page 225)
about 8 Christmas roses or roses (see page 235)
about 20 marzipan or bought holly leaves and berries (see page 233)
about 10 marzipan or bought ivy leaves (see page 233)
about 1 metre/1 yard red or green ribbon, 2.5 cm/1 inch wide (optional)

1 Smoothly ice the top of the cake giving it two coats. Leave to dry.
2 Stand the cake on a turntable or upturned plate. Add a little extra icing (confectioners') sugar to the icing to make it stiff enough to stand up in stiff peaks.
3 Spread the icing round the sides of the cake quite thickly but evenly. If using the ribbon, run a palette knife or spatula around the sides of the cake to give a flat strip wide enough for the ribbon.
4 Using a palette knife or the handle of a spoon, pull the icing up into peaks all round the sides of the cake. The peaks on the top edge can be made to tip over onto the top of the cake to give an attractive edging. Leave to dry.
5 For the decoration, arrange a pretty circle of the flowers, leaves and berries around the top of the cake about 2.5 cm/1 inch in from the edge of the rough icing. When it is as you want, attach each piece with a small dab of icing. Leave to dry.
6 Tie the ribbon around the sides of the dry cake (if used).

Christmas Tree Cake

This cake is iced smoothly all over before adding the decorations which are also made, so it will take rather longer to prepare than the other two designs. (See step-by-step illustrations, page 235.)

20 cm/8 inch round or square Christmas cake covered with marzipan
royal icing made with 4 egg whites (see page 225)
yellow liquid food colouring
8 marzipan Christmas trees (see page 233)
56 silver balls

1 Smoothly ice the top and sides of the cake giving them two coats. Leave to dry. The cake may be covered with fondant icing, if preferred.
2 Colour about 2 tablespoons of the icing a pale yellow and put into a piping bag fitted with a plain No. 2 writing nozzle. Put about 2 tablespoons of white icing into another piping bag again fitted with a plain No. 2 writing nozzle. Keep in a polythene bag.
3 Draw a square on a sheet of wax or greaseproof paper, large enough to fit 4 Christmas trees with their tips almost touching in the centre and allowing about 1 cm/½ inch from the tree tubs. Cut out this square and place it centrally on the cake.
4 Take the bag of white icing and pipe around the outside of this square keeping the lines straight but not touching the paper, then pipe another square about 1 cm/⅓ inch outside the first one, again using white icing. Leave to dry, then remove the paper from the centre.
5 Position the Christmas trees in the centre of the square with the tops almost touching and tubs halfway along each side of the iced square and attach with icing.
6 Take the bag of yellow icing and pipe a straight line of yellow over the white lines, doing the inside one first and then the outer one. Leave to dry.
7 Position the other trees on the sides of the cake equidistant between those on the top of the cake and attach with icing.
8 Fill an icing bag fitted with a small star nozzle with white icing and pipe a series of graduated-sized stars from directly below the tree tubs on top of the cake, starting with quite a large star and following with 3 smaller stars in a straight line towards the edge of the cake. Pipe a line of 3 graduated stars about 2.5 cm/1 inch away from the first line on both sides. Repeat under the other tubs.
9 Pipe a border of stars all round the top edge of the cake keeping neat and even. Leave to dry a little and then pipe another row of smaller stars on the side of the cake just under the top ones.
10 Using the same nozzle, pipe a series of stars on the sides of the cake equidistant from the Christmas trees with a vertical line of 4 stars decreasing in size in the centre and vertical lines of 3 stars on each side. Leave to dry.
11 Finally, pipe a row of medium-sized stars all around the base of the cake to attach to the board and give an attractive finish. Leave to dry.

BIRTHDAY CAKES

These can be made of sponge or fruit mixtures, depending greatly on the taste of the person who is having the birthday. Icings too can be formal with marzipan and royal icing or fondant icing, or much softer, using butter cream. Decorations suitable for any occasion can easily be bought, but it can be prettier to add a few simple marzipan flowers and leaves and perhaps a name.

Butter Cream Rose Cake

20 cm/8 inch round sandwich or layer cake
a little apricot glaze (see page 222)
2 recipe quantities butter cream (see page 223)
colourings and flavourings
about 7 marzipan roses of varying sizes (see page 234)
a few marzipan or silver rose leaves (see page 233)

1 Put the cake on a silver cake board and brush all over with apricot glaze.
2 Make up the butter cream and colour it lightly with whatever you choose. Pale pink, yellow, peach or green all look good. Spread an even layer over the top of the cake and finish off with a palette knife or spatula by running it backwards and forwards across the top of the cake to give a surface of smooth evenly-spaced lines.
3 Spread more of the butter cream evenly around the sides of the cake (preferably standing it on a turntable) and then run a serrated-edged icing comb all round the sides or use a fork to make wavy lines.
4 Tint the rest of the butter cream about two shades darker than the rest of the cake. Put a small amount of it into a piping bag fitted with a No. 2 writing nozzle and keeping even with one of the lines on top of the cake pipe out the name of the person or Happy Birthday.
5 Put the rest of the butter cream into a piping bag fitted with a medium star nozzle and pipe a shell border or a row of stars around the top edge of the cake, then pipe a heavier row of shells or stars around the base of the cake.
6 Arrange the roses (in a colour to blend or contrast with the main icing) and the leaves in an attractive spray on top of the cake above the writing. Leave to set.
7 If liked, a ribbon may be tied round the cake just before serving, but it is wise to put a strip of wax or greaseproof paper between the ribbon and cake to prevent the grease from the icing marking the ribbon.

Note: This cake can be decorated in the same way using royal icing by smoothly icing the cake first after covering with marzipan and adding the decorations when dry, or by covering first in bought fondant icing and then adding the decoration in butter cream or royal icing. With these two methods the top of the cake will be smoothly iced and not ridged as with the butter cream.

Anniversary Cake

20–25 cm/8–10 inch square sponge cake
a little apricot glaze (see page 222)
2 recipe quantities chocolate butter cream (see page 223)
chocolate vermicelli or coarsely grated chocolate
glacé cherries
silver leaves or chocolate leaves (see page 233)

1 Stand the cake on a cake board and brush all over with apricot glaze.
2 Spread a thin layer of butter cream all round the sides of the cake, then coat the sides in chocolate vermicelli or grated chocolate by putting the coating on a sheet of paper and rolling the cake in it.
3 Replace the cake on the board attaching with a dab of butter cream.
4 Cover the top of the cake with butter cream, finishing it as for the rose cake above. Mark two diagonal lines across the cake with a knife about a quarter of the way into the cake.
5 Put a little butter cream into a piping bag fitted with a No. 2 writing nozzle and pipe out the words Happy Anniversary or whatever you want between the two marked lines.
6 Put the rest of the butter cream into a piping bag fitted with a star nozzle and first pipe a line of shells across the two marked lines on top of the cake. Next pipe a shell edging all round the top edge of the cake and finally pipe another shell edging around the base of the cake to attach it to the board.
7 Put 1, 2 or 3 whole glacé cherries on top of the cake in the corners with leaves of chocolate or silver around them to represent flowers; and use halved or quartered cherries to place around the top shell border and the base to complete the decoration. Leave to dry.

This cake may be decorated in different flavoured butter cream and the cake baked in whatever flavour you prefer, and it can be used equally well for a birthday cake.

NOVELTY CAKES

Children, in particular, like to have a surprise novelty cake for their birthday. Some of the designs you see are so complicated and take a great deal of time and expertise to produce, but lovely cakes can be prepared quite simply. Use a basic Victoria sandwich cake or quick mix cake for the base and then cut out to the shape required or assemble as required. A little patience is needed but the result is sure to please some little boy or girl.

Making a Paper Icing Bag (see page 232)

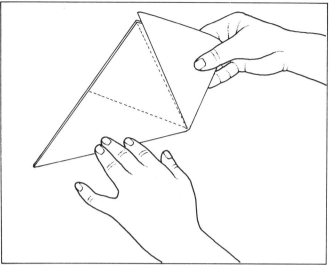

1   *Having folded the square of paper in half to form a triangle, then in half again, open out the smaller triangle and fold the bottom half of the triangle up to the folded line.*

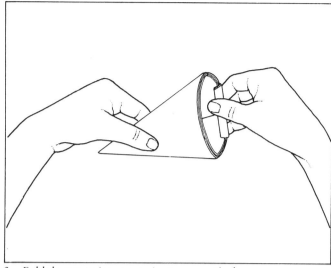

3   *Fold the top point over twice to secure the bag.*

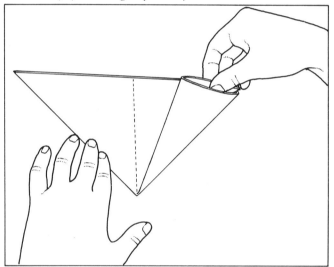

2   *Continue to fold the bag over to each fold, creasing it firmly each time until completed.*

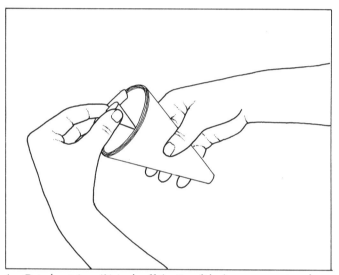

4   *Cut about 1 cm/½ inch off the tip of the bag, open out and insert the nozzle.*

Butterfly Cake

(See step-by-step illustrations, page 234.)

3 egg Victoria sandwich or quick mix cake baked in two 20 cm/8 inch round cake tins, any flavour (see pages 210 and 208)
2 recipes quantities butter cream (see page 223)
a little apricot glaze (see page 222)
food colouring, coloured balls, candles and holders

1   Use some butter cream to sandwich the cakes together.
2   Cut the cake evenly in half and position the halves, back to back, on a cake board at a slightly slanting angle so the 'wings' are wider apart at the top.
3   Brush the cake all over with apricot glaze.
4   Colour about two-thirds of the icing any colour you choose, but keep it a pastel shade. Use to spread all round the sides and over the top of the cake. Use a serrated icing comb or fork to pull round the sides of the cake evenly to give an attractive finish.
5   Leave the rest of the butter cream white or tint it a darker shade than the basic cake, or a contrasting colour. Put most of it into a piping bag fitted with a star nozzle. Pipe a shell or star border around the base of the cakes to give two 'wings' then do the same on the top of the cake. Inside the top border of icing on each wing pipe two separate wing shapes, one larger than the other, to represent the insect's two sets of wings, by outlining with a continuous line of shells or stars.
6   Pipe a 'body' between the wings with a backwards and forwards line using the star nozzle.
7   Put the remaining butter cream into a piping bag fitted with a No. 2 writing nozzle and pipe a lacework design inside the shapes on the wings. This is simply a freehand squiggly line which looks rather like lace.
8   Use coloured balls to place along the shell borders for decoration and add two candles and holders at the head to represent the antennae (or chocolate matchsticks can be used) and leave to set.

Holy and Ivy Cake (see page 228) *and Teddy Bears Picnic Maypole Cake* (see page 232)

Teddy Bear's Picnic Maypole Cake

2 recipe quantities Victoria sandwich mixture or quick mix cake baked in two 25 cm/10 inch round cake tins, any flavour (see pages 210 and 208)
2 recipe quantities butter cream, any flavour (see page 223)
a little raspberry jam or lemon cheese or curd
liquid food colouring
about 2 packets chocolate finger biscuits (milk or plain)
75 g/3 oz/³⁄4 cup desiccated coconut
5–8 little bear figures
a thin stick for the maypole (about 30 cm/12 inches long)
6–9 coloured ribbons (very narrow)
a few artificial or marzipan flowers and leaves

1   Sandwich the cakes together with a layer of vanilla butter cream and one of raspberry jam or lemon cheese or curd. Stand on a cake board.
2   Colour or flavour the butter cream to blend with or contrast with the cake and spread a layer all round the sides of the cake. Stick chocolate finger biscuits (cut to size) all round the outside of the cake so the tops of the biscuits are just above the top of the cake.
3   Soak the coconut in cold water coloured green or yellow then drain thoroughly and dry the coloured coconut in a clean cloth.
4   Spread a layer of butter cream over the top of the cake and sprinkle with an even layer of the coloured coconut.
5   Put the butter cream into a piping bag fitted with a star nozzle and pipe a circle of stars on top of the cake just touching the biscuits. Then pipe another row of stars around the base of the cake.
6   Place the figures of bears evenly round the top edge of the cake. Cover the maypole with foil and wind a ribbon down it to make it pretty. Attach the same number of coloured ribbons as bears to the top of the pole and then stick the pole right through the centre of the cake to the board so it stands up firmly. Spread out a ribbon to each bear.
7   Complete the decoration with flowers and leaves between the bears and around the base of the maypole. Leave to set.

Note: Other figures of animals or children can be used. If for a birthday, each figure can hold a candle, and afterwards the figures could be given to the children as presents.

PIPING TECHNIQUES

The piping in this chapter is very simple, but there are a few important points to note to help make the job easier. Practice does make perfect and it is a good idea to practice piping straight lines, stars, shells or whatever onto a working surface before you try them on the actual cake. This will help tremendously and also give you a chance to see what size the stars, etc., should be to give the best effect. If you want to try on something similar to a cake, use an upturned cake tin – the icing will soon wash off.

Icing bags can be of various types. Most experts prefer a home-made bag made from wax or greaseproof paper because it can be made to take any icing nozzle and is very pliable and easy to hold. There are many types of plastic fabric or nylon bags available, which require a metal or plastic screw inserted into the bag and then the matching type of metal nozzles that either screw directly onto the screw connector or are sandwiched between the connector and a screw-on collar. These are very good and easy to use, but you must only buy the nozzle that fits your particular make of connector; other makes just won't fit. You can also buy an icing pump which again has nozzles to screw on. This is a much more cumbersome object and, because it is rigid, prevents you getting the 'feel' of the icing as it comes out, so it may come out in fits and starts rather than always smoothly – making it difficult to produce fine work.

TO MAKE A PAPER ICING BAG
1   Cut a piece of good quality wax or greaseproof paper to a 25–30 cm/10–12 inch square. Fold in half to form a triangle.
2   Fold the triangle in half to make a smaller triangle and press the folds firmly.
3   Open out the smaller triangle and fold the bottom half of the triangle up to the folded line, creasing firmly.
4   Continue to fold the bag over to each fold, creasing it firmly each time until completed.
5   Secure the outside join with sticky tape or fold the top point over twice to secure the bag. Cut about 1 cm/½ inch off the tip of the bag, open out and insert the nozzle.

TO FILL AN ICING BAG
1   Fill the bag half to two-thirds full with icing – no more or it will be difficult to manage and burst out the top.
2   Push the icing well down in the bag and into the nozzle, fold over the top carefully once and then again, continuing to push the icing downwards all the time. All types of bags are filled in this way. It is important that the icing is packed down well without any air pockets in it, or as the icing is piped out the air will burst out causing the icing to break and more than likely spoil what you are actually doing.

TO HOLD AN ICING BAG
1   For paper icing bags, it is easiest to open your hand and place the bag across your palm with the tip towards the ends of your fingers. Place the thumb on the folded end of the bag (to keep in the icing), then fold over the four fingers to hold the bag tightly.
2   Use the other hand to steady the bag and apply a steady pressure to the bag until the icing begins to come out of the nozzle.
3   With a nylon bag, place the thumb and forefinger round the icing in the bag and twist the bag tightly two or three times to prevent the icing coming out or moving up the bag, then hold the bag tightly over the twist, again with the thumb and forefinger and with the rest of the fingers folded over the bag. Apply pressure with the other hand.

CONSISTENCY OF ICINGS

1 It is most important to use an icing of the correct consistency for piping and this will differ with various types of piping.
2 With royal icing for dots, shells, rosettes, etc., it should be stiff enough to stand in well-formed but not hard peaks, but for writing it must be slacker or the icing will break – but it must not be too soft or it will not hold its shape.
3 Glacé icing to be used for piping lines, lacework or writing needs to be stiffer than that used to coat a cake – simply add a little extra sifted icing (confectioners') sugar.
4 Butter cream should be stiff enough to pull into softish peaks, but not too firm or it will not pipe evenly. Butter cream can be used to work designs of shells, stars and rosettes as well as for writing.

PIPING

As I have already said, it takes practice to perfect but the following points should help:

1 Always begin with the tip of the nozzle wiped clean or it will not be easy to start the piping.
2 Place the tip of the nozzle where the piping is to begin and then keeping a steady pressure on the icing as it begins to emerge lift the nozzle up off the surface. If you keep the nozzle on the surface it is almost impossible to keep a straight line and the actual icing will be mis-shapen as it cannot come out of the nozzle cleanly.
3 Break off the icing sharply with a down and up movement.
4 If the icing ends in a blob, remove the excess with a hat pin or fine skewer.
5 When piping straight lines, hold the nozzle at least 2.5 cm/1 inch above the surface, this makes it much easier to keep the line straight and you can move it quite easily before it touches the surface should the line waver.
6 When using a star nozzle, always finish off sharply with a quick down and up movement or there will not be a clean tip to the shape.
7 Paper and nylon icing bags can be refilled, but do not add too much icing and remember to push well down and then squeeze out the icing until you come to the new lot or a large explosion of air will spoil the icing when you hit the new icing put into the bag.

DECORATIONS

There are many types of decoration you can make from marzipan or moulding fondant icing as well as chocolate and other ingredients. The following are used in the cakes described in this chapter, but many others can be devised by yourself when you get the general idea of how to begin.

Chocolate Leaves – select a number of real rose leaves that are not too big and are unblemished. Wash in cold water and dry thoroughly. Melt a small amount of plain or milk chocolate in a small bowl and, using a paint brush, paint the underside of each leaf with melted chocolate. Leave until firm and then paint on a second coat. Leave until quite set – the refrigerator will hasten the process – and then peel off the leaf, leaving a chocolate leaf ready to use as a decoration. These leaves will store well for up to 2 weeks in a small rigid airtight container between layers of tissue or wax or greaseproof paper.

Marzipan Holly Leaves and Berries – take a small quantity of marzipan and tint it a deep green by moulding in green, blue and possibly a touch of brown liquid food colouring. Continue to knead until evenly coloured. Roll out the marzipan thinly to a strip and cut into rectangles about 2.5–4 cm/1–1½ inches long and 2 cm/¾ inch wide. Using a tiny round cutter or the base of a piping nozzle, take cuts out of the edges of the leaves to represent a holly leaf. Mark a vein down the centre with a knife, and leave to dry, putting some leaves over a wooden spoon handle to give a curved effect. Lay others on non-stick paper. For the berries, tint a small amount of marzipan a deep red and roll into tiny balls. Leave these to dry by the leaves.

Marzipan Ivy Leaves – draw several sizes of ivy leaves on paper and cut out, or use real ivy leaves as a pattern if you can find them. Tint a small quantity of marzipan green, but not such a dark colour as for the holly, and then roll out thinly. Place the paper patterns on the marzipan and cut round them with a small sharp knife. Mark veins with a knife and leave to dry on non-stick paper.

Rose Leaves – again use a fairly dark green marzipan and roll out thinly. Copy some real rose leaves and cut out similar shapes. Mark the veins and then make tiny indentations around the edge of each leaf with a knife if you want the leaves to look really authentic. These leaves can be left flat to dry or laid over wooden spoon handles.

Marzipan Christmas Trees – draw a simple pattern for a Christmas tree and cut out. Place this pattern on some thinly rolled out dark green marzipan and cut around it. Tint a little marzipan red and roll out thinly. Cut out a small piece to represent a tub and attach to the base of the tree. Leave on non-stick paper to dry. The tips of the tree branches can be 'decorated' by sticking a silver ball onto each branch with a small dab of icing.

Butterfly Cake (see page 230)

1   *Having covered the cake with butter cream, use a serrated icing comb or fork to pull round the sides of the cake evenly to give an attractive finish.*

3   *Fill the inner wing shapes with a lacework design.*

2   *Pipe a shell or star border around the base and top of the cakes, then pipe two separate wing shapes on each wing.*

4   *Decorate with coloured balls and candles to represent the antennae.*

Marzipan (or Fondant) Roses – roses can be made in a variety of colours similar to any you would find in the garden. Yellow marzipan makes good roses and so does the white variety for roses to be used on Christmas cakes.

1   Roll out the marzipan very thinly between two sheets of polythene or non-stick paper and cut out several circles of about 1 cm/½ inch, then cut out more circles, each about 3 mm/⅛ inch larger than before.

2   Hold the circle at one side and with the other hand carefully press out the rest of the circle until very thin and almost transparent. Carefully roll this up to represent the centre of the rose.

3   Continue to make the petals from the circles in the same way and add one at a time by wrapping round the previous petal, keeping the thick part at the base and folding the petals so they look real. Use a slightly larger piece of marzipan for each petal.

4   When the rose seems large enough (or small enough for a bud) open out the top petals a little and trim off the base. Leave to dry on non-stick paper.

5   For a small rose use about 4 petals, but a large rose can have 7 or 8 until the size you want is achieved. Take care not to press the central part too firmly or into a point, or the flower will become elongated and look more like a cabbage than a rose.

6   When quite dry, the roses can be stored in an airtight container between layers of tissue or wax or grease-proof paper. Do not put brightly-coloured moulded flowers onto a white cake until quite dry or they will stain the icing and spoil the effect. Flowers will take several days in a warm place to dry out.

Christmas Tree Cake (see page 228)

1   Pipe around the outside of the square of wax or greaseproof paper on top of the cake, keeping the lines straight but not touching the paper.

3   Having piped a double border of stars around the top edge of the cake, using the same piping nozzle, pipe a series of stars on the sides of the cake.

2   Pipe a series of graduated stars from directly below the tree tubs.

4   Complete the cake by piping a row of stars all around the base of the cake.

Christmas Roses – these are made from white marzipan or fondant icing. Take tiny scraps of it and shape into tiny petals with rounded edges. Each flower requires 5 petals and they are pinched together at the centre. Lay on non-stick paper to dry and then pipe 5 or 7 small dots of yellow royal icing in the centre to form the stamen and leave to dry again.

It is one thing learning how to cook the food so it looks and tastes fantastic. It is quite another thing to learn how to put a well balanced meal together.

The first thing to think about is that, as you are entertaining, your presence is required with your guests even though you are also the cook. This means the meal must be planned so you are not going to be kept in the kitchen all the time – except when the meal is over! If the meal is to be a three course one, then make sure at least one and preferably two of the courses are to be served cold, so they can be prepared in advance with only the final preparation required at the last minute.

Never serve three creamy dishes at a meal; not only will you pile on the calories for everyone concerned, but you may have a guest who is not particularly keen on cream, and you will end up with a very rich and possibly sickly meal. Avoid also too many spicy dishes, especially if to be served together or following one another. If you want to serve something rather different or, possibly, some sort of shellfish, and you don't know your guests' taste, it is wise to ask if they like shellfish.

When it comes to vegetables, I have left the choice up to you, but it is a good idea to serve two vegetables – one of which should be a green vegetable of some sort and another type of vegetable, possibly in a sauce, (Don't for instance serve cabbage and sprouts; carrots and parsnips or French (snap) beans and runner (green) beans.) Also serve some type of potatoes, rice or pasta to blend with your main course.

TWO COURSE MEALS

The following ideas are suitable for main courses or evening meals and should be accompanied with two vegetables. A salad makes a good alternative to vegetables, especially in the summer, but excellent winter salads can also be served.

Steak and Kidney Pie Blackcurrant Sorbet	Hungarian Goulash Lemon Meringue Pie
Lamb and Orange Risotto Rhubarb Snow	Somerset Pork Queen of Puddings
Veal Fricassée Winter Fruit Salad	Oxtail Casserole Raspberry Mousse
Fish Pie Chocolate Soufflé	Cidered Fish Casserole Pineapple Upside Down Pudding

THREE COURSE MEALS

These meals can easily be cut down to two courses, without using the starter, or for a change cutting out the dessert and serving fresh fruit or cheese and biscuits, if preferred.

Avocado Vinaigrette Chicken with Coconut Fruit Pie	Endive, Onion and Egg Salad Turkey Beanpot Pecan Pie
Cauliflower and Caper Salad Rabbit with Mustard Bread and Butter Pudding	Vegetable Soup with Oatmeal Baked Stuffed Herrings Mince Pies
Cream of Cucumber Soup Boston Style Bean Casserole Stewed Fruits	Tomato and Onion Salad Liver Marsala Rhubarb and Apple Crumble
Creamy Mushroom Soup Chicken Goujons Peach Melba	Grilled Grapefruit Steak and Kidney Pie Hazelnut Meringues

ENTERTAINING MENUS

With the following menus, at least one of the courses can be made in advance and then just served up when required. The recipes that can be prepared in advance are marked with a *. This should help you to plan the meal and make the actual cooking much easier. Don't forget too, that the vegetables can be prepared earlier in the day, the table can be laid and all the coffee things put out ready. If you are serving cheese do take it out of the refrigerator in good time to allow it to return to room temperature and 'breathe' so that the true flavour and texture are apparent. Coffee can be served at the dinner table, or the guests can remove to the sitting room to drink their coffee.

French Onion Soup * Sage and Bacon Stuffed Pork Sherry Syllabub *	Liver and Bacon Pâté * Poached Salmon * French Apple Flan *
Stuffed Eggs* Saltimbocca Apples and Oranges Bristol *	Minestrone Soup * Port Fillet in a Crust Fruit Brûlée
Cream of Mussel Soup * Pot Roast Peanut Chicken Crêpes Suzettes *	Coquille St Jacques * Pot Roast Venison Lemon Cheesecake *
Mushrooms à la Grecque * Duck with Cumberland Sauce Pineapple Mousse *	Consommé * Roast Pheasant Jalousie *
Grapefruit and Avocado Salad * Carbonnade of Beef * Crème Brûlée *	Crab with Avocado * Coq au Vin * Olde Englishe Trifle *
Carrot and Coriander Soup * Brisket Pot Roast Charlotte Russe *	Cheese Aigrettes Noisettes of Lamb Lemon Soufflé *

Index